THE ROAD TO
CHARACTER

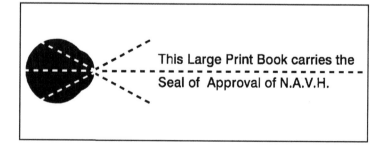

This Large Print Book carries the
Seal of Approval of N.A.V.H.

THE ROAD TO CHARACTER

DAVID BROOKS

LARGE PRINT PRESS
A part of Gale, Cengage Learning

GALE
CENGAGE Learning·

Farmington Hills, Mich • San Francisco • New York • Waterville, Maine
Meriden, Conn • Mason, Ohio • Chicago

GALE
CENGAGE Learning

LIBRARY OF CONGRESS CATALOGING-IN-PUBLICATION DATA

Brooks, David, 1961–
    The road to character / by David Brooks. — Large print edition.
    pages cm. — (Thorndike Press large print basic)
    ISBN 978-1-4104-8278-5 (hardcover) — ISBN 1-4104-8278-2 (hardcover)
    1. Character. 2. Virtues. 3. Humility. I. Title.
BF818.B764 2015b
170'.44—dc23   2015018366

ISBN 13: 978-1-59413-937-6 (pbk.)
ISBN 10: 1-59413-937-7 (pbk.)

Published in 2016 by arrangement with Random House, an imprint and division of Penguin Random House LLC

Printed in Mexico
4 5 6 7 8 9 21 20 19 18 17

To my parents,
Lois and Michael Brooks

CONTENTS

INTRODUCTION:
ADAM II

Recently I've been thinking about the difference between the résumé virtues and the eulogy virtues. The résumé virtues are the ones you list on your résumé, the skills that you bring to the job market and that contribute to external success. The eulogy virtues are deeper. They're the virtues that get talked about at your funeral, the ones that exist at the core of your being — whether you are kind, brave, honest or faithful; what kind of relationships you formed.

Most of us would say that the eulogy virtues are more important than the résumé virtues, but I confess that for long stretches of my life I've spent more time thinking about the latter than the former. Our education system is certainly oriented around the résumé virtues more than the eulogy ones. Public conversation is, too — the self-help tips in magazines, the nonfiction bestsellers. Most of us have clearer strategies for how to achieve career success than we do for how to develop a profound character.

One book that has helped me think about these two sets of virtues is *Lonely Man of Faith,* which was written by Rabbi Joseph Soloveitchik in 1965. Soloveitchik noted that there are two accounts of creation in Genesis and argued that these represent the two opposing sides of our nature, which he called Adam I and Adam II.

Modernizing Soloveitchik's categories a bit, we could say that Adam I is the career-oriented, ambitious side of our nature. Adam I is the external, résumé Adam. Adam I wants to build, create, produce, and discover things. He wants to have high status and win victories.

Adam II is the internal Adam. Adam II wants to embody certain moral qualities. Adam II wants to have a serene inner character, a quiet but solid sense of right and wrong — not only to do good, but to be good. Adam II wants to love intimately, to sacrifice self in the service of others, to live in obedience to some transcendent truth, to have a cohesive inner soul that honors creation and one's own possibilities.

While Adam I wants to conquer the world, Adam II wants to obey a calling to serve the world. While Adam I is creative and savors his own accomplishments, Adam II sometimes renounces worldly success and status for the sake of some sacred purpose. While Adam I asks how things work, Adam II asks why things exist, and what ultimately we are here for. While Adam I wants to venture forth, Adam II wants to return to his roots and savor the warmth of a family meal. While Adam I's motto is "Success," Adam II experiences life as a moral drama. His motto is "Charity, love, and redemption."

Soloveitchik argued that we live in the contradiction between these two Adams. The outer, majestic Adam and the inner, humble Adam are not fully reconcilable. We are forever caught in self-confrontation. We are called to fulfill both personae, and must master the art of living forever within the tension between these two natures.

The hard part of this confrontation, I'd add, is that Adams I and II live by different logics. Adam I — the creating, building, and discovering Adam — lives by a straightforward utilitarian logic. It's the logic of economics. Input leads to output. Effort leads to reward. Practice makes perfect. Pursue self-interest. Maximize your utility. Impress the world.

Adam II lives by an inverse logic. It's a

11

moral logic, not an economic one. You have to give to receive. You have to surrender to something outside yourself to gain strength within yourself. You have to conquer your desire to get what you crave. Success leads to the greatest failure, which is pride. Failure leads to the greatest success, which is humility and learning. In order to fulfill yourself, you have to forget yourself. In order to find yourself, you have to lose yourself.

To nurture your Adam I career, it makes sense to cultivate your strengths. To nurture your Adam II moral core, it is necessary to confront your weaknesses.

THE SHREWD ANIMAL

We live in a culture that nurtures Adam I, the external Adam, and neglects Adam II. We live in a society that encourages us to think about how to have a great career but leaves many of us inarticulate about how to cultivate the inner life. The competition to succeed and win admiration is so fierce that it becomes all-consuming. The consumer marketplace encourages us to live by a utilitarian calculus, to satisfy our desires and lose sight of the moral stakes involved in everyday decisions. The noise of fast and shallow communications makes it harder to

12

hear the quieter sounds that emanate from the depths. We live in a culture that teaches us to promote and advertise ourselves and to master the skills required for success, but that gives little encouragement to humility, sympathy, and honest self-confrontation, which are necessary for building character.

If you are only Adam I, you turn into a shrewd animal, a crafty, self-preserving creature who is adept at playing the game and who turns everything into a game. If that's all you have, you spend a lot of time cultivating professional skills, but you don't have a clear idea of the sources of meaning in life, so you don't know where you should devote your skills, which career path will be highest and best. Years pass and the deepest parts of yourself go unexplored and unstructured. You are busy, but you have a vague anxiety that your life has not achieved its ultimate meaning and significance. You live with an unconscious boredom, not really loving, not really attached to the moral purposes that give life its worth. You lack the internal criteria to make unshakable commitments. You never develop inner constancy, the integrity that can withstand popular disapproval or a serious blow. You find yourself doing things that other people approve of, whether these things are right for you or not. You foolishly judge other people by their abilities, not by their worth. You do not have a strategy to build character, and without that, not only your inner life but also your external life will eventually fall to pieces.

This book is about Adam II. It's about how some people have cultivated strong character. It's about one mindset that people through the centuries have adopted to put iron in their core and to cultivate a wise heart. I wrote it, to be honest, to save my own soul.

I was born with a natural disposition toward shallowness. I now work as a pundit and columnist. I'm paid to be a narcissistic blowhard, to volley my opinions, to appear more confident about them than I really am, to appear smarter than I really am, to appear better and more authoritative than I really am. I have to work harder than most people to avoid a life of smug superficiality. I've also become more aware that, like many people these days, I have lived a life of vague moral aspiration — vaguely wanting to be good, vaguely wanting to serve some larger purpose, while lacking a concrete moral vocabulary, a clear understanding of how to live a rich inner life, or even a clear knowledge of how character is developed and depth is achieved.

I've discovered that without a rigorous focus on the Adam II side of our nature, it is easy to slip into a self-satisfied moral mediocrity. You grade yourself on a forgiving curve. You follow your desires wherever they take you, and you approve of yourself so long as you are not obviously hurting anyone else. You figure that if the people around you seem to like you, you must be good enough. In the process you end up slowly turning yourself into something a little less impressive than you had originally hoped. A humiliating gap opens up between your actual self and your desired self. You realize that the voice of your Adam I is loud but the voice of your Adam II is muffled; the life plan of Adam I is clear, but the life plan of Adam II is fuzzy; Adam I is alert, Adam II is sleepwalking.

I wrote this book not sure I could follow the road to character, but I wanted at least to know what the road looks like and how other people have trodden it.

THE PLAN

The plan of this book is simple. In the next chapter I will describe an older moral ecology. It was a cultural and intellectual tradition, the "crooked timber" tradition, that emphasized our own brokenness. It was a tradition that demanded humility in the face of our own limitations. But it was also a tradition that held that each of us has the power to confront our own weaknesses, tackle our own sins, and that in the course of this confrontation with ourselves we build character. By successfully confronting sin and weakness we have the chance to play our role in a great moral drama. We can shoot for something higher than happiness. We have a chance to take advantage of everyday occasions to build virtue in ourselves and be of service to the world.

Then I will describe what this character-building method looks like in real life. I'm going to do this through biographical essays, which are also moral essays. Since Plutarch, moralists have tried to communicate certain standards by holding up exemplars. You can't build rich Adam II lives simply by reading sermons or following abstract rules. Example is the best teacher. Moral improvement occurs most reliably when the heart is warmed, when we come into contact with people we admire and love and we consciously and unconsciously bend our lives to mimic theirs.

This truth was hammered home to me after I wrote a column expressing frustration with how hard it is to use the classroom experience to learn how to be good. A veterinarian named Dave Jolly sent me an email that cut to the chase:

The heart cannot be taught in a classroom intellectually, to students mechanically taking notes. . . . Good, wise hearts are obtained through lifetimes of diligent effort to dig deeply within and heal lifetimes of scars. . . . You can't teach it or email it or tweet it. It has to be discovered within the depths of one's own heart when a person is finally ready to go looking for it, and not before.

The job of the wise person is to swallow the frustration and just go on setting an example of caring and digging and diligence in their own lives. What a wise person teaches is the smallest part of what they give. The totality of their life, of the way they go about it in the smallest details, is what gets transmitted.

Never forget that. The message is the person, perfected over lifetimes of effort that was set in motion by yet another wise person now hidden from the recipient by the dim mists of time. Life is much bigger than we think, cause and effect intertwined in a vast moral structure that keeps pushing us to do better, become better, even when we dwell in the most painful confused darkness.

Those words explain the methodology of this book. The subjects of the portraits that follow in chapters 2 through 10 are a diverse set, white and black, male and female, religious and secular, literary and nonliterary. None of them is even close to perfect. But they practiced a mode of living that is less common now. They were acutely aware of their own weaknesses. They waged an internal struggle against their sins and emerged with some measure of self-respect. And when we think of them, it is not primarily what they accomplished that we remember — great though that may have been — it is who they were. I'm hoping their examples will fire this fearful longing we all have to be better, to follow their course.

In the final chapter I wrap these themes up. I describe how our culture has made it harder to be good, and I summarize this "crooked timber" approach to life in a series of specific points. If you're impatient for the condensed message of this book, skip to the end.

Occasionally, even today, you come across certain people who seem to possess an impressive inner cohesion. They are not leading fragmented, scattershot lives. They have achieved inner integration. They are calm, settled, and rooted. They are not blown off course by storms. They don't crumble in adversity. Their minds are consistent and their hearts are dependable. Their virtues are not the blooming virtues you see in smart college students; they are the ripening virtues you see in people who have lived a little and have learned from joy and pain.

Sometimes you don't even notice these people, because while they seem kind and cheerful, they are also reserved. They possess the self-effacing virtues of people who are inclined to be useful but don't need to prove anything to the world: humility, restraint, reticence, temperance, respect, and soft self-discipline.

They radiate a sort of moral joy. They answer softly when challenged harshly. They are silent when unfairly abused. They are dignified when others try to humiliate them, restrained when others try to provoke them. But they get things done. They perform acts of sacrificial service with the same modest everyday spirit they would display if they were just getting the groceries. They are not thinking about what impressive work they are doing. They are not thinking about themselves at all. They just seem delighted by the flawed people around them. They just recognize what needs doing and they do it.

They make you feel funnier and smarter when you speak with them. They move through different social classes not even aware, it seems, that they are doing so. After you've known them for a while it occurs to you that you've never heard them boast, you've never seen them self-righteous or doggedly certain. They aren't dropping little hints of their own distinctiveness and accomplishments.

They have not led lives of conflict-free tranquillity, but have struggled toward maturity. They have gone some way toward solving life's essential problem, which is that, as Aleksandr Solzhenitsyn put it, "the line separating good and evil passes not through states, nor between classes, nor between political parties either — but right through every human heart."

These are the people who have built a strong inner character, who have achieved a certain depth. In these people, at the end of this struggle, the climb to success has surrendered to the struggle to deepen the soul. After a life of seeking balance, Adam I bows down before Adam II. These are the people we are looking for.

CHAPTER 1
THE SHIFT

On Sunday evenings my local NPR station rebroadcasts old radio programs. A few years ago I was driving home and heard a program called *Command Performance,* which was a variety show that went out to the troops during World War II. The episode I happened to hear was broadcast the day after V-J Day, on August 15, 1945.

The episode featured some of the era's biggest celebrities: Frank Sinatra, Marlene Dietrich, Cary Grant, Bette Davis, and many others. But the most striking feature of the show was its tone of self-effacement and humility. The Allies had just completed one of the noblest military victories in human history. And yet there was no chest beating. Nobody was erecting triumphal arches.

"Well, it looks like this is it," the host, Bing Crosby, opened. "What can you say at a time like this? You can't throw your skimmer in the air. That's for run-of-the mill holidays. I guess all anybody can do is thank God it's over." The mezzo-soprano Risë Stevens came on and sang a solemn version of "Ave Maria," and then Crosby came back on to summarize the mood: "Today, though, our deep-down feeling is one of humility."

That sentiment was repeated throughout the broadcast. The actor Burgess Meredith read a passage written by Ernie Pyle, the war correspondent. Pyle had been killed just a few months before, but he had written an article anticipating what victory would mean: "We won this war because our men are brave and because of many other things — because of Russia, England, and China and the passage of time and the gift of nature's materials. We did not win it because destiny created us better than all other people. I hope that in victory we are more grateful than proud."

The show mirrored the reaction of the nation at large. There were rapturous celebrations, certainly. Sailors in San Francisco commandeered cable cars and looted liquor stores. The streets of New York's garment district were five inches deep in confetti.[1] But the mood was divided. Joy gave way to solemnity and self-doubt.

This was in part because the war had been

such an epochal event, and had produced such rivers of blood, that individuals felt small in comparison. There was also the manner in which the war in the Pacific had ended — with the atomic bomb. People around the world had just seen the savagery human beings are capable of. Now here was a weapon that could make that savagery apocalyptic. "The knowledge of victory was as charged with sorrow and doubt as with joy and gratitude," James Agee wrote in an editorial that week for *Time* magazine.

But the modest tone of *Command Performance* wasn't just a matter of mood or style. The people on that broadcast had been part of one of the most historic victories ever known. But they didn't go around telling themselves how great they were. They didn't print up bumper stickers commemorating their own awesomeness. Their first instinct was to remind themselves they were not morally superior to anyone else. Their collective impulse was to warn themselves against pride and self-glorification. They intuitively resisted the natural human tendency toward excessive self-love.

I arrived home before the program was over and listened to that radio show in my driveway for a time. Then I went inside and turned on a football game. A quarterback threw a short pass to a wide receiver, who was tackled almost immediately for a two-yard gain. The defensive player did what all professional athletes do these days in moments of personal accomplishment. He did a self-puffing victory dance, as the camera lingered.

It occurred to me that I had just watched more self-celebration after a two-yard gain than I had heard after the United States won World War II.

This little contrast set off a chain of thoughts in my mind. It occurred to me that this shift might symbolize a shift in culture, a shift from a culture of self-effacement that says "Nobody's better than me, but I'm no better than anyone else" to a culture of self-promotion that says "Recognize my accomplishments, I'm pretty special." That contrast, while nothing much in itself, was like a doorway into the different ways it is possible to live in this world.

LITTLE ME

In the years following that *Command Performance* episode, I went back and studied that time and the people who were prominent then. The research reminded me first of all that none of us should ever wish to go back to the culture of the mid-twentieth century. It was a more racist, sexist, and anti-Semitic culture. Most of us would not have had the opportunities we enjoy if we had lived back then. It was also a more boring culture, with bland food and homogeneous living arrangements. It was an emotionally cold culture. Fathers, in particular, frequently were unable to express their love for their own children. Husbands were unable to see the depth in their own wives. In so many ways, life is better now than it was then.

But it did occur to me that there was perhaps a strain of humility that was more common then than now, that there was a moral ecology, stretching back centuries but less prominent now, encouraging people to be more skeptical of their desires, more aware of their own weaknesses, more intent on combatting the flaws in their own natures and turning weakness into strength. People in this tradition, I thought, are less likely to feel that every thought, feeling, and achievement should be immediately shared with the world at large.

The popular culture seemed more reticent in the era of *Command Performance*. There were no message T-shirts back then, no exclamation points on the typewriter keyboards, no sympathy ribbons for various diseases, no vanity license plates, no bumper stickers with personal or moral declarations. People didn't brag about their college affiliations or their vacation spots with little stickers on the rear windows of their cars. There was stronger social sanction against (as they would have put it) blowing your own trumpet, getting above yourself, being too big for your britches.

The social code was embodied in the self-effacing style of actors like Gregory Peck or Gary Cooper, or the character Joe Friday on *Dragnet.* When Franklin Roosevelt's aide Harry Hopkins lost a son in World War II, the military brass wanted to put his other sons out of harm's way. Hopkins rejected this idea, writing, with the understatement more common in that era, that his other sons shouldn't be given safe assignments just because their brother "had some bad luck in the Pacific."[2]

Of the twenty-three men and women who served in Dwight Eisenhower's cabinets, only one, the secretary of agriculture, published a memoir afterward, and it was so discreet as to be soporific. By the time the Reagan administration rolled around, twelve of his thirty cabinet members published memoirs, almost all of them self-advertising.[3]

When the elder George Bush, who was raised in that era, was running for president, he, having inculcated the values of his childhood, resisted speaking about himself. If a speechwriter put the word "I" in one of his speeches, he'd instinctively cross it out. The staff would beg him: You're running for president. You've got to talk about yourself. Eventually they'd cow him into doing so. But the next day he'd get a call from his mother. "George, you're talking about yourself again," she'd say. And Bush would revert to form. No more I's in the speeches. No more self-promotion.

THE BIG ME

Over the next few years I collected data to suggest that we have seen a broad shift from a culture of humility to the culture of what you might call the Big Me, from a culture that encouraged people to think humbly of themselves to a culture that encouraged people to see themselves as the center of the universe.

It wasn't hard to find such data. For example, in 1950, the Gallup Organization asked high school seniors if they considered themselves to be a very important person. At that point, 12 percent said yes. The same question was asked in 2005, and this time it wasn't 12 percent who considered themselves very important, it was 80 percent.

Psychologists have a thing called the narcissism test. They read people statements and ask if the statements apply to them. Statements such as "I like to be the center of attention . . . I show off if I get the chance because I am extraordinary . . . Somebody should write a biography about me." The median narcissism score has risen 30 percent in the last two decades. Ninety-three percent of young people score higher than the middle score just twenty years ago.[4] The largest gains have been in the number of people who agree with the statements "I am an extraordinary person" and "I like to look at my body."

Along with this apparent rise in self-esteem, there has been a tremendous increase in the desire for fame. Fame used to rank low as a life's ambition for most people. In a 1976 survey that asked people to list their life goals, fame ranked fifteenth out of sixteen. By 2007, 51 percent of young people reported that being famous was one of their top personal goals.[5] In one study, middle school girls were asked who they would most like to have dinner with. Jennifer Lopez came in first, Jesus Christ came in second, and Paris Hilton third. The girls were then asked which of the following jobs they would like to have. Nearly twice as many said they'd rather be a celebrity's personal assistant — for example, Justin Bieber's — than president of Harvard. (Though, to be fair, I'm pretty sure the president of Harvard would also rather be Justin Bieber's personal assistant.)

As I looked around the popular culture I kept finding the same messages everywhere: You are special. Trust yourself. Be true to yourself. Movies from Pixar and Disney are constantly telling children how wonderful they are. Commencement speeches are larded with the same clichés: Follow your passion. Don't accept limits. Chart your own course. You have a responsibility to do great things because you are so great. This is the gospel of self-trust.

As Ellen DeGeneres put it in a 2009 commencement address, "My advice to you is to be true to yourself and everything will be fine." Celebrity chef Mario Batali advised graduates to follow "your own truth, expressed consistently by you." Anna Quindlen urged another audience to have the courage to "honor your character, your intellect, your inclinations, and, yes, your soul by listening to its clean clear voice instead of following the muddied messages of a timid world."

In her mega-selling book *Eat, Pray, Love* (I am the only man ever to finish this book), Elizabeth Gilbert wrote that God manifests himself through "my own voice from within my own self. . . . God dwells within you as you yourself, exactly the way you are."[6]

I began looking at the way we raise our children and found signs of this moral shift. For example, the early Girl Scout handbooks preached an ethic of self-sacrifice and self-effacement. The chief obstacle to happiness, the handbook exhorted, comes from the overeager desire to have people think about you.

By 1980, as James Davison Hunter has pointed out, the tone was very different. *You Make the Difference: The Handbook for Cadette and Senior Girl Scouts* was telling girls to pay *more* attention to themselves: "How can you get more in touch with *you*? What are *you* feeling? . . . Every option available to you through Senior Scouting can, in some way, help you to a better understanding of yourself. . . . Put yourself in the 'center stage' of your thoughts to gain perspective on your own ways of feeling, thinking and acting."[7]

The shift can even be seen in the words that flow from the pulpit. Joel Osteen, one of the most popular megachurch leaders today, writes from Houston, Texas. "God didn't create you to be average," Osteen says in his book *Become a Better You.* "You were made to excel. You were made to leave a mark on this generation. . . . Start [believing] 'I've been chosen, set apart, destined to live in victory.' "[8]

THE HUMBLE PATH
As years went by and work on this book continued, my thoughts returned to that episode of *Command Performance.* I was haunted by the quality of humility I heard in those voices.

There was something aesthetically beautiful about the self-effacement the people on that program displayed. The self-effacing person is soothing and gracious, while the self-promoting person is fragile and jarring. Humility is freedom from the need to prove you are superior all the time, but egotism is a ravenous hunger in a small space — self-concerned, competitive, and distinction-hungry. Humility is infused with lovely emotions like admiration, companionship, and gratitude. "Thankfulness," the Archbishop of Canterbury, Michael Ramsey, said, "is a soil in which pride does not easily grow."[9]

There is something intellectually impressive about that sort of humility, too. We have, the psychologist Daniel Kahneman writes, an "almost unlimited ability to ignore our ignorance."[10] Humility is the awareness that there's a lot you don't know and that a lot of what you think you know is distorted or wrong.

This is the way humility leads to wisdom. Montaigne once wrote, "We can be knowledgeable with other men's knowledge, but we can't be wise with other men's wisdom." That's because wisdom isn't a body of information. It's the moral quality of knowing what you don't know and figuring out a way to handle your ignorance, uncertainty, and limitation.

The people we think are wise have, to some degree, overcome the biases and overconfident tendencies that are infused in our nature. In its most complete meaning, intellectual humility is accurate self-awareness from a distance. It is moving over the course of one's life from the adolescent's close-up view of yourself, in which you fill the whole canvas, to a landscape view in which you see, from a wider perspective, your strengths and weaknesses, your connections and dependencies, and the role you play in a larger story.

Finally, there is something morally impressive about humility. Every epoch has its own preferred methods of self-cultivation, its own ways to build character and depth. The people on that *Command Performance* broadcast were guarding themselves against some of their least attractive tendencies, to be prideful, self-congratulatory, hubristic.

Today, many of us see our life through the metaphor of a journey — a journey through the external world and up the ladder of success. When we think about making a difference or leading a life with purpose, we often think of achieving something external — performing some service that will have an impact on the world, creating a successful company, or doing something for the community.

Truly humble people also use that journey metaphor to describe their own lives. But they also use, alongside that, a different metaphor, which has more to do with the internal life. This is the metaphor of self-confrontation. They are more likely to assume that we are all deeply divided selves, both splendidly endowed and deeply flawed — that we each have certain talents but also certain weaknesses. And if we habitually fall for those temptations and do not struggle against the weaknesses in ourselves, then we will gradually spoil some core piece of ourselves. We will not be as good, internally, as we want to be. We will fail in some profound way.

For people of this sort, the external drama up the ladder of success is important, but the inner struggle against one's own weaknesses is the central drama of life. As the popular minister Harry Emerson Fosdick put it in his 1943 book *On Being a Real Person,* "The beginning of worth-while living is thus the confrontation with ourselves."[11]

Truly humble people are engaged in a great effort to magnify what is best in themselves and defeat what is worst, to become strong in the weak places. They start with an acute awareness of the bugs in their own nature. Our basic problem is that we are self-centered, a plight beautifully captured in the famous commencement address David Foster Wallace gave at Kenyon College in 2005:

> Everything in my own immediate experience supports my deep belief that I am the absolute center of the universe; the realest, most vivid and important person in existence. We rarely think about this sort

of natural, basic self-centeredness because it's so socially repulsive. But it's pretty much the same for all of us. It is our default setting, hard-wired into our boards at birth. Think about it: there is no experience you have had that you are not the absolute center of. The world as you experience it is there in front of YOU or behind YOU, to the left or right of YOU, on YOUR TV or YOUR monitor. And so on. Other people's thoughts and feelings have to be communicated to you somehow, but your own are so immediate, urgent, real.

This self-centeredness leads in several unfortunate directions. It leads to selfishness, the desire to use other people as means to get things for yourself. It also leads to pride, the desire to see yourself as superior to everybody else. It leads to a capacity to ignore and rationalize your own imperfections and inflate your virtues. As we go through life, most of us are constantly comparing and constantly finding ourselves slightly better than other people — more virtuous, with better judgment, with better taste. We're constantly seeking recognition, and painfully sensitive to any snub or insult to the status we believe we have earned for ourselves.

Some perversity in our nature leads us to put lower loves above higher ones. We all love and desire a multitude of things: friendship, family, popularity, country, money, and so on. And we all have a sense that some loves are higher or more important than other loves. I suspect we all rank those loves in pretty much the same way. We all know that the love you feel for your children or parents should be higher than the love you have for money. We all know the love you have for the truth should be higher than the love you have for popularity. Even in this age of relativism and pluralism, the moral hierarchy of the heart is one thing we generally share, at least most of the time.

But we often put our loves out of order. If someone tells you something in confidence and then you blab it as good gossip at a dinner party, you are putting your love of popularity above your love of friendship. If you talk more at a meeting than you listen, you may be putting your ardor to outshine above learning and companionship. We do this all the time.

People who are humble about their own nature are moral realists. Moral realists are aware that we are all built from "crooked timber" — from Immanuel Kant's famous line, "Out of the crooked timber of humanity, no straight thing was ever made." People in this "crooked-timber" school of humanity have an acute awareness of their own flaws and believe that character is built in the struggle against their own weaknesses. As Thomas Merton wrote, "Souls are like athletes that need opponents worthy of them, if they are to be tried and extended and pushed to the full use of their powers."[12]

You can see evidence of the inner struggle in such people's journals. They are exultant on days when they win some small victory over selfishness and hard-heartedness. They are despondent on days when they let themselves down, when they avoid some charitable task because they were lazy or tired, or fail to attend to a person who wanted to be heard. They are more likely see their life as a moral adventure story. As the British writer Henry Fairlie put it, "If we acknowledge that our inclination to sin is part of our natures, and that we will never wholly eradicate it, there is at least something for us to do in our lives that will not in the end seem just futile and absurd."

I have a friend who spends a few moments in bed at night reviewing the mistakes of his day. His central sin, from which many of his other sins branch out, is a certain hardness of heart. He's a busy guy with many people making demands on his time. Sometimes he is not fully present for people who are asking his advice or revealing some vulnerability. Sometimes he is more interested in making a good impression than in listening to other people in depth. Maybe he spent more time at a meeting thinking about how he might seem impressive than about what others were actually saying. Maybe he flattered people too unctuously.

Each night, he catalogs the errors. He tallies his recurring core sins and the other mistakes that might have branched off from them. Then he develops strategies for how he might do better tomorrow. Tomorrow he'll try to look differently at people, pause more before people. He'll put care above prestige, the higher thing above the lower thing. We all have a moral responsibility to be more moral every day, and he will struggle to inch ahead each day in this most important sphere.

People who live this way believe that character is not innate or automatic. You have to build it with effort and artistry. You can't be the good person you want to be unless you wage this campaign. You won't even achieve enduring external success unless you build a solid moral core. If you don't have some inner integrity, eventually your Watergate, your scandal, your betrayal, will happen. Adam I ultimately depends upon Adam II.

Now, I have used the word "struggle" and "fight" in the previous passages. But it's a mistake to think that the moral struggle against internal weakness is a struggle the way a war is a struggle or the way a boxing match is a struggle — filled with clash of arms and violence and aggression. Moral realists sometimes do hard things, like standing firm against evil and imposing intense self-discipline on their desires. But character is built not only through austerity and hardship. It is also built sweetly through love and pleasure. When you have deep friendships with good people, you copy and then absorb some of their best traits. When you love a person deeply, you want to serve them and earn their regard. When you experience great art, you widen your repertoire of emotions. Through devotion to some cause, you elevate your desires and organize your energies.

Moreover, the struggle against the weaknesses in yourself is never a solitary struggle. No person can achieve self-mastery on his or her own. Individual will, reason, compassion, and character are not strong enough to consistently defeat selfishness, pride, greed, and self-deception. Everybody needs redemptive assistance from outside — from family, friends, ancestors, rules, traditions, institutions, exemplars, and, for believers, God. We all need people to tell us when we are wrong, to advise us on how to do right, and to encourage, support, arouse, co-operate, and inspire us along the way.

There's something democratic about life viewed in this way. It doesn't matter if you work on Wall Street or at a charity distributing medicine to the poor. It doesn't matter if you are at the top of the income scale or at the bottom. There are heroes and schmucks in all worlds. The most important thing is whether you are willing to engage in moral struggle against yourself. The most important thing is whether you are willing to engage this struggle well — joyfully and compassionately. Fairlie writes, "At least if we recognize that we sin, know that we are individually at war, we may go to war as warriors do, with something of valor and zest and even mirth."[13] Adam I achieves success by winning victories over others. But Adam II builds character by winning victories over the weaknesses in himself.

The people in this book led diverse lives. Each one of them exemplifies one of the activities that lead to character. But there is one pattern that recurs: They had to go down to go up. They had to descend into the valley of humility to climb to the heights of character.

The road to character often involves moments of moral crisis, confrontation, and recovery. When they were in a crucible moment, they suddenly had a greater ability to see their own nature. The everyday self-deceptions and illusions of self-mastery were shattered. They had to humble themselves in self-awareness if they had any hope of rising up transformed. Alice had to be small to enter Wonderland. Or, as Kierkegaard put it, "Only the one who descends into the underworld rescues the beloved."

But then the beauty began. In the valley of humility they learned to quiet the self. Only by quieting the self could they see the world clearly. Only by quieting the self could they understand other people and accept what they are offering.

When they had quieted themselves, they had opened up space for grace to flood in. They found themselves helped by people they did not expect would help them. They found themselves understood and cared for by others in ways they did not imagine beforehand. They found themselves loved in ways they did not deserve. They didn't have to flail about, because hands were holding them up.

Before long, people who have entered the valley of humility feel themselves back in the uplands of joy and commitment. They've thrown themselves into work, made new friends, and cultivated new loves. They realize, with a shock, that they've traveled a long way since the first days of their crucible. They turn around and see how much ground they have left behind. Such people don't come out healed; they come out different. They find a vocation or calling. They commit themselves to some long obedience and dedicate themselves to some desperate lark that gives life purpose.

Each phase of this experience has left a residue on such a person's soul. The experience has reshaped their inner core and given it great coherence, solidity, and weight. People with character may be loud or quiet, but they do tend to have a certain level of self-respect. Self-respect is not the same as self-confidence or self-esteem. Self-respect is not based on IQ or any of the mental or physical gifts that help get you into a competitive college. It is not comparative. It is not earned by being better than other people at something. It is earned by being better than you used to be, by being dependable in times of testing, straight in times of temptation. It emerges in one who is morally dependable. Self-respect is produced by inner triumphs, not external ones. It can only be earned by a person who has endured some internal temptation, who has confronted their own weaknesses and who knows, "Well, if worse comes to worst, I can endure that. I can overcome that."

The sort of process I've just described can happen in big ways. In every life there are huge crucible moments, altering ordeals, that either make you or break you. But this process can also happen in daily, gradual ways. Every day it's possible to recognize small flaws, to reach out to others, to try to correct errors. Character is built both through drama and through the everyday.

What was on display in *Command Performance* was more than just an aesthetic or a style. The more I looked into that period, the more I realized I was looking into a different moral country. I began to see a different view of human nature, a different attitude about what is important in life, a different formula for how to live a life of character and depth. I don't know how many people in those days hewed to this different moral ecology, but some people did, and I found that I admired them immensely.

My general belief is that we've accidentally left this moral tradition behind. Over the last several decades, we've lost this language, this way of organizing life. We're not bad. But we are morally inarticulate. We're not more selfish or venal than people in other times, but we've lost the understanding of how character is built. The "crooked timber" moral tradition — based on the awareness of sin and the confrontation with sin — was an inheritance passed down from generation to generation. It gave people a clearer sense of how to cultivate the eulogy virtues, how to develop the Adam II side of their nature. Without it, there is a certain superficiality to modern culture, especially in the moral sphere.

The central fallacy of modern life is the belief that accomplishments of the Adam I realm can produce deep satisfaction. That's false. Adam I's desires are infinite and always leap out ahead of whatever has just been achieved. Only Adam II can experience deep satisfaction. Adam I aims for happiness, but Adam II knows that happiness is insufficient. The ultimate joys are moral joys. In the pages ahead, I will try to offer some real-life examples of how this sort of life was lived. We can't and shouldn't want to return to the past. But we can rediscover this moral tradition, relearn this vocabulary of character, and incorporate it into our own lives.

You can't build Adam II out of a recipe book. There is no seven-point program. But we can immerse ourselves in the lives of outstanding people and try to understand the wisdom of the way they lived. I'm hoping you'll be able to pick out a few lessons that are important to you in the pages ahead, even if they are not the same ones that seem important to me. I'm hoping you and I will both emerge from the next nine chapters slightly different and slightly better.

CHAPTER 2
THE SUMMONED SELF

Today, the area around Washington Square Park in Lower Manhattan is surrounded by New York University, expensive apartments, and upscale stores. But back in 1911, there were nice brownstones on the northern side of the park and factories on its eastern and southern sides, drawing young and mostly Jewish and Italian immigrant workers. One of the nice homes was owned by Mrs. Gordon Norrie, a society matron descended from two of the men who signed the Declaration of Independence.

On March 25, Mrs. Norrie was just sitting down to tea with a group of friends when they heard a commotion outside. One of her guests, Frances Perkins, then thirty-one, was from an old but middle-class Maine family, which could also trace its lineage back to the time of the Revolution. She had attended Mount Holyoke College and was working at the Consumers' League of New York, lobbying to end child labor. Perkins spoke in the upper-crust tones befitting her upbringing — like Margaret Dumont in the old Marx Brothers movies or Mrs. Thurston Howell III — with long flat *a*'s, dropped *r*'s, and rounded vowels, "tom*aahhh*to" for "tomato."

A butler rushed in and announced that there was a fire near the square. The ladies ran out. Perkins lifted up her skirts and sprinted toward it. They had stumbled upon the Triangle Shirtwaist Factory, one of the most famous fires in American history. Perkins could see the eighth, ninth, and tenth floors of the building ablaze and dozens of workers crowding around the open windows. She joined the throng of horrified onlookers on the sidewalk below.

Some saw what they thought were bundles of fabric falling from the windows. They thought the factory owners were saving their best material. As the bundles continued to fall, the onlookers realized they were not bundles at all. They were people, hurling themselves to their death. "People had just begun to jump as we got there," Perkins would later remember. "They had been holding on until that time, standing in the windowsills, being crowded by others behind them, the fire pressing closer and closer, the smoke closer and closer.[1]

"They began to jump. The window was too crowded and they would jump and they hit the sidewalk," she recalled. "Every one of them was killed, everybody who jumped was killed. It was a horrifying spectacle."[2]

The firemen held out nets, but the weight of the bodies from that great height either yanked the nets from the firemen's hands or the bodies ripped right through. One woman grandly emptied her purse over the onlookers below and then hurled herself off.

Perkins and the others screamed up to them, "Don't jump! Help is coming." It wasn't. The flames were roasting them from behind. Forty-seven people ended up jumping. One young woman gave a speech before diving, gesticulating passionately, but no one could hear her. One young man tenderly helped a young woman onto the windowsill. Then he held her out, away from the building, like a ballet dancer, and let her drop. He did the same for a second and a third. Finally, a fourth girl stood on the windowsill; she embraced him and they shared a long kiss. Then he held her out and dropped her, too. Then he himself was in the air. As he fell, people noticed, as his pants ballooned out, that he wore smart tan shoes. One reporter wrote, "I saw his face before they covered it. You could see in it that he was a real man. He had done his best."[3]

The fire had started at about 4:40 that afternoon, when somebody on the eighth floor threw a cigarette or a match into one of the great scrapheaps of cotton left over from the tailoring process. The pile quickly burst into flames.

Somebody alerted the factory manager, Samuel Bernstein, who grabbed some nearby buckets of water and dumped them on the fire. They did little good. The cotton scraps were explosively flammable, more so than paper, and there was roughly a ton of the stuff piled on the eighth floor alone.[4]

Bernstein dumped more buckets of water on the growing fire, but by this point they had no effect whatsoever, and the flames were spreading to the tissue paper patterns hanging above the wooden work desks. He ordered workers to drag a fire hose from a nearby stairwell. They opened the valve, but there was no pressure. As a historian of the fire, David Von Drehle, has argued, Bernstein made a fatal decision in those first three minutes. He could have spent the time fighting the fire or evacuating the nearly five hundred workers. Instead, he battled the exploding fire, to no effect. If he had spent

51

the time evacuating, it is possible that nobody would have died that day.[5]

When Bernstein finally did take his eyes off the wall of fire, he was astonished by what he saw. Many of the women on the eighth floor were taking the time to go to the dressing room to retrieve their coats and belongings. Some were looking for their time cards so they could punch out.

Eventually, the two factory owners up on the tenth floor were alerted to the fire, which had already consumed the eighth floor and was spreading quickly to their own. One of them, Isaac Harris, gathered a group of workers and figured it was probably suicidal to try to climb down through the fire. "Girls, let us go up on the roof! Get on the roof!" he bellowed. The other owner, Max Blanck, was paralyzed by fear. He stood frozen with a look of terror on his face, holding his youngest daughter in one arm and his elder daughter's hand with the other.[6] A clerk, who was evacuating with the firm's order book, decided to throw it down and save his boss's life instead.

Most of the workers on the eighth floor were able to get out, but the workers on the ninth floor had little warning until the fire was already upon them. They ran like terrified schools of fish from one potential exit to another. There were two elevators, but they were slow and overloaded. There was no sprinkler system. There was a fire escape, but it was rickety and blocked. On normal days the workers were searched as they headed home, to prevent theft. The factory had been designed to force them through a single choke point in order to get out. Some of the doors were locked. As the fire surrounded them, the workers were left to make desperate life-and-death decisions with limited information in a rising atmosphere of fire, smoke, and terror.

Three friends, Ida Nelson, Katie Weiner, and Fanny Lansner, were in the changing room when the screams of "Fire!" reached them. Nelson decided to sprint for one of the stairwells. Weiner went to the elevators and saw an elevator car descending the shaft. She hurled herself into space, diving onto the roof. Lansner took neither course and didn't make it out.[7]

Mary Bucelli later described her own part in the vicious scramble to get out first: "I can't tell you because I gave so many pushes and kicks. I gave and received. I was throwing them down wherever I met them," she said of her co-workers. "I was only looking for my own life. . . . At a moment like that, there is big confusion and you must understand that you cannot see anything. . . . You see a multitude of things, but you can't distinguish anything. With the confusion and the fight that you take, you can't distinguish anything."[8]

Joseph Brenman was one of the relatively few men in the factory. A crowd of women were pushing between him and the elevators. But they were small, and many of them were faint. He shoved them aside and barreled his way onto the elevator and to safety.

The fire department arrived quickly but its ladders could not reach the eighth floor. The water from its hoses could barely reach that high, just enough to give the building exterior a light dousing.

SHAME

The horror of the Triangle Shirtwaist fire traumatized the city. People were not only furious at the factory owners, but felt some deep responsibility themselves. In 1909 a young Russian immigrant named Rose Schneiderman had led the women who worked at Triangle and other factories on a strike to address the very issues that led to the fire disaster. The picketers were harassed by company guards. The city looked on indifferently, as it did upon the lives of the poor generally. After the fire there was a collective outpouring of rage, fed by collective guilt at the way people had self-centeredly gone about their lives, callously indifferent to the conditions and suffering of the people close around them. "I can't begin to tell you how disturbed the people were everywhere," Frances Perkins remembered. "It was as though we had all done something wrong. It shouldn't have been. We were sorry. Mea culpa! Mea culpa!"[9]

A large memorial march was held, and then a large meeting, with all the leading citizens of the city. Perkins was on stage as a representative of the Consumers' League when Rose Schneiderman electrified the crowd: "I would be a traitor to those poor burned bodies if I were to come here to talk good fellowship. We have tried you, good people of the public — and we have found you wanting!

"The old Inquisition had its rack and its thumbscrews and its instruments of torture with iron teeth. We know what these things are today: the iron teeth are our necessities, the thumbscrews are the high-powered and swift machinery close to which we must work, and the rack is here in the firetrap structures that will destroy us the minute they catch fire. . . .

"We have tried you, citizens! We are trying

you now and you have a couple of dollars for the sorrowing mothers and brothers and sisters by way of a charity gift. But every time the workers come out in the only way they know to protest against conditions which are unbearable, the strong hand of the law is allowed to press down heavily upon us. . . . I can't talk fellowship to you who are gathered here. Too much blood has been spilled!"[10]

The fire and its aftershocks left a deep mark on Frances Perkins. Up until that point she had lobbied for worker rights and on behalf of the poor, but she had been on a conventional trajectory, toward a conventional marriage, perhaps, and a life of genteel good works. After the fire, what had been a career turned into a vocation. Moral indignation set her on a different course. Her own desires and her own ego became less central and the cause itself became more central to the structure of her life. The niceties of her class fell away. She became impatient with the way genteel progressives went about serving the poor. She became impatient with their prissiness, their desire to stay pure and above the fray. Perkins hardened. She threw herself into the rough and tumble of politics. She was willing to take morally hazardous action if it would prevent another catastrophe like the one that befell the women at the Triangle factory. She was willing to compromise and work with corrupt officials if it would produce results. She pinioned herself to this cause for the rest of her life.

SUMMONED

Today, commencement speakers tell graduates to follow their passion, to trust their feelings, to reflect and find their purpose in life. The assumption behind these clichés is that when you are figuring out how to lead your life, the most important answers are found deep inside yourself. When you are young and just setting out into adulthood, you should, by this way of thinking, sit down and take some time to discover yourself, to define what is really important to you, what your priorities are, what arouses your deepest passions. You should ask certain questions: What is the purpose of my life? What do I want from life? What are the things that I truly value, that are not done just to please or impress the people around me?

By this way of thinking, life can be organized like a business plan. First you take an inventory of your gifts and passions. Then you set goals and come up with some metrics to organize your progress toward those goals. Then you map out a strategy to achieve your purpose, which will help you distinguish those things that move you toward your goals from those things that seem urgent but are really just distractions. If you define a realistic purpose early on and execute your strategy flexibly, you will wind up leading a purposeful life. You will have achieved self-determination, of the sort captured in the oft-quoted lines from William Ernest Henley's poem "Invictus": "I am the master of my fate / I am the captain of my soul."

This is the way people tend to organize their lives in our age of individual autonomy. It's a method that begins with the self and ends with the self, that begins with self-investigation and ends in self-fulfillment. This is a life determined by a series of individual choices. But Frances Perkins found her purpose in life using a different method, one that was more common in past eras. In this method, you don't ask, What do I want from life? You ask a different set of questions: What does life want from me? What are my circumstances calling me to do?

In this scheme of things we don't create our lives; we are summoned by life. The important answers are not found inside, they are found outside. This perspective begins not within the autonomous self, but with the concrete circumstances in which you happen to be embedded. This perspective begins with an awareness that the world existed long before you and will last long after you, and that in the brief span of your life you have been thrown by fate, by history, by chance, by evolution, or by God into a specific place with specific problems and needs. Your job is to figure certain things out: What does this environment need in order to be made whole? What is it that needs repair? What tasks are lying around waiting to be performed? As the novelist Frederick Buechner put it, "At what points do my talents and deep gladness meet the world's deep need?"

Viktor Frankl described this sort of call in his famous 1946 book *Man's Search for Meaning*. Frankl was a Jewish psychiatrist in Vienna who was rounded up in 1942 by the Nazis and sent to a ghetto and then to a series of concentration camps. His wife, mother, and brother died in the camps. Frankl spent most of his time in camp laying tracks for railway lines. This was not the life he had planned for himself. This was not his passion, or his dream. This is not what he would be doing if he were marching to the beat of his own drummer. But this was the life events had assigned to him. And it became clear to him that what sort of person he would wind up being depended upon what sort of inner decision he would make in response to his circumstances.

"It did not really matter what we expected from life," he wrote, "but rather what life expected from us. We needed to stop asking the meaning of life, and instead think of ourselves as those who were being questioned by life — daily and hourly."[11] Frankl concluded that fate had put a moral task and an intellectual task before him. It had given him an assignment.

His moral task was to suffer well, to be worthy of his sufferings. He could not control how much he suffered, or whether or when he would end up in the gas chamber or as a corpse by the side of the road, but he could control his inner response to his sufferings. The Nazis tried to dehumanize and insult their victims, and some prisoners went along with this degradation or retreated into their memories of a happier past. But some prisoners struggled against the insults and fortified their own integrity. "One could make a victory of those experiences, turning life into

60

an inner triumph," Frankl realized. One could struggle against the insults by asserting small acts of dignity, not necessarily to change your outer life or even your ultimate fate, but to strengthen the beams and pillars of your inner structure. He could exercise what he called an "inner hold," a rigorous control of his own inner state, a disciplined defense of his own integrity.

"Suffering had become a task on which we did not want to turn our backs," Frankl wrote.[12] Once he became aware of the task events had assigned to him, he understood the meaning and ultimate purpose of his life and the opportunity the war had given him to realize that purpose. And once he understood the meaning of these events, survival itself became easier. As Nietzsche observed, "He who has a why to live for can bear almost any how."

Frankl's other assignment was to take the circumstances into which he had been put and turn them into wisdom he could take to the world. Frankl had been given a great intellectual opportunity, the opportunity to study human beings under the most horrific conditions. He had the chance to share his observations with his fellow prisoners, and, if he survived, he figured he could spend the rest of his life sharing this knowledge with the world beyond.

When he had the mental energy, he spoke with groups of prisoners, telling them to take their lives seriously and struggle to preserve their inner hold. He told them to focus their minds upward on the image of a loved one, to preserve, share, and strengthen love for their absent wife or child or parent or friend, even in the midst of circumstances that conspire to destroy love, even though the loved one, having been sent to a different camp, might already be dead. Amid the grit and grime and the corpses one could still rise upward: "I called to the Lord from my narrow prison and he answered me in the freedom of space." One could, Frankl wrote, still participate in a rapturous passion for one's beloved and thus understand the full meaning of the words "The angels are lost in perpetual contemplation of an infinite glory."

He told potential suicides that life had not stopped expecting things from them, and that something in the future was still expected of them. In the darkness after lights out, he told his fellow prisoners that someone was watching them — a friend, a wife, somebody alive or dead, or God — who did not want to be disappointed.[13] Life, he concluded, "ultimately means taking the responsibility to find the right answer to its problems and to fulfill the tasks which it constantly sets before the individual."[14]

Few people are put in circumstances that horrific and extreme, but all of us are given gifts, aptitudes, capacities, talents, and traits that we did not strictly earn. And all of us are put in circumstances that call out for action, whether they involve poverty, suffering, the needs of a family, or the opportunity to communicate some message. These circumstances give us the great chance to justify our gifts.

Your ability to discern your vocation depends on the condition of your eyes and ears, whether they are sensitive enough to understand the assignment your context is giving you. As the Jewish Mishnah puts it, "It's not your obligation to complete the work, but neither are you free to desist from beginning it."

VOCATION

Frankl, like Perkins, had a vocation. A vocation is not a career. A person choosing a career looks for job opportunities and room for advancement. A person choosing a career is looking for something that will provide financial and psychological benefits.

If your job or career isn't working for you, you choose a different one.

A person does not choose a vocation. A vocation is a calling. People generally feel they have no choice in the matter. Their life would be unrecognizable unless they pursued this line of activity.

Sometimes they are called by indignation. Frances Perkins witnessed the Triangle fire and was indignant that this tear in the moral fabric of the world could be permitted to last. Other people are called by an act. A woman picks up a guitar and from that moment knows that she is a guitarist. Playing is not something she does; a guitarist is who she is. Still other people are called by a Bible verse or a literary passage. One summer morning in 1896, Albert Schweitzer came upon the biblical passage "Whosoever would save his life shall lose it and whosoever shall lose his life for my sake shall save it." He knew at the moment he was called to give up his very successful career as a musical scholar and organist to go into medicine and become a jungle doctor.

A person with a vocation is not devoted to civil rights, or curing a disease, or writing a great novel, or running a humane company because it meets some cost-benefit analysis.

Such people submit to their vocations for reasons deeper and higher than utility and they cling to them all the more fiercely the more difficulties arise. Schweitzer would write, "Anybody who proposes to do good must not expect people to roll any stones out of his way, and must calmly accept his lot even if they roll a few more onto it. Only force that in the face of obstacles becomes stronger can win."[15]

It is important to point out how much the sense of vocation is at odds with the prevailing contemporary logic. A vocation is not about fulfilling your desires or wants, the way modern economists expect us to do. A vocation is not about the pursuit of happiness, if by "happiness" you mean being in a good mood, having pleasant experiences, or avoiding struggle and pain. Such a person becomes an instrument for the performance of the job that has been put before her. She molds herself to the task at hand. While serving as an instrument in the fight against Soviet tyranny, Aleksandr Solzhenitsyn put it this way: "It makes me happier, more secure, to think that I do not have to plan and manage everything for myself, that I am only a sword made sharp to smite the unclean forces, an enchanted sword to cleave and disperse them. Grant, O Lord, that I may not break as I strike! Let me not fall from Thy hand!"

And yet people with vocations are generally not morose. In the first place, there is the joy they typically take in their own activities. Dorothy L. Sayers, best known today as a mystery writer but also a respected scholar and theologian in her time, used to make a distinction between serving the community and serving the work. People who seek to serve the community end up falsifying their work, she wrote, whether the work is writing a novel or baking bread, because they are not single-mindedly focused on the task at hand. But if you serve the work — if you perform each task to its utmost perfection — then you will experience the deep satisfaction of craftsmanship and you will end up serving the community more richly than you could have consciously planned. And one sees this in people with a vocation — a certain rapt expression, a hungry desire to perform a dance or run an organization to its utmost perfection. They feel the joy of having their values in deep harmony with their behavior. They experience a wonderful certainty of action that banishes weariness from even the hardest days.

The Triangle Shirtwaist Factory fire wasn't

the only event that defined Frances Perkins's purpose in life, but it was a major one. This horror had been put in front of her. And like many people, she found a fiercer resolve amid a flood of righteous rage. It wasn't just that so many people had died — after all, they could not be brought back to life; it was also the "ongoing assault on the common order that the fire came to symbolize." There is a universal way people should be treated, a way that respects their dignity as living creatures, and this way was being violated by their mistreatment. The person who experiences this kind of indignation has found her vocation.

THE RIGOROUS CHILDHOOD

Perkins was born on Beacon Hill in Boston on April 10, 1880. Her ancestors had come over in the great Protestant migration in the middle of the seventeenth century, settling first in Massachusetts and then in Maine. One ancestor, James Otis, was an incendiary Revolutionary War hero. Another, Oliver Otis Howard, served as a general in the Civil War before founding Howard University, the historically black college in Washington, D.C. Howard visited the Perkins home when Frances was fifteen. Because he had lost his arm in the war,

Frances served as his scribe.[16]

The Perkinses had been farmers and brickmakers through the centuries, mostly near the Damariscotta River east of Portland, Maine. Frances's mother was a member of the large Bean family. They gave their daughter a traditional Yankee upbringing: parsimonious, earnest, and brutally honest. In the evenings, Fred Perkins read Greek poetry and recited Greek plays with friends. He began to teach Frances Greek grammar when she was seven or eight. Frances's mother was heavy, artistic, and assertive. When Frances was ten, her mother took her to a hat shop. The fashionable hats of the day were narrow and tall, with feathers and ribbons. But Susan Bean Perkins plopped a low-crowned, simple, three-cornered hat onto Frances's head. What she said next reflects a very different sort of child rearing than is common today. While today we tend to tell children how wonderful they are, in those days parents were more likely to confront children with their own limitations and weaknesses. They were more likely to confront them with an honesty that can seem brutal to us today:

"There, my dear, that is your hat," her mother said. "You should always wear a hat something like this. You have a very broad face. It's broader between the two cheekbones than it is up at the top. Your head is narrower above the temples than it is at the cheekbones. Also, it lops off very suddenly into your chin. The result is you always need to have as much width in your hat as you have width in your cheekbones. Never let yourself get a hat that is narrower than your cheekbones, because it makes you look ridiculous."[17]

These days, New England Yankee culture has been diluted by the softening influence of the global culture, but then it was still hard and distinct. Yankees were reticent, self-reliant, egalitarian, and emotionally tough. Sometimes that toughness devolved into frigidity. But sometimes it was motivated by and intermixed with a fierce love and tenderness. New Englanders tended to have an acute awareness of their own sinfulness, and they worshipped a God who demonstrated his love through restraint and correction. They worked hard. They did not complain.

One evening, Perkins, then a young woman, came downstairs wearing a new party dress. Her father told her that it made her look ladylike. Perkins reflected later, "Even if I had ever succeeded in making myself look pretty — which, mind you, I'm not saying I ever succeeded in doing — my father would never have told me. That would have been a sin."[18]

The Yankees also combined what you might call social conservatism with political liberalism. Traditional and stern in their private lives, they believed in communal compassion and government action. They believed that individuals have a collective responsibility to preserve the "good order." Even in the mid-eighteenth century, the New England colonies had levels of taxation for state and local governments that were twice as high as the levels in colonies such as Pennsylvania and Virginia. They also put tremendous faith in education. For the past 350 years, New England schools have been among the best in the United States. New Englanders have, to this day, some of the highest levels of educational attainment in the nation.[19]

Perkins's parents saw to it that she was educated, but she never earned good grades. She had a natural facility with words, and in high school she used her glibness to slide by. She then went off to Mount Holyoke College, a member of the class of 1902. The rules at the college, and at colleges generally, were, again, very different from the rules today. Today, students live more or less unsupervised in their dorms. They are given the freedom to conduct their private lives as they see fit. Then, they were placed under restrictions, many of which seem absurd now, that were designed to inculcate deference, modesty, and respect. Here are some of the rules that formed part of the deference code when Perkins entered Holyoke: "Freshmen should keep a respectful silence in the presence of sophomores. Freshmen meeting a sophomore on the campus should bow respectfully. No Freshman shall wear a long skirt or hair high on head before the mid-year examinations."[20] Perkins survived the restraint, and the hazing that went along with this class structure, and became one of the social stars of her class, elected class president her senior year.

Today, teachers tend to look for their students' intellectual strengths, so they can cultivate them. But a century ago, professors tended to look for their students' moral weaknesses, so they could correct them. A Latin teacher, Esther Van Dieman, diagnosed Perkins's laziness, her tendency to be too easy on herself. Van Dieman used Latin grammar the way a drill instructor might use forced marches, as an ordeal to cultivate industriousness. She forced Perkins to work, hour upon hour, on precise recitations of the Latin verb tenses. Perkins would burst into tears in frustration and boredom, but later expressed appreciation for the enforced discipline: "For the first time I became conscious of character."[21]

Perkins was interested in history and literature, and she floundered badly in chemistry. Nonetheless, her chemistry teacher, Nellie Goldthwaite, hounded her into majoring in chemistry. The idea was that if she was tough enough to major in her weakest subject, she'd be tough enough to handle whatever life threw at her. Goldthwaite urged Perkins to take the hardest courses even if it meant earning mediocre grades. Perkins took the challenge. Goldthwaite became her faculty adviser. Years later, Perkins told a student with the school's alumnae quarterly, "The undergraduate mind should concentrate on the scientific courses, which temper the human spirit, harden and refine it, and make of it a tool with which one may tackle any kind of material."[22]

Mount Holyoke was the sort of school that leaves a permanent mark on its students. It did not see its role, as modern universities tend to, in purely Adam I cognitive terms. It was not there merely to teach people how to think. It was not there merely to help students question their assumptions. Instead, it successfully performed the broader role of college: helping teenagers become adults. It inculcated self-control. It helped its students discover new things to love. It took young women and ignited their moral passions by giving them a sense that humans are caught in a web of good and evil and that life is an epic struggle between these large forces. A dozen voices from across the institution told students that while those who lead flat and unremarkable lives may avoid struggle, a well-lived life involves throwing oneself into struggle, that large parts of the most worthy lives are spent upon the rack, testing moral courage and facing opposition and ridicule, and that those who pursue struggle end up being happier than those who pursue pleasure.

Then it told them that the heroes in this struggle are not the self-aggrandizing souls who chase after glory; they are rather the heroes of renunciation, those who accept some arduous calling. Then it tried to cut down their idealism and make it permanent by criticizing mere flights of compassion and self-congratulatory sacrifice. It emphasized that performing service is not something you do out of the goodness of your heart but as a debt you are repaying for the gift of life.

Then it gave them concrete ways to live this life of steady, heroic service. Over the decades, Mount Holyoke sent hundreds of women to missionary and service jobs in northwest Iran, Natal in southern Africa, and Maharashtra in western India. "Do what nobody else wants to do; go where nobody else wants to go," the school's founder, Mary Lyon, implored her students.

In 1901 a new president arrived, Mary Woolley, one of the first women to graduate from Brown and a biblical studies scholar. She wrote an essay titled "Values of College Training for Women" for *Harper's Bazaar* that captures the tone of high moral ambition that characterized life at the school. "Character is the main object for education," she declared, continuing, "A true perspective implies poise." Today, the word "poise" suggests social grace. But in that day it referred to the deeper qualities of steadiness and balance. "The lack of these qualities is often the weak place in the armor, and good impulses, high purposes, real ability, fail of their end."[23]

The Mount Holyoke education was dominated by theology and the classics — Jerusalem and Athens. The students were to take from religion an ethic of care and compassion, and from the ancient Greeks and Romans a certain style of heroism — to be courageous and unflinching in the face of the worst the world could throw at you. In her *Harper's Bazaar* essay, Woolley quoted the Stoic philosopher Epictetus: "To live in the presence of great truths and eternal laws, to be led by permanent ideals, that is what keeps a man patient when the world ignores him and calm and unspoiled when the world praises him." Perkins and Woolley would remain friends until Woolley's death.

Perkins also went to college at a time when the social gospel movement was at its most influential. In response to urbanization and industrialization, the leaders of the movement, including Walter Rauschenbusch, rejected the individualistic and privatized religion that was prevalent in many genteel churches. It is not enough, Rauschenbusch argued, to heal the sinfulness in each individual human heart. There is also suprapersonal sin — evil institutions and social structures that breed oppression and suffering. The leaders of the social gospel movement challenged their listeners to test and purify themselves by working for social reform. The real Christian life, they said, is not a solitary life of prayer and repentance. It is a life of sacrificial service, which involves practical solidarity with the poor and membership in a larger movement working to repair God's kingdom on earth.

As class president, Perkins helped select her class motto, "Be ye steadfast." The full verse, which Perkins read to her classmates in their final prayer meeting, is from 1 Corinthians. "Therefore my beloved brethren, be ye steadfast, unmovable, always abounding in the work of the Lord, forasmuch as ye know that your labor is not in vain in the Lord."

Holyoke took Perkins, who had been taught, because of her sex and because of her stature, to think lowly of herself, and it persuaded her and the other women that she could do something heroic. But it achieved this task in an ironic way. It didn't tell her that she was awesome and qualified for heroism. It forced her to confront her natural weaknesses. It pushed her down. It pushed her down and then taught her to push herself upward and outward. Perkins came to Holyoke sweet and glib, diminutive and charming. She left stronger, fortified, ardent for service and clearly unsuited to the narrow bourgeois world in which she'd grown up. When Frances Perkins's mother came to see her daughter graduate from Mount Holyoke, she remarked in a tone of dismay, "I don't recognize my daughter Fanny anymore. I can't understand it. She's a stranger to me."[24]

TENDER TOUGHNESS

Perkins knew she wanted some sort of heroic life, but she struggled after graduation to find a specific role. She was too inexperienced to be a social worker; the agencies would not hire her. She tried teaching at an upscale school for girls in Lake Forest, Illinois, but it was uninspiring. Eventually she also commuted in to Chicago and became involved with Hull House.

Hull House was a settlement house cofounded by Jane Addams, the leading American social reformer of her day. The idea was to give women a new range of service careers, to link the affluent with the poor, and to re-create the sense of community that had been destroyed by the disruptions of industrialization. It was modeled after Toynbee Hall in London, in which affluent university men organized social gatherings with the poor in the same manner in which they would organize them with one another.

At Hull House, affluent women lived among the poor and working classes, serving as counselors, assistants, and advisers and taking on projects to make their lives better. They offered job training, child care, a savings bank, English lessons, even art classes.

Today, community service is sometimes used as a patch to cover over inarticulateness about the inner life. Not long ago, I asked the head of a prestigious prep school how her institution teaches its students about character. She answered by telling me how many hours of community service the students do. That is to say, when I asked her about something internal, she answered by talking about something external. Her assumption seemed to be that if you go off and tutor poor children, that makes you a good person yourself.

And so it goes. Many people today have deep moral and altruistic yearnings, but, lacking a moral vocabulary, they tend to convert moral questions into resource allocation questions. How can I serve the greatest number? How can I have impact? Or, worst of all: How can I use my beautiful self to help out those less fortunate than I?

The atmosphere at Hull House was quite different. The people who organized the place had a specific theory about how to build character, equally for those serving the poor and for the poor themselves.

Addams, like many of her contemporaries, dedicated her life to serving the needy, while being deeply suspicious of compassion. She was suspicious of its shapelessness, the way compassionate people tended to ooze out sentiment on the poor to no practical effect. She also rejected the self-regarding taint of the emotion, which allowed the rich to feel good about themselves because they were doing community service. "Benevolence is the twin of pride," Nathaniel Hawthorne had written. Addams had no tolerance for any pose that might put the server above those being served.

As with all successful aid organizations, she wanted her workers to enjoy their work, to love their service. At the same time, she wanted them to hold their sentiments in check and to struggle relentlessly against any feelings of superiority. At Hull House, social workers were commanded to make themselves small. They were commanded to check their sympathies and exercise scientific patience as they investigated the true needs of each individual. The social worker was to be a practical adviser, almost in the manner of today's management consultant — to investigate options, offer friendship and counsel, but never let her own opinions prevail over the decisions of the beneficiaries. The idea was to let the poor determine their own lives rather than becoming dependent upon others.

Addams observed a phenomenon one still sees frequently today: Many people graduate from college energetic, lively, and impressive, but by age thirty they have become duller and more cynical versions of themselves. Their ambitions have shrunk. At school, Addams wrote in her memoir, *Twenty Years at Hull House,* students are taught to be self-sacrificial and self-forgetting, to put the good of society above the good of their ego. But when they graduate they are told to look out for themselves, to settle down into marriage and, perhaps, career. The young women are effectively asked to repress their desire to right wrongs and alleviate suffering. "The girl loses something vital out of her life to which she is entitled," Addams wrote. "She is restricted and unhappy; her elders, meanwhile, are unconscious of the situation and we have all the elements of tragedy."[25] Addams saw Hull House not only as a place to help the poor; it was a place where the affluent could surrender to an ennobling vocation. "The final return of the deed is upon the head of the doer," Addams wrote.[26]

Perkins spent as much time at Hull House

as possible, first staying over for weekends, then longer stretches. When she left, she had more of a scientific mentality — data must be gathered. She knew how to navigate the landscape of poverty. She also had more courage. Her next job was with an organization in Philadelphia founded by a Hull House alumna. Bogus employment agencies were luring immigrant women into boardinghouses, sometimes drugging them and forcing them into prostitution. Perkins exposed 111 of these places by applying for such jobs herself, confronting the pimps face-to-face. Then, in 1909, with some experience under her belt, she joined Florence Kelley in New York at the National Consumers League. Kelley was a hero and inspiration to Perkins. "Explosive, hot-tempered, determined, she was no gentle saint," Perkins would later write. "She lived and worked like a missionary, no sacrifice too great, no effort too much. She was a deeply emotional and profoundly religious woman, although the expression was often unconventional."[27] While at the Consumers' League, Perkins lobbied against child labor and other atrocities.

In New York, she also fell in with the bohemian Greenwich Village crowd: Jack Reed, who later became involved in the

Russian Revolution; Sinclair Lewis, who once proposed marriage to her, at least semiseriously; and Robert Moses, who was part of the counterculture then but who would go on to become the domineering uber-engineer of New York City.

RETICENCE

Perkins was getting a bit tougher at every step along the way — at Mount Holyoke, at Hull House — and yet she was also getting more idealistic, more fervent about her cause. The Triangle Factory fire was the moment when those two processes took a definitive leap.

The United States ambassador to the United Nations, Samantha Power, perceptively observes that some people put themselves "at stake" when they get involved in a cause. That is to say, they feel that their own reputation and their own identity are at stake when decisions are made. They are active in the cause in part because of what it says about them, and they want their emotions and their identity and their pride to be validated along the way. Perkins was not "at stake" after the fire. She went to work in Albany, lobbying the state legislature for worker safety legislation. She left behind the prejudices of her upscale New York social set. She left behind the gentility of progressive politics. She would compromise ruthlessly if it meant making progress. Her mentor, Al Smith, a rising figure in New York politics, told Perkins that before long, the genteel progressives would lose interest in any cause. If you want to usher real change, he told her, you have to work with the sleazy legislators and the rough party pols. You have to be practical, subordinate your personal purity to the cause. Perkins learned that in a fallen world it is often the "tainted" people who help you do the most good. In Albany she began to work closely with the denizens of the Tammany Hall political machine, who were regarded with horror in the polite circles in which she had previously traveled.

In Albany, Perkins also learned how to deal with older men. One day she was standing by the elevators of the state capitol when a crude little senator named Hugh Frawley came out and started describing the confidential details of the backroom negotiations and moaning about the shameful work he was compelled to perform. Swept up in self-pity, he cried, "Every man's got a mother, you know."

Perkins kept a folder titled "Notes on the Male Mind" and recorded this episode in it. It played a major role in her political education: "I learned from this that the way men take women in political life is to associate them with motherhood. They know and respect their mothers — 99 percent of them do. It's a primitive and primary attitude. I said to myself, 'That's the way to get things done. So behave, dress, and so comport yourself that you remind them subconsciously of their mothers.' "[28]

Perkins was then thirty-three, and perky, though certainly not beautiful. Up until then, she had dressed in the conventional fashion of the day. But from that point on she began dressing like a mother. She wore somber black dresses with white bow ties at the neck. She wore pearls and a black tricorn hat and adopted a matronly demeanor. The press picked up on the change and started calling her "Mother Perkins" for the way she led sixty-something state legislators. She despised the nickname, but she found that the method worked. She suppressed her sexuality, her femininity, and even part of her identity in order to win the confidence of the old men around her. It's a questionable tactic today, when women should not have to suppress themselves to succeed, but in the 1920s, it was necessary.

Among other projects, Perkins lobbied

furiously for a bill to limit the workweek to 54 hours. She tried to befriend the machine bosses to get them to support the bill. They did their best to deceive and outmaneuver her, but she won support from some of the rank and file. "Me sister was a poor girl and she went to work when she was young," one machine pol, Big Tim Sullivan, confided to her. "I feel kind sorry for them poor girls that work the way you say they work. I'd like to do them a good turn. I'd like to do you a good turn."[29]

When the 54-hour workweek bill finally came to a vote, the legislators exempted one of the most egregious but politically influential industries, the canners. The activists for the bill had spent the previous months insisting that there could be no exemptions. All industries, especially the canners, had to be covered by the legislation. At the crucial moment, Perkins stood at the edge of the legislative chamber. On the spot, she had to decide whether to accept this deeply flawed bill or reject it as a matter of principle. Her colleagues argued vociferously for rejecting it. Instead, she took half a loaf. She told legislators her organization would support the bill. "This is my responsibility. I'll do it and hang for it if necessary."[30] Many Progressives were indeed outraged. But her tough-minded mentor, Florence Kelley, completely endorsed her decision. Forever after Perkins was known as a "half-a-loaf girl," in public or private life, as someone who would take as much as circumstances allowed.[31]

Around this time she met Paul Wilson, a handsome, wellborn progressive, who became a close aide to New York's reformist mayor, John Purroy Mitchel. Wilson fell in love with Perkins and slowly won her over. "Before you came into my life," she wrote to him, "it was a lonesome place — cold and raw and trembling except on the outside. . . . You stormed into my heart somehow and I could never let you go."[32]

The courtship was odd. Perkins's letters to Wilson are romantic, earnest, and passionate. But with her friends and co-workers she was extremely reticent, and decades later she would deny that she had ever felt strong emotions. They were married on September 26, 1913, at Grace Church in Lower Manhattan. They did not invite their friends or tell them of the wedding in advance. Perkins and Wilson informed their families, but too late for them to attend. Perkins dressed for the wedding alone in her apartment on Waverly Place and probably walked over. The two witnesses were just people who happened to be in the building at the time. There was no luncheon or tea afterward.

When she described her decision to marry in later years, she adopted the matter-of-fact tone that you might use for making a dental appointment. "There was a New England pride in me," Perkins said decades later. "I wasn't anxious to get married. To tell the truth, I was reluctant. I was no longer a child but a grown woman. I hadn't wanted to marry. I liked life better in a single harness."[33] But people were constantly asking her when she would find a husband, so she decided to get it out of the way, thinking, "I know Paul Wilson well. I like him. . . . I enjoy his friends and company and I might as well marry and get it off my mind."

Their first years were relatively happy. They lived in a gracious townhouse on Washington Square, not far from where Perkins had been drinking tea when the Triangle fire erupted. Wilson served in the mayor's office. Perkins continued with her social work. Their home became a center for political activists of the day.

Soon things began to deteriorate. John Mitchel was voted out of office. Wilson had an affair with a society lady, which caused a furor and then was never mentioned again. Perkins began to feel stifled in the marriage and asked for a separation. "I've made some wretched blunders," Perkins wrote to Wilson. "I've become a different kind of person with a lesser degree of working efficiency and paler kind of spiritual efficiency."[34]

Then she got pregnant. The boy died shortly after birth. Perkins was consumed by grief, but that, too, was never mentioned again. Afterward, Perkins became executive secretary of the Maternity Center Association, a voluntary organization that sought to lower maternal and infant death rates. She also had a daughter, Susanna, named after the wife of the second governor of the Plymouth Colony.

Perkins wanted to have another child, but by 1918 Wilson was showing signs of mental illness. He seems to have been manic-depressive. He couldn't withstand any pressure. "It was always up and down. He was sometimes depressed, sometimes excited," Perkins said later. From 1918 on there were never anything but very short periods of reasonably comfortable accommodations to life. In one of these manic phases, Wilson invested his life's savings in a gold scheme and was wiped out. Perkins was sometimes afraid to be alone with him, because he was prone to violent rages and was much stronger than she was. He would spend significant parts of the next several decades in asylums and institutional care, where Perkins would visit him on weekends. When he was home he was unable to handle any responsibility. He had a nurse — euphemistically known as a secretary — to look after him. "He was becoming a kind of nonperson," Perkins's biographer, George Martin, wrote, "someone to be talked at rather than with."[35]

Her New England reticence kicked in. She called the loss of their family fortune "this accident," and she realized she would have to work to support the family. She pushed such "accidents" "into the background. I haven't brooded over them and had a Freudian collapse."[36] For the next several decades she tried to rope off her private life, conceal it from public view. This attitude was partly a product of her Yankee upbringing. But she was also reticent as a matter of philosophy and conviction. She believed that private emotions were too intricate to be exposed to public glare; she would have been horrified by the culture of exposure that is so prevalent today.

There is a general struggle between two philosophic dispositions, what the social critic Rochelle Gurstein calls the party of reticence and the party of exposure. The party of reticence believes that the tender emotions of the inner world are brutalized and polluted when they are exposed to the glare of public exhibition. The party of exposure believes that anything secret is suspect and that life works better when everything is brought out into the open and discussed. Perkins was definitely a member of the party of reticence. She stood with those who believe that everything that is complex, nuanced, contradictory, paradoxical, and mysterious about private sensations is reduced to banality when it is paraded about and summarized in pat phrases. Damage is done when people bring intimate things before mere acquaintances or total strangers. Precious emotions are lifted out of the context of trust and intimacy and trampled. Therefore people should keep what is private, private. Though she was a believer in government when it came to serving the poor and protecting the weak, she had a strong aversion to government when it trampled the right to privacy.

There was a cost to this philosophy. She was not superbly introspective. She did not excel at intimacy. She did not have a particularly happy private life. It is hard to know what would have happened if her husband had not spent so much time in mental institutions, but it is likely that her public vocation would have crowded out her energy and capacity for private intimacy nonetheless. She was built for the public campaign. She did not receive love well, or give it, or display vulnerability. Even her care for her daughter often took the form of a moral improvement crusade, which backfired. Frances exerted iron control over herself and expected it in her daughter.

But that daughter, Susanna, inherited her father's manic temperament. Starting when she was sixteen, when Perkins moved to Washington to serve in the Roosevelt administration, they seldom shared a home. Throughout her life, Susanna suffered severe bouts of depression. Susanna married a man who conducted a flagrant affair. By the 1940s, she was something of a hippie, twenty years before the term existed. She became involved with various counter-cultural groups. She developed a fixation on the Romanian sculptor Constantin Brancusi. She went out of her way to shock polite society and embarrass her mother. Perkins once invited Susanna to a society event and begged her to dress appropriately. Susanna chose a flamboyant green dress and wore her hair piled wildly atop her head, with garish flowers adorning her hair and neck.

"I have given way to morbid superstition that I am the cause of others' nervous collapse, my husband, my daughter," Perkins confessed. "[It] frightens and oppresses me."[37] Susanna was never really able to work and was supported by Frances. Even at age seventy-seven, Frances turned over her rent-controlled apartment in New York so that Susanna would have a place to live. She had to take a job to pay her daughter's bills.

Every virtue can come with its own accompanying vice. The virtue of reticence can yield the vice of aloofness. Perkins was not emotionally vulnerable to those close to her. Her public vocation never completely compensated for her private solitude.

DUTY

New York's governor Al Smith was Perkins's first and greatest political love. He was loyal, approachable, voluble and a man with the common touch. Smith also gave Perkins her first big break in government. He appointed her to the Industrial Commission, the body that regulated workplace conditions across the Empire State. The job brought a generous $8,000 a year salary and put Perkins in the middle of the major strikes and industrial disputes. She was not only a rare woman in a man's world, she was in the manliest precincts of the man's world. She'd travel to factory towns and throw herself in the middle of bitter disputes between energized labor organizers and determined corporate executives. There is no boasting in any of her reminiscences that this was a brave and even reckless thing to do. To her, this was simply a job that needed doing. The word "one" plays a crucial role in her descriptions of her own life. Sometimes she would use the formulation "I did this," but more often her diction was formal and archaic: "One did this . . ."

Nowadays we think of the use of "one" as pompous and starched. But for Perkins it was simply a way to avoid the first person pronoun. It was a way to suggest that any proper person would of course be duty-bound to do what she had done under the circumstances.

During the 1910s and 1920s in Albany, Perkins also had occasion to work with Franklin Delano Roosevelt. He did not impress her. She found him shallow and a bit arrogant. He had a habit of throwing his head back as he spoke. Later, when he was president, that gesture suggested confidence and buoyant optimism. But when he was young, Perkins just thought it made him look supercilious.

Roosevelt disappeared from Perkins's life when he suffered his polio attack. When he returned, she felt he had changed. He almost never spoke of his illness, but Perkins felt it "purged the slightly arrogant attitude he had displayed."[38]

One day, as Roosevelt was reentering politics, Perkins sat on a stage and watched him drag himself up to the podium to deliver a speech. His hands, supporting his weight on the podium, never stopped trembling. Perkins realized that after the speech, someone would have to cover his awkward movements as he lurched down from the stand. She gestured to a woman behind her, and as he concluded, they hurried up to Roosevelt, nominally to congratulate him, but actually to shield his movements with their skirts. Over the years, this became a routine.

Perkins admired the way Roosevelt gratefully and humbly accepted help. "I began to see what the great teachers of religion meant when they said that humility is the greatest of virtues," she later wrote, "and if you can't learn it, God will teach it to you by humiliation. Only so can a man be really great, and it was in those accommodations to necessity that Franklin Roosevelt began to approach the stature of humility and inner integrity which made him truly great."[39]

When Roosevelt was elected governor of New York, he offered Perkins the job of Industrial Commissioner. She wasn't sure she should take it, because she wasn't sure she could successfully manage an agency. "I believe that such talent as I may have for public service lies much more in the judicial and legislative work of the Department than in the administrative," she wrote in a note to Roosevelt. On the day he offered her the job, she told him that she would give him a day to reconsider, to consult with others. "If anyone says it's unwise to appoint me or will make trouble with the leaders, just disregard today. . . . I'm not going to tell anyone so you're not sewed up."[40]

Roosevelt responded, "That's very decent, I must say, but I'm not going to change my mind." He was pleased to appoint a woman to such a senior job, and Perkins's reputation as a public servant was exemplary. As one biographer, George Martin, put it, "As an administrator she was good, perhaps even more than good; as a judge or legislator she was quite extraordinary. She had a judicial temperament and a strong sense in all situations of what was fair. She was always open to new ideas and yet the moral purpose of the law, the welfare of mankind, was never overlooked."[41]

When he was elected president, Roosevelt asked Perkins to become his secretary of labor. Again, she resisted. When rumors of her potential nomination circulated during the transition, Perkins wrote FDR a letter saying that she hoped they were untrue. "You are quoted as saying that the newspaper predictions on cabinet posts are 80 percent wrong. I write to say that I honestly hope that what they've been printing about me is among the 80 percent of incorrect items. I've had my 'kick' out of the gratifying letters etc., but for your own sake and that of the U.S.A. I think that someone straight from the ranks of some group of organized workers should be appointed — to establish firmly the principle that labor is in the President's councils."[42] She also touched lightly on her family problems, which she feared might become a distraction. Roosevelt wrote a little squib on a piece of scratch paper and sent it back: "Have considered your advice and don't agree."[43]

Perkins's grandmother had told her that when somebody opens a door, you should always walk through. So Perkins confronted FDR with terms if she was to become his labor secretary. If she were to join the cabinet, FDR would have to commit to a broad array of social insurance policies: massive unemployment relief, a giant public works program, minimum wage laws, a Social Security program for old age insurance, and the abolition of child labor. "I suppose you are going to nag me about this forever," Roosevelt told her. She confirmed she would.

Perkins was one of only two top aides to stay with Roosevelt for his entire term as president. She became one of the tireless champions of the New Deal. She was central to the creation of the Social Security system. She was a major force behind many of the New Deal jobs programs such as the Civilian Conservation Corps, the Federal Works Agency, and the Public Works Administration. Through the Fair Labor Standards Act she established the nation's first minimum wage law and its first overtime law. She sponsored federal legislation on child labor and unemployment insurance. During World War II she resisted calls to draft women, sensing that women would benefit more over the long run if they could take the jobs that were being abandoned by drafted men.

Perkins excelled at reading Franklin Roosevelt. After he died, Perkins wrote a biographical work, *The Roosevelt I Knew*, which remains one of the most astute character sketches ever written about the man. Overshadowing all Roosevelt's decisions, Perkins wrote, "was his feeling that nothing in human judgment is final. One may courageously take the step that seems right today because it can be modified tomorrow if it does not work well." He was an improviser, not a planner. He took a step and adjusted, a step and adjusted. Gradually a big change would emerge.

This mentality develops, she continued, in "a man who is more an instrument than an engineer. The prophets of Israel would have called him an instrument of the Lord. The prophets of today could only explain his type of mind in terms of psychology, about which they know so pitiably little."[44]

Perkins devised a strategy to deal with this man who was prone to changing his mind and shifting direction depending upon who was the last adviser he encountered. Before her meeting with the president she would prepare a one-page memo outlining the concrete options before him. They would go over her outline and Roosevelt would state his preference. Then Perkins would force him to repeat himself: "Do you authorize me to go ahead with this? Are you sure?"

They would have a little more discussion, and then Perkins would underline his decision a second time: "Are you sure you want item number one? Do you want items number two and three? You understand that this is what we do and this is who is opposed?" The purpose of this exercise was to sear a photograph of the decision into Roosevelt's memory. Then she would ask him a third time, asking him whether he explicitly remembered his decision and understood the opposition he would face. "Is that all right? Is it still okay?"

FDR did not always stand up for Perkins when she needed it. He was too slippery a politician to extend loyalty downward all of the time. She was not popular with many of the men in the cabinet. For one thing, she had a tendency to go on at meetings. She was certainly not popular with the press. Her sense of privacy and her fierce desire to protect her husband prevented her from hanging around with reporters or ever letting down her guard. The reporters, in turn, were unsympathetic.

As the years went by, she became exhausted by the job. Her reputation waned.

Twice she sent Roosevelt a letter of resignation and twice he rejected it. "Frances, you can't go now. You mustn't put this on me now," Roosevelt pleaded. "I can't think of anybody else. I can't get used to anyone else. Not now! Do stay there and don't say anything. You are all right."

In 1939 she became the target of impeachment proceedings. The case revolved around an Australian longshoreman named Harry Bridges who led a general strike in San Francisco. Bridges's critics called him a Communist and demanded that he be deported for subversive activities. When the Soviet Union fell and the files were opened, it turned out they were right. Bridges was a Communist agent, known by the code name Rossi.[45]

But at the time, that wasn't so clear. Deportation hearings, operated by the Labor Department, dragged on. In 1937, more evidence against Bridges surfaced, and in 1938, the department began proceedings to deport him. These proceedings were blocked by a court decision, which was then appealed to the Supreme Court. The delay inflamed Bridges's critics, which included business groups and the leaders of rival unions.

Perkins bore the brunt of their criticism.

Why was the labor secretary shielding a subversive? One congressman accused her of being a Russian Jew and a Communist herself. In January 1939, J. Parnell Thomas of New Jersey introduced impeachment charges against her. The press coverage was brutal. Franklin Roosevelt was given a chance to rise to her defense, but, wary of soiling his own reputation by association, he just let her hang out there. Most of her allies in Congress remained silent, too. The Federation of Women's Clubs also refused to defend her. *The New York Times* wrote an ambiguous editorial. The common sentiment was that she was in fact a Communist, and nobody wanted to get in the line of fire of those who were persecuting her. It was left to the Tammany Hall pols to remain reliably steadfast beside her.

Perkins's grandmother had always told her that when social disaster strikes, "all are to act as though nothing had happened." Perkins soldiered on. Her description of that period is awkwardly phrased but revealing. "Of course if I had wept at all, or if I'd let myself down at all, I would have disintegrated," Perkins said later. "That's the kind of person which we New Englanders are. We disintegrate if we do these things. All the qualities in us of integrity and the ability to keep our heads clear and make decisions and take actions that are influenced by our personal suffering or personal effect on ourselves, that integrity would have been scattered, and I would not have had that inner core within myself which makes it possible for me to rely upon myself under the guidance of God to do the right thing."[46]

Put in plain language, Perkins was aware that there was a fragility within herself. If she relaxed the hold she had on herself, then all might fall apart. Over the years, Perkins had made frequent visits to the All Saints Convent in Catonsville, Maryland. She would go to the convent for two or three days at a time, gathering for prayers five times a day, eating simple meals, and tending the gardens. She spent most of those days in silence, and when the nuns came to mop her floor, they sometimes had to mop around her, for she was on her knees in prayer. During the impeachment crisis, Perkins visited the convent whenever she could. "I have discovered the rule of silence is one of the most beautiful things in the world," she wrote to a friend. "It preserves one from the temptation of the idle world, the fresh remark, the wisecrack, the angry challenge. . . . It is really quite remarkable what it does for one."[47]

She also reflected on a distinction that had once seemed unimportant to her. When a person gives a poor man shoes, does he do it for the poor man or for God? He should do it for God, she decided. The poor will often be ungrateful, and you will lose heart if you rely on immediate emotional rewards for your work. But if you do it for God, you will never grow discouraged. A person with a deep vocation is not dependent on constant positive reinforcement. The job doesn't have to pay off every month, or every year. The person thus called is performing a task because it is intrinsically good, not for what it produces.

Finally, on February 8, 1939, Perkins was able to meet her accusers. She appeared before the House Judiciary Committee as it considered articles of impeachment against her. She delivered a long and detailed recitation of the administrative procedures initiated against Bridges, the reasons for them, and the legal constraints preventing further action. The questions ranged from the skeptical to the brutal. When opponents made vicious charges against her, she asked them to repeat their question, believing that no person can be scurrilous twice. The photographs of the hearing make her look haggard and exhausted, but she impressed the committee with her detailed knowledge of the case.

Eventually, in March, the committee ruled that there were insufficient facts to support impeachment. She was cleared, but the report was vague and elliptical. It generated little press coverage and her reputation was permanently marred. Unable to resign, she soldiered on in the administration for another six years, helping out mostly behind the scenes. She was stoic about it all, never showing any public weakness or any self-pity. After her government service ended, when she could have written a memoir to give her side of the story, she declined.

During the Second World War, she served as an administrative troubleshooter. She urged Roosevelt to do something to help European Jewry. She became alarmed by the way federal action was beginning to infringe on privacy and civil liberties.

When FDR died in 1945, she was finally released from the cabinet, though President Truman asked her to serve on the Civil Service Commission. Instead of writing that memoir, she wrote a book about Roosevelt. It was a tremendous success, but it contains very little autobiography.

Perkins did not really experience private

joy until the end of her life. In 1957, a young labor economist asked her to teach a course at Cornell. The job paid about $10,000 a year, scarcely more than she had earned decades before as New York Industrial Commissioner, but she needed the money to pay for her daughter's mental health care.

At first, she lived in residential hotels during her time in Ithaca, but she was then invited to live in a small bedroom at Telluride House, a sort of fraternity house for some of Cornell's most gifted students. She was delighted by the invitation. "I feel like a bride on her wedding night!" she told friends.[48] While there, she drank bourbon with the boys and tolerated their music at all hours.[49] She attended the Monday house meetings, though she rarely spoke. She gave them copies of Baltasar Gracian's *The Art of Worldly Wisdom,* a seventeenth-century guidebook by a Spanish Jesuit priest on how to retain one's integrity while navigating the halls of power. She became close friends with Allan Bloom, a young professor who would go on to achieve fame as the author of *The Closing of the American Mind.* Some of the boys had trouble understanding how this small, charming, and unassuming old lady could have played such an important historical role.

She did not like airplanes and traveled alone by bus, sometimes having to make four or five connections to get to a funeral or a lecture. She tried to destroy some of her papers, to foil future biographers. She traveled with a copy of her will in her handbag, so that if she died she "wouldn't cause any trouble."[50] She died alone, in a hospital, on May 14, 1965, at age eighty-five. A few of the Telluride House boys served as pallbearers, including Paul Wolfowitz, who would go on to serve in the Reagan and Bush administrations. The minister read the "be ye steadfast" passage from 1 Corinthians that Perkins herself had read upon her graduation from Mount Holyoke College more than six decades before.

If you look back at her college yearbook photo, you see a small, cute, almost mousy young lady. It would be hard to foresee from that vulnerable expression that she would be able to endure so much hardship — the mental illnesses of her husband and daughter, the ordeal of being the solitary woman in a hypermasculine world, the decades of political battles and negative press.

But it would also be hard to foresee how much she would accomplish throughout the hardship. She faced her own weaknesses — laziness, glibness — early in life and steeled herself for a life of total commitment. She suppressed her own identity so she could lobby for her cause. She took on every new challenge and remained as steadfast as her motto. She was, as Kirstin Downey would put it in the title of her fine biography, "The Woman Behind the New Deal."

On the one hand she was a fervent liberal activist, of the sort we are familiar with today. But she combined this activism with reticent traditionalism, hesitancy, and a puritanical sensibility. Daring in politics and economics, she was conservative in morality. She practiced a thousand little acts of self-discipline to guard against self-indulgence, self-glorification, or, until the impeachment and the end of her life, self-reflection. Her rectitude and reticence pinched her private life and made her bad at public relations. But it helped her lead a summoned life, a life in service to a vocation.

Perkins didn't so much choose her life. She responded to the call of a felt necessity. A person who embraces a calling doesn't take a direct route to self-fulfillment. She is willing to surrender the things that are most dear, and by seeking to forget herself and submerge herself she finds a purpose that defines and fulfills herself. Such vocations almost always involve tasks that transcend a lifetime. They almost always involve throwing yourself into a historical process. They involve compensating for the brevity of life by finding membership in a historic commitment. As Reinhold Niebuhr put it in 1952:

Nothing that is worth doing can be achieved in our lifetime; therefore we must be saved by hope. Nothing which is true or beautiful or good makes complete sense in any immediate context of history; therefore we must be saved by faith. Nothing we do, however virtuous, can be accomplished alone; therefore we are saved by love. No virtuous act is quite as virtuous from the standpoint of our friend or foe as it is from our standpoint. Therefore we must be saved by the final form of love, which is forgiveness.[51]

Chapter 3
Self-Conquest

Ida Stover Eisenhower was born in 1862 in the Shenandoah Valley of Virginia, one of eleven children. Her childhood was more or less a series of catastrophes. When she was a young girl, Union soldiers invaded her home, hunting for her two teenage brothers. They threatened to burn down the barn and ransacked the town and surrounding country. Her mother died when Ida was nearly five, and her father died when she was eleven.

The children were scattered among distant relations. Ida became the assistant cook for the large household that was putting her up. She baked pies, pastries, and meats, darned socks, and patched clothing. She was not, however, sad and pitiable. From the start, she had spark and drive and pushed daringly against her hardships. She was an overworked orphan, but folks in town remembered her as something of a tomboy, wiry and unafraid, galloping bareback through town on any borrowed horse, and one time falling and breaking her nose.

Girls were generally not educated beyond eighth grade at the time, but Ida, who in early adolescence had memorized 1,365 Bible verses in six months on her own, possessed a tremendous drive to improve herself, in both Adam I and Adam II terms. One day, when she was fifteen, her host family went off on a family outing, leaving her alone. She packed her belongings and sneaked away, walking to Staunton, Virginia. She got a room and a job and enrolled herself in the local high school.

She graduated, taught for two years, and at twenty-one came into a $1,000 inheritance. She used $600 of that (more than $10,000 today) to buy an ebony piano, which was to remain the most treasured possession of her life. The rest she devoted to her education. She hitched on with a Mennonite caravan heading west, though she was not a Mennonite, and settled with her brother at the grandly named Lane University in Lecompton, Kansas. There were fourteen freshmen the year Ida matriculated, and classes were held in the parlor of a residential house.

Ida studied music. She was, according to faculty reports, not the brightest student, but she was diligent, and she earned good grades through hard digging. Her classmates found a joyful, gregarious personality and an extremely optimistic nature, and they elected her valedictorian.[1] She also met her temperamental opposite while at Lane, a dour and stubborn fellow named David Eisenhower. Inexplicably, they fell in love, and they remained together for life. Their children could not remember a serious argument between them, though David gave Ida ample cause.

They were married within the River Brethren church, a small orthodox sect that believed in plain dress, temperance, and pacifism. After a daring girlhood, Ida devoted herself to a strict, but not too strict, life. The women of the River Brethren sect wore bonnets as part of their religious garb. One day Ida and a friend decided they no longer wanted to wear the bonnets. They were ostracized at church, forced to sit alone in the back. But eventually they won the day and were readmitted, bonnetless, into the community. Ida was strict in her faith but fun-loving and humane in practice.

David opened a store with a partner named Milton Good near Abilene, Kansas.

Later, after the store failed, David told his family that Good had disappeared and stolen all the store's money. That was a face-saving lie, which his sons appeared to believe. The fact is that David Eisenhower was solitary and difficult. He seems to have abandoned the business or had a falling-out with his partner. After the business collapsed, David left for Texas, leaving Ida with an infant son at home and another on the way. "David's decision to quit the store and abandon his pregnant wife is incomprehensible," the historian Jean Smith writes. "He had no job lined up or a profession on which to fall back."[2]

David eventually found a job doing manual labor in a railroad yard. Ida followed him to Texas and set up home in a shack along the tracks, where Dwight was born. By the time Ida was twenty-eight, they'd hit bottom. They had $24.15 in cash and few possessions except the piano back in Kansas, and David had no marketable skills.[3]

The extended Eisenhower family came to the rescue. David was offered a job at a creamery in Abilene, and they moved back to Kansas and back to the middle class. Ida raised five boys, all of whom would go on to remarkable success and all of whom would spend their lives revering her. Dwight would later call her "the finest person I've ever known."[4] In *At Ease,* the memoir composed late in life, Ike revealed how much he idolized her, though his prose, characteristically, was restrained: "Her serenity, her open smile, her gentleness with all and her tolerance of their ways, despite an inflexible religious conviction and her own strict pattern of personal conduct, made even a brief visit with Ida Eisenhower memorable for a stranger. And for her sons, privileged to spend a boyhood in her company, the memories are indelible."[5]

There was no drinking, card playing, or dancing in the house. There was not much demonstrated love. Dwight's father was quiet, somber, and inflexible, while Ida was warm and down to earth. But there were Ida's books, her tutelage, and her commitment to education. Dwight became an avid reader of classical history, reading about the battles of Marathon and Salamis and heroes like Pericles and Themistocles. There was also Ida's vibrant, funny personality, and her maxims, which came in a steady, tough-minded flow: "God deals the cards and we play them," "Sink or swim," "Survive or perish." The family prayed and read the Bible every day, the five brothers taking turns and forfeiting the right to be the reader when they stumbled over a line. Though Dwight was not religious later in life, he was steeped in the biblical metaphysic and could cite verses with ease. Ida, though devout herself, strongly believed that religious views were a matter of personal conscience and not to be imposed on others.

During Eisenhower's presidential campaigns, Abilene was portrayed as an idyllic, Norman Rockwell piece of rural America. In reality, it was a harsh environment covered by a thick code of respectability and propriety. Abilene had gone from boomtown to Bible Belt, from whorehouses to schoolmarms, without any of the intervening phases. Victorian morality was reinforced by puritan rigor, what one historian has called Augustinianism come to America.

Ida began raising her boys in a house Ike would later calculate to be about 833 square feet. Thrift was essential, self-discipline a daily lesson. Before modern medicine, with sharp tools and hard physical labor to be done, there was a greater chance of accidents and more catastrophic consequences when they came. One year an invasion of grasshoppers ruined the crops.[6] Dwight suffered a leg infection as a teenager and refused to let the doctors amputate because it would have ended his football career. He slipped in and out of consciousness and had one of his brothers sleep on the threshold of his room to prevent the doctor from cutting off the leg while Ike was asleep. Once, when Dwight was babysitting his three-year-old brother, Earl, he left a pocketknife open on a windowsill. Earl got up on a chair, tried to grasp the knife, but it slipped from his hands and plunged into his eye, damaging the eye and producing a lifelong sense of guilt in Dwight.

Somebody should write a history of how the common death of children shaped culture and beliefs. It must have created a general sense that profound suffering was not far off, that life was fragile and contained unbearable hardships. After Ida lost one son, Paul, she converted to the sect that would later become the Jehovah's Witnesses, in search of a more personal and compassionate expression of faith. Eisenhower himself would later lose his own firstborn son, Doud Dwight, known in the family as "Icky," an experience that darkened his world ever after. "This was the greatest disappointment and disaster in my life," he would write decades later, "the one I have never been able to forget completely.

Today, when I think of it, even now as I write about it, the keenness of our loss comes back to me as fresh and terrible as it was in that long dark day soon after Christmas, 1920."[7]

The fragility and remorselessness of this life demanded a certain level of discipline. If a single slip could produce disaster, with little in the way of a social safety net to cushion the fall; if death, or drought, or disease, or betrayal could come crushingly at any moment; then character and discipline were paramount requirements. This was the shape of life: an underlying condition of peril, covered by an ethos of self-restraint, reticence, temperance, and self-wariness, all designed to minimize the risks. People in that culture developed a moral abhorrence of anything that might make life even more perilous, like debt or childbirth out of wedlock. They developed a stern interest in those activities that might harden resilience.

Any child raised by Ida Eisenhower was going to value education, but the general culture placed much less emphasis on it than ours does now. Of the two hundred children who entered first grade with Dwight in 1897, only thirty-one graduated with him from high school. Academics were

116

less important because you could get a decent job without a degree. What mattered more to long-term stability and success was having steady habits, the ability to work, the ability to sense and ward off sloth and self-indulgence. In that environment, a disciplined work ethic really was more important than a brilliant mind.

One Halloween evening, when he was about ten, Eisenhower's older brothers received permission to go out trick-or-treating, a more adventurous activity in those days than it is now. Ike wanted to go with them, but his parents told him he was too young. He pleaded with them, watched his brothers go, and then became engulfed by uncontrolled rage. He turned red. His hair bristled. Weeping and screaming, he rushed out into the front yard and began pounding his fists against the trunk of an apple tree, scraping the skin off and leaving his hands bloody and torn.

His father shook him, lashed him with a hickory switch, and sent him up to bed. About an hour later, with Ike sobbing into his pillow, his mother came up and sat silently rocking in the chair next to his bed. Eventually she quoted a verse from the Bible: "He that conquereth his own soul is greater than he who taketh a city."

As she began to salve and bandage his wounds, she told her son to beware the anger and hatred burning inside. Hatred is a futile thing, she told him, which only injures the person who harbors it. Of all her boys, she told him, he had the most to learn about controlling his passions.

When he was seventy-six, Eisenhower wrote, "I have always looked back on that conversation as one of the most valuable moments of my life. To my youthful mind, it seemed to me that she talked for hours, but I suppose the affair was ended in fifteen or twenty minutes. At least she got me to acknowledge that I was wrong and I felt enough ease in my mind to fall off to sleep."[8]

That concept — conquering your own soul — was a significant one in the moral ecology in which Eisenhower grew up. It was based on the idea that deep inside we are dual in our nature. We are fallen, but also splendidly endowed. We have a side to our nature that is sinful — selfish, deceiving, and self-deceiving — but we have another side to our nature that is in God's image, that seeks transcendence and virtue. The essential drama of life is the drama to construct character, which is an engraved set of disciplined habits, a settled disposition to do good. The cultivation of Adam II was seen as a necessary foundation for Adam I to flourish.

SIN

Today, the word "sin" has lost its power and awesome intensity. It's used most frequently in the context of fattening desserts. Most people in daily conversation don't talk much about individual sin. If they talk about human evil at all, that evil is most often located in the structures of society — in inequality, oppression, racism, and so on — not in the human breast.

We've abandoned the concept of sin, first, because we've left behind the depraved view of human nature. In the eighteenth and even the nineteenth century, many people really did embrace the dark self-estimation expressed in the old Puritan prayer "Yet I Sin": "Eternal Father, Thou art good beyond all thought, but I am vile, wretched, miserable, blind . . ." That's simply too much darkness for the modern mentality.

Second, in many times and many places, the word "sin" was used to declare war on pleasure, even on the healthy pleasures of sex and entertainment. Sin was used as a pretext to live joylessly and censoriously. "Sin" was a word invoked to suppress the pleasures of the body, to terrify teenagers about the perils of masturbation.

Furthermore, the word "sin" was abused by the self-righteous, by dry-hearted scolds who seem alarmed, as H. L. Mencken put it, by the possibility that someone somewhere might be enjoying himself, who always seem ready to rap somebody's knuckles with a ruler on the supposition that that person is doing wrong. The word "sin" was abused by people who embraced a harsh and authoritarian style of parenting, who felt they had to beat the depravity out of their children. It was abused by those who, for whatever reason, fetishize suffering, who believe that only through dour self-mortification can you really become superior and good.

But in truth, "sin," like "vocation" and "soul," is one of those words that it is impossible to do without. It is one of those words — and there will be many in this book — that have to be reclaimed and modernized.

Sin is a necessary piece of our mental furniture because it reminds us that life is a moral affair. No matter how hard we try to reduce everything to deterministic brain chemistry, no matter how hard we try to reduce behavior to the sort of herd instinct that is captured in big data, no matter how hard we strive to replace sin with nonmoral words, like "mistake" or "error" or "weakness," the most essential parts of life are matters of individual responsibility and moral choice: whether to be brave or cowardly, honest or deceitful, compassionate or callous, faithful or disloyal. When modern culture tries to replace sin with ideas like error or insensitivity, or tries to banish words like "virtue," "character," "evil," and "vice" altogether, that doesn't make life any less moral; it just means we have obscured the inescapable moral core of life with shallow language. It just means we think and talk about these choices less clearly, and thus become increasingly blind to the moral stakes of everyday life.

Sin is also a necessary piece of our mental furniture because sin is communal, while error is individual. You make a mistake, but we are all plagued by sins like selfishness and thoughtlessness. Sin is baked into our nature and is handed down through the generations. We are all sinners together. To be aware of sin is to feel intense sympathy toward others who sin. It is to be reminded that as the plight of sin is communal, so the solutions are communal. We fight sin together, as communities and families, fighting our own individual sins by helping others fight theirs.

Furthermore, the concept of sin is necessary because it is radically true. To say you are a sinner is not to say that you have some black depraved stain on your heart. It is to say that, like the rest of us, you have some perversity in your nature. We want to do one thing, but we end up doing another. We want what we should not want. None of us wants to be hard-hearted, but sometimes we are. No one wants to self-deceive, but we rationalize all the time. No one wants to be cruel, but we all blurt things out and regret them later. No one wants to be a bystander, to commit sins of omission, but, in the words of the poet Marguerite Wilkinson, we all commit the sin of "unattempted loveliness."

We really do have dappled souls. The same ambition that drives us to build a new company also drives us to be materialistic and to exploit. The same lust that leads to children leads to adultery. The same confidence that can lead to daring and creativity can lead to self-worship and arrogance.

Sin is not some demonic thing. It's just our perverse tendency to fuck things up, to favor the short term over the long term, the lower over the higher. Sin, when it is committed over and over again, hardens into loyalty to a lower love.

The danger of sin, in other words, is that it feeds on itself. Small moral compromises on Monday make you more likely to commit other, bigger moral compromises on Tuesday. A person lies to himself and soon can no longer distinguish when he is lying to himself and when he isn't. Another person is consumed by the sin of self-pity, a passion to be a righteous victim that devours everything around it as surely as anger or greed.

People rarely commit the big sins out of the blue. They walk through a series of doors. They have an unchecked problem with anger. They have an unchecked problem with drinking or drugs. They have an unchecked problem of sympathy. Corruption breeds corruption. Sin is the punishment of sin.

The final reason sin is a necessary part of our mental furniture is that without it, the whole method of character building dissolves. From time immemorial, people have achieved glory by achieving great external things, but they have built character by struggling against their internal sins. People become solid, stable, and worthy of self-respect because they have defeated or at least struggled with their own demons. If you take away the concept of sin, then you take away the thing the good person struggles against.

The person involved in the struggle against sin understands that each day is filled with moral occasions. I once met an employer who asks each job applicant, "Describe a time when you told the truth and it hurt you." He is essentially asking those people if they have their loves in the right order, if they would put love of truth above love of career.

In places like Abilene, Kansas, the big sins, left unchallenged, would have had very practical and disastrous effects. Sloth could lead to a failure of a farm; gluttony and inebriation to the destruction of a family; lust to the ruination of a young woman; vanity to excessive spending, debt, and bankruptcy.

In places like that, people had an awareness not only of sin but of the different kinds of sins and the different remedies for each. Some sins, such as anger and lust, are like wild beasts. They have to be fought through habits of restraint. Other sins, such as mockery and disrespect, are like stains. They can be expunged only by absolution, by apology, remorse, restitution, and cleansing. Still others, such as stealing, are like a debt. They can be rectified only by repaying what you owe to society. Sins such as adultery, bribery, and betrayal are more like treason than like crime; they damage the social order. Social harmony can be rewoven only by slowly recommitting to relationships and rebuilding trust. The sins of arrogance and pride arise from a perverse desire for status and superiority. The only remedy for them is to humble oneself before others.

In other words, people in earlier times inherited a vast moral vocabulary and set of moral tools, developed over centuries and handed down from generation to generation. This was a practical inheritance, like learning how to speak a certain language, which people could use to engage their own moral struggles.

CHARACTER

Ida Eisenhower was funny and warm-hearted, but stood sentry against backsliding. She forbade dancing and card games and drinking in her home precisely because her estimation of the power of sin was so high. Since self-control is a muscle that tires easily, it is much better to avoid temptation in the first place rather than try to resist it once it arises.

In raising her boys she showed them bottomless love and warmth. She allowed them more freedom to get into scrapes than parents generally do today. But she did demand that they cultivate the habit of small, constant self-repression.

Today, when we say that somebody is repressed, we tend to mean it as a criticism. It means they are uptight, stiff, or unaware of their true emotional selves. That's because we live in a self-expressive culture. We tend to trust the impulses inside the self and distrust the forces outside the self that seek to push down those impulses. But in this earlier moral ecology, people tended to distrust the impulses inside the self. These impulses could be restrained, they argued, through habit.

In 1877, the psychologist William James wrote a short treatise called "Habit." When you are trying to lead a decent life, he wrote, you want to make your nervous system your ally and not your enemy. You want to engrave certain habits so deep that they will become natural and instinctual. James wrote that when you set out to engrave a habit — say, going on a diet or always telling the truth — you want to launch yourself with as "strong and decided an initiative as possible." Make the beginning of a new habit a major event in your life. Then, "never suffer an exception" until the habit is firmly rooted in your life. A single slip undoes many fine acts of self-control. Then take advantage of every occasion to practice your habit. Practice a gratuitous exercise of self-discipline every day. Follow arbitrary rules. "Asceticism of this sort is like the insurance which a man pays on his house of goods. The tax does him no good at the time, and may possibly never bring him a return. But if the fire does come, his having paid it will be his salvation from ruin."

What William James and Ida Eisenhower were trying to inculcate, in their different ways, was steadiness over time. Character, as the Yale law professor Anthony T. Kronman has put it, is "an ensemble of settled dispositions — of habitual feelings and desires."[9] The idea is largely Aristotelian. If you act well, eventually you will be good. Change your behavior and eventually you rewire your brain.

Ida emphasized the importance of practicing small acts of self-control: following the rules of etiquette when sitting at the table, dressing in one's Sunday best when going to church, keeping the Sabbath afterward, using formal diction in letter writing as a display of deference and respect, eating plain food, avoiding luxury. If you are in the army, keep your uniform neat and your shoes polished. If you are at home, keep everything tidy. Practice the small outward disciplines.

In the culture of that time, people also believed that manual labor was a school for character. In Abilene, everybody, from business owners to farmers, did physical labor every day, greasing the buggy axles, shoveling coal, sifting the unburned lumps from the stove ash. Eisenhower grew up in a home with no running water, and the boys' chores began at dawn — waking up at five to build the morning fire, hauling water from the well — and continued through the day — carrying a hot lunch to their father at the creamery, feeding the chickens, canning up to five hundred quarts of fruit annually, boiling the clothing on washday, raising corn to be sold for spending money, digging trenches when plumbing became available, and wiring the house when electricity came to town. Ike grew up in an atmosphere that is almost the inverse of the way many children are raised today. Today's children are spared most of the manual labor Dwight had to perform, but they are not given nearly as much leeway to roam over forests and town when the chores were done. Dwight had a great deal of assigned work, but also a great deal of freedom to roam around town.

David Eisenhower, Dwight's father, practiced this sort of disciplined life in a harsh and joyless way. He was defined by his punctilious sense of rectitude. He was rigid, cool, and strictly proper. After his bankruptcy he had a horror of taking on any debt, of slipping even a bit. When he was a manager at his company he forced his employees to save 10 percent of their salary every month. They had to report to him what they had done with their 10 percent, either putting it in the bank or investing it in stocks. He wrote down each answer each month, and if he was not satisfied with their report, they lost their job.

He seemed never to relax, never taking his boys out hunting or fishing or playing with them much at all. "He was an inflexible man with a stern code," one of the boys, Edgar, was to recall. "Life to him was a very serious proposition, and that's the way he lived it, soberly and with due reflection."[10]

Ida, on the other hand, always had a smile on her lips. She was always willing to be a little naughty, to violate her sense of rectitude, even taking a shot of alcohol if the situation warranted. Ida seemed to understand, as her husband did not, that you can't rely just on self-control, habit, work, and self-denial to build character. Your reason and your will are simply too weak to defeat your desires all the time. Individuals are strong, but they are not self-sufficient. To defeat sin you need help from outside.

Her character-building method had a tender side as well. Fortunately, love is the law of our nature. People like Ida understand that love, too, is a tool to build character. The tender character-building strategy is based on the idea that we can't always resist our desires, but we can change and reorder our desires by focusing on our higher loves. Focus on your love for your children. Focus on your love of country. Focus on your love for the poor and downtrodden. Focus on your love of your hometown or alma mater. To sacrifice for such things is sweet. It feels good to serve your beloved. Giving becomes cheerful giving because you are so eager to see the things you love prosper and thrive.

Pretty soon you are behaving better. The parent focusing on the love of his or her children will drive them to events day after day, will get up in the middle of the night when they are sick, will drop everything when they are in crisis. The lover wants to sacrifice, to live life as an offering. A person motivated by such feelings will be a bit less likely to sin.

Ida demonstrated that it is possible to be strict and kind, disciplined and loving, to be aware of sin and also aware of the possibility of forgiveness, charity, and mercy. Decades later, when Dwight Eisenhower took the presidential oath of office, Ida asked him to have the Bible open to 2 Chronicles 7:14: "If my people, which are called by my name, shall humble themselves, and pray, and seek my face, and turn from their wicked ways; then I will hear from heaven, and will forgive their sin, and will heal their land." The most powerful way to fight sin is by living in a sweet, loving way. It's how you do the jobs you do, whether it's a prestigious job or not. As others have noted, God loves adverbs.

SELF-CONTROL

Dwight seems to have belonged to the category of those who believe that religion is good for society but who are not religious themselves. There's no evidence that he had an explicit sense of God's grace or any theological thoughts about redemption. But he inherited both his mother's garrulous nature and her sense that that nature had to be continually repressed and conquered. He just held these beliefs in secular form.

He was rambunctious from birth. His childhood was remembered in Abilene for a series of epic brawls. At West Point, he was defiant, rebellious, and misbehaving. He ran up a string of demerits, for gambling, smoking, and general disrespectfulness. At graduation, he ranked 125th out of 164 men for discipline. Once he was demoted from sergeant to private for dancing too exuberantly at a ball. He was also bedeviled, throughout his military career and his presidency, with the barely suppressed temper that his parents had seen on that Halloween evening. Throughout his military career, his subordinates came to look for the telltale signs of his looming fury, such as certain set expressions that signaled an imminent profanity-laced explosion. Dubbed "the terrible-tempered Mr. Bang" by a World War II journalist, Eisenhower's capacity for rage was always there, just under the surface.[11] "It was like looking into a Bessemer furnace," one of his aides, Bryce Harlow, recalled. His wartime doctor, Howard Snyder, noticed the "twisted cord-like temple arteries standing out on the side of his head" just before one of Eisenhower's explosions. "Ike's subordinates were awed by his capacity for rage," his biographer Evan Thomas wrote.[12] Eisenhower's appointments secretary, Tom Stephens, noticed that the president tended to wear brown whenever he was in a foul temper. Stephens would see Eisenhower from the office window. "Brown suit today!" he would call out to the staff as forewarning.[13]

Ike was even more divided than most of us. He was a master of army expletives, but he almost never cursed in front of women. He would turn away if someone told a dirty joke.[14] He was reprimanded at West Point for habitually smoking cigarettes in the halls, and by the end of the war he was a four-pack-a-day smoker. But one day he quit cold turkey: "I simply gave myself an order." "Freedom," he would later say in his 1957 State of the Union address, "has been defined as the opportunity for self-discipline."[15]

His internal torment could be convulsive. By the end of World War II, his body was a collection of aches and pains. He spent the nights staring at the ceiling, racked by insomnia and anxiety, drinking and smoking, tortured by throat infections, cramps, spiking blood pressure. But his capacity for self-repression — what might be called noble hypocrisy — was also immense. He was not naturally good at hiding his emotions. He had a remarkably expressive face. But day by day he put on a false front of confident ease and farm-boy garrulousness. He became known for his sunny, boyish temperament. Evan Thomas writes that Ike told his grandson, David, that that smile "came not from some sunny feel-good philosophy but from getting knocked down by a boxing coach at West Point. 'If you can't smile when you get up from a knockdown,' the coach said, 'you're never going to lick an opponent.' "[16] He thought it was necessary to project easy confidence in order to lead the army and win the war:

I firmly determined that my mannerisms and speech in public would always reflect the cheerful certainty of victory — that any pessimism and discouragement I might ever feel would be reserved for my pillow. To translate this conviction into tangible results, I adopted a policy of circulating through the whole force to the full limit imposed by physical considerations. I did my best to meet everyone from general to private with a smile, a pat on the back and a definite interest in his problems.[17]

He devised stratagems for dismissing his true passions. For example, in his diaries he made lists of people who offended him as a way of sealing off his anger toward them. When he felt a surge of hatred, he refused to let it rule him. "Anger cannot win. It cannot even think clearly," he noted in his diary.[18] Other times he would write an offender's name on a piece of paper and then drop it into the wastebasket, another symbolic purging of emotion. Eisenhower was not an authentic man. He was a passionate man who lived, as much as his mother did, under a system of artificial restraints.

ORGANIZATION MAN

Ida sent Ike off from Abilene to West Point on June 8, 1911. She remained an ardent pacifist, determinedly opposed to the soldier's vocation, but she told her son, "It is your choice." She saw the train off, went home, and shut herself in her room. The remaining boys could hear her sobbing through the door. His brother Milton later told Ike it was the first time he had ever heard their mother cry.[19]

Ike graduated from West Point in the class of 1915. He thus spent his early career in the shadow of World War I. Trained for combat, he never saw action in the war that was supposed to end all wars. He never even left the United States. He spent those years training troops, coaching football, and doing logistics. He lobbied furiously to be sent to war, and in October 1918, when he was twenty-eight, he received orders. He was to ship out to France on November 18. The war, of course, ended on November 11. It was a bitter blow. "I suppose we'll spend the rest of our lives explaining why we didn't get into this war," he lamented in a letter to a fellow officer. Then he made an uncharacteristically unrestrained vow: "By God, from now on I am cutting myself a swath that will make up for this."[20]

That vow didn't immediately come true. Eisenhower was promoted to lieutenant colonel in 1918, in advance of his coming deployment. He would not be promoted again for twenty years, until 1938. The army had a glut of officers who'd been elevated during the war, and there were not many openings for advancement in an army that by the 1920s was shrinking and assuming a marginal role in American life. His career stagnated, while the careers of his civilian brothers zoomed ahead. By the time he was in his forties, he was easily the least accomplished of the boys in the Eisenhower family. He was in middle age. He did not receive his first star until he was fifty-one. Nobody expected great things of him.

During these interwar years Ike served as an infantry officer, football coach, and staff officer, intermittently attending school at the Infantry Tank School, the Command and General Staff School, and eventually the War College. Ike would occasionally unleash his frustration at the bureaucratic bungling of his institution, at the way it smothered his opportunities and wasted his talents. But on the whole, his response was amazingly restrained. He became the classic Organization Man. From Ida's rules of conduct, Ike slid easily into the military code of conduct. He subsumed his own desires for the sake of the group.

He wrote in one of his memoirs that by the time he was in his thirties he had learned "the basic lesson of the military — that the proper place for a soldier is where he is ordered by his superiors."[21] He was given a run-of-the-mill assignment. "I found no better cure than to blow off steam in private and then settle down to the job at hand."[22]

As a staff officer — never a coveted or glamorous role — Eisenhower learned to master procedure, process, teamwork, and organization. He learned the secrets of thriving within the organization. "When I go to a new station I look to see who is the strongest and ablest man on the post. I forget my own ideas and do everything in my power to promote what he says is right."[23] Later, in *At Ease,* he wrote, "Always try to associate yourself closely and learn as much as you can from those who know more than you, who do better than you, who see more clearly than you." He was a fanatic about both preparation and then adaptation: "The plans are nothing, but the planning is everything," he would say. Or, "Rely on planning, but never trust plans."

He also gained a perspective on himself. He began carrying around an anonymous little poem:

Take a bucket, fill it with water,
Put your hand in — clear up to the wrist.
Now pull it out; the hole that remains
Is a measure of how much you'll be
    missed. . . .

The moral of this quaint example:
To do just the best that you can,
Be proud of yourself, but remember,
There is no Indispensible Man![24]

In 1922, Eisenhower was ordered to Panama, where he joined the 20th Infantry Brigade. Two years in Panama did two things for Ike. First, it allowed him a change of scene after the death of his firstborn son, Icky. Second, it introduced him to General Fox Connor. As the historian Jean Edward Smith put it, "Fox Connor was understatement personified: self-possessed, soft-spoken, eminently formal, and polite — a general who loved reading, a profound student of history, and a keen judge of military talent."[25] Connor was completely devoid of theatricality. From Connor Ike learned the maxim "Always take your job seriously, never yourself."

Fox Connor served as the beau ideal of the humble leader. "A sense of humility is a quality I have observed in every leader whom I have deeply admired," Eisenhower later wrote. "My own conviction is that every leader should have enough humility to accept, publicly, the responsibility for the mistakes of the subordinates he has himself selected and, likewise, to give them credit, publicly, for their triumphs." Connor, Ike continued, "was a practical officer, down to earth, equally at home in the company of the most important people in the region and with any of the men in the regiment. He never put on airs of any kind, and he was as open and honest as any man I have ever known. . . . He has held a place in my affections for many years that no other, not even a relative, could obtain."[26]

Connor also revived Ike's love of the classics, military strategy, and world affairs. Eisenhower called his service under Connor "a sort of graduate school in military affairs and the humanities, leavened by the comments and discourses of a man who was experienced in his knowledge of men and their conduct. . . . It was the most interesting and constructive [period] of my life." On a visit to Panama, Ike's boyhood friend Edward "Swede" Hazlett noted that Eisenhower had "fitted up the 2nd story screened porch of their quarters as a rough study, and here, with drawing board and texts, he put in his spare time re-fighting the campaigns of the old masters."[27]

At the same time, Ike was particularly affected by the training of a horse, "Blackie." In his memoirs, he wrote:

In my experience with Blackie — and earlier with allegedly incompetent recruits at Camp Colt — is rooted my enduring conviction that far too often we write off a backward child as hopeless, a clumsy animal as worthless, a worn-out field as beyond restoration. This we do largely out of our own lack of willingness to take the time and spend the effort to prove ourselves wrong: to prove that a difficult boy can become a fine man, that an animal can respond to training, that the field can regain its fertility.[28]

General Connor arranged for Eisenhower to attend the Command and General Staff School at Fort Leavenworth, Kansas. He would graduate first in his class of 245 officers. Like Blackie, he was not to be written off.

In 1933, after graduating from the War College as one of the youngest officers ever to attend, Eisenhower was appointed General Douglas MacArthur's personal assistant. For the next several years, Eisenhower worked with MacArthur, primarily in the Philippines, helping that nation prepare for its independence. Douglas MacArthur was the theatrical one. Ike respected MacArthur but was put off by his grandiosity. He described MacArthur as "an aristocrat, but as for me, I'm just folks."[29]

Under MacArthur, Eisenhower met the ultimate test of his temper. Their small office rooms adjoined, separated by only a slatted door. "He called me to his office by raising his voice,"[30] Eisenhower remembered. "He was decisive, personable, and he had one habit that never ceased to startle me. In reminiscing or in telling stories, he talked of himself in the third person."[31]

Several times, Ike asked to leave his staff assignment. MacArthur denied the request, insisting Eisenhower's work in the Philippines was far more important than anything he could do as a mere lieutenant colonel in the American army.

Ike was disappointed, but he remained with MacArthur for six more years, working behind the scenes with more and more planning work falling on his shoulders.[32] Ike remained respectful in his boss's presence but eventually came to detest MacArthur for the way he put himself above the institution. After one of MacArthur's more memorable acts of egomania, Eisenhower erupted in the privacy of his diary:

But I must say it is almost incomprehensible that after 8 years of working for him, writing every word he publishes, keeping his secrets, preventing him from making too much of an ass of himself, trying to advance his interests while keeping myself in the background, he should suddenly turn on me. He'd like to occupy a throne room surrounded by experts in flattery; while in a dungeon beneath, unknown to the world, would be a bunch of slaves doing his work and producing the things that, to the public, would represent the brilliant accomplishment of his mind. He's a fool, but worse he is a puking baby.[33]

Eisenhower served loyally and humbly, putting himself inside the mind of his superior, adopting his perspectives as his own, getting his work done efficiently and on time. In the end, the officers he served — MacArthur included — ended up promoting him. And when the great challenge of his life came during World War II, Ike's ability to repress his own passions served him well. He never greeted war with a sense of romantic excitement, the way his lifelong colleague George S. Patton did. He saw it as another hard duty to be endured. He had learned to focus less on the glamor and excitement of wartime heroics and more on the dull, mundane things that would prove to be the keys to victory. Preserving alliances with people you might find insufferable. Building enough landing craft to make amphibious invasions possible. Logistics.

Eisenhower was a masterful wartime commander. He suppressed his own frustrations in order to keep the international alliance together. He ferociously restrained national prejudices, which he felt as acutely as anyone, in order to keep the disparate armies on the same team. He passed credit for victories on to his subordinates and, in one of the most famous unsent messages in world history, was willing to put the blame for failures upon himself. This was the memo he was going to release if the D-Day invasion failed. "Our landings . . . have failed . . . and I have withdrawn the troops," he wrote. "My decision to attack at this time and place was based upon the best information available. The troops, the air and the Navy did all that bravery and devotion could do. If any blame or fault attaches to the attempt it is mine alone."

Eisenhower's disciplined and self-regulating life had its downsides. He was not a visionary. He was not a creative thinker. In war, he was not a great strategist. As president, he was often oblivious to the most consequential emerging historical currents of his time — from the civil rights movement to the menace of McCarthyism. He was never good with abstract ideas. He behaved disgracefully in failing to defend General George C. Marshall from attacks upon his patriotism, to his great regret and shame later on. And all that artificial self-restraint could make him cold when he should have been warm, ruthlessly practical when he should have been chivalrous and romantic. His behavior toward his mistress, Kay Summersby, at the end of the war is repellent. Summersby had served, and presumably, loved Eisenhower through the hardest years of his life. He did not give her even the benefit of a good-bye. One day, she found that her name had been dropped from his travel roster. She received an icy typewritten note from Ike on official Army stationery: "I am sure you understand that I am personally much distressed that an association that has been so valuable to me has to be terminated in this particular fashion but it is by reasons over which I have no control. . . . I hope that you will drop me a note from time to time — I will always be interested in how you are getting along."[34] He had become so practiced at suppressing his own emotions that in this moment he was even able to suppress any hint of compassion, any ember of gratitude.

Eisenhower was occasionally aware of his shortcomings. Thinking of his hero George Washington, he said, "I've often felt the deep wish that the Good Lord had endowed me with his clarity of vision in big things, his strength of purpose and his genuine greatness of mind and spirit."[35]

But for some, life is the perfect school; it teaches them exactly those lessons they will need later on. Eisenhower was never a flashy man, but two outstanding traits defined the mature Eisenhower, traits that flowed from his upbringing and that he cultivated over time. The first was his creation of a second self. Today, we tend to live within an ethos of authenticity. We tend to believe that the "true self" is whatever is most natural and untutored. That is, each of us has a certain sincere way of being in the world, and we should live our life being truthful to that authentic inner self, not succumbing to the pressures outside ourself. To live artificially, with a gap between your inner nature and your outer conduct, is to be deceptive, cunning, and false.

Eisenhower hewed to a different philosophy. This code held that artifice is man's nature. We start out with raw material, some good, some bad, and this nature has to be pruned, girdled, formed, repressed, molded, and often restrained, rather than paraded in public. A personality is a product of cultivation. The true self is what you have built from your nature, not just what your nature started out with.

Eisenhower was not a sincere person. He hid his private thoughts. He recorded them in his diary, and they could be scathing. Of Senator William Knowland, he wrote, "In his case, there seems to be no final answer to the question, 'How stupid can you get?' "[36] But in public he wore a costume of affability, optimism, and farm-boy charm. As president, he was perfectly willing to appear stupider than he really was if it would help him perform his assigned role. He was willing to appear tongue-tied if it would help him conceal his true designs. Just as he learned to suppress his anger as a boy, he learned to suppress his ambitions and abilities as an adult. He was reasonably learned in ancient history, admiring especially the crafty Athenian leader Themistocles, but he never let that on. He did not want to appear smarter than other people, or somehow superior to the average American. Instead he cultivated the image of simple, unlearned charm. As president he would supervise a detailed meeting about an arcane topic, issuing clear and specific instructions about what was to be done. Then he would go out to a press conference and massacre the English language in an effort to disguise his designs. Or he would just pretend the whole subject was over his head: "That's just too complicated for a dumb bunny like me."[37] He was willing to appear more stupid than he really was. (This is how we know he was not a New Yorker.)

Ike's simplicity was strategic. After his death, his vice president, Richard Nixon, recollected, "[Ike] was a far more complex and devious man than most people realized, and in the best sense of these words. Not shackled to a one-track mind, he always applied two, three, or four lines of reasoning to a single problem. . . . His mind was quick and facile."[38] He was a famously good poker player. "Ike's wide smile, open as the Kansas sky," Evan Thomas writes, "concealed a deep secretiveness. He was honorable but occasionally opaque, outwardly amiable but inwardly seething."[39]

Once, before a press conference, his press secretary, Jim Hagerty, informed him of an increasingly delicate situation in the Formosa Strait. Ike smiled and said, "Don't worry, Jim, if that question comes up, I'll just confuse them." Predictably, the question was raised by journalist Joseph Harsch.

Good-naturedly, Eisenhower responded:

The only thing I know about war is two things: the most changeable factor in war is human nature in its day-by-day manifestation; but the only unchanging factor about war is human nature. And the next thing is that every war is going to astonish you in the way it occurred and the way it is carried out. . . . So I think you just have to wait, and that is the kind of prayerful decision that may some day face a president.[40]

After the conference, Thomas writes, "Eisenhower himself joked that he must have given fits to Russian and Chinese translators trying to explain to their bosses what he meant."[41]

Ike's double nature could make it hard for people to really know him. "I don't envy you trying to figure Dad out," John Eisenhower told the biographer Evan Thomas. "I can't figure him out." After his death, his widow, Mamie, was asked whether she had really known her husband. "I'm not sure anyone did," she replied.[42] But self-repression helped Eisenhower to control his natural desires and to fulfill the tasks assigned to him, both by his military superiors and by history. He looked simple and straightforward, but his simplicity was a work of art.

MODERATION

His final trait which ripened with his full maturity was moderation.

Moderation is a generally misunderstood virtue. It is important to start by saying what it is not. Moderation is not just finding the midpoint between two opposing poles and opportunistically planting yourself there. Neither is moderation bland equanimity. It's not just having a temperate disposition that doesn't contain rival passions or competing ideas.

On the contrary, moderation is based on an awareness of the inevitability of conflict. If you think that the world can fit neatly together, then you don't need to be moderate. If you think all your personal qualities can be brought together into simple harmony, you don't need to hold back, you can just go whole hog for self-actualization and growth. If you think all moral values point in the same direction, or all political goals can be realized all at once by a straightforward march along one course, you don't need to be moderate, either. You can just head in the direction of truth as quickly as possible.

Moderation is based on the idea that things do not fit neatly together. Politics is likely to be a competition between legitimate opposing interests. Philosophy is likely to be a tension between competing half-truths. A personality is likely to be a battleground of valuable but incompatible traits. As Harry Clor put it in his brilliant book *On Moderation,* "The fundamental division in the soul or psyche is at the root of our need for moderation." Eisenhower, for example, was fueled by passion and policed by self-control. Neither impulse was entirely useless and neither was entirely benign. Eisenhower's righteous rage could occasionally propel him toward justice, but it could occasionally blind him. His self-control enabled him to serve and do his duty, but it could make him callous.

The moderate person contains opposing capacities to the nth degree. A moderate person can start out hot on both ends, both fervent in a capacity for rage and fervent in a desire for order, both Apollonian at work and Dionysian at play, both strong in faith and deeply doubtful, both Adam I and Adam II.

A moderate person can start out with these divisions and rival tendencies, but to live a coherent life, the moderate must find a series of balances and proportions. The moderate is forever seeking a series of temporary arrangements, embedded in the specific situation of the moment, that will help him or her balance the desire for security with the desire for risk, the call of liberty with the need for restraint. The moderate knows there is no ultimate resolution to these tensions. Great matters cannot be settled by taking into account just one principle or one viewpoint. Governing is more like sailing in a storm: shift your weight one way when the boat tilts to starboard, shift your weight the other way when it tilts to port — adjust and adjust and adjust to circumstances to keep the semblance and equanimity of an even keel.

Eisenhower understood this intuitively. Writing to Swede, his boyhood friend, in his second term as president, he mused "Possibly I am something like a ship which, buffeted and pounded by wind and wave, is still afloat and manages in spite of frequent tacks and turnings to stay generally along its plotted course and continues to make some, even if slow and painful, headway."[43]

As Clor observes, the moderate knows she cannot have it all. There are tensions between rival goods, and you just have to

152

accept that you will never get to live a pure and perfect life, devoted to one truth or one value. The moderate has limited aspirations about what can be achieved in public life. The paradoxes embedded into any situation do not allow for a clean and ultimate resolution. You expand liberty at the cost of encouraging license. You crack down on license at the cost of limiting liberty. There is no escaping this sort of trade-off.

The moderate can only hope to have a regulated character, stepping back to understand opposing perspectives and appreciating the merits of each. The moderate understands that political cultures are traditions of conflict. There are never-ending tensions that pit equality against achievement, centralization against decentralization, order and community against liberty and individualism. The moderate doesn't try to solve those arguments. There are no ultimate solutions. The moderate can only hope to achieve a balance that is consistent with the needs of the moment. The moderate does not believe there are some policy solutions that are right for all times (this seems obvious, but the rule is regularly flouted by ideologues in nation after nation). The moderate does not admire abstract schemes but understands that it is necessary to legislate along the grain of human nature, and within the medium in which she happens to be placed.

The moderate can only hope to be disciplined enough to combine in one soul, as Max Weber put it, both warm passion and a cool sense of proportion. He aims to be passionate about his ends but deliberate about the proper means to realize them. The best moderate is blessed with a spirited soul and also the proper character to tame it. The best moderate is skeptical of zealotry because he is skeptical of himself. He distrusts passionate intensity and bold simplicity because he know that in politics the lows are lower than the highs are high — the damage leaders do when they get things wrong is greater than the benefits they create when they get things right. Therefore caution is the proper attitude, an awareness of the limits the foundation of wisdom.

For many people at the time and for many years after, Eisenhower seemed like an emotionally flat simpleton with a passion for Western novels. His star has risen among historians as his inner turmoil has become better appreciated. And at the end of his presidency, he delivered a speech that still stands today as a perfect example of moderation in practice.

Ike's speech came at a crucial pivot point in American politics and even public morality. On January 20, 1961, John F. Kennedy gave an inaugural address that signaled a cultural shift. Kennedy's speech was meant to indicate a new direction in the march of history. One generation and one era was ending and another generation would, as he put it, "begin anew." There would be a "new endeavor" and "a new world of law." The possibilities, he argued, were limitless. "Man holds in his mortal hands the power to abolish all forms of human poverty," he declared. Kennedy issued a call to uninhibited action. "We shall pay any price, bear any burden, meet any hardship. . . ." He called on his listeners not just to tolerate problems, but to end them: "Together let us explore the stars, conquer the deserts, eradicate disease." It was the speech of a man supremely confident in himself. It inspired millions of people around the world and set the tone and standard for political rhetoric ever since.

Three days earlier, however, Eisenhower had given a speech that epitomized the worldview that was fading away. Whereas Kennedy emphasized limitless possibilities, Eisenhower warned against hubris. Whereas

Kennedy celebrated courage, Eisenhower celebrated prudence. Whereas Kennedy exhorted the nation to venture boldly forth, Eisenhower called for balance.

The word "balance" recurs throughout his text — a need to balance competing priorities, "balance between the private economy and the public economy, balance between the cost and hoped-for advantages, balance between the clearly necessary and the comfortably desirable, balance between our essential requirements as a nation and the duties imposed by the nation upon the individual; balance between the actions of the moment and the national welfare of the future. Good judgment seeks balance and progress; lack of it eventually finds imbalance and frustration."

Eisenhower warned the country against belief in quick fixes. Americans, he said, should never believe that "some spectacular and costly action could become the miraculous solution to all current difficulties." He warned against human frailty, particularly the temptation to be shortsighted and selfish. He asked his countrymen to "avoid the impulse to live only for today, plundering, for our own ease and convenience, the precious resources of tomorrow." Echoing the thrifty ethos of his childhood, he reminded the nation that we cannot "mortgage the material assets of our grandchildren without risking the loss also of their political and spiritual heritage."

He warned, most famously, about the undue concentration of power, and the way unchecked power could lead to national ruin. He warned first about the military-industrial complex — "a permanent armaments industry of vast proportions." He also warned against "a scientific-technological elite," a powerful network of government-funded experts who might be tempted to take power away from the citizenry. Like the nation's founders, he built his politics on distrust of what people might do if they have unchecked power. He communicated the sense that in most times, leaders have more to gain from being stewards of what they have inherited than by being destroyers of what is there and creators of something new.

This was the speech of a man who had been raised to check his impulses and had then been chastened by life. It was the speech of a man who had seen what human beings are capable of, who had felt in his bones that man is a problem to himself. It was the speech of a man who used to tell his advisers "Let's make our mistakes slowly," because it was better to proceed to a decision gradually than to rush into anything before its time. This is the lesson that his mother and his upbringing had imparted to him decades before. This was a life organized not around self-expression, but self-restraint.

CHAPTER 4
STRUGGLE

On the night of April 18, 1906, when she was eight years old, Dorothy Day was living in Oakland, California.

She had, as usual, said her prayers at bedtime. She was the only religiously observant member of her household and had become, as she wrote later, "disgustingly, proudly pious."[1] She had always had a sense, she wrote in her diary decades later, of an immanent spiritual world.

The earth began shaking. When the rumbling began, her father rushed into the children's bedroom, snatched her two brothers, and rushed for the front door. Her mother grabbed her baby sister from Dorothy's arms. Her parents apparently figured Dorothy could take care of herself. She was left alone in her brass bed as it rolled back and forth across the polished floor. The night of the San Francisco earthquake, she felt that God was visiting her. "The earth became a sea which rocked our house in a most tumultuous manner," she recalled.[2] She could hear the water in the rooftop tank splashing above her head. These sensations "were linked up with my idea of God as a tremendous Force, a frightening impersonal God, a Hand stretched out to seize me, His child, and not in love."[3]

When the earth settled, the house was a mess. There were broken dishes all over the floor, along with books, chandeliers, and pieces of the ceiling and chimney. The city was in ruins, too, temporarily reduced to poverty and need. But in the days after, Bay Area residents pulled together. "While the crisis lasted, people loved each other," she wrote in her memoir decades later. "It was as though they were united in Christian solidarity. It makes one think of how people could, if they would, care for each other in times of stress, unjudgingly in pity and love."

As the writer Paul Elie has put it, "A whole life is prefigured in that episode" — the crisis, the sense of God's nearness, the awareness of poverty, the feeling of loneliness and abandonment, but also the sense that that loneliness can be filled by love and community, especially through solidarity with those in deepest need.[4]

Day was born with a passionate, ideal nature. Like Dorothea, the main character in George Eliot's novel *Middlemarch,* her nature demanded that she live an ideal life. She was unable to be satisfied with mere happiness, being in a good mood, enjoying the normal pleasures that friendships and accomplishments bring. As Eliot put it, "Her flame quickly burned up that light fuel; and, fed from within, soared after some illimitable satisfaction, some object which would never justify weariness, which would reconcile self-despair with the rapturous consciousness of life beyond self." Day needed spiritual heroism, some transcendent purpose for which she could sacrifice.

CHILDREN'S CRUSADE

Dorothy's father had been a journalist, but the newspaper printing plant burned down in the quake and his job was gone. The family possessions lay in ruins. Day experienced the family's humiliating descent into poverty. Her father moved them to Chicago, where he set out to write a novel that was never published. A distant, distrustful man, he forbade his children to leave the house without permission or to invite friends in.

Day remembered Sunday dinners marked by gloomy silence but for the sound of everybody chewing. Her mother did her best, but she suffered four miscarriages, and one night she fell into hysterics, smashing every dish in the home. The next day she was back to normal. "I lost my nerve," she explained to her children.

In Chicago, Day noticed that her own family was much less affectionate than the families around her. "We were never hand holders. We were always withdrawn and alone, unlike Italians, Poles, Jews and other friends who I had who were fresh and spontaneous in their affections." She went to church and sang hymns with neighboring families. In the evenings she got on her knees and inflicted her piety on her sister: "I used to plague my sister with my long prayers. I would kneel until my knees ached and I was cold and stiff. She would beg me to come to bed and tell her a story." One day she had a conversation with her best friend, Mary Harrington, about a certain saint. Later in life, writing her memoirs, Day couldn't remember exactly which saint they were talking about, but she remembered "my feeling of lofty enthusiasm, and how my heart almost burst with desire to take part in such high endeavor. One verse of the Psalms often comes to mind, 'Enlarge Thou my heart, O Lord, that Thou mayst enter in.' . . . I was filled with a natural striving, a thrilling recognition of the possibilities of spiritual adventure."[5]

Parents in those days did not feel it necessary to entertain their children. Day remembered spending happy hours on the beach with her friends, fishing in creeks for eels, running away to an abandoned shack at the edge of a swamp, setting up a fantasy world and pretending that they would live there alone forever. Day also remembered long days of intolerable boredom, especially over the summer break. She tried to ease the tedium by doing household chores and reading. She read Charles Dickens, Edgar Allan Poe, and *The Imitation of Christ* by Thomas à Kempis, among other books.

With adolescence came a fascination with sex. She knew right away that she was thrilled by it, but she also had been taught that it was dangerous and evil. One afternoon, when she was fifteen, Day was out in a park with her baby brother. The weather was perfect. The world was full of life, and there must have been boys around. In a letter she wrote at the time to her best friend, she describes a "wicked thrilling feeling at my heart." In the next passage, she remonstrates herself priggishly, "It is wrong to think so much about human love. All those feelings and cravings that come to us are sexual desires. We are prone to have them at this age, I suppose, but I think they are impure. It is sensual and God is spiritual."

In her superb memoir *The Long Loneliness,* she reprints long passages from this letter. Her fifteen-year-old self continued, "How weak I am. My pride forbids me to write this and to put it down on paper makes me blush, but all the old love comes back to me. It is a lust of the flesh and I know that unless I forsake all sin, I will not gain the kingdom of heaven."

The letter has all the self-involvement and paint-by-numbers self-righteousness that you'd expect in a precocious teenager. She's got the basic concept of her religion down, but not the humanity and the grace. But there's also an arduous spiritual ambition at work. "Maybe if I stayed away from books more this restlessness would pass. I am reading Dostoyevsky." She resolves to fight her desires: "Only after a hard bitter struggle with sin and only after we have overcome it, do we experience blessed joy and peace. . . . I have so much work to do to overcome my sins. I am working always, always on guard, praying without ceasing to overcome all physical sensations to be purely spiritual."

Reflecting on that letter in *The Long Loneliness*, which was published when she was in her fifties, Day confessed that it "was filled with pomp and vanity and piety. I was writing of what interested me most, the conflict of flesh and spirit, but I was writing self-consciously and trying to pretend to myself I was being literary."[6] But that letter displays some of the features that would eventually make Day one of the most inspiring religious figures and social workers of the twentieth century: her hunger to be pure, her capacity for intense self-criticism, her desire to dedicate herself to something lofty, her tendency to focus on hardship and not fully enjoy the simple pleasures available to her, her conviction that fail as she might, and struggle as she would, God would ultimately redeem her from her failings.

BOHEMIA

Day was one of three students in her high school to win a college scholarship, thanks to her excellence in Latin and Greek. She went to the University of Illinois, where she cleaned and ironed to pay for room and board and was an indifferent student. She threw herself, willy-nilly, into activities that she hoped would lead to an epic life. She joined the writers' club, accepted for an essay in which she described what it was like to go without food for three days. She also joined the Socialist Party, broke from religion, and began doing what she could to offend the churchgoers. She decided the sweetness of girlhood was gone. It was time to be at war with society.

At age eighteen, after a couple of years at Illinois, she decided that college life was unsatisfying. She moved to New York to become a writer. She wandered the city for months, desperately lonely: "In all that great city of seven millions, I found no friends; I had no work, I was separated from my fellows. Silence in the midst of city noises oppressed me. My own silence, the feeling that I had no one to talk to overwhelmed me so that my very throat was constricted; my heart was heavy with unuttered thoughts; I wanted to weep my loneliness away."[7]

During this lonely period she became indignant at the poverty she saw in New York, its different smell from the poverty she had seen in Chicago. "Everyone must go through something analogous to a conversion," she would later write, "conversion to an idea, a thought, a desire, a dream, a vision — without vision the people perish. In my teens I read Upton Sinclair's *The Jungle* and Jack London's *The Road* and became converted to the poor, to a love for and desire to be always with the poor and suffering — the workers of the world. I was converted to the idea of the Messianic mission of the proletariat." Russia was very much on people's minds then. Russian writers defined the spiritual imagination. The Russian Revolution inflamed young radicals' visions for the future. Dorothy's closest college friend, Rayna Simons, moved to Moscow to be part of that future, and died of illness after a few months there. In 1917, Day attended a rally celebrating the Russian Revolution. She felt a sense of exaltation; the victory of the masses was at hand.

Dorothy finally found work at a radical paper, *The Call,* for five dollars a week. There she covered labor unrest and the lives of factory workers. She interviewed Leon Trotsky one day and a millionaire's butler the next. Newspaper life was intense. She was carried along by events, not reflecting on them, just letting them sweep over her.

Although more an activist than an aesthete, she fell in with a bohemian crowd, with the critic Malcolm Cowley, the poet Allen Tate, and the novelist John Dos Passos. She formed a deep friendship with the radical writer Michael Gold. They would walk along the East River for hours, happily talking about their reading and their dreams. Occasionally, Gold would break into joyful song, in Hebrew or Yiddish. She had a close though apparently platonic relationship with the playwright Eugene O'Neill, who shared her obsessions with loneliness, religion, and death. Day's biographer Jim Forest writes that Dorothy would sometimes put O'Neill to bed, drunk and shaking with the terrors, and hold him until he fell asleep. He asked her to have sex with him, but she refused.

She protested on behalf of the working classes. But the most vital dramas of her life were going on inside. She had become an even more avid reader, especially of Tolstoy and Dostoyevsky.

It's hard now to recapture how seriously people took novel reading then, or at least how seriously Day and others took it — reading important works as wisdom literature, believing that supreme artists possessed insights that could be handed down as revelation, trying to mold one's life around the heroic and deep souls one found in books. Day read as if her whole life depended upon it.

Fewer people today see artists as oracles

and novels as a form of revelation. The cognitive sciences have replaced literature as the way many people attempt to understand their own minds. But Day was "moved to the depths of my being" by Dostoyevsky. "The scene in *Crime and Punishment* where the young prostitute reads from the New Testament to Raskolnikov, sensing sin more profound than her own; that story, 'The Honest Thief'; those passages in *The Brothers Karamazov;* Mitya's conversion in jail, the very legend of the Grand Inquisitor, all this helped to lead me on." She was especially drawn to the scene in which "Father Zossima spoke glowingly of that love for God which resulted in a love for one's brother. The story of his conversion to love is moving, and that book, with its picture of religion, had a lot to do with my later life."[8]

She didn't just read Russian novels, she seemed to live them out. She was a heavy drinker and barfly. Malcolm Cowley wrote that gangsters loved her because she could drink them under the table, though that is hard to believe, given her rail-thin frame. The tragedies of her raucous life were there, too. A friend named Louis Holladay took an overdose of heroin and died in her arms.[9] In her memoir, she describes her moves from one rancid and airless apartment to another, but even she, self-critical as she was, leaves out some of the messiness. She leaves out her promiscuity, calling it "a time of searching" and referring vaguely to "the sadness of sin, the unspeakable dreariness of sin."[10]

In the spring of 1918, she volunteered as a nurse at King's County Hospital as a deadly flu epidemic swept through the city and the world. (More than 50 million people died of it between March 1918 and June 1920.)[11] She began work at six each morning and worked twelve-hour days, changing linens, emptying bedpans, administering shots, enemas, and douches. The hospital was run like a military unit. When the head nurse entered the ward, the junior nurses stood at attention. "I liked the order of life and the discipline. By contrast the life that I had been leading seemed disorderly and futile," she recalled. "One of the things that this year in the hospital made me realize is that one of the hardest things in the world is to organize ourselves and discipline ourselves."[12]

She met a newspaperman named Lionel Moise at the hospital. They had a tumultuous physical relationship. "You are hard," she wrote to him lustfully. "I fell in love with you because you are hard." She got pregnant. He told her to get an abortion, which she did (also neglecting to mention it in her memoirs). One night, after he dumped her, she unhooked the gas pipe from the heater in her apartment and attempted suicide. A neighbor found her in time.

In her memoirs she writes that she left the hospital job because it eventually made her numb to suffering, and it left her no time to write. She neglected to mention that she had also agreed to marry a man twice her age named Berkeley Tobey, a rich man from the Northwest. They traveled to Europe together, and after the trip was over, she left him. In her memoirs she describes it as a solo trip, embarrassed that she had used Tobey for a chance to go to Europe. "I didn't want to write what I was ashamed of," she would later tell the journalist Dwight MacDonald. "I felt I had used him and was ashamed."[13]

She also, crucially, was arrested twice, first in 1917 at age twenty and then in 1922 at age twenty-five. The first time, it was in the name of political activism. She had become active in advocating for the rights of women; she was arrested for taking part in a suffragist protest in front of the White House and sentenced, with the rest of the protesters, to thirty days in jail. The prisoners began a hunger strike, but Day, sitting there gnawed by hunger, soon slipped into a deep depression. She flipped from feeling solidarity with the hunger strikers to feeling that it was all somehow wrong and meaningless. "I lost all consciousness of any cause. I had no sense of being a radical. I could only feel darkness and desolation all around me. . . . I had an ugly sense of the futility of human effort, man's helpless misery, the triumph of might. . . . Evil triumphed. I was a petty creature, filled with self-deception, self-importance, unreal, false, and rightly scorned and punished."[14]

In jail she asked for a Bible and read it intensely. Other prisoners told her stories of the solitary confinement cells where prisoners would be locked up for six months at a time. "Never would I recover from this wound, this ugly knowledge I had gained of what men were capable of in their treatment of each other."[15]

Day was taking a stand against injustice, but she was doing it without an organizing transcendent framework. She seems to have felt, unconsciously and even then, that for her, activism without faith would fail.

Her second imprisonment was even more

172

emotionally devastating. She had gone to stay with a friend, a drug addict, in her apartment on Skid Row, in a building that served as both a whorehouse and a residence for members of the IWW, the radical union. The police raided the place, looking for subversives. The cops assumed that Day and her friend were prostitutes. They were forced to stand out on the street, semiclad, before they were hauled off to jail.

She was a victim of the Red hysteria of the time. But she also felt she was a victim of her own imprudence and lack of integrity. She took the arrest as an indictment of her scattered life. "I do not think that ever again, no matter of what I am accused, can I suffer more than I did then of shame and regret, and self-contempt. Not only because I had been caught, found out, branded, publicly humiliated, but because of my own consciousness that I deserved it."[16]

These are episodes of extraordinary self-scrutiny and self-criticism. Looking back years later, Day took a dim view of her own rowdy life. She saw it as a form of pride, as an attempt to define what was good and bad for herself, without reference to anything larger. "The life of the flesh called to me as a good and wholesome life, regardless of man's laws, which I felt rebelliously were made for the repression of others. The strong could make their own law, live their own lives; in fact they were beyond good and evil. What was good and what was evil? It is easy enough to stifle conscience for a time. The satisfied flesh has its own law."

But Day was not just lost in a world of shallow infatuations, tumultuous affairs, fleshly satisfaction, and selfishness. Her extreme self-criticism flowed from a deep spiritual hunger. She used the word "loneliness" to describe this hunger. For many of us, that word brings to mind solitude. And Day was indeed solitary, and she did suffer from it. But Day also used the word "loneliness" to describe spiritual isolation. She had a sense that there was some transcendent cause or entity or activity out there and that she would be restless until she found it. She was incapable of living life on the surface only — for pleasures, success, even for service — but needed a deep and total commitment to something holy.

CHILDBIRTH

Day had spent her twenties throwing herself down different avenues, looking for a vocation. She tried politics. She took part in protests and marches. But they didn't satisfy. Unlike Frances Perkins, she was unfit for the life of politics, with its compromises, self-seeking, shades of gray, and dirty hands. She needed a venue that would involve internal surrender, renunciation of self, commitment to something pure. She looked back on her early activism with disquiet and self-criticism. "I do not know how sincere I was in my love of the poor and my desire to serve them. . . . I wanted to go on picket lines, to go to jail, to write, to influence others and so make my mark on the world. How much ambition and how much self-seeking there was in all of this."[17]

Then Day went the literary route. She wrote a novel about her disordered early life called *The Eleventh Virgin,* which was accepted by a New York publisher and optioned for $5,000 by a Hollywood studio.[18] But this sort of literature did not cure the longing, either, and the book would eventually make her feel ashamed — she later thought of buying up every existing copy.

She thought that romantic love might satisfy her longing. She fell in love with a man named Forster Batterham, and they lived together, unmarried, in a house on Staten Island that Day bought with the proceeds of her novel. She describes Forster romantically in *The Long Loneliness* as an anarchist, an Englishman by descent, and a biologist. In fact, the truth is more prosaic. He made gauges in a factory; he had grown up in North Carolina and gone to Georgia Tech. He had an interest in radical politics.[19] But Day's love for him was real. She loved him for his convictions, for his stubborn attachment to them, for his love of nature. She would, after their disagreements about fundamental things had become clear, still beg him to marry her. Day was still a passionate, sexual woman, and her lust for him was real, too. "My desire for you is a painful rather than pleasurable emotion," she wrote in a letter that was released after her death. "It is a ravishing hunger which makes me want you more than anything in the world. And makes me feel as though I could barely exist until I saw you again." On September 21, 1925, during one of their separations, she wrote to him, "I made myself a beautiful new nightie, all lacie and exotic, also several new pairs of panties which you will be interested in I am sure. I think of you much and dream of you every night and if my dreams could affect you over long distance, I am sure they would keep you awake."

When you read of Day and Batterham living their secluded life in Staten Island, reading, talking, making love, you get the impression that they, like many young couples newly in love, were trying to build what Sheldon Vanauken would call a "Shining Barrier," a walled garden, cut off from the world, in which their love would be pure. Ultimately, Day's longing could not be contained within the Shining Barrier. Living with Batterham, taking long walks with him on the beach, she still felt a desire for something more. Among other things, she wanted a child. She felt her house was empty without one. In 1925, at age twenty-eight, she was thrilled when she learned she was pregnant. Batterham did not share her feelings. A self-styled radical, a modern man, he did not believe in bringing more human beings into the world. He certainly did not believe in the bourgeois institution of marriage, and he would never consent to marry her.

While she was pregnant, it occurred to Day that most of the descriptions of childbirth had been written by men. She set out to rectify this. Shortly after giving birth, she wrote an essay on the experience, which eventually appeared in the *New Masses*. Day vividly described the physical struggle of the birth itself:

Earthquake and fire swept my body. My spirit was a battleground on which thousands were butchered in a most horrible manner. Through the rush and roar of the cataclysm which was all about me I heard the murmur of the doctor and answered the murmur of the nurse in my head. In a white blaze of thankfulness I knew that ether was forthcoming.

When her daughter Tamar arrived, she was overwhelmed by gratitude: "If I had written the greatest book, composed the greatest symphony, painted the most beautiful painting or carved the most exquisite figure, I could not have felt the more exalted creator than I did when they placed my child in my arms." She felt the need for someone to thank. "No human creature could receive or contain so vast a flood of love and joy as I often felt after the birth of my child. With this came the need to worship, to adore."[20]

But whom to thank? Whom to worship? A sense of God's reality and immanence came upon her, particularly on her long walks, when she found herself praying. She had trouble praying on her knees, but while she was walking, words of gratitude, praise, and obedience seemed to leap from her. A walk that began in misery could end in exultation.

Day was not answering the question of whether God exists. She was simply made aware of a presence beyond herself. She was surrendering to the belief that independent of one's own will, there is something significant that gives shape to life. If the life of a radical was a life of assertion and agency, a desire to steer history, she was turning to a life of obedience. God was in charge. As she later put it, she came to see that "worship, adoration, thanksgiving, supplication — these were the noblest acts of which men were capable of in this life."[21] The birth of her child began her transformation from a scattered person to a centered one, from an unhappy bohemian to a woman who had found her calling.

Day had no obvious outlet for her faith. She was a member of no church. She was not comfortable with theology or traditional religious doctrines. But she felt hunted by God. "How can there be no God," she asked Forster, "when there are all these beautiful things?"

Her attention turned to the Catholic Church. It was not church history that drew her, or papal authority, or even the political and social positions taken by the church. She knew nothing about Catholic theology and only knew the Church itself as a backward and politically reactionary force. It was the people, not theology. It was the Catholic immigrants she had covered and served — their poverty, their dignity, their communal spirit, and their generosity toward those who were down and out. Day's friends told her that she didn't need a religious institution to worship God, certainly not one as retrograde as the Catholic Church, but Day's experience as a radical taught her to associate herself as closely as possible with those who were suffering, to join in their walk, which meant joining their church.

She observed that Catholicism already organized the lives of many poor urban families. It had won their allegiance. They poured into its churches on Sundays and holy days and in moments of joy and mourning. In the same way, the Catholic faith would provide structure for her life, and she hoped it would provide structure for her daughter. "We all crave order, and in the book of Job, hell is described as a place where no order is. I felt that 'belonging' to a church would bring order into [Tamar's] life, which I felt was lacking in my own."[22]

Day's adult faith was warmer and more joyful than the faith she'd experienced as a teenager. Day was particularly attracted to Saint Teresa of Avila, the sixteenth-century Spanish mystic and nun whose experiences closely paralleled Day's own: the deeply spiritual childhood, the terror in the face of her own sinfulness, the occasional moments of what could be described as sexual ecstasy in His presence, the intense ambition to reform human institutions and serve the poor.

Teresa lived a life of renunciation. She slept under a single woolen blanket. There was no heat in her convent except for a stove in one room. Her days were filled with prayer and penance. But she also possessed a lightness of spirit. Day said she loved the fact that Saint Teresa wore a bright red dress the day she entered the convent. She loved the fact that one day Teresa shocked her fellow nuns by taking out castanets and dancing. When she was the Mother Superior and the nuns under her became melancholy, she had the kitchen serve them steak. Teresa said that life is like a "night spent in an uncomfortable inn," so you might as well do what you can to make it more pleasant.

Day was becoming a Catholic, but she

wasn't close to any practicing Catholics. But she encountered a nun walking down a street and asked her for instruction. The nun was shocked by Day's ignorance of Catholic teaching and berated her for it, but she welcomed her in. Day began attending services weekly, even when she didn't feel like it. She asked herself, "Do I prefer the Church or my own will?" She decided that even though she would have found it more pleasant to spend Sunday mornings reading the papers, she preferred the church to her own will.

The path to God eventually meant breaking with Forster. He was scientific, skeptical, and empirical. He bet his life on a material universe, clinging to his conviction as fiercely as Day ultimately would to her view of a divinely created one.

Their separation took some time and required much tearing. One day, over a meal, Forster asked the questions many of Day's radical friends were asking: Had she lost her mind? Who was pushing her to an archaic and backward institution like the Church? Who was the secret person in her life corrupting her in this way?

Day was surprised by the passion and power behind his questions. Finally she quietly said, "It is Jesus. I guess it is Jesus

Christ who is the one who is pushing me to the Catholics."[23]

Forster turned white and went silent. He didn't move. He just sat there glaring at her. She asked if they could talk some more about religion. He didn't answer her at all, or nod, or shake his head. Then he clasped his hands together on the table in a gesture that reminded Day of the way schoolboys act when they want their teachers to think they are good. He sat for several seconds in this posture, then raised his clasped hands and brought them smashing down on the table, rattling the cups and dishes. Day was terrified that he would lose control and start striking her with his clasped hands. But he didn't. He got up and told Day that she was mentally disturbed. Then he walked around the table once and went out of the house.[24]

These scenes did not end their love, or their lust, for each other. Day still pleaded with Forster to marry her and to give Tamar a real father. Even after she had effectively renounced him for the Church, she wrote to him, "I dream of you every night — that I am lying in your arms and can feel your kisses and it is torture to me, but so sweet too. I do love you more than anything else in the world, but I cannot help my religious sense, which tortures me unless I do as I believe right."[25]

Dorothy's love for Forster paradoxically opened her up to faith. Her love for him broke through her shell and exposed the soft and more vulnerable regions of the heart to other loves. It provided her with a model. As Day put it, "It was through a whole love, both physical and spiritual, I came to know God."[26] This is a more mature understanding than her tendency, as a teenager, to divide the world between flesh on one side and spirit on the other.

CONVERSION

The conversion process was a dreary, joyless affair. Day, being Day, made it hard on herself. She criticized herself at each moment, doubting her own motives and practices. She was divided between the radicalism of her former self and the devotion to the Church that her new life required. One day, walking to the post office, she was enveloped with scorn for her own faith. "Here you are in a stupor of content. You are biological. Like a cow. Prayer for you is like the opiate of the people." She kept repeating that phrase in her head: "The opiate of the people." But, she reasoned as she continued her walk, she wasn't praying to escape pain. She was praying because she was happy, because she wanted to thank God for her happiness.[27]

She had Tamar baptized in July 1927. There was a party afterward, and Forster brought some lobsters he had caught. But then he quarreled with Day, telling her again that it was all just so much mumbo-jumbo, and then he left.

She officially joined the church on December 28, 1927. The moment brought her no consolation. "I had no sense of peace, no joy, no conviction that what I was doing was right. It was just something that I had to do, a task to be gotten through."[28] As she performed the sacraments, the Baptism, Penance, Holy Eucharist, she felt herself a hypocrite. She went through the motions, getting down on her knees, coldly. She was afraid somebody might see her. She was afraid she was betraying the poor and going over to the losing side of history, to an institution lined up on the side of property, of the powerful and the elites. "Are you sure of yourself?" she asked herself. "What kind of affectation is this? What act is this you are going through?"

Self-critical as always, Day questioned herself over the following months and years, wondering whether her faith was deep or practical enough: "How little, how puny my work had been since becoming a Catholic, I thought. How self-centered, how ingrown, how lacking in a sense of community! My summer of quiet reading and prayer, my self-absorption seemed sinful as I watched my brothers in their struggle, not for themselves but for others."[29]

In choosing religion, she chose an arduous path. It is often said that religion makes life easier for people, provides them with the comforting presence of a loving and all-knowing father. That is certainly not how Day experienced it. She experienced it as difficult self-conflict, the sort of self-conflict that Joseph Soloveitchik described in a famous footnote in his book *Halakhic Man.* Here is an abridged version of that footnote:

This popular ideology contends that the religious experience is tranquil and neatly ordered, tender and delicate; it is an enchanted stream for embittered souls and still waters for troubled spirits. The person "who comes in from the field, weary" (Gen. 25:29), from the battlefield and campaigns of life, from the secular domain which is filled with doubts and fears, contradictions and refutations, clings to religion as does a baby to its mother and finds in her lap "a shelter for his head, the nest of his forsaken prayers" and there is comforted for his disappointments and tribulations. This Rousseauian ideology left its stamp on the entire Romantic movement from the beginning of its growth until its final (tragic!) manifestations in the consciousness of contemporary man. Therefore, the representatives of religious communities are inclined to portray religion, in a wealth of colors that dazzle the eye, as a poetic Arcadia, a realm of simplicity, wholeness, and tranquillity. This ideology is intrinsically false and deceptive. That religious consciousness in man's experience, which is most profound and most elevated, which penetrates to the very depths and ascends to the very heights, is not that simple and comfortable.

On the contrary, it is exceptionally complex, rigorous, and tortuous. Where you find its complexity, there you find its greatness. The consciousness of *homo religiosis* flings bitter accusations against itself and immediately is filled with regret, judges its desires and yearnings with excessive severity, and at the same time steeps itself in them, casts derogatory aspersions on its own attributes, flails away at them, but also subjugates itself to them. It is in a condition of spiritual crisis, of psychic ascent and descent, of contradiction arising from affirmation and negation, self-abnegation and self-appreciation. Religion is not, at the outset, a refuge of grace and mercy for the despondent and desperate, an enchanted stream for crushed spirits, but a raging clamorous torrent of man's consciousness with all its crises, pangs, and torments.

Early in her religious journey, Day met three women who were in love but weren't sleeping with the men they intended to marry, even though it was obvious how much they wanted to. Day looked at their self-denial and began to feel "that Catholicism was something rich and real and fascinating. . . . I saw them wrestling with moral problems, with the principles by which they lived, and this made them noble in my eyes."[30]

Day attended mass daily, which meant rising at dawn. She prayed according to the monastic rhythms through the day. She dedicated time each day to the religious disciplines, reading the scripture, saying the rosary. She fasted and went to confession.

These rituals could become routine, like playing the scales for a musician, but Day found the routine, even when it was dull, necessary: "Without the sacraments of the church, primarily the Eucharist, the Lord's Supper, as it is called, I certainly do not think that I could go on. . . . I do not always approach it from need, or with joy and thanksgiving. After 38 years of almost daily communion, one can confess to a routine, but it is like the routine of taking daily food."[31]

These routines created a spiritual center for her life. From the fragmentation of her early life she moved toward integration.

LIVING OUT THE GOSPEL

Day was now in her early thirties. The great depression was biting with full force. In 1933 she started a newspaper called *The Catholic Worker* to mobilize the proletariat and apply Catholic social teaching toward the goal of creating a society in which it is easier for people to be good. It wasn't only a newspaper; it was a movement, located in ramshackle offices in Lower Manhattan, with everybody working for free. Within three years it had a circulation of 150,000, with distribution in five hundred parishes across the country.[32]

The newspaper hosted a soup kitchen, feeding as many as fifteen hundred each morning. It sponsored a series of hospitality houses for the indigent, providing nearly fifty thousand nights of lodging between 1935 and 1938. Day and her colleagues also organized and inspired more than thirty other hospitality houses across the United States and in England. They eventually opened and inspired agrarian communes from California to Michigan to New Jersey. They organized marches and events. These were, in part, efforts to build community, to heal the loneliness that marks human existence.

To Day, separation was sin: separation from God, separation from one another. Unity was holiness: the fusion between people and spirits. *The Catholic Worker* fused a lot of things together. It was a newspaper but also an activist aid organization. It was a religious publication, but it also advocated for economic change. It was about inner life, but also political radicalism. It brought the rich and poor into contact. It joined theology and economics, material concerns and spiritual ones, body and soul.

Day insisted on being radical, to get down to the roots of social problems. The paper was Catholic, but she embraced a philosophy of personalism, which is an affirmation of the dignity of each person, created in the image of God. Being a personalist, Day had a suspicion of bigness, whether it was big government or big corporations. Day even had a suspicion of big philanthropy. She was constantly urging her co-workers to "stay small": Start your work from where you live, with the small concrete needs right around you. Help ease tension in your workplace. Help feed the person right in front of you. Personalism holds that we each have a deep personal obligation to live simply, to look after the needs of our brothers and sisters, and to share in the happiness and misery they are suffering. The personalist brings his whole person to serve another whole person. This can only be done by means of intimate contact within small communities.

Day spent the rest of her life, until her death on November 29, 1980, as a Catholic worker, working on the newspaper and serving bread and soup to the poor and mentally disabled. She wrote eleven books and more than a thousand articles. The service work was prosaic. This was before computers and copiers. Each month the staff had to type out tens of thousands of address labels in order to send the paper out to subscribers. The reporters sold the paper themselves on the street. Day felt that it was not enough to just care for the poor, "one must live with them, share with them their suffering too. Give up one's privacy, and mental and spiritual comforts as well as physical."[33] She didn't just visit the shelters and hospitality houses from the comfort of her own home. She lived in the hospitality houses herself, with those she was serving.

The work was relentless — endlessly serving coffee and soup, raising money, writing articles for the paper. "Breakfast a thick slice of dry bread," Day wrote in her diary one day, "and some very bad coffee. I dictate a dozen letters. My brain is a fog. I am too weak to climb stairs. I have prescribed for myself this day in bed but I keep thinking it is my spirit that is all wrong. I am surrounded by repellent disorder, noise, people, and have no spirit of inner solitude or poverty."[34]

We sometimes think of saints, or of people who are living like saints, as being ethereal, living in a higher spiritual realm. But often enough they live in an even less ethereal way than the rest of us. They are more fully of this earth, more fully engaged in the dirty, practical problems of the people around them. Day and her colleagues slept in cold rooms. They wore donated clothes.

They did not receive salaries. Day's mind was not engaged by theology most of the time, but by how to avoid this or that financial crisis, or arrange for this person to get that treatment. In a 1934 journal entry she described the activities of a single day, a mixture of the sacred and the profane: she woke up, got to mass, made breakfast for the staff, answered mail, did the bookkeeping, read some literature, wrote an inspirational message to be mimeographed and handed out. Then a relief worker came in looking for a confirmation outfit for a twelve-year-old girl, then a convert came in to share his religious writings, then a Fascist came by to whip up hatred among the residents, then an art student arrived with some drawings of Saint Catherine of Siena, and so on and so on.

The atmosphere was similar to the one Albert Schweitzer, the German medical missionary, described at his hospital in the African jungle. He did not hire idealists for that hospital, nor did he hire people who had a righteous sense of how much they were giving to the world. He certainly did not hire people who set out "to do something special." He only wanted people who would perform constant acts of service with the no-nonsense attitude that they will simply do what needs doing. "Only a person who feels his preference to be a matter of course, not something out of the ordinary, and who has no thought of heroism but only of a duty undertaken with sober enthusiasm, is capable of being the sort of spiritual pioneer the world needs."[35]

Day was not a naturally social creature. She had a writer's personality, somewhat aloof and often craving solitude. But she forced herself to be with people, almost all day, every day. Many of those she served had mental disabilities, or suffered from alcoholism. Bickering was constant. The guests could be rude, nasty, and foul-mouthed. Yet she forced herself to sit at the table and focus on the specific person in front of her. That person might be drunk and incoherent, but Day would sit, showing respect and listening.

She would carry notebooks with her and use spare moments to write, journal entries for herself and a constant string of columns, essays, and reports for others. Other people's sins became an occasion to reflect on her own greater ones. As she wrote one day in her journal: "Drunkenness and all the sins which follow in its wake are so obviously ugly and monstrous, and mean such unhappiness for the poor sinner that it is all the more important that we do not judge or condemn. In the eyes of God the hidden subtle sins must be far worse. We must make every effort of will to love more and more — to hang on to each other with love. They should serve to show us the hideousness of our own sins so that we truly repent and abhor them."[36]

She guarded against spiritual pride, against the feeling of self-righteousness that might come over her because she was doing good works. "I have to stop myself sometimes," she wrote. "I have found myself rushing from one person to another — soup bowls and more soup bowls, plates of bread and more plates of bread, with the gratitude of the hungry becoming a loud din in my ears. The hunger of my ears can be as severe as someone else's stomach hunger; the joy of hearing those expressions of gratitude."[37] The sin of pride is around every corner, Day believed, and there are many corners even in a charity house. To serve others is to live under a great temptation.

SUFFERING

As a young woman, day followed the mode of Dostoyevsky — her life was filled with drinking and disorder even while she was God-haunted. But, as Paul Elie notes, internally she was not a Dostoyevskyan; she was a Tolstoyan. She was not a trapped animal compelled to suffer by circumstance; she ardently chose suffering. At each step along the way, when most people would have sought out comfort and ease — what economists call self-interest or what psychologists call happiness — she chose a different route, seeking discomfort and difficulty in order to satisfy her longing for holiness. She wasn't just choosing to work at a nonprofit institution in order to have a big impact; she was seeking to live in accord with the Gospels, even if it meant sacrifice and suffering.

When most people think about the future, they dream up ways they might live happier lives. But notice this phenomenon. When people remember the crucial events that formed them, they don't usually talk about happiness. It is usually the ordeals that seem most significant. Most people shoot for happiness but feel formed through suffering.

Day was unusual, maybe even perverse, in that she sometimes seemed to seek out suffering as a road to depth. She probably observed, as we all do, that people we call deep have almost always endured a season of suffering, or several such seasons. But she seemed to seek out those seasons, and to avoid some of the normal pleasures of life that would have brought simple earthly happiness. She often sought out occasions for moral heroism, occasions to serve others in acts of enduring hardship.

For most of us, there is nothing intrinsically noble about suffering. Just as failure is sometimes just failure (and not your path to becoming the next Steve Jobs), suffering is sometimes just destructive, to be exited or medicated as quickly as possible. When it is not connected to some larger purpose beyond itself, suffering shrinks or annihilates people. When it is not understood as a piece of a larger process, it leads to doubt, nihilism, and despair.

But some people can connect their suffering to some greater design. They place their suffering in solidarity with all the others who have suffered. These people are clearly ennobled by it. It is not the suffering itself that makes all the difference, but the way it is experienced. Think of the way Franklin Roosevelt came back deeper and more empathetic after being struck by polio. Often, physical or social suffering can give people an outsider's perspective, an attuned awareness of what others are enduring.

The first big thing suffering does is it drags you deeper into yourself. The theologian Paul Tillich wrote that people who endure suffering are taken beneath the routine busyness of life and find they are not who they believed themselves to be. The pain involved in, say, composing a great piece of music or the grief of having lost a loved one smashes through a floor they thought was the bottom floor of their soul, revealing a cavity below, and then it smashes through that floor, revealing another cavity, and so on and so on. The person in pain descends to unknown ground.

Suffering opens up ancient places of pain that had been hidden. It exposes frightening experiences that had been repressed, shameful wrongs that had been committed. It spurs some people to painfully and carefully examine the basement of their own soul. But it also presents the pleasurable sensation that one is getting closer to the truth. The pleasure in suffering is that you feel you are getting beneath the superficial and approaching the fundamental. It creates what modern psychologists call "depressive realism," an ability to see things exactly the way they are. It shatters the comforting rationalizations and pat narratives we tell about ourselves as part of our way of simplifying ourselves for the world.

Then, too, suffering gives people a more

accurate sense of their own limitations, of what they can control and not control. When people are thrust down into these deeper zones, thrust into lonely self-scrutiny, they are forced to confront the fact that they can't determine what goes on there.

Suffering, like love, shatters the illusion of self-mastery. Those who suffer can't tell themselves to stop feeling pain, or to stop missing the one who has died or gone. And even when tranquillity begins to come back, or in those moments when grief eases, it is not clear where that relief comes from. The healing process, too, feels as though it's part of some natural or divine process beyond individual control. For people in this striving culture, in this Adam I world where everything is won by effort, exertion, and control, suffering teaches dependence. It teaches that life is unpredictable and that the meritocrat's efforts at total control are an illusion.

Suffering, oddly, also teaches gratitude. In normal times we treat the love we receive as a reason for self-satisfaction (I deserve to be loved), but in seasons of suffering we realize how undeserved this love is and how it should in fact be a cause for thanks. In proud moments we refuse to feel indebted, but in humble moments, people know they don't deserve the affection and concern they receive.

People in this circumstance also have a sense that they are swept up in some larger providence. Abraham Lincoln suffered through depression through his life and then suffered through the pain of conducting a civil war, and emerged with the sense that Providence had taken control of his life, that he was a small instrument in a transcendent task.

It's at this point that people in the midst of difficulty begin to feel a call. They are not masters of the situation, but neither are they helpless. They can't determine the course of their pain, but they can participate in responding to it. They often feel an overwhelming moral responsibility to respond well to it. They may start their suffering asking "Why me?" or "Why evil?" But they soon realize the proper question is "What am I supposed to do if I am confronted with suffering, if I am the victim of evil?"

People who seek this proper response to their ordeal sense that they are at a deeper level than the level of personal happiness. They don't say, "Well, I'm fighting a lot of pain over the loss of my child. I should try to balance my hedonic account by going to a lot of parties and whooping it up."

The right response to this sort of pain is not pleasure. It's holiness. I don't mean that in a purely religious sense. I mean seeing the pain as part of a moral narrative and trying to redeem something bad by turning it into something sacred, some act of sacrificial service that will put oneself in fraternity with the wider community and with eternal moral demands. Parents who have lost a child start foundations; their dead child touches the lives of people they never met. Suffering simultaneously reminds us of our finitude and pushes us to see life in the widest possible connections, which is where holiness dwells.

Recovering from suffering is not like recovering from a disease. Many people don't come out healed; they come out different. They crash through the logic of individual utility and behave paradoxically. Instead of recoiling from the sorts of loving commitments that often lead to suffering, they throw themselves more deeply into them. Even while experiencing the worst and most lacerating consequences, some people double down on vulnerability and become available to healing love. They hurl themselves deeper and more gratefully into their art, loved ones, and commitments.

This way, suffering becomes a fearful gift, very different from that other gift, happiness, conventionally defined. The latter brings pleasure, but the former cultivates character.

SERVICE

As the decades wore on, news of Dorothy day's example spread. She has inspired generations of young Catholics because she wasn't merely a champion of Catholic social teaching, but a concrete living example. Catholic social teaching is based, in part, on the idea that each life has equal dignity, that the soul of a drug-addled homeless person is just as invaluable as the most laudable high achiever. It is based on the conviction that God has a special love for the poor. As it says in Isaiah, "True worship is to work for justice and care for the poor and oppressed." This teaching emphasizes that we are one human family. God's servants are therefore called upon to live in solidarity with one another, in community. Day formed her organization around these principles.

The Long Loneliness was published in 1952. It sold well and has been in print ever since. As her work became famous, her houses attracted flocks of admirers, and that, too, presented its own spiritual challenges. "I get tired of hearing people say how wonderful it is, what we do. Lots of times it's not as wonderful as they think. We are overworked, or feel tired and irritable, and we have heard some rude remark from someone in the line and our patience is exhausted and we're ready to explode."[38] Still, she was afraid she and her flock would be corrupted by this admiration. It also made her feel lonely.

Surrounded by people almost all the time, Day was often isolated from those she loved. Her family was estranged from her, mystified by her Catholicism. After Forster, she never loved another man and remained celibate the rest of her life. "It was years before I awakened without that longing for a face pressed against my breast, an arm about my shoulder. The sense of loss was there. It was a price I had paid."[39] It's not clear why she felt she had to pay this price, to bear this loneliness and this chastity, but she did.

Living in the hospitality houses, going on long lecture tours, even meant being away from her daughter, Tamar. "It took me hours to get to sleep," she wrote in her diary in 1940. "I miss Tamar terribly, unhappily at night, but in the day not sadly. My nights are always sadness and desolation and it seems as soon as I lie down, I am on a rack of bitterness and pain. Then in the day I am again strong enough to make an act of faith and love and go on in peace and joy."[40]

She was a single mother leading a diverse and demanding social movement. She traveled often, while a parade of others looked after Tamar. She often felt she was failing as a mother. Tamar grew up within the Catholic Worker family when she was young, and then went to boarding school when she got older. While she was sixteen, Tamar fell in love with a volunteer at *The Catholic Worker* named David Hennessy. Dorothy told Tamar she was too young to marry. She ordered her not to write to David for a year and to return his letters unopened. She wrote to David urging him to leave her daughter alone, but David returned those letters without reading them.

The couple persevered, finally marrying, with Dorothy's blessing, when Tamar was eighteen, on April 19, 1944. They moved to a farm in Easton, Pennsylvania, where Tamar gave birth to the first of the nine grandchildren she was to present to her mother. The marriage between Tamar and

David lasted until the end of 1961, when they divorced. David was unemployed for long periods and struggled with mental illness. Tamar eventually moved back near a Catholic Worker farm on Staten Island. People described her as a gentle, hospitable person, without the propulsive spiritual longing her mother wrestled with. She accepted people as they were and loved them unconditionally. She died in 2008, at the age of eighty-two, in New Hampshire. Tamar remained wedded to the Social Worker movement, but she had precious little time to spend with her mother.

IMPACT

Torn between competing demands and vocations, day was restless through much of her adult life. At times she even thought of leaving the newspaper. "The world is too much with me in the Catholic Worker. The world is suffering and dying. I am not suffering and dying in the CW. I am writing and talking about it."[41] She also thought about becoming invisible, about getting a job in a hospital as a maid, about finding a room to live in somewhere, preferably next door to a church: "There in the solitude of the city, living and working with the poor, to learn to pray, to work, to suffer, to be silent."

In the end, she decided not to leave. She built a series of communities, around the newspaper, the hospitality houses, the rural communes. The communities provided her with families and joy.

"Writing," she wrote in one column in 1950, "is an act of community. It is a letter, it is comforting, consoling, helping, advising on our part as well as asking for it on yours. It is part of our human association with each other. It is an expression of our love and concern for each other."[42]

She returned to this theme again and again, wrestling with her divided self: her solitary nature and also her craving for others. "The only answer in this life, to the loneliness we are all bound to feel, is community," she wrote. "The living together, working together, sharing together, loving God and loving our brother, and living close to him in community so we can show our love for Him."[43] At the end of *The Long Loneliness* she cries out, in one of her great bursts of gratitude,

> I found myself, a barren woman, the joyful mother of children. It is not easy always to be joyful, to keep in mind the duty to

delight. The most significant thing about The Catholic Worker is poverty, some say. The most significant thing about The Catholic Worker is community, others say. We are not alone anymore. But the final word is love. At times it has been, in the words of Father Zossima, a harsh and dreadful thing, and our very faith in love has been tried through fire.

We cannot love God unless we love each other, and to love we must know each other. We know Him in the breaking of bread, and we know each other in the breaking of bread, and we are not alone anymore. Heaven is a banquet and life is a banquet, too, even with a crust, where there is companionship.[44]

It may seem from the outside as if Day was doing the sort of community service that young people are called upon to do these days — serving soup, providing shelter. But in fact, her life rested on very different foundations and pointed in very different directions than the lives of many do-gooders today.

The Catholic Worker movement was meant to ease the suffering of the poor, but that was not its main purpose or organizing principle. The main idea was to provide a model of what the world would look like if Christians really did lead the lives that the Gospels command and love. It was not only to help the poor, but to address their own brokenness, that people served. "Going to bed at night with the foul smell of unwashed bodies. Lack of privacy," Day wrote in her diary. "But Christ was born in a [manger] and a stable is apt to be unclean and odorous. If the Blessed Mother could endure it, why not I."[45]

As the journalist Yishai Schwartz has written, for Day, "every significant action only attains its significance because of its relation to the Divine." Every time she found somebody a piece of clothing, that was an act of prayer. Day was revolted by "the idea of doled-out charity," which denigrates and disrespects the poor. For her, each act of service was a gesture upward to the poor and toward God, and the fulfillment of an internal need. Day felt it was necessary, Schwartz writes, to "internalize poverty as a private virtue," to embrace poverty as a way to achieve communion with others and come closer to God. To separate community service from prayer would have been to separate it from its life-altering purpose.

The loneliness, suffering, and pain Dorothy Day endured have a sobering effect on anybody who reads her diaries. Does God really call for this much hardship? Did she not renounce too many of the simple pleasures that the world provides? In some sense she did. But in some sense this is a false impression left by overreliance on her diaries and her own writing. Like many people, Day's mood was darker in her journals than it was in her daily life. She didn't write when happy; she was engaged in the activities that made her happy. She wrote when she was brooding about something and used her diaries to contemplate the sources of her pain.

The diaries give the impression of someone in torment, but the oral histories give the impression of someone who was constantly surrounded by children, by dear friends, by admiration and a close community. As one admirer, Mary Lathrop, put it, "She had an enormous capacity for close friendships. Really quite extraordinary. Each friendship was unique, and she had many, many of them — people who loved her, and people that she loved."[46]

Others remembered her intense love of music and the sensual things of the world. As Kathleen Jordan put it, "there was Dorothy's deep sense of beauty. . . . I'd interrupt her during the opera time [while she was listening to the Metropolitan Opera on the radio]. I'd walk in and see her almost in ecstasy. That taught me a great deal about what proper prayer meant to her. . . . She used to say, 'Remember what Dostoyevsky said: "Beauty will save the world." ' We would see that in her. She didn't separate the natural and supernatural."[47]

NANETTE

By 1960, more than three decades had passed since she had left Forster Batterham. He had spent almost all of those years living with an innocent and charming woman named Nanette. When cancer struck Nanette, Forster called on Dorothy once again, to minister to her as she died. Of course Day responded without a second thought. For several months she spent much of each day with Nanette on Staten Island. "Nanette has been having a very hard time," Day recounted in the diary, "not only pressure but pain all through her. She lay there and cried pitifully today. There is so little one can do, except just be there and say nothing. I told her how hard it was to comfort her, one could only keep the silence in the face of suffering, and she said bitterly, 'Yes, the silence of death.' I told her I would say a rosary."[48]

Day did what sensitive people do when other people are in trauma. We are all called at certain moments to comfort people who are enduring some trauma. Many of us don't know how to react in such situations, but others do. In the first place, they just show up. They provide a ministry of presence. Next, they don't compare. The sensitive person understands that each person's ordeal is unique and should not be compared to anyone else's. Next, they do the practical things — making lunch, dusting the room, washing the towels. Finally, they don't try to minimize what is going on. They don't attempt to reassure with false, saccharine sentiments. They don't say that the pain is all for the best. They don't search for silver linings. They do what wise souls do in the presence of tragedy and trauma. They practice a passive activism. They don't bustle about trying to solve something that cannot be solved. The sensitive person grants the sufferer the dignity of her own process. She lets the sufferer define the meaning of what is going on. She just sits simply through the nights of pain and darkness, being practical, human, simple, and direct.

Forster, on the other hand, behaved terribly through the ordeal. He kept running away, leaving Nanette with Dorothy and the other caregivers. "Forster in a sad state," Day wrote in her diary, "resolutely refusing to spend time with Nanette. Nanette in a sad state all day, legs swelling badly, also stomach. Later in the evening she cried out she was losing her mind and screamed continually."[49]

Day found herself suffering with Nanette and fighting off anger toward Forster. "I get so impatient at him and his constant fleeing from her, his self-pity and his weeping that I feel hard and must fight to overcome it. Such fear of sickness and death."

On January 7, 1960, Nanette asked to be baptized. The next day she died. Day remembered her final hours: "This morning at 8:45 Nanette died after an agony of two days. The Cross was not as hard as this, she said. People in concentration camps suffered like this, she said, showing her arms. She died peacefully after a slight hemorrhage. She had a slight smile, calm and peaceful."

APOTHEOSIS

When the radicalism of the late 1960s came along, Day became active in the peace movement, and in many of the other political activities of the era, but she couldn't have been more different from those radicals in her fundamental approach to life. They preached liberation, freedom, and autonomy. She preached obedience, servitude, and self-surrender. She had no patience for the celebration of open sexuality and the lax morality. She was repelled when some young people wanted to use a Dixie cup to serve the sacramental wine. She was out of step with the spirit of the counterculture and complained about all the rebellious young people: "All this rebellion makes me long for obedience — hunger and thirst for it."

In 1969 she wrote a journal entry disagreeing with those who sought to build community outside the permanent disciplines of the Church. Day had always understood the flaws in the Catholic Church, but she also understood the necessity of the structure. The radicals around her saw only the flaws and wanted to throw everything away. "It is as though the adolescents had just discovered their parents were fallible and they are so shocked they want to throw out the institutions of the home and go in for 'community.' . . . They call them 'young adults' but it seems to me they are belated adolescents with all the romanticism that goes with it."

The years confronting genuine dysfunction in the shelters had made Day realistic. "I can't bear romantics," she told one interviewer. "I want a religious realist." Much of the activism she saw around her was far too easy and self-forgiving. She had paid a terrible price to perform community service and to practice her faith — the breakup of her relationship with Forster, the estrangement from her family. "For me, Christ was not bought for thirty pieces of silver, but with my heart's blood. We buy not cheap on this market."

All around her people were celebrating nature and natural man, but Day believed that natural man is corrupt and is only saved by repressing natural urges. "We must be pruned to grow," she wrote, "and cutting hurts the natural man. But if this corruption is to put on incorruption, if one is to *put on Christ,* the new man, pain of one kind or another is inevitable. And how joyful a thought that in spite of one's dullness and lethargy one is indeed growing in the spiritual life."

The word "counterculture" was used a lot in the late 1960s, but Day was living according to a true counterculture, a culture that stood athwart not only the values of the mainstream culture of the day — the commercialism, the worship of success — but also against the values of the Woodstock counterculture the media was prone to celebrate — the antinomianism, the intense focus on the liberated individual and "doing your own thing." The Woodstock counterculture seemed, superficially, to rebel against mainstream values, but as the ensuing decades have demonstrated, it was just a flipside version of the culture of the Big Me. Both capitalism and Woodstock were about the liberation of self, the expression of self. In commercial society you expressed self by shopping and building a "lifestyle." In Woodstock culture you expressed self by casting off restraint and celebrating yourself. The bourgeois culture of commerce could merge with the bohemian culture of the 1960s precisely because both favored individual liberation, both encouraged people to measure their lives by how they were able to achieve self-gratification.

Day's life, by contrast, was about the surrender of self and ultimately the transcendence of self. Toward the end of her life she would occasionally appear on television talk shows. There is a simplicity and directness to her presence on these shows, and great self-possession. Through

215

The Long Loneliness and her other writings she practiced a sort of public confession, which has attracted people ever since. She was open about her interior life, as Frances Perkins and Dwight Eisenhower never were. She was the opposite of reticent. The premise behind her confession was not mere self-revelation, though. It was the idea that in the long run our problems are all the same. As Yishai Schwartz writes, "Confessions are meant to reveal universal truths through specific examples. Through introspection and engagement with the priest, the penitent uses her experiences to transcend her own life. Confession is thus a private moral act with a public moral purpose. For in reflecting on private decisions, we better understand the problems and struggles of humanity — itself composed of billions of individuals struggling with their own decisions." Day's confessions were theological, too. Her attempts to understand herself and humanity were really efforts to understand God.

She certainly never achieved complete spiritual tranquillity and self-satisfaction. On the day she died, there was a card inserted into the final page of her journal, inscribed with a prayer of penance from Saint Ephraim the Syrian that begins, "O

Lord and master of my life, take from me the spirit of sloth, faintheartedness, lust of power and idle talk. But give to thy servant rather the spirit of chastity, humility, patience and love."

But over the course of her life, she built a steady inner structure. Her work for others yielded a certain steadiness in herself, which was so absent in the early years. And at the end there was gratitude. For her tombstone inscription she simply chose the words DEO GRATIAS. Toward the close of her life she met with Robert Coles, a Harvard child psychiatrist, who had become a friend and confidant. "It will soon be over," she told him. And then she described a moment when she tried to make a literary summation of her life. She had been writing all those years and it would have been natural to write a memoir. She sat down one day to compose something like that. She told Coles what happened:

I try to think back; I try to remember this life that the Lord gave me; the other day I wrote down the words "a life remembered," and I was going to try to make a summary for myself, write what mattered most — but I couldn't do it. I just sat there and thought of our Lord, and His visit to us all those centuries ago, and I said to myself that my great luck was to have had Him on my mind for so long in my life!

Coles wrote, "I heard the catch in her voice as she spoke, and soon her eyes were a little moist, but she quickly started talking of her great love for Tolstoy, as if, thereby, she had changed the subject."[50] That moment represents a calm apotheosis, a moment when after all the work and all the sacrifice and all the efforts to write and change the world, the storm finally abates and a great calm comes over. Adam I lies down before Adam II. The loneliness ends. At the culmination of that lifetime of self-criticism and struggle there was thankfulness.

CHAPTER 5
SELF-MASTERY

George Catlett Marshall was born in 1880 and grew up in Uniontown, Pennsylvania. Uniontown was a small coal city, with a population of about thirty-five hundred, just then being transformed by industrialization. His father was a successful businessman — thirty-five years old when George was born — who had established himself as a figure of some consequence in town. He was proud of his old southern family. Supreme Court Justice John Marshall was a distant relative. His father was also somewhat stiff and reserved, especially at home, where he played the role of lord of the manor.

In midlife, though, Marshall's father sold his coal business and invested in a real estate scheme around the Luray Caverns in Virginia, which quickly went bankrupt. He lost all the wealth it had taken him twenty years to acquire. He retreated from the world, spending his time on family genealogy. The family began its descent. Later in life, George Marshall would remember trips to a hotel kitchen, where they would ask for leftover scraps to serve as dog food and the occasional stew. It was "painful and humiliating," he would later remember, "a black spot on my boyhood."[1]

Marshall was not a bright, sparkling boy. When he was nine, his father enrolled him in the local public school. His placement was determined by an interview with the school superintendent, Professor Lee Smith. The man asked him a series of simple questions to gauge Marshall's intelligence and preparation, but Marshall could not answer them. As his father looked on, he hemmed and hawed, stuttered and squirmed. Later, after he had led the U.S. Army through World War II, served as secretary of state, and won the Nobel Peace Prize, Marshall still remembered that excruciating episode, when he had so publicly failed his father. His father, Marshall recalled, "suffered very severely"[2] from the embarrassment.

Marshall lagged academically. He developed a terror of any sort of public presentation, an intense fear of being laughed at by other students, and a painful self-consciousness that inevitably fueled more failure and humiliation. "I did not like school," he would recall later in life. "The truth is I was not even a poor student. I was simply not a student, and my academic record was a sad affair."[3] He grew mischievous and troublesome. After his sister Marie called him the "dunce of the class," she found a frog in her bed that night. When visitors he did not approve of came to the house, he dropped water bombs off the roof onto unsuspecting heads. But he was also ingenious. He started a small business transporting groups of girls across a creek on a raft he built himself.[4]

After elementary school, he wanted to follow his older and favored brother Stuart to the Virginia Military Institute. He would later recall in an interview with his great biographer, Forrest Pogue, his brother's cruel response:

When I was begging to go to VMI, I overheard Stuart talking to my mother; he was trying to persuade her not to let me go because he thought I would disgrace the family name. Well, that made more of an impression on me than all the instructors, parental pressure or anything else. I decided right then that I was going to wipe his eye. I did finally get ahead of what my brother had done. That was the first time I had ever done that, and it was where I really learned my lesson. The urgency to succeed came from hearing that conversation; it had a psychological effect on my career.[5]

This is a common trait among modest people who achieve extraordinary success. It's not that they were particularly brilliant or talented. The average collegiate GPA for a self-made millionaire is somewhere in the low B range. But at some crucial point in their lives, somebody told them they were too stupid to do something and they set out to prove the bastards wrong.

Marshall was not totally without family warmth and support. While his father was perpetually disappointed in his son, his mother rejoiced in him, offering unconditional love and support. She sold the last of her family's property so he could go away to college, including the lot in Uniontown upon which she had been hoping to build a house of her own.[6] Marshall also had learned from his humiliations in school and at home that his rise in the ranks of life would not come from his natural talent. It would come from grinding, the dogged plod, and self-discipline. When Marshall got to VMI (he seems to have been admitted without having to take the entrance exam), he found a way of living and a pattern of discipline exactly to his liking.

He arrived at VMI in 1897 and was instantly drawn to its southern traditions. VMI had a moral culture that brought together several ancient traditions: a chivalric devotion to service and courtesy, a stoic commitment to emotional self-control, and a classical devotion to honor. The school was haunted by the memories of southern chivalry: of the Civil War general Stonewall Jackson, a former professor there; of the 241 cadets, some as young as fifteen, who marched out on May 15, 1864, to turn back a Union force at the Battle of New Market; and by the ghost of the Confederate hero Robert E. Lee, who served as a beau ideal of what a man was supposed to be.

VMI taught Marshall a sense of reverence, the imaginative ability to hold up a hero in his mind to copy in all appropriate ways, to let him serve as a standard by which to judge himself. Not long ago, there was a great move to debunk heroes. Even today, the word "irreverent" is often used as a high compliment. But in the world of Marshall's youth, there was a greater intent to cultivate a capacity for veneration. The work of the

Roman biographer Plutarch is based on the premise that the tales of the excellent can lift the ambitions of the living. Thomas Aquinas argued that in order to lead a good life, it is necessary to focus more on our exemplars than on ourselves, imitating their actions as much as possible. The philosopher Alfred North Whitehead argued, "Moral education is impossible without the habitual vision of greatness." In 1943, Richard Winn Livingstone wrote, "One is apt to think of moral failure as due to weakness of character: more often it is due to an inadequate ideal. We detect in others, and occasionally in ourselves, the want of courage, of industry, of persistence, which leads to defeat. But we do not notice the more subtle and disastrous weakness, that our standards are wrong, that we have never learned what is good."[7]

By cultivating the habit of reverence — for ancient heroes, for the elderly, for leaders in one's own life — teachers were not only offering knowledge of what greatness looks like, they were trying to nurture a talent for admiration. Proper behavior is not just knowing what is right; it is having the motivation to do what is right, an emotion that propels you to do good things.

School days were filled with tales —

sometimes false or romanticized tales — of the great paragons of history, Pericles, Augustus, Judah Maccabee, George Washington, Joan of Arc, Dolley Madison. Character, James Davison Hunter has written, does not require religious faith. "But it does require a conviction of a truth made sacred, abiding as an authoritative presence within consciousness and life, reinforced by habits institutionalized within a moral community. Character, therefore, resists expedience; it defies hasty acquisition. This is undoubtedly why Søren Kierkegaard spoke of character as 'engraved,' deeply etched."[8]

VMI was an academically mediocre institution, and Marshall was not then a good student. But it held up heroes who were regarded as sacred. And the school certainly taught the habits of institutionalized self-discipline. Throughout his adult life, Marshall displayed a strong desire to be as close to flawless in all things as possible. Against the current advice, he absolutely did sweat the "small stuff."

VMI also taught renunciation, the ability to forgo small pleasures in order to enjoy great ones. VMI was a place where young men from mostly privileged backgrounds went to get toughened up, to renounce the luxuries they might have enjoyed at home and to acquire the hardness they would need to be worthy of the struggle of life. Marshall bought into the ascetic culture and its rigors. First-year students were compelled to sleep with their large dorm windows wide open, so that in winter they might awake covered in snow.

The week before he was due to arrive at the institute, Marshall was stricken with typhoid fever, and he was forced to show up a week after the other cadets. It was tough enough for the first-year students, and Marshall's sickly pallor and Northern accent drew unwanted attention from his seniors. He was called "Yankee rat" and "Pug" for his relatively snub-nosed appearance. "Rat" Marshall filled his days with undesirable chores, cleaning toilets a good deal. In his memory of the period, it did not occur to him to rebel or resent the treatment. "I think I was more philosophical about this sort of thing than a great many boys. It was part of the business, and the only thing to do was accept it as best you could."[9]

In one hazing ritual early in his rat tenure, Marshall was forced to squat naked over a bayonet that had been jammed into a hole in the floor. The ordeal was called "sitting on infinity," and it was a rite of passage.

While a crowd of upperclassmen looked on, he strained to keep himself from collapsing onto the point. Finally he could take it no longer and fell. He did not fall straight down, but to one side, so he emerged with a deep but mendable wound to his right rear. Hazing that brutal was against regulations, even by the standards of the day, and the upperclassmen rushed him to the medical center, fearing what he might say. But Marshall did not report his tormentors, and he immediately won the regard of the corps for his staunch silence. One of his ex-classmates said, "By the time that episode was over nobody cared about his accent. He could have talked double Dutch and they'd have accepted it. He was in."[10]

Marshall still did not excel academically at VMI. But he excelled at drilling, neatness, organization, precision, self-control, and leadership. He mastered the aesthetic of discipline, having the correct posture, erect carriage, crisp salute, direct gaze, well-pressed clothing, and the way of carrying the body that is an outward manifestation of inner self-control. During one football game in his first or second year he badly tore a ligament in his right arm but refused to report the injury to a doctor. It would heal on its own (over the next two years)."[11]

A day in the life of a VMI cadet is marked by the succession of saluting one does to one's superiors, and since Marshall could not lift his right arm above his elbow without pain, it must have been two years of discomfort.

This starchy formality is not in vogue today. We carry ourselves in ways that are more natural and relaxed. We worry about appearing artificial. But those in Marshall's military world were more likely to believe that great individuals are made, not born, and that they are made through training. Change happens from the outside in. It is through the exercise of drill that a person becomes self-regulating. It is through the expression of courtesy that a person becomes polite. It is through the resistance to fear that a person develops courage. It is through the control of facial expressions that one becomes sober. The act precedes the virtue.

The point of all this was to separate instant emotion from action, to reduce the power of temporary feelings. A person might feel fear, but he would not act on it. A person might desire sweets, but would be able to repress the urge to eat them. The stoic ideal holds that an emotion should be distrusted more often than trusted. Emotion robs you of agency, so distrust desire. Distrust anger, and even sadness and grief. Regard these things as one might regard fire: useful when tightly controlled, but a ravaging force when left unchecked.

People in this mold try to control emotion with the constant firebreaks of decorum. Hence all those strict Victorian manners. They policed emotional expression in order to reduce their vulnerability. Hence the elaborate formal way of addressing each other. People in this mold — and all his life, Marshall was one of them — were deliberately austere and undramatic. Marshall scorned the theatricality of a Napoleon or a Hitler or even the histrionic display of two generals who would work with him, Douglas MacArthur and George S. Patton.

"By means not always subtle," one of Marshall's biographers wrote, "the man whose mettle was fit for tempering grew from control to self-control, until in the end he imposed by his own desire those restraints upon himself which he could hardly brook when he first encountered them."[12]

Marshall was not funny or emotionally vibrant or self-reflective. He refused to keep a diary, because he thought the exercise might cause him to focus too much on himself and his own reputation, or on how others might view him in the future. Diary keeping, he told Robert E. Lee's biographer Douglas Southall Freeman in 1942, might unconsciously cause "self-deception or hesitation in reaching decisions" when, in war, he needed to focus objectively on "the business of victory."[13] Marshall never got around to writing his autobiography. *The Saturday Evening Post* once offered him more than $1 million to tell his story, but he turned it down. He did not want to embarrass himself or any of the other generals.[14]

The whole object of VMI training was to teach Marshall how to exercise controlled power. The idea was that power exaggerates the dispositions — making a rude person ruder and a controlling person more controlling. The higher you go in life, the fewer people there are to offer honest feedback or restrain your unpleasant traits. So it is best to learn those habits of self-restraint, including emotional self-restraint, at an early age. "What I learned at VMI was self-control, discipline, so that it was ground in," he would recall later.

In his last year at VMI, Marshall was named first captain, the Institute's highest rank. He completed his four years without a single demerit. He developed the austere commanding presence that would forever mark his personality. He excelled at anything to do with soldiering and was the unquestioned leader of his class.

A letter of recommendation from John Wise, the president of VMI, praised Marshall's accomplishment in the unique tone of the school: Marshall was "one of the fittest pieces of food for gunpowder turned out by this mill for many years."[15]

At an astonishingly early age, Marshall had constructed the sort of ordered mind that military men and women have generally admired. "That person then, whoever it may be," Cicero wrote in *Tusculan Disputations,* "whose mind is quiet through consistency and self-control, who finds contentment in himself, who neither breaks down in adversity nor crumbles in fright, nor burns with any thirsty need nor dissolves into wild and futile excitement, that person is the wise one we are seeking, and that person is happy."

THE SERVICE

There is always an interesting moment in the lives of successful people when they first learn how to work. For Marshall, that moment came at VMI.

To get an appointment to the U.S. Army, he needed political support. He went to Washington and showed up at the White House without an appointment. He worked his way up to the second floor, where one of the ushers told him it was impossible for him just to burst in and see the president. But Marshall sneaked into the Oval Office with a larger group, and after they left, he stated his case to President McKinley. Whether McKinley intervened is unclear, but in 1901, Marshall was permitted to take the army entrance exam, and in 1902 he received his commission.

Like Eisenhower, Marshall was a late bloomer. He worked professionally, he served other men, but he did not rise spectacularly. He was such a valuable aide, his superiors sometimes held him back from getting his own command. "Lt. Col. Marshall's special fitness is staff work," one general wrote. "I doubt that in this, whether it be teaching or practice, he has any equal in the army today."[16] He was such a genius at the dull, background work of military life, especially logistics, that he was not pushed forward to the fighting edge. By age thirty-nine, at the end of his service in World War I, he was still only a temporary lieutenant colonel, surpassed by younger men who had held combat commands. He suffered grievously with each disappointment.

But he was slowly acquiring skills. During postgraduate training at Fort Leavenworth, Marshall became an autodidact, compensating for his lamentable academic record. He was shuffled to the Philippines and across the American South and Midwest, serving as engineering officer, ordnance officer, post quartermaster, post commissary officer, and in other undistinguished staff positions. Each day passed to the rhythm of his daily chores and minor accomplishments. However, his attention to detail and endurance would serve him later on. As he later observed, "The truly great leader overcomes all difficulties, and campaigns and battles are nothing but a long series of difficulties to be overcome."[17]

He sublimated his ego: "The less you agree with the policies of your superiors, the more energy you must direct to their accomplishment." Biographers have scoured his life, and the most striking feature is what they don't find — any moment of clear moral failure. He made many poor decisions, but there is no clear moment when he committed adultery, betrayed his friends, told an egregious lie, or let himself and others down.

Though promotions did not come, Marshall began to develop a reputation as a legendary master of organization and administration. It was not exactly the glamor side of military life. In 1912, he organized maneuvers involving 17,000 officers and men in the United States. In 1914, during a training exercise in the Philippines, he effectively commanded an invading force of 4,800 men to tactically outmaneuver and defeat the defending force.

In World War I, Marshall served as an assistant to the chief of staff of the American Expeditionary Force (AEF) for the 1st Division in France. It was the first division ever fielded by the American Army in Europe, and, contrary to popular belief, Marshall saw more action and ducked more shot, shells, and gas attacks than many other Americans in the war. His assignment was to keep AEF headquarters informed about the frontline supplies, position, and morale of the men. Much of his time was spent on or near the front in France, jumping in and out of trenches, checking in with the soldiers, and taking note of what they most desperately needed.

The moment he returned safely to headquarters, he would report to the chief and begin mapping out logistics for the next massive movement of men to or from the line. In one operation, he organized the movement of 600,000 men and 900,000 tons of supplies and ammunition from one sector to another part of the front. It was the most complicated logistics problem of the war, and Marshall's performance became legendary, earning him the temporary nickname "Wizard."

During October 1917, Marshall's unit received a visit from General John "Blackjack" Pershing, the senior U.S. commander in the war. Pershing ripped into the unit for its poor training and performance, upbraiding Marshall's immediate commanding officer General William Sibert and Sibert's chief of staff, who had arrived only two days earlier. Marshall, then a captain, decided it was time for what he called a "sacrifice play." He stepped forward and attempted to explain the situation to the general. An already irate Pershing silenced Marshall and turned away. Marshall then did something that could have cost him his career. He placed his hand on Pershing's arm to prevent him from leaving. He vehemently countered the old man, overwhelming him with a torrent of facts about the failures of Pershing's own headquarters, about poor supplies, the misplacement of the troops, the lack of motor transport, and many other hurdles not to be overlooked.

There was a long silence and everyone stood amazed by Marshall's effrontery. Pershing looked at him narrowly and responded defensively, "Well, you have to appreciate the problems we have."

Marshall shot back, "Yes, General, but we have them every day and many a day, and we have to solve every one of them by night."

Pershing said nothing and stalked off angrily. Marshall's colleagues thanked him and told him his career was finished. Instead, Pershing remembered the younger man, hired him, and became his most important mentor.

Marshall was shocked by the letter he received summoning him to join the General Staff at its headquarters in Chaumont. He ached for a promotion that would position him to lead men into battle. However, he packed his bags immediately and said good-bye to the men he had known for more than a year. Tucked between war reports, Marshall wrote an uncharacteristically sentimental description of his departure:

It was hard to preserve one's composure to these men with whom I had been so intimately associated for over a year in France. We had been prisoners and our trials and tribulations had seemed to bind us very close to one another. I can see them now — gathered in the broad doorway of the chateau. The friendly jests and affectionate farewells, as I got into the Cadillac, made a deep impression on my mind, and I drove off hardly daring to wonder when and where would be our next meeting.[18]

Six days later, the 1st Division joined the great counterattack that would lead to the retreat of the German army, and within seventy-two hours most of the men in that doorway, and every field officer, battalion commander, and the four lieutenants of the 1st Division, were casualties, either dead or wounded.

In 1918 in France, Marshall was close to being promoted to brigadier general. The war ended and it would take him eighteen long years to get his first star. He returned home, where he spent five years under Pershing in Washington doing paperwork. He served his superior officers but received few promotions for himself. Through it all,

Marshall worked on his profession and served his institution, the U.S. Army.

INSTITUTIONS

Today, it is unusual to meet someone with an institutional mindset. We live in an age of institutional anxiety, when people are prone to distrust large organizations. This is partly because we've seen the failure of these institutions and partly because in the era of the Big Me, we put the individual first. We tend to prize the freedom to navigate as we wish, to run our lives as we choose, and never to submerge our own individual identities in conformity to some bureaucracy or organization. We tend to assume that the purpose is to lead the richest and fullest individual life, jumping from one organization to the next as it suits our needs. Meaning is found in these acts of self-creation, in the things we make and contribute to, in our endless choices.

Nobody wants to be an Organization Man. We like start-ups, disruptors, and rebels. There's less prestige accorded to those who tend to the perpetual reform and repair of institutions. Young people are raised to think that big problems can be solved by a swarm of small, networked NGOs and social entrepreneurs. Big hierarchical organizations are dinosaurs.

This mentality has contributed to institutional decay. As the editor Tina Brown has put it, if everybody is told to think outside the box, you've got to expect that the boxes themselves will begin to deteriorate.

People who possess an institutional mindset, as Marshall did, have a very different mentality, which begins with a different historical consciousness. In this mindset, the primary reality is society, which is a collection of institutions that have existed over time and transcend generations. A person is not born into an open field and a blank social slate. A person is born into a collection of permanent institutions, including the army, the priesthood, the fields of science, or any of the professions, like being a farmer, a builder, a cop, or a professor.

Life is not like navigating through an open field. It is committing oneself to a few of the institutions that were embedded on the ground before you were born and will be here after you die. It is accepting the gifts of the dead, taking on the responsibility of preserving and improving an institution and then transmitting that institution, better, on to the next generation.

Each institution comes with certain rules,

obligations, and standards of excellence. Journalism imposes habits that help reporters keep a mental distance from those they cover. Scientists have certain methods they use to advance and verify knowledge one step at a time. Teachers treat all their students equally and invest extra hours to their growth. In the process of subordinating ourselves to the institutions we inhabit, we become who we are. The customs of the institution structure the soul, making it easier to be good. They guide behavior gently along certain time-tested lines. By practicing the customs of an institution, we are not alone; we are admitted into a community that transcends time.

With this sense of scope, the institutionalist has deep reverence for those who came before and the rules he has temporarily taken delivery of. The rules of a profession or an institution are not like practical tips on how to best do something. They are deeply woven into the identities of the people who practice them. A teacher's relationship to the craft of teaching, an athlete's relationship to his or her sport, a doctor's commitment to the craft of medicine, is not an individual choice that can be easily renounced when the psychic losses exceed the psychic benefits. These are life-shaping and life-defining commitments. Like finding a vocation, they are commitments to something that transcends a single lifetime.

A person's social function defines who he or she is. The commitment between a person and an institution is more like a covenant. It is an inheritance to be passed on and a debt to be repaid.

The technical tasks of, say, being a carpenter are infused with a deep meaning that transcends the task at hand. There are long periods when you put more into your institutions than you get out of them, but service to the institution provides you with a series of fulfilling commitments and a secure place in the world. It provides you with a means to submerge your ego, to quiet its anxieties and its relentless demands.

Marshall conformed his life to the needs of his organization. Very few people in the course of the last century aroused as much reverence as Marshall did, even in his own lifetime, even among people who knew him well. There were also few people who felt entirely comfortable around him — Eisenhower included. The cost of his perfect self-denial and self-control was aloofness. While in uniform, he never let his hair down or allowed people into the intimacy of his own soul. He maintained his composure in all circumstances.

LOVE AND DEATH

Marshall did have a private life. It was starkly separated from his public role. Today we bring our work home, returning work emails on our phones. But for Marshall, these were two separate spheres, with different emotions and patterns of conduct. The home was a haven in a heartless world. Marshall's home life centered on his wife, Lily.

George Marshall wooed Elizabeth Carter Coles, known to her friends as Lily, while in his final year at VMI. They took long carriage rides, and at night he risked expulsion by sneaking off grounds to be with her. George was six years Lily's junior, and several other senior classmates and senior VMI graduates — including Marshall's older brother Stuart — had done their best to win her fancy. She was a striking, dark beauty and the reigning belle of Lexington. "I was much in love," he recalled, and it was for keeps.[19]

They married shortly after his graduation in 1902. He felt himself extraordinarily lucky to have won her, and he carried that gratitude with him forever after. His attitude toward Lily can be described as constant and extremely solicitous. Shortly after their marriage, he discovered that she suffered from a thyroid condition that gave her an extremely weak heart. She would have to be treated as a semi-invalid all her life. They could never risk having children. There would always be the possibility of sudden death by exertion. But Marshall's devotion and gratitude to his wife only deepened.

Marshall was pleased to put himself in her service, supplying her with little surprises, compliments, and comforts, always giving the greatest attention to the smallest details. She would never be allowed to rise to retrieve that needlepoint basket she had forgotten upstairs. Marshall was playing the role of the chivalric knight in service to his lady. Lily sometimes looked upon this with wry amusement. She was more rugged and capable than he thought, but it gave him such pleasure to look after her.

In 1927, when Lily was fifty-three, her heart condition worsened. She was taken to Walter Reed Hospital, and on August 22 an operation was performed. Her recovery was slow but steady. Marshall was in his element, catering to her every need, and Lily seemed to be recovering. On September 15, she was told that she could return home the next day. She sat down to send her mother a note. She wrote the word "George," slumped over, and passed away. The doctors said it was her excitement over returning home that elevated her pulse irregularly.

Marshall was teaching classes at the War College in Washington at that moment. A guard interrupted his lecture and called him to the telephone. They went into a little office where Marshall took the call, listened for a few moments, and then put his head on his arms on the desk. The guard asked if there was any way he could be of assistance. Marshall replied with quiet formality. "No, Mr. Throckmorton, I just had word my wife, who was to join me here today, has just died."

The formality of that phrasing, the pause to remember the guard's name (Marshall was not good with names), perfectly captured his emotional self-control, his self-discipline at all times.

Marshall was stricken by his wife's death. He filled his home with photographs of her, so that she looked out at him from nearly every vantage point in every room. Lily had been not only his sweet wife but his most trusted confidante, and, it seemed, his only one. Only she had been privileged to see the burden he carried and help him bear it.

Suddenly and brutally, he was alone and adrift.

General Pershing, who had lost a wife and three daughters, wrote a note of condolence. Marshall replied that he missed Lily desperately: "Twenty-six years of most intimate companionship, something I have never known since I was a mere boy, leave me lost in my best efforts to adjust myself to future prospects in life. If I had been given to club life or other intimacies with men outside of athletic diversion, or if there was a campaign on or other pressing duty that demanded concentrated effort, then I think I could do better. However, I will find a way."[20]

Lily's death changed Marshall. Once taciturn, he softened and became conversational, as if he could charm visitors into staying and filling the lonely hours. Over the years his letters became more thoughtful, more openly compassionate. Despite his commitment to the service, and several periods when work consumed him, Marshall had never been a workaholic. Careful not to strain his own health, he broke off work in late afternoon to garden, go horseback riding, or take a walk. Whenever possible, he encouraged, even ordered, his staff to do the same.

PRIVACY

Marshall was a private man. That is to say, he made a stronger distinction than many people today make between the private and public spheres, between those people he considered intimates and everybody else. He could be witty and tell long funny stories to people within the inner circle of his trust and affection, but his manner to the larger population was defined by courtliness and a certain reserved charm. Very rarely did he call anyone by their first name.

This code of privacy is different from the one that is common in the era of Facebook and Instagram. This privacy code, which he shared with Frances Perkins, is based on the notion that this zone of intimacy should be breached only gradually, after long reciprocity and trust. The contents of the private world should not instantly be shared online or in conversation; they should not be tweeted.

Marshall's polite social manner matched his polite inner makeup. The French philosopher André Comte-Sponville argues that politeness is the prerequisite for the great virtues: "Morality is like a politeness of the soul, an etiquette of inner life, a code of duties."[21] It is a series of practices that make you considerate of others.

Marshall was unfailingly considerate, but his formality made it hard for him to develop friendships. He strongly disapproved of gossip, he frowned at off-color stories, and he never enjoyed the garrulous relationships with men that Ike specialized in.

Marshall's early biographer, William Frye, wrote:

Marshall was one of those controlled and disciplined people who find both incentive and reward deep within themselves, who require neither urging nor applause from many men. Such people are terribly alone, without the release most find in the easy sharing of mind and heart with many people. For all their self-sufficiency, they are incomplete; and if they are fortunate, they find completion in one or two others. There are not more than two, usually — the heart opened to a lover, the mind to a friend.[22]

REFORMER

Marshall finally found respite from his grief with an assignment that consumed his energies. At the end of that year, he was asked to lead the Infantry School program at Fort Benning, Georgia. Marshall was conservative in manners, but he was not a traditional-ist when it came to operations. All his life he pushed against what he regarded as the stifling traditionalism of the army way of doing things. In his four years there, he revolutionized officer training, and since many of the most important officers of World War II passed through Fort Benning during his time there, he revolutionized the U.S. Army, too.

The lesson plans he inherited were built on the ridiculous premise that in battle, offi-cers would have complete information about their troops' positions and the enemy's. He sent them out on maneuvers without maps or with outdated ones, telling them that in a real war, the maps would be either absent or worse than useless. He told them the crucial issue is usually *when* a decision should be made as much as *what* the decision should be. He told them that mediocre solutions undertaken in time were better than perfect solutions undertaken too late. Until Marshall, professors wrote their lectures and simply read them out to the class. Marshall prohibited the practice. He cut the supply systems manual from 120 pages down to 12, to make training a citizen force easier and to allow greater discretion down the chain of command.

Even his success and reforms did not speed his promotions. The army had its own seniority system. But as the 1930s wore on and the Fascist threat became clearer, personal merit began to count for more. Eventually, Marshall received a series of large promotions, leapfrogging senior but less admired men, all the way to Washington and the centers of power.

THE GENERAL

In 1938, Franklin Roosevelt held a cabinet meeting to discuss strategy for an arms buildup. FDR argued that the next war would be largely determined by air and sea power, not ground troops. He went around the room, looking for agreement, and was met with general assent. Finally he turned to Marshall, the new deputy chief of staff, and asked, "Don't you think so, George?"

"I am sorry, Mr. President, but I don't at all." Marshall made the case for land forces. FDR looked startled and called the meeting to a close. It was the last time the president would presume to call Marshall by his first name.

In 1939, FDR had to replace the outgoing chief of staff, the top position in the U.S. military. Marshall at that time ranked thirty-fourth in seniority, but the contest came down to him and Hugh Drum. Drum was a talented general, but also a bit pompous, and he organized a lavish campaign for the job, lining up of letters of endorsement and organizing a series of positive articles in the press. Marshall refused to campaign and squashed efforts by others to campaign on his behalf. But he did have key friends in the White House, the most important of whom was Harry Hopkins, an FDR intimate who was an architect of the New Deal. FDR went with Marshall, though there was little personal warmth between them.

War is a series of blunders and frustrations. At the outset of the Second World War, Marshall understood he would have to ruthlessly cull the incompetent from their jobs. By this time he was married to his second wife, Katherine Tupper Brown, a glamorous former actress with a strong personality and an elegant manner who would become Marshall's constant companion. "I cannot afford the luxury of sentiment," he told her. "Mine must be cold logic. Sentiment is for others. I cannot allow myself to get angry, that would be fatal — it is too exhausting. My brain must be kept clear. I cannot afford to appear tired."[23]

The culling process was brutal. Marshall ended the careers of hundreds of colleagues.

"He was once our dear friend, but he ruined my husband," a senior officer's wife observed after her husband had been shoved aside.[24] One evening he told Katherine, "I get so tired of saying 'No,' it takes it out of me." Organizing his department while war loomed, Marshall observed, "It is not easy to tell men where they have failed. . . . My days seem to be filled with situations and problems where I must do the difficult, the hard thing."[25]

A vintage Marshall performance was given at a meeting with the press in London in 1944. He entered the room without any papers and began by instructing each reporter to ask a question while he listened. After thirty-plus questions, Marshall explained in detail the situation of the war, addressing the larger visions, strategic goals, and technical details, shifting his eyes deliberately to a different face every few sentences. Then he finished, forty minutes later, and thanked the reporters for their time.

World War II had its share of cinematic generals, like MacArthur and Patton, but most, like Marshall and Eisenhower, were anticinematic. They were precise organizers, not flamboyant showmen. Marshall detested generals who screamed and pounded tables.

He favored the simple, spare uniform rather than the more decorated uniform favored by generals today, with their placards of ribbons forming a billboard across their chests.

During this time Marshall developed an astounding reputation. The general view was summarized by the CBS war correspondent Eric Sevareid: "a hulking, homely man of towering intellect, the memory of an unnatural genius, and the integrity of a Christian saint. The atmosphere of controlled power he exuded made one feel oneself a physical weakling, and his selfless devotion to duty [was] beyond all influences of public pressure or personal friendship."[26] Speaker of the House Sam Rayburn said no other American had equal influence with Congress: "We are in the presence of a man who is telling the truth as he sees it." As Truman's secretary of state Dean Acheson put it, "the thing that stands out in everybody's recollection of General Marshall is the immensity of his integrity."

That integrity did not win him immediate favor with everybody. He held a soldier's contempt for politics and remembered his particular disgust when he once met with President Roosevelt to tell him that the plans for the North African invasion were ready. The president clapped his hands together in mock prayer and said, "Please make it before election day."[27] Marshall's deputy chief of staff, Tom Handy, later explained in an interview:

It's no use saying General Marshall was an easy man, because he wasn't. He could be extremely rigid. But he had a terrific influence and power, especially over the British and Congress. I think FDR envied him this. I think that the basis was that they knew, in Marshall's case, there was no underhanded or selfish motive. The British knew that he was not out to make American points or British points, but trying to win the war the best way. The Congress knew he was talking to them straight, with no politics involved.[28]

The quintessential Marshall moment came in the middle of the war. The Allies were planning Operation Overlord, the invasion of France, but still no overall commander had been selected. Marshall secretly craved the assignment and was widely accepted as the most qualified for it. This would be among the most ambitious military operations ever attempted, and whoever commanded it would be performing a great service to the cause and would go down in history as a result of it. The other Allied leaders, Churchill and Stalin, told Marshall that he would get the job. Eisenhower assumed Marshall would get the job. Roosevelt knew that if Marshall asked for the job, he would have to give it to him. He had earned it, and his stature was so high.

But Roosevelt relied on Marshall to be nearby in Washington, whereas the Overlord commander would go to London. FDR may also have had doubts about Marshall's austere personality. Commanding Overlord would mean managing political alliances, and a warm touch might come in handy. The controversy flared. Several senators argued that Marshall was needed in Washington and should not get the job. From his hospital bed, General Pershing pleaded with FDR to give Marshall a command in the field.

Still, everyone presumed that Marshall would command. In November 1943, Roosevelt visited Eisenhower in North Africa and nearly said as much: "You and I know who the Chief of Staff was during the last years of the Civil War, but practically no one else knows. . . . I hate to think that fifty years from now practically nobody will know who George Marshall was. That is one of the reasons why I want George to have the big command — he is entitled to establish his place in history as a great general."

Still Roosevelt had doubts. "It is dangerous to monkey with a winning team,"[29] he said. He sent Harry Hopkins to gauge Marshall's feelings about the appointment. Marshall would not be drawn in. He told Hopkins that he had served with honor. He would not ask for anything. He would "go along good-heartedly with whatever decision the president made."[30] In an interview with Forrest Pogue decades later, Marshall explained his behavior: "I was determined that I should not embarrass the President one way or the other — that he must be able to deal in this matter with a perfectly free hand in whatever he felt was the best interest [of the country]. . . . I was utterly sincere in the desire to avoid what had happened so much in other wars — the consideration of the feelings of the individual rather than the good of the country."[31]

FDR called Marshall into his office on December 6, 1943. Roosevelt beat around the bush for several awkward minutes, raising subjects of minor importance. Then he asked Marshall if he wanted the job. If

Marshall had simply uttered the word "Yes," he presumably would have gotten the job. Still, Marshall refused to be drawn in. Marshall told Roosevelt to do what he thought best. Marshall insisted that his own private feelings should have no bearing on the decision. Again and again, he refused to express his preference one way or the other.

FDR looked at him. "Well, I didn't feel I could sleep at ease if you were out of Washington." There was a long silence. Roosevelt added, "Then it will be Eisenhower."[32]

Inwardly, Marshall must have been crushed. Somewhat gracelessly, Roosevelt asked him to transmit the decision to the Allies. As chief of staff, Marshall was compelled to write the order himself: "The immediate appointment of General Eisenhower to command of 'Overlord' operation has been decided on." He generously saved the slip of paper and sent it to Ike: "Dear Eisenhower. I thought you might like to have this as a memento. It was written very hurriedly by me as the final meeting broke up yesterday, the President signing it immediately. G.C.M."[33]

It was the greatest professional disappointment of Marshall's life, and it came about because he refused to express his own desires. But that, of course, was the code he lived by.

When the war in Europe was over, it was Eisenhower, not Marshall, who returned to Washington as the triumphant conqueror. Still, Marshall was overcome with pride. John Eisenhower remembered the scene of his father's return to Washington: "It was on that day that I saw General Marshall completely unbend. Standing behind Ike and eschewing the glare of the photographers, he beamed on Ike and Mamie with a kindly, fatherly expression. There was nothing of the normally aloof George Marshall in his demeanor that day. Then he faded into the background and let Ike take the stage for the rest of the day — a motorcade down the streets of Washington, a visit to the Pentagon."[34]

In a personal letter, Churchill wrote to Marshall, "It has not fallen to your lot to command the great armies. You have had to create them, organize them, and inspire them."[35] Outshone by the men he had promoted, Marshall had become known simply as the "organizer of victory."

FINAL TASKS

Marshall spent his postwar life trying to retire. On November 26, 1945, there was a simple ceremony at the Pentagon and Marshall was released from duty as the army chief of staff. He drove to Dodona Manor, the home he and Katherine had bought in Leesburg, Virginia. They walked through the sunny yard, looking forward to years of leisure and retirement. Katherine went upstairs to rest before dinner and heard the phone ring as she climbed. An hour later, she came downstairs to find Marshall stretched out ashen-faced on a chaise longue listening to the radio. The news broadcast announced that the U.S. ambassador to China had just resigned and that George Marshall had accepted the president's request to take his place. The phone call had been President Truman asking Marshall to leave immediately. "Oh, George," she said, "how *could* you?"[36]

The job was thankless, but he and Katherine remained in China for fourteen months, trying to negotiate away an inevitable civil war between the Chinese Nationalists and Communists. On the return flight home from his first major failed mission, Marshall, now sixty-seven, was asked again by the president for another favor — to serve as secretary of state. Marshall accepted and hung up.[37] In his new position, he enacted the Marshall Plan

— although he never called it anything but its official name, the European Recovery Plan — and President Roosevelt's wish that Marshall be long remembered by history came true.

There were other duties that followed: president of the American Red Cross, secretary of defense, chair of the U.S. delegation to the coronation of Elizabeth II. There were highs — winning the Nobel Prize — and lows — becoming the object of a hate campaign by Joe McCarthy and his allies. As each job was offered, Marshall felt the tug of obligation. He made some good decisions and some bad ones — he opposed the formation of the State of Israel. He was continually accepting assignments he did not want.

Some people seem to have been born into this world with a sense of indebtedness for the blessing of being alive. They are aware of the transmission of generations, what has been left to them by those who came before, their indebtedness to their ancestors, their obligations to a set of moral responsibilities that stretch across time.

One of the purest expressions of this attitude is a letter sent home by a Civil War soldier named Sullivan Ballou to his wife on the eve of the first battle of Bull Run, early in the war. Ballou, an orphan, knew the pain of growing up without a father. Nonetheless, he wrote to his wife, he was willing to die to pay the debt he owed to his ancestors:

If it is necessary that I should fall on the battlefield for my country, I am ready. . . . I know how strongly American Civilization now leans upon the triumph of the government, and how great a debt we owe to those who went before us through the blood and suffering of the Revolution. And I am willing — perfectly willing — to lay down all my joys in this life, to help maintain this Government, to help pay that debt.

But, my dear wife, when I know that with my own joys I lay down nearly all of yours, and replace them in this life with cares and sorrows — when, after having eaten for long years the bitter fruit of the orphanage myself, I must offer it as their only sustenance to my dear little children — is it weak or dishonorable, while the banner of my purpose floats calmly and proudly in the breeze, that my unbounded love for you, my darling wife and children, should struggle in fierce, though useless, contest with my love of country? . . .

Sarah, my love for you is deathless, it seems to bind me to you with mighty cables that nothing but Omnipotence could break; and yet my love of Country comes over me like a strong wind and bears me irresistibly on with all these chains to the battlefield. . . . I have, I know, but few and small claims upon Divine Providence, but something whispers to me — perhaps it is the wafted prayer of my little Edgar — that I shall return to my loved ones unharmed. If I do not, my dear Sarah, never forget how much I love you, and when my last breath escapes me on the battlefield it will whisper your name.

Of course, Ballou did fight the next day at Bull Run, and he did die. Like Marshall, he did have the sense that he couldn't find fulfillment outside of his obligations to community and country.

We live in a society that places great emphasis on personal happiness, defined as not being frustrated in the realization of your wants. But old moral traditions do not die. They waft down the centuries and re-inspire new people in new conditions. Marshall lived in the world of airplanes and the nuclear bomb, but in many ways he was formed by the moral traditions of classical

Greece and Rome. His moral make-up owed something to Homer, to the classical emphasis on courage and honor. It owed something to the Stoics, with their emphasis on moral discipline. But particularly later in life it also owed something to the ancient Athenian Pericles, who embodied the style of leadership that we call magnanimity, or great-souled.

The magnanimous leader of Greece's golden age had a high but accurate view of his own virtue. He put himself in a different category from most people around him, understanding that he had been blessed by unusual good fortune. This understanding strained his relations with those around him. He could seem solitary and detached, reserved and dignified, except with a few close friends. He navigated the world with a qualified friendliness, genial to people but never quite exposing his inner feelings, thoughts, and fears.[38] He hid his vulnerabilities and detested the thought that he might be dependent on others. As Robert Faulkner writes in *The Case for Greatness*, he is not a joiner, a team player, or a staffer: "He does not put his shoulder to any ordinary wheel, especially if he must take a secondary role. Neither is he eager for reciprocity."[39] He is fond of granting favors but ashamed to receive them. He was, as Aristotle put it, "Not capable of leading his life to suit anyone else."[40]

The magnanimous leader does not have a normal set of social relations. There is a residual sadness to him, as there is in many grandly ambitious people who surrender companionship for the sake of their lofty goals. He can never allow himself to be silly or simply happy and free. He is like marble.

The magnanimous leader is called upon by his very nature to perform some great benefit to his people. He holds himself to a higher standard and makes himself into a public institution. Magnanimity can only really be expressed in public or political life. Politics and war are the only theaters big enough, competitive enough, and consequential enough to call forth the highest sacrifices and to elicit the highest talents. The man who shelters himself solely in the realms of commerce and private life is, by this definition, less consequential than one who enters the public arena.

By the time of Pericles, the great-souled leader was supposed to carry himself with steadiness and sobriety. He was supposed to be more judicious and self-disciplined than the hot-tempered Homeric heroes. Most of all, he was supposed to provide some public benefit on a grand scale. He was supposed to save his people in a time of peril or transform them to fit the needs of a new age.

The great-souled man may not be a good man — he may not always be kind, compassionate, considerate, and pleasant — but he is a great man. He wins great honors because he is worthy of them. He achieves a different style of happiness, defined by the popularizer of Greek thought, Edith Hamilton, as "the exercise of vital powers along lines of excellence in a life affording them scope."

DEATH

In 1958, Marshall checked in to Walter Reed Hospital for the removal of a cyst on his face. His goddaughter, Rose Wilson, came to visit, stunned at how old he suddenly looked.

"I have so much time to remember now," he told her, recalling a time when as a boy he went tobogganing with his father in Uniontown. "Colonel Marshall," she replied, "I'm sorry your father didn't live long enough to know what a great son he had. He would have been very proud of you."

"Do you think so?" Marshall answered.

"I'd like to believe he would have approved of me."

Marshall continued to weaken. Every corner of the earth seemed to respond to the general's illness. Messages arrived from Winston Churchill and General Charles de Gaulle, Mao Tse-tung and Chiang Kai-shek, Joseph Stalin and General Dwight Eisenhower, Marshal Tito and Field Marshal Bernard Montgomery.[41] Thousands of letters from ordinary people poured in. President Eisenhower came to visit three times. Truman visited. Winston Churchill, then eighty-four, also visited. Marshall was in a coma by then, and Churchill could do no more than stand in the doorway weeping as he looked at the small body of the man he had once known.

He died on October 16, 1959, just shy of his eightieth birthday. General Tom Handy, his old deputy chief of staff, had once asked him about the arrangements for his funeral but Marshall cut him off. "You don't have to worry about it. I've left all the necessary instructions."[42] These instructions were opened after his death. They were remarkable: "Bury me simply, like any ordinary officer of the U.S. Army who has served his country honorably. No fuss. No elaborate ceremonials. Keep the service short, confine the guest-list to the family. And above everything, do it quietly."[43]

At his express order, there was no state funeral. There was no lying in state in the Capitol rotunda. His body lay in state at the Bethlehem Chapel of the National Cathedral for twenty-four hours so friends could pay their respects. In attendance at the funeral were family, a few colleagues, and his old wartime barber, Nicholas J. Totalo, who had cut the general's hair in Cairo, Teheran, Potsdam, and later at the Pentagon.[44] Then there was a short, plain service at Fort Myer in Arlington, Virginia, using the standard Order for the Burial of the Dead from the Book of Common Prayer, with no eulogy.

CHAPTER 6
DIGNITY

The most prominent civil rights leader in America at the time *Command Performance* aired was A. Philip Randolph. He was the African American leader who organized and called for marches, who met with the president, and whose fame and moral authority helped shape the movement.

Randolph was born in 1899, near Jacksonville, Florida. His father was a minister in an African Methodist Episcopal church, but the church paid so little that he made most of his income as a tailor and butcher, while his wife worked as a seamstress.

Randolph, who was not a religious person, recalled, "My father preached a racial religion. He spoke to the social condition of his flock, and always reminded them that the AME church was the first black militant institution in America."[1] The elder Randolph also took his two boys to political meetings run by blacks. He introduced them to successful black men. And he told and retold the stories of black exemplars throughout history: Crispus Attucks, Nat Turner, Frederick Douglass.

The family lived lives of highly respectable poverty. The home was kept impeccably neat. They followed a code of old-fashioned propriety, discipline, and etiquette. Randolph's parents practiced perfect elocution and taught their son to pronounce every syllable of each word so that throughout his life, words like "responsibility" came out as a long, stately procession: "re-spons-a-bil-i-tay."

Confronted by humiliating racism, they hewed to a code of moral refinement and gentlemanly conduct that jarred with their material circumstances. The elder Randolph, the biographer Jervis Anderson wrote, "was, very simply, a self-made gentleman, one who was guided by the values of civility, humility, and decency, inspired by religious and social service, and utterly devoted to the idea of dignity."[2]

At school, Randolph was taught by two white New England schoolmarms who had come south to educate black underprivileged children, and whom Randolph would later call "two of the finest teachers who ever lived." Miss Lillie Whitney taught Randolph Latin and math, while Miss Mary Neff taught him literature and drama. Tall and athletic, Randolph excelled at baseball, but he developed a love of Shakespeare and drama that would last. In the final decades of his wife's life, when she was confined to a wheelchair, Randolph would read Shakespeare to her each day.

Most people are the product of their circumstances, but Randolph's parents, his teachers, and he himself created a moral ecology that transcended circumstances, a way of behaving that was always slightly more elevated, slightly more formal, and much more dignified than that of the world around him. Throughout his life, Randolph's carriage was always proper and upright. C. L. Dellums, a colleague and labor leader, remembered, "Randolph learned to sit erect and walk erect. You almost never saw him leaning back, reclining. No matter how enjoyable the occasion, you look around and there's Randolph just as straight as if there was a board in his back."[3]

His voice was soft, deep, and serene. He had an accent that people described as a cross between upper-class Boston and West Indian. He spoke in biblical cadences and used archaic words like "verily" and "vouchsafe."[4]

He fought any tendency toward looseness or moral laziness with constant acts of self-mastery, whether small acts of personal conduct or large acts of renunciation. His staff marveled at the way women threw themselves at him during his travels and the gentle way he turned them aside. "I don't think a man ever lived who women begged and chased more than that man," Dellums would recall to a biographer, "They tried everything but rape. Webster and I had a joke between us that we followed the chief around to handle the overflow. And they were the most beautiful women. . . . It was always depressing having to get out of there. I've seen women try everything, plead with him to come up to their hotel room, for a nightcap or something. He would just say, 'Sorry, I'm tired. I had a hard day. We better call it a night.' Sometimes I'd say to him, 'Chief? You kidding me?' "[5]

He did not believe in self-exposure. Outside of his writing, which could be tough and polemical, he did not often criticize others. His formality often kept people from feeling that they really knew him; even Bayard Rustin, one of his closest colleagues, always called him "Mr. Randolph." He was not interested in money and suspected that personal luxury was morally corrupting. Even when he was an old man and globally famous, he rode the bus home from work every day. One day he was mugged in the hallway of his building. The muggers found $1.25 on him, but no watch or jewelry of any kind. When some donors tried to raise money for him, to enhance his lifestyle, he shut them down, saying, "I am sure you know that I have no money and, at the same time, don't expect to get any. However, I would not think of having a movement started to raise money for me and my family. It is the lot of some people to be poor and it is my lot, which I do not have any remorse about."[6]

These qualities — his incorruptibility, his reticent formality, and above all his dignity — meant it was impossible to humiliate him. His reactions and internal state were determined by himself, not by the racism or even by the adulation that later surrounded him. Randolph's significance was in establishing a certain model for how to be a civil rights leader. He exuded self-mastery and, like George C. Marshall, left a string of awed admirers in his wake. "It is hard to make anyone who has never met him believe that A. Philip Randolph must be the greatest man who has lived in the U.S. this century," the columnist Murray Kempton wrote. "But it is harder yet to make anyone who has ever known him believe anything else."

PUBLIC-SPIRITEDNESS

The chief challenges of Randolph's life were: How do you take imperfect people and organize them into a force for change? How do you amass power while not being corrupted by power? Even in the midst of one of the noblest enterprises of the century, the civil rights movement, leaders like Randolph were filled with self-suspicion, feeling they had to be on the lookout for their own laxity, their own sinfulness, feeling that even in the midst of fighting injustice it is still possible to do horrible wrong.

There's a reason the civil rights leaders were transfixed by the book of Exodus. The Israelites in that book were a divided, shortsighted, and petulant people. They were led by a man, Moses, who was meek, passive, and intemperate and who felt himself inadequate to the task. The leaders of the movement had to tackle the insoluble dilemmas of Mosaic leadership: how to reconcile passion with patience, authority with power sharing, clarity of purpose with self-doubt.[7]

The solution was a certain sort of public-spiritedness. Today, when we use the phrase "public-spirited," we tend to mean someone who gathers petitions, marches and protests, and makes his voice heard for the public good. But in earlier eras it meant someone who curbed his own passions and moderated his opinions in order to achieve a larger consensus and bring together diverse people. We think of public-spiritedness as self-assertion, but historically it has been a form of self-government and self-control. The reticent and sometimes chilly George Washington exemplified this version of public-spiritedness.[8] Randolph exemplified it, too. He combined political radicalism with personal traditionalism.

Sometimes his advisers would get fed up with his unfailing politeness. "Every now and then," Bayard Rustin told Murray Kempton, "I think he permits good manners to get in the way. . . . Once I complained about that and he answered, 'Bayard, we must with good manners accept everyone. Now is the time for us to learn good manners. We will need them when this is over, because we must show good manners after we have won.' "[9]

THE GENTEEL RADICAL

Randolph began his career by moving from Florida to Harlem, arriving in April, 1911, a month after the Triangle factory fire. He became active in theater groups, and with his elocution and presence seemed on the verge of becoming a Shakespearean actor until his parents squelched the idea. He briefly attended City College, where he read Karl Marx voraciously. He helped start a series of racial magazines, bringing Marxism to the black community. In one editorial he called the Russian Revolution "the greatest achievement of the twentieth century." He opposed U.S. entry into World War I, believing the war only served the interests of munitions makers and other industrialists. He crusaded against Marcus Garvey's Back-to-Africa movement. In the middle of that fight some anonymous enemy sent Randolph a box containing a threatening note and a severed human hand.

At the same time he was getting arrested for violating antisedition legislation, his personal life became even more bourgeois and upstanding. Randolph married a genteel woman from a prominent Harlem family. On Sunday afternoons they enjoyed taking part in the weekly promenades. People got dressed up in their finest clothes — gaiters, canes, boutonnieres, spats, and fancy hats — and strolled down Lenox Avenue or 135th Street, exchanging greetings and pleasantries with neighbors along the way.

By the early 1920s, Randolph had begun to move into labor organizing. He helped start a half dozen small trade unions, organizing waiters, waitresses, and other disaffected groups. In June 1925, Randolph was approached by a few Pullman car porters who were looking for a charismatic, educated leader who could build a union for them. The Pullman Company provided luxury railway sleeping cars that were leased to railroads. The patrons were served by squads of liveried black men who shined shoes, changed linens, and brought food. After the Civil War, the founder, George Pullman, had hired ex-slaves to do this work, believing they would be a docile labor force. The porters had tried to unionize as early as 1909, but had always been beaten back by the company.

Randolph accepted the challenge and spent the next twelve years trying to create a porters' union and win concessions from the company. He traveled around the country trying to persuade porters to join the union, at a time when the slightest whiff of union activity could cost them their job or get them beaten. Randolph's primary tool was his manner. As one union member would recall, "He gripped you. You would have to be without feeling to pull yourself away from him. You felt by him the way the disciples felt by the Master. You may not know it right then, but when you got home to yourself, and got to thinking what he had said, you would just have to be a follower of him, that's all."[10]

The work was slow, but over the next four years the union grew to nearly seven thousand members. Randolph learned that the rank and file didn't like it when he criticized the company, to which they still felt loyal. They did not share his more general critique of capitalism, so he changed tactics. He made it a fight for dignity. Randolph also decided he would reject all donations from sympathetic whites. This would be a victory blacks would organize and win on their own.

Then the Depression hit, and the company struck back, firing or threatening any employee who voted to strike. By 1932, union membership was down to 771. Offices had closed in nine cities. Randolph and the headquarters staff were evicted for failure to pay rent. Randolph's salary, which had been ten dollars a week, fell to nothing.

Always a polished, sharp-dressed man, his clothes became tattered and worn. Union activists were beaten in cities from Kansas City to Jacksonville. In 1930 an Oakland loyalist named Dad Moore wrote a determined letter a month before his death:

> My back is against the wal but I will Die before I will Back up one inch. I am fiting not for myself but for 12,000 porters and maids, and there children. . . . I has bin at Starvasion Door but it had not change my mind, for just as the night folows the Day we are gointer win. Tell all the men in your Dist that they should folow Mr. Randolph as they would follow Jes Christ.[11]

NONVIOLENT RESISTANCE

The black press and the black churches turned against the union for being overly aggressive. In New York, Mayor Fiorello La Guardia offered Randolph a city job paying $7,000 a year, but Randolph turned it down.

The tide turned in 1933 with the election of Franklin Roosevelt and a change in the labor laws. Still, company executives had trouble wrapping their minds around the fact that to settle the labor dispute they would have to sit down as equals with the black porters and their representatives. It wasn't until July 1935 that the company and union leadership met in a room in Chicago to begin negotiations. An agreement was finally reached two years later. The company agreed to a reduction in the work month from 400 to 240 hours and agreed to increase the company's total pay package by $1,250,000 a year. Thus ended one of the longest and most bitter labor fights of the twentieth century.

By this time Randolph was the most famous African American organizer in the country. Having broken decisively with the Marxism of his youth, he spent the next years in a series of brutal fights to purge Soviet-dominated organizations from the labor movement. Then, in the early 1940s, with the country mobilizing for war, a new injustice pressed down on the black community. The factories were hauling in workers in droves to build planes, tanks, and ships, but they were not hiring blacks.

On January 15, 1941, Randolph issued a statement calling for a giant march on Washington if this discrimination was allowed to continue. "We loyal Negro American citizens demand the right to work and fight for our country," he declared. He formed the March on Washington Committee and realistically expected they could bring ten thousand or perhaps twenty or thirty thousand blacks together for a protest march on the Mall.

The prospect of the march alarmed the nation's leadership. Roosevelt asked Randolph to come see him for a meeting at the White House.

"Hello, Phil," the president said when they were together. "Which class were you in at Harvard?"

"I never went to Harvard, Mr. President," Randolph responded.

"I was sure you did. Anyway, you and I share a kinship in our great interest in human and social justice."

"That's right, Mr. President."

Roosevelt launched into a series of jokes and political anecdotes, but Randolph eventually cut him off.

"Mr. President, time is running on. You are quite busy, I know. But what we want to talk with you about is the problem of jobs for Negroes in defense industries."

Roosevelt offered to call some company heads and urge them to hire blacks.

"We want you to do more than that," Randolph replied. "We want something concrete. . . . We want you to issue an executive order making it mandatory that Negroes be permitted to work in these plants."

"Well, Phil, you know I can't do that. If I issue an executive order for you, then there'll be no end of other groups coming here and asking me to issue executive orders for them, too. In any event I couldn't do anything unless you called off this march of yours. Questions like this can't be settled with a sledgehammer."

"I'm sorry, Mr. President, the march cannot be called off." Randolph, bluffing a bit, vowed to bring a hundred thousand marchers.

"You can't bring a hundred thousand Negroes to Washington," Roosevelt protested, "somebody might get killed."

Randolph insisted. The impasse lasted until Mayor La Guardia, who was at the meeting, jumped in. "It is clear Mr. Randolph is not going to call off the march, and I suggest we all begin to seek a formula."[12] Six days before the march was due to take place, Roosevelt signed Executive Order 8802, banning discrimination in the defense industries. Randolph called off the march, amid much opposition from civil rights leaders who wanted to use it to push other causes such as discrimination in the armed forces themselves.

After the war, Randolph pushed more

broadly for worker rights and desegregation. His great power, as always, derived from his obvious moral integrity, his charisma, his example as an incorruptible man in service to a cause. He was, however, not a meticulous administrator. He had trouble concentrating his energies on a single cause. The unabashed admiration he inspired in the people around him could threaten organizational effectiveness. "There is, especially in the National Office, an unhealthy degree of leader-worship of Mr. Randolph," one outside analyst of the 1941 March on Washington organization observed, "which paralyzes action and prevents an intelligent working out of policy."[13]

But Randolph had one more important contribution to make to the civil rights movement. In the 1940s and 1950s he was among those who championed nonviolent resistance as a tactic to advance the civil rights cause. Influenced by Mahatma Gandhi and some of the early labor movement tactics, he helped form the League of Non-Violent Civil Disobedience Against Military Segregation in 1948.[14] Against most of the established civil rights groups, which advocated education and reconciliation over confrontation and contention,

Randolph argued for restaurant sit-ins and "prayer protests." As he told the Senate Armed Services Committee in 1948, "Ours would be [a movement] of non-resistance. . . . We would be willing to absorb the violence, absorb the terrorism, to face the music and to take whatever comes."

This tactic of nonviolence relied on intense self-discipline and renunciation of the sort Randolph had practiced his entire life. One of the aides who influenced Randolph and was influenced by him was Bayard Rustin. A few decades younger, Rustin shared many qualities with his mentor.

RUSTIN

Bayard Rustin grew up in West Chester, Pennsylvania, and was raised by his grandparents. He was well into boyhood before he learned that the person he thought was his older sister was actually his mother. His father, who suffered from alcoholism, lived in the town but had no role in Rustin's life.

Rustin remembered his grandfather as having "the most erect carriage of any person you have ever seen. None of us can remember a single unkindness in him." His grandmother had been raised a Quaker and was one of the first black women in the county to receive a high school education. She impressed upon Bayard the need for calm, dignity, and relentless self-control. "One just doesn't lose one's temper" was one of her favorite maxims. His mother also ran a summer Bible camp, with emphasis on the book of Exodus, which Bayard attended every day. "My grandmother," he recalled, "was thoroughly convinced that when it came to matters of the liberation of black people, we had much more to learn from the Jewish experience than we had to learn out of Matthew, Mark, Luke and John."[15]

In high school Rustin was a good athlete and wrote poetry. Like Randolph, he spoke in a proper, almost British accent, which could appear haughty to those who first met him. His classmates teased him for his excessive dignity. One high school classmate recalled, "He spoke biblical poetry. And Browning. He would tackle you and then get up and recite a poem."[16] As a freshman he became the first black student in forty years to win his high school's oratory prize. By senior year he made the all-county football team, and he was a class valedictorian. He developed a passion for opera, Mozart, Bach, and Palestrina, and George Santayana's novel *The Last Puritan* was one of his favorite books. On his own he also read Will and Ariel Durant's *The Story of Civilization,* which, he testified, was like "taking a whiff of something that simply opens your nostrils except that it happened in my brain."[17]

Rustin went off to college at Wilberforce University in Ohio and then Cheney State in Pennsylvania. While in college he realized he was gay. The realization did not induce too much emotional turmoil — he had been raised in a tolerant family and was to live more or less openly as a homosexual for his entire life — but it did cause him to move to New York, where there was at least an underground gay culture and a bit more acceptance.

Once in Harlem, he went in multiple directions at once, joining leftist organizations and also volunteering to help organize Randolph's March on Washington effort. He joined a Christian pacifist organization, the Fellowship of Reconciliation (FOR), and quickly emerged as a rising star of the movement. Pacifism was a way of life for Rustin. It provided him with both a path to inner virtue and a strategy for social change. The path to inner virtue meant suppressing personal anger and the violent tendencies inside. "The only way to reduce ugliness in the world is to reduce it in yourself," Rustin would say.[18] As a strategy for change, pacifism, he later wrote in a letter to Martin Luther King, "rests upon two pillars. One is resistance, continuous military resistance. The evildoer is subjected to pressure so that he never is permitted to rest. Second it projects good-will against ill-will. In this way, nonviolent resistance is a force against apathy in our own ranks."[19]

Throughout his late twenties, Rustin traveled for FOR, electrifying audiences around the country. He staged constant acts of civil disobedience, which quickly became legendary in pacifist and civil rights circles. In 1942 in Nashville he insisted upon riding in the white section of a public bus. The driver called the police. Four officers arrived and beat him while Rustin maintained a passive, Gandhian demeanor. As David McReynolds, a member of FOR, later recalled, "Not only was he the Fellowship's most popular lecturer but he was also a genius at tactical matters. Bayard was being groomed by FOR to become an American Gandhi."[20]

In November 1943, when he received his draft notice, Rustin decided he would take a stance of noncooperation and go to jail rather than serve in one of the rural labor camps as a conscientious objector. At that time, one out of every six inmates in federal prison was a prisoner of conscience. These inmates thought of themselves as the shock troops of pacifism and civil rights. Locked away, Rustin aggressively defied the prison's segregationist policies. He insisted upon eating in the Whites Only part of the dining hall. During free time he stationed himself in the Whites Only part of the cell block. Sometimes his agitation got him in trouble with the other prisoners. On one occasion a white prisoner went after him, bashing him with a mop handle, landing blows on Rustin's head and body. Once again, Rustin went into a Gandhian pose of nonresistance. He simply repeated over and over again, "You can't hurt me." Eventually the mop handle snapped. Rustin suffered a broken wrist and bruises across his head.

Word of Rustin's exploits soon spread beyond prison walls, to the wider press and activist circles. In Washington, officials at the Federal Bureau of Prisons, under the leadership of James Bennett, classified Rustin as a "notorious offender," in the same category as Al Capone. As his biographer John D'Emilio put it, "Throughout Rustin's 28-month imprisonment, Bennett was plagued by letters from subordinates who pleaded for advice on what to do about Rustin, and from Rustin's supporters on the outside who kept an eye on his treatment."[21]

PROMISCUITY

Rustin behaved heroically, but there was also an arrogance and an anger and sometimes a recklessness in his behavior that was not in keeping with his stated beliefs. On October 24, 1944, he felt compelled to send a letter to the warden apologizing for his behavior at a disciplinary hearing. "I am quite ashamed that I lost my temper and behaved rudely," he wrote.[22] There was also a recklessness to his sexual life. Rustin was gay at a time when gay life was pushed underground, when there was no public affirmation for gays and lesbians. But there was a relentlessness to Rustin's search for partners that even his lovers found disturbing. His speaking tours before and after prison involved constant rounds of seduction. One long-term lover complained that "coming home one day and finding him in bed with somebody else was not my idea of fun."[23] In prison he was flagrant about his sexual interests and was several times caught performing fellatio on other prisoners.

The prison authorities eventually convened a disciplinary hearing. At least three prisoners testified that they had seen Rustin performing oral sex. At first Rustin lied, vehemently denying the charges. When authorities announced they were putting him in a separate part of the prison as punishment, he wrapped his arms and legs around a swivel chair, resisted the guards, and ended up in isolation.

News of the incident spread across activist circles nationwide. Some of his supporters were upset to learn he was gay, but Rustin had never really hidden that. Mostly they were upset because his sexual activities undermined the example he had been setting as a disciplined, heroic resister. In a movement that called upon its leaders to be peaceful, self-restrained, and self-purifying, Rustin had been angry, arrogant, lax, and self-indulgent. A. J. Muste, the leader of FOR and Rustin's mentor, wrote him a harsh letter:

> You have been guilty of gross misconduct, especially reprehensible in a person making the claims to leadership and — in a sense — moral superiority which you were making. Furthermore, you have deceived everybody, including your own comrades and most devoted friends. . . . You are still far from facing re-

ality in yourself. In the self that has been and still is you, there is nothing to respect, and you must ruthlessly cast out *everything* in you, which prevents you from facing that. Only so can your true self come to birth — through fire, anguish complete and child-like humility. . . . You remember Psalm 51: "Have mercy upon me, O God, according to thy loving kindness — wash me thoroughly from mine iniquities and cleanse me from my sin. . . . against thee only have I sinned and done this evil in thy sight. . . . Create me a clean heart, O God, and renew a right spirit within me."[24]

In a later letter, Muste made it clear that it was not Rustin's homosexuality he was objecting to, but his promiscuity: "How utterly horrible and cheap where there is no discipline, no form in the relationship." Just as an artist with the freest vision, the most powerful creative urge, submits to the severest discipline, so, too, must a lover tame his impulses in order to reach "the discipline, the control, the effort to understand the other."

With promiscuity, Muste continued, "we come close to the travesty and denial of love, for if love means depth, means understanding above the ordinary . . . means exchange of life blood, how can that happen among an indefinite number of people?"

Rustin initially resisted Muste's harsh judgment, but eventually, after weeks in isolation, he surrendered, writing a long, heartfelt letter in reply:

When success was imminent in our racial campaign my behavior stopped progress. . . . I have misused the confidence that negroes here had in my leadership; I have caused them to question the moral basis of non-violence; I have hurt and let down my friends over the country. . . . I am a traitor (by our means of thought) just as surely as an army captain who willfully exposed military positions during a battle. . . . I have really been dedicated to my "ego." I have thought in terms of my power, my time, my energy and of giving them to the great struggle. I have thought in terms of my voice, my ability, my willingness to go into the non-violent vanguard. I have not humbly accepted God's gifts to me. . . . [This] has led, I now see, first to arrogance and pride and then to weakness, to artificiality and failure.[25]

A few months later Rustin was permitted to travel home, with an accompanying guard, to visit his dying grandfather. While on the way home, Rustin met up with Helen Winnemore, a fellow activist and an old friend. Winnemore told Rustin she loved him and wanted to be his life companion, to give him the heterosexual relationship, or at least cover, so that he could continue his work. In a letter to his longtime male lover, Davis Platt, Rustin summarized the offer Winnemore had made, paraphrasing her words:

Now since I believe that once redeemed your power for service and redemption of others will be vast, and since I believe your greatest immediate need is for real love, real understanding, and confidence, I tell you without shame of the love I have for you, of my desire to be with you thru light and darkness, to give all that I possess that the goodness within you shall live and flower. Men must see the goodness that potentially is yours and glorify your creator. This, Bayard, she went on to say in effect, this [is the] love I have for you and I offer it joyfully not for myself or for you alone, but for all mankind, which would profit by what your integration would mean — and then for a long time we were silent.[26]

Rustin was touched by Winnemore's offer. "Never had I heard such unselfish love speak in a woman. Never had I sensed a more simple and complete offering." He did not take Winnemore up on her offer, but he regarded it as a sign from God. The memory of their conversation brought him "a joy that is almost beyond understanding — a flash of light in the right direction — a new hope . . . a sudden reevaluation . . . a light on the road I know I should travel."[27]

Rustin vowed to curb his arrogance, the spirit of anger that had marred his pacifist activities. He also rethought his sex life. He fundamentally accepted Muste's critique of his promiscuity. Rustin worked on his relationship with his longtime lover Davis Platt, exchanging a series of long, searching letters with him in the hopes that one truly loving relationship would serve as a barricade against lust and promiscuity.

Rustin remained in prison until June 1946. Upon his release he immediately became active again in the civil rights movement. In North Carolina, he and some fellow activists sat at the front of a segregated bus and were beaten and nearly lynched. In

Reading, Pennsylvania, he extracted an apology from a hotel manager after a clerk denied him a room. In St. Paul, Minnesota, he conducted a sit-in until he was given a room. On a train from Washington to Louisville he sat in the middle of the dinner car from breakfast straight through lunchtime as the waiters refused to serve him.

When A. Philip Randolph called off a resistance campaign, Rustin harshly criticized his mentor for issuing a statement that was nothing more than a "weasel worded, mealy mouthed sham."[28] He was quickly ashamed of himself, and he avoided Randolph for the next two years. When they finally met again, "I was so nervous I was shaking, waiting for his wrath to descend upon me." Randolph laughed it off and resumed their relationship.

Rustin went on speaking tours around the world, a star once again. He also continued to seduce men at every stop. Eventually Platt threw him out of their apartment. Then, in 1953, while on a speaking engagement in Pasadena, he was arrested at just after three in the morning. He was performing oral sex on two men in a car when two county police officers approached and arrested him for lewd vagrancy.

He was sentenced to sixty days in jail, and his reputation would never fully recover. He had to dissociate himself from his activist organizations. He tried unsuccessfully to get a job as a publicist for a publishing house. A social worker suggested he get a job cleaning bathrooms and hallways in a hospital.

BACKSTAGE

Some people try to recover from scandal by starting where they were and simply continuing through life. Some people strip themselves down and start again from the bottom. Rustin eventually understood that his new role was to serve his good cause, but in the background.

Rustin slowly recommitted himself to the civil rights movement. Instead of being the star speaker, leader, and organizer, he would forever after be mostly in the shadows, working behind the scenes, receiving no credit, shifting the glory to others, like his friend and protégé, Martin Luther King, Jr. Rustin wrote for King, spread ideas through King, introduced King to labor leaders, pushed him to talk about economic as well as civil rights issues, tutored him on nonviolent confrontation and the Gandhian philosophy, and organized one action after another on King's behalf. Rustin was a significant player in the Montgomery bus boycott. King wrote a book about the boycott, but Rustin asked him to take out all references to his own role. When asked to sign some public statement on behalf of this or that stand, he generally refused.

Even this backstage role was fragile. In 1960, Adam Clayton Powell, the pastor and then congressman from New York City, let it be known that if King and Rustin did not bow to his demands on a certain tactical matter, he would accuse them of having a sexual affair. Randolph urged King to stand by Rustin, since the charge was so obviously bogus. King hesitated. Rustin handed in his resignation from the Southern Christian Leadership Conference in the hope that King would reject it. Instead, King quietly accepted it, much to Rustin's dismay. King dropped Rustin personally as well, no longer calling upon him for advice, sending the occasional bland note as a cover for his decision to cut him off.

In 1962, Rustin turned fifty, largely unknown. Of all the major civil rights leaders, Randolph was the one who had stuck by him most steadfastly. One day, as they were sitting around in Harlem, Randolph began reminiscing about the World War II era march on Washington that never took place. Rustin sensed immediately that it was time to complete that dream and organize a "mass descent" on the nation's capital. The marches and protests across the South had begun to shake the foundations of the old order, Rustin believed. The election of John F. Kennedy made Washington once again relevant. It was time to force federal action through mass confrontation.

At first, the major civil rights organizations such as the Urban League and the NAACP were skeptical or completely hostile. They did not want to offend legislators or members of the administration. A confrontational march might reduce their access to those in power and lessen their ability to exercise influence from the inside. In addition, there had long been a basic difference of outlook within the civil rights movements that involved not just a debate about strategy but also a deep difference of opinion about morality and human nature.

As David L. Chappell argues in his book *A Stone of Hope,* there were really two civil rights movements. The first was northern and highly educated. People in this group tended to have an optimistic view of history and human nature. Without thinking much about it, they perceived the arc of history as a gradual ascent, a steady accumulation of more scientific and psychological knowledge, a steady achievement of greater prosperity, a steady growth of progressive legislation, and a gentle rise from barbarism to decency.

They believed that racism was such a clear violation of America's founding documents that the main job for the civil rights activist was to appeal to reason and the better angels of people's nature. As education levels increased, as consciousness was raised, as prosperity and economic opportunity spread, then more and more people would gradually see that racism was wrong, that segregation was unjust, and they would rise to combat it. Education, prosperity, and social justice would rise together. All good things are compatible and mutually reinforcing.

People in this camp tended to believe in conversation over confrontation, consensus over aggression, and civility over political force.

There was a second camp, Chappell argues, that emerged from the biblical prophetic tradition. Its leaders, including King and Rustin, cited Jeremiah and Job. In this world, they argued, the just suffer while the unjust prosper. Being right does not necessarily lead to being victorious. Man is a sinner at the core of his being. He will rationalize the injustices that benefit him. He will not give up his privileges even if you can persuade him they are unjust. Even people on the righteous side of a cause can be corrupted by their own righteousness, can turn a selfless movement into an instrument to serve their own vanity. They can be corrupted by whatever power they attain and corrupted by their own powerlessness.

Evil, King declared, is "rampant" in the universe. "Only the superficial optimist who refuses to face the realities of life fails to see this patent fact."[29] People in this realist camp, who were mostly southern and religious, had contempt for the northern faith in gradual natural progress. "This particular sort of optimism has been discredited by the brutal logic of events," King continued. "Instead of assured progress in wisdom and decency, man faces the ever present possibility of swift relapse not merely to animalism, but into such calculated cruelty as no other animal can practice."[30]

The optimists, members of this camp argued, practice idolatry. They worship man and not God, and when they do worship God it is a God who merely possesses human qualities in extreme form. As a result they overestimate the power of human goodwill, idealism, and compassion and their own noble intentions. They are too easy on themselves, too complacent about their own virtue, and too naïve about the resolve of their opponents.

Randolph, King, and Rustin had this more austere view of their struggle. The defenders of segregation would not lie down, and people of goodwill would not be persuaded to act if there was any risk to themselves. The civil rights activists themselves could not rely on their own goodwill or their own willpower, because very often they would end up perverting their own cause. If there was to be any progress, it was necessary not just to be engaged, one had to utterly surrender to the movement, at the cost of one's own happiness and fulfillment and possibly life. This attitude of course fueled a fierce determination, which many of their more optimistic secular allies could not match. As Chappell put it, "Civil rights activists drew from illiberal sources to supply the determination that liberals lacked, but needed."[31] The biblical lens didn't protect the realists from pain and suffering, but it explained that pain and suffering were inevitable and redemptive.

One consequence of this attitude was that the prophetic realists were much more aggressive. They took it as a matter of course that given the sinful nature of man, people could not be altered merely by education, consciousness raising, and expanded opportunity. It was wrong to put one's faith in historical processes, human institutions, or human goodness. As Rustin put it, American blacks look "upon the middle class idea of long term educational and cultural changes with fear and mistrust."[32]

Instead, change comes through relentless pressure and coercion. That is to say, these biblical realists were not Tolstoyan, they were Gandhian. They did not believe in merely turning the other cheek or trying to win people over with friendship and love alone. Nonviolence furnished them with a series of tactics that allowed them to remain on permanent offense. It allowed them to stage relentless protests, marches, sit-ins, and other actions that would force their opponents to do things against their own will. Nonviolence allowed the biblical realists to aggressively expose the villainy of their foes, to make their enemies' sins work against them as they were exposed in ever more brutal forms. They compelled their foes to commit evil deeds because they themselves were willing to absorb evil. Rustin endorsed the idea that extreme behavior was required to make the status quo crumble. He saw Jesus as "this fanatic whose insistence on love thrust at the very pillars of a stable society."[33] Or, as Randolph put it, "I feel morally obligated to disturb and keep disturbed the conscience of Jim Crow America."[34]

Even in the midst of these confrontations, Randolph, Rustin, and the other civil rights activists were in their best moments aware that they were in danger of being corrupted by their own aggressive actions. In their best moments they understood that they would become guilty of self-righteousness because their cause was just; they would become guilty of smugness as their cause moved successfully forward; they would become vicious and tribal as group confronted group; they would become more dogmatic and simplistic as they used propaganda to mobilize their followers; they would become more vain as their audiences enlarged; their hearts would harden as the conflict grew more dire and their hatred for their enemies deepened; they would be compelled to make morally tainted choices as they got closer to power; the more they altered history, the more they would be infected by pride.

Rustin, who had been so undisciplined in his sexual life, saw nonviolence as a means a protester could use to discipline himself against these corruptions. Nonviolent protest in this view is different from normal protest. It demands relentless self-control. The Gandhian protester must step into race riots without ever striking out, must face danger while remaining calm and communicative, must confront with love those who deserve to be hated. This requires physical self-discipline, marching into danger slowly and deliberately, keeping one's arms curled around one's head as the blows rain down. It requires emotional discipline, resisting the urge to feel resentment, maintaining a spirit of malice toward none and charity toward all. It requires above all the ability to absorb suffering. As King put it, the people who had suffered for so long had to endure more suffering if they were to end their oppression: "Unearned suffering is redemptive."[35]

The nonviolent path is an ironic path: the weak can triumph by enduring suffering; the oppressed must not fight back if they hope to defeat their oppressor; those on the side of justice can be corrupted by their own righteousness.

This is the inverted logic of people who

see around them a fallen world. The mid-century thinker most associated with this ironic logic is Reinhold Niebuhr. People like Randolph, Rustin, and King thought along Niebuhrian lines, and were influenced by him. Niebuhr argued that, beset by his own sinful nature, man is a problem to himself. Human actions take place in a frame of meaning too large for human comprehension. We simply can't understand the long chain of consequences arising from what we do, or even the origins of our own impulses. Neibuhr argued against the easy conscience of modern man, against moral complacency on every front. He reminded readers that we are never as virtuous as we think we are, and that our motives are never as pure as in our own accounting.

Even while acknowledging our own weaknesses and corruptions, Niebuhr continued, it is necessary to take aggressive action to fight evil and injustice. Along the way it is important to acknowledge that our motives are not pure and we will end up being corrupted by whatever power we manage to attain and use.

"We take and must continue to take morally hazardous actions to preserve our civilization," Niebuhr wrote in the middle of the Cold War. "We must exercise our power. But we ought neither to believe that a nation is capable of perfect disinterestedness in its exercise nor become complacent about particular degrees of interest and passion which corrupt the justice by which the exercise of power is legitimized."[36]

Behaving in this way, he continued, requires the innocence of a dove and the shrewdness of a serpent. The ultimate irony is that in any struggle "we could not be virtuous if we were really as innocent as we pretended to be."[37] If we were truly innocent we couldn't use power in the ways that are necessary to achieve good ends. But if you adopt a strategy based on self-doubt and self-suspicion, then you can achieve partial victories.

CULMINATION

At first Rustin and Randolph had trouble rallying civil rights leaders around the idea of a March on Washington. But the violent protests in Birmingham, Alabama, during the spring of 1963 changed the mood. The whole world saw the Birmingham police force setting dogs on teenage girls, unleashing water cannons, and hurling boys into walls. The images mobilized the Kennedy administration to prepare civil rights legislation, and they persuaded nearly everybody in the civil rights movement that the time was right for a mass descent on the nation's capital.

Rustin, as the chief organizer of the march, expected to be named the official director. But at a crucial meeting, Roy Wilkins of the NAACP objected: "He's got too many scars." King vacillated and finally Randolph stepped in, saying he would himself serve as director of the march. This would give him the right to appoint a deputy, and he would appoint Rustin, who would be director in all but name. Wilkins was outmaneuvered.

Rustin oversaw everything from the transportation systems to the toilet facilities to the speaker lineup. To avoid confrontation with the D.C. police he organized a corps of black off-duty policemen and gave them training in nonviolence. They were to surround the marchers and prevent clashes.

Two weeks before the march, the segregationist senator Strom Thurmond went on the Senate floor and lambasted Rustin for being a sexual pervert. He introduced the Pasadena police booking slip into the Congressional Record. As John D'Emilio points out in his outstanding biography *Lost Prophet,* Rustin instantly and inadvertently became one of the most visible homosexuals in America.

Randolph leaped to Rustin's defense: "I am dismayed there are in this country men who, wrapping themselves in the mantle of Christian morality, would mutilate the most elementary conceptions of human decency, privacy and humility in order to persecute other men."[38] Since the march was only two weeks away, the other civil rights leaders had no choice but to defend Rustin as well. Thurmond ended up doing Rustin a great favor.

The Saturday before the march, Rustin issued a final statement that summed up his policy of tightly controlled aggression. The march, he declared, "will be orderly, but not subservient. It will be proud, but not arrogant. It will be non-violent but not timid."[39] On the day, Randolph spoke first. Then John Lewis brought the gigantic crowd to full roar with a fiery, aggressive speech. Mahalia Jackson sang and King delivered his "I have a dream" speech.

He ended with the refrain from the old spiritual, "Free at last! Free at last! Thank God Almighty we are free at last!" Then Rustin, playing a master of ceremonies role, mounted the podium and reintroduced Randolph. Randolph led the crowd in a pledge to continue the struggle: "I pledge that I will not relax until victory is won. . . . I will pledge my heart and my mind and my body unequivocally and without regard to personal sacrifice, to the achievement of social peace through social justice."

After the march, Rustin and Randolph found each other. As Rustin would later recall, "I said to him, 'Mr. Randolph, it looks like your dream has come true.' And when I looked into his eyes, tears were streaming down his cheeks. It is the one time I can recall that he could not hold back his feelings."[40]

In the final decades of his life, Rustin cut his own path, working hard to end apartheid in South Africa, bucking the civil rights establishment in New York City during a crucial teachers' strike in 1968, defending the ideal of integration against more nationalist figures like Malcolm X. In those final years, he did find personal peace, in the form of a long-term relationship with a man named Walter Naegle. Rustin almost never spoke about his private life in public, but he did tell an interviewer, "The most important thing is that after many years of seeking, I've finally found a solid, ongoing relationship with one individual with whom I have everything in common, everything. . . . I spent years looking for exciting sex instead of looking for a person who was compatible."

The story of A. Philip Randolph and Bayard Rustin is the story of how flawed people wield power in a fallen world. They shared a worldview based on an awareness of both social and personal sin, the idea that human life is shot through with veins of darkness. They learned, Randolph instantly and Rustin over a lifetime, to build an inner structure to contain the chaotic impulses within. They learned that sinfulness is battled obliquely through self-giving, by directing life away from the worst tendencies. They were extremely dignified in their bearing. But this same sense made them aggressive in their outward strategy. They knew that dramatic change, when it is necessary, rarely comes through sweet suasion. Social sin requires a hammering down of the door by people who are simultaneously aware that they are unworthy to be so daring.

This is a philosophy of power, a philosophy of power for people who combine extreme conviction with extreme self-skepticism.

CHAPTER 7
LOVE

"A human life, I think," George Eliot wrote, "should be well rooted in some spot of native land, where it may get the love of tender kinship for the face of the earth, for the labors men go forth to, for the sounds and accents that haunt it, for whatever will give that early home a familiar unmistakable difference amidst the future widening of knowledge."[1]

Eliot's native spot was in Warwickshire, in the middle of England, a gentle, soft, unremarkable landscape. From her home she could see both the ancient rolling farmland and also the new and grimy coal mines, the economic clash that gave the Victorian era its special intensity. She was born with the name Mary Anne Evans on November 22, 1819.

Her father began as a carpenter but rose through self-discipline and an eye for opportunity and ended up as a very successful land agent. He supervised other people's properties and became moderately rich in the process. She adored him. When she became a novelist, she would use his traits — practical knowledge, unlettered wisdom, a loyal devotion to his work — as the basis for several of her more admirable characters. After he died she kept his wire-rimmed glasses as a reminder of his watchful eyes and his perspective on the world.

Her mother, Christiana, was in ill health through most of Mary Anne's girlhood. She lost twin boys eighteen months after Mary Anne's birth, and she sent her surviving children away to boarding schools to spare herself the physical effort of raising them. Mary Anne seems to have felt the loss of her mother's affection acutely, responding with what one biographer, Kathryn Hughes, calls "an infuriating mix of attention-seeking and self-punishing behavior."[2] She was, on the surface, a precocious, strong-willed, somewhat awkward girl, more comfortable in the company of adults than with other children, but there was something deeply needy about her.

Hungry for affection and terrified of being abandoned, she turned her attention, as a young girl, to her older brother, Isaac. When he returned on visits from school she followed him about, badgering him with questions about every particular of his life. For a time he returned her love, and they enjoyed "little spots of time," perfect days playing in the grass and streams. But then he grew older, got a pony, and lost interest in the bothersome little girl. She was left weeping and abandoned. This was a pattern — her desperate need for love and some man's exasperated refusal — that would dominate the first thirty years of her life. As her final husband, John Cross, would put it, "In her moral development she showed, from the earliest years, the trait that was most marked in her all through life — namely the absolute need of some one person who should be all in all to her, and to whom she should be all in all."[3]

In 1835 her mother fell ill with breast cancer. Mary Anne, who had been sent away to boarding school at age five to spare her mother's health, was called back at age sixteen to tend to it. There's no record that she suffered any great grief when her mother finally succumbed to the disease, but her formal education was over, and she took over the role of supervising the household, almost as her father's surrogate wife.

In her famous preface to *Middlemarch,* Eliot writes about the crisis of vocation that many young women feel. They experience a great yearning inside, she wrote, a spiritual ardor to devote their energies in some substantial, heroic, and meaningful direction. They are propelled by moral imagination, the urge to do something epic and righteous with their life. These young women, "fed from within," soared after some "illimitable satisfaction, some object which would never justify weariness, which would reconcile self-despair with the rapturous consciousness of life beyond self." And yet Victorian society provided so few avenues for their energy that their "loving heartbeats and sobs after an unattainable goodness tremble off and are dispersed among hindrances, instead of centering in some long-recognizable deed."

Mary Anne was driven by that moral ardor, that spiritual perfectionism. In her late teens and early twenties, she became something of a religious nut. She came of age in a time when society was in great religious tumult. Science was beginning to expose cracks in the Church's description of human creation. The spread of unbelief made morality a problem; many Victorians clung more ferociously to stern moral precepts even as their doubts about the existence of God increased. Among the faithful, there were efforts to make the church more vibrant and more spiritual. John Henry Newman and the Oxford Movement tried to return Anglicanism to its Catholic roots, tried to restore a sense of reverence for tradition and medieval ritual. The evangelicals democratized the faith, creating more charismatic services and emphasizing individual prayer, individual conscience, and each individual's direct relationship with God.

During her teenage years, Mary Anne was caught up in the religious fervor and, in her self-centered immaturity, came to embody many of religion's most priggish and unattractive aspects. Her faith was long on self-admiring renunciation and short on delight or humane sympathy. She gave up reading fiction, believing that a morally serious person should focus on the real world and not imaginary ones. She forswore wine and as manager of her household forced those around her into abstinence as well. She adopted a severe and puritanical mode of dress. Music, which had once been a source of great joy, was now, she decided, permissible only when it accompanied worship. At social events she could be counted on to disapprove of the vulgar humanity and then to fall into fits of weeping. At one party, she wrote a friend, "the oppressive noise that accompanied the dancing" made it impossible for her to "maintain the Protestant character of a True Christian."[4] She developed a headache, slipped into hysterics, and vowed to reject "all invitations of a dubious character."

D. H. Lawrence once wrote, "It was really George Eliot who started it all. It was she who started putting the action inside." In her teenage years, Mary Anne lived melodramatically and narcissistically, full of solitary internal anguish, struggle, and resignation. She was trying to lead a life of martyrdom and surrender. But she was artificially narrowing herself, amputating every humane and tender piece that didn't fit into a rigid frame. Her behavior was filled with affectation, less about being a saint than about getting herself admired for being a saint. There was a painful and ostentatious self-consciousness in her letters from this period, and even in her bad early poetry: "oh Saint! oh would that I could claim / The privileg'd, the honored name / And confidently take my stand / Though lowest in a saintly band!" one biographer, Frederick R. Karl, sums up the common view: "Except for her high intelligence, Mary Ann, in 1838, at close to nineteen, sounds intolerable."[5]

Fortunately, her roving mind couldn't be contained for long. She was too intelligent not to be able to observe herself accurately. "I feel that my besetting sin is the one of all others most destroying, as it is the fruitful parent of them all, Ambition, a desire insatiable for the esteem of my fellow creatures," she wrote in a letter. "This seems the center whence all my actions proceed."[6] At some level she understood that her public righteousness was just a play for attention. Furthermore, she was just too curious to stay in a self-imposed mental straitjacket for very long. She was too hungry for knowledge. Her reading could not be contained within narrow banks.

She was still reading biblical commentary, but she was also learning Italian and German, reading Wordsworth and Goethe. Her reading stretched to include the Romantic poets, including Shelley and Byron, whose lives certainly did not conform to the strictures of her faith.

Soon she was reading widely in the sciences, including John Pringle Nichol's *The Phenomena and Order of the Solar System* and Charles Lyell's *Principles of Geology,* a book that paved the way for Darwin's account of evolution. Christian writers were rising up to defend the biblical account of creation. She read their books, too, but they backfired with her. They were so unpersuasive in rebutting the findings of the new science that they only served to reinforce Mary Anne's growing doubts.

She was profoundly influenced by a book titled *An Inquiry Concerning the Origin of Christianity* by Charles Hennell, which she bought in 1841 at the age of twenty-one. Hennell parsed through each of the Gospels, trying to determine what could be established as fact and what was later embellishment. He concluded that there was insufficient evidence to prove that Jesus was divinely born, or that he had performed any miracles, or that he had been resurrected from the dead. Hennell concluded that Jesus was a "noble minded reformer and sage, martyred by crafty priests and brutal soldiers."[7]

For most of this time, Mary Anne had nobody close to her intellectual level with whom she could discuss what she was reading. She invented a word to describe her condition: "non-impartitive." She received information but could not digest it through conversation.

But then she learned that Hennell's youngest sister, Cara, lived nearby. Cara's husband, Charles Bray, was a successful ribbon merchant who had written his own religious tract, "The Philosophy of Necessity." It held that the universe was governed by unchanging rules ordained by God, but that God was not active in the world. It was man's duty to discover these rules and improve the world along their lines. Bray believed people should spend less time praying and more time involved in social reform. The Brays were bright, intellectual, unconventional thinkers who would go on to lead unconventional lives. Though they remained married, Charles fathered six children with their cook, and Cara had a close and possibly sexual friendship with Edward Noel, a relative of Lord Byron, who had three children of his own and an estate in Greece.

Mary Anne was introduced to the Brays by a mutual friend, perhaps in order to bring the Brays back into the fold of orthodox Christianity. If that was her intent, it didn't work. By the time Mary Anne settled into their lives, she herself was already drifting away from the faith. The Brays immediately recognized her as a kindred spirit. She began socializing with them more and more, delighted to have found intellectual peers at last. They did not cause her defection from Christianity, but they catalyzed it.

It was dawning on Mary Anne that her growing disbelief would cause her no end of trouble. It would mean a rupture with her father, the rest of her family, and polite society generally. It would make it very hard for her to find a husband. In the society of her time, agnosticism meant ostracism. But she pushed on bravely toward what her heart and head told her was truth. "I wish to be among the ranks of that glorious crusade that is seeking to set Truth's Holy Sepulcher free from usurped domination," she wrote in a letter to a friend.[8]

As that sentence indicates, Mary Anne was not renouncing the spirit of religion even while she was coming to renounce Christianity. She discounted Christian teaching, and the divinity of Jesus, but she did not doubt, especially at this age, the existence of God. She rejected Christianity on realist grounds, out of distaste for anything abstract or fantastical. She did it after exhaustive reading, but she did not do it coldly or by the use of dry reason. Rather, she loved life with such an earthy passion that she had trouble accepting the idea that this world was subsidiary to some other world that obeyed different laws. She came to feel she could achieve a state of grace not through surrender but through her own moral choices, by living a virtuous and rigorous life. With this philosophy Mary Anne put a heavy burden on herself, and on her own conduct.

In January 1842, Mary Anne told her father that she would no longer accompany him to church. His response was to withdraw into what one biographer called a cold and sullen rage. Mary Anne was not only defying her father and God, as he saw it; she was also choosing to dishonor her family and to cast it into social disgrace. On the first Sunday after her refusal, Mary Anne's father went to church, but he noted simply and coldly in his diary, "Mary Anne did not go."

The next few weeks were spent in what Mary Anne called a "Holy War." She lived at home at loggerheads with her father. He broke off contact with her but fought back in different ways. He enlisted friends and relatives to come plead with her to attend church, if only on prudence grounds. If she continued on this path, they warned, she would spend her life poor, cast out, isolated. These very plausible predictions had no effect on her. Her father also asked clergy and other knowledgeable scholars to come and persuade her by force of reason that Christianity was the true doctrine. They came, they argued, they were defeated. Mary Anne had already read every book they cited to make their case, and she had her responses.

Finally, her father decided to relocate the family. If Mary Anne was going to make herself unmarriageable, there was no use keeping the big house that had been rented to catch her a husband.

Mary Anne tried to reopen conversation with her father by writing him a letter. First, she made clear why she could no longer be a Christian. She said she regarded the Gospels as "histories consisting of mingled truth and fiction, and while I admire and cherish much of what I believe to have been the moral teaching of Jesus himself, I consider the system of doctrines built upon the facts of his life . . . to be most dishonorable to God and most pernicious in its influence on individual and social happiness."

It would be rank hypocrisy, she told him, to appear to worship in the home of a doctrine she thought pernicious. She wrote that she would like to go on living with her father, but if he wanted her to leave, "I can cheerfully do it if you desire it and shall go with deep gratitude for all the tenderness and rich kindness you have never been tired of showing me. So far from complaining I shall joyfully submit if as a proper punishment for the pain I have most unintentionally given you, you determine to appropriate any provision you may have intended to make for my future support to your other children whom you may consider more deserving."

At the first dawn of her adulthood, Mary Anne was not only renouncing the faith of her family. She was willing to go out into the world without a home, without an inheritance, without a husband, and without prospects. She concluded with a declaration of love: "As a last vindication of herself from one who has no one to speak for her I may be permitted to say that if ever I loved you I do so now, if ever I sought to obey the laws of my Creator and to follow duty wherever it may lead me I have that determination now and the consciousness of this will support me though every being on earth were to frown on me."

This letter, remarkable for a woman so young, shows many of the traits the world would later come to see in George Eliot: an intense intellectual honesty, an arduous desire to live according to the strictures of her conscience, an amazing bravery in the face of social pressure, a desire to strengthen her character by making the necessary hard choices, but also a bit of egotism, a tendency to cast herself as the star of her own melodrama, an intense desire for the love of men even as she puts that love at risk.

After a few months, they compromised. Mary Anne agreed to accompany her father to church, so long as he and everybody else understood that she was not a Christian and a believer in the doctrines of the faith.

It looks like a capitulation, but it wasn't entirely. Mary Anne's father must have realized the cruelty in his rejection of his daughter. He bent. Meanwhile, Mary Anne came to see and regret the thick vein of self-aggrandizement that was running through her protest. She came to see that she was taking a secret delight in being the center of a town scandal. She regretted the pain she was causing her father.

Moreover, she knew there was something self-indulgent in the way she had taken an uncompromising stance. Within a month she was writing a friend saying that she deplored her "impetuosity both of feeling and judging." Later she said she deeply regretted this collision with her father, which might have been avoided with a little subtlety and management. Yes, she had an obligation to follow her individual conscience, she concluded, but it was her moral duty to mute her own impulses by considering their effect on others and on the social fabric of the community. By the time Mary Anne Evans became the novelist George Eliot, she was an avowed enemy of that kind of stark grandstanding. By middle age, she was a meliorist and a gradualist, believing that people and society were best reformed by slow stretching, not by sudden rupture. She was capable of making brave and radical moves in line with her own convictions, as we shall see, but she also believed in the importance of social niceties and conventions. She believed that society is held together by a million restraints on individual will, which enmesh the individual within a common moral world. When people behave on the basis of uncompromising individual desire, she came to believe, they might set off a selfish contagion in those around them. She cloaked her own radical path in all the trappings of respectability. She became a courageous freethinker with a faith in ritual, habit, and convention. The Holy War with her father was important in teaching her that lesson.

Within a few months, Mary Anne and her father were reconciled. Her admiration for him and moral dependence upon him was expressed in a letter she wrote shortly after his death seven years after the Holy War: "What shall I be without my Father? It will seem as if part of my moral nature were gone. I had a horrid vision of myself last night becoming earthly sensual and devilish for want of that purifying restraining influence."

NEEDINESS

Intellectually, Mary Anne was mature. The intensive reading she had done throughout her adolescence produced an impressive depth of knowledge and a capacity for observation and judgment. At the level of the mind, Mary Anne was well on the central journey of her life, the transformation that would take her from a self-absorbed adolescent to an adult whose maturity was measured by an unsurpassed ability to enter into other people's feelings.

Emotionally, though, she was still something of a basket case. By the time she was twenty-two it became a joke in her circle that Mary Anne fell in love with everyone she met. These relationships followed a general pattern. Desperate for affection, she would throw herself at some man, usually a married or otherwise unavailable one. Dazzled by her conversation, he would return her attention. Mistaking his intellectual engagement for romantic love, she would become emotionally embroiled, hoping their love would fill some void in herself. Finally he would reject her or flee, or his wife would force her out of the picture. Mary Anne would be left awash in tears, or crippled by migraines.

Mary Anne's romantic forays might have been successful if she had been conventionally pretty, but as Henry James, then a young and handsome man, reported, she was "magnificently ugly — deliciously hideous." A series of men simply couldn't get around her heavy jaw and plain horse-like features, though finer spirits eventually came to see the beauty within. In 1852, an American visitor, Sara Jane Lippincott, described the effect her conversation had on her appearance: "Miss Evans certainly impressed me at first as exceedingly plain, with her aggressive jaw and her evasive blue eyes. Neither nose, nor mouth nor chin were to my liking; but, as she grew interested and earnest in conversation, a great light flashed over or out of her face, till it seemed transfigured, while the sweetness of her rare smile was something quite indescribable."[9]

Men came. Mary Anne fell. Men went.

She had an infatuation with a music instructor and with Charles Hennell, the author. She became entangled with a young man named John Sibree who was studying for the ministry. Sibree didn't return her affection, but after conversations with her, he gave up his clerical career, though he had nothing else to fall back on.

Later she attached herself with disturbing intensity to a married, four-foot-tall, middle-aged artist named François d'Albert Durade. Once, and for about a day, she developed an infatuation with a man who was actually single, but she lost interest in him by the morrow.

Friends would invite Mary Anne to stay in their homes. Before long she'd be involved in some sort of passionate intimacy with the father of the family. Dr. Robert Brabant was a much older, cultivated doctor who gave Mary Anne access to his library and asked her to come live with his family. Before long they were completely entwined. "I am in a little heaven here, Dr. Brabant being its archangel," she wrote in a letter to Cara; "time would fail me to tell of all his charming qualities. We read, walk and talk together, and I am never weary of his company." Before long Dr. Brabant's wife put her foot down. Either Mary Anne would leave the house or she would. Mary Anne had to flee in disgrace.

The oddest imbroglio happened in the home of John Chapman, publisher of the *Westminster Review,* which Mary Anne would eventually write for and edit. Chapman was already living with his wife and a mistress when Mary Anne moved in. Before long the three women were competing for Chapman's affections. As the Eliot biographer Frederick R. Karl puts it, the situation had all the makings of a country house farce, with slammed doors, couples sneaking out for walks, hurt feelings, and tearful, angry scenes. If there was too much calm one day, Chapman would stir the drama by showing a love letter from one woman to one of the others. Eventually the wife and the mistress formed an alliance against Mary Anne. Once again she had to flee amid whispers of scandal.

Biographers generally argue that the absence of maternal love created a hole at the center of Mary Anne's being, which she desperately tried to fill for the rest of her life. But there was also some narcissism here, the love of her own love, the love of her own nobility, of feeling the sweep of one's own passion. She made a drama of herself and indulged in it, enjoying the attention, luxuriating in her own capacity for emotional depth, and savoring the sense of her own epic importance. People who see themselves as the center of their solar system, often get enraptured by their own terrible but also delicious suffering. People who see themselves as a piece of a larger universe and a longer story rarely do.

She would later write, "to be a poet is to have a soul so quick to discern, that no shade of quality escapes it, and so quick to feel, that discernment is but a hand playing with finely ordered variety of chords of emotion — a soul in which knowledge passes instantaneously into feeling, and feeling flashes back as a new organ of knowledge." Mary Anne had that kind of soul. Feeling and action and thought were the same thing. But she had no person to attach her passion to, and no work to give it discipline and shape.

AGENCY

In 1852, at age thirty-two, Mary Anne fell in love with the philosopher Herbert Spencer, the only one of the men thus far in her life who was close to her intellectual equal. They went to the theater together and talked constantly. Spencer liked her company but could not overcome his own narcissism and her ugliness. "The lack of physical attraction was fatal," Spencer would write decades later. "Strongly as my judgment prompted, my instincts would not respond."

In July she wrote him a letter that was both pleading and bold. "Those who have known me best have already said that if ever I loved any one thoroughly my whole life must turn upon that feeling, and I find they said truly," she declared. She asked him not to forsake her: "If you become attached to someone else, then I must die, but until then I could gather courage to work and make life valuable, if only I had you near me. I do not ask you to sacrifice anything — I would be very glad and cheerful and never annoy you. . . . You will find that I can be satisfied with very little, if I am delivered from the dread of losing it."

Finally, she added a climactic flourish: "I suppose no woman ever before wrote such a letter as this — but I am not ashamed of it, for I am conscious in the light of reason and true refinement I am worthy of your respect and tenderness, whatever gross men or vulgar-minded women might think of me."[10]

This letter represents a pivotal moment in Eliot's life, with its mixture of pleading vulnerability and strong assertion. After the years of disjointed neediness, the iron was beginning to enter her soul and she became capable of that declaration of her own dignity. You might say that this moment was Eliot's agency moment, the moment when she began the process by which she would stop being blown about by her voids and begin to live according to her own inner criteria, gradually developing a passionate and steady capacity to initiate action and drive her own life.

The letter didn't solve her problems. Spencer still rejected her. She remained insecure, especially about her writing. But her energies were roused. She exhibited growing cohesion and at times amazing courage.

This agency moment can happen, for many people, surprisingly late in life. Sometimes you see lack of agency among the disadvantaged. Their lives can be so blown about by economic disruption, arbitrary bosses, and general disruption that they lose faith in the idea that input leads to predictable output. You can offer programs to improve their lives, but they may not take full advantage of them because they don't have confidence that they can control their own destinies.

Among the privileged, especially the privileged young, you see people who have been raised to be approval-seeking machines. They may be active, busy, and sleepless, but inside they often feel passive and not in control. Their lives are directed by other people's expectations, external criteria, and definitions of success that don't actually fit them.

Agency is not automatic. It has to be given birth to, with pushing and effort. It's not just the confidence and drive to act. It's having engraved inner criteria to guide action. The agency moment can happen at any age, or never. Eliot began to display signs of emotional agency when she was with Spencer, but it came to mature fruition only after she met George Lewes.

ONE TRUE LOVE

The story of George Eliot's love for George Lewes is almost always told from her perspective, as the great passion that gave coherence to her soul, that took her from a self-absorbed and desperate girl and provided her with the love she craved and the emotional support and security she required. But the story can equally well be told from Lewes's perspective, as the central element in his journey from fragmentation to integrity.

Lewes came from a long lineage of family chaos. His grandfather was a comic actor who was married three times. His father was married to one woman in Liverpool and had four children by her, then left and set up a new household with another woman in London with whom he had three boys before he disappeared forever to Bermuda.

Lewes grew up moderately poor and educated himself by going to Europe and schooling himself in the leading Continental authors such as Spinoza and Comte, who were then largely unknown in England. He returned to London and supported himself with his pen, writing on any subject for anybody who would pay. In an age that was beginning to favor specialization and earnestness, he was slighted as a superficial journeyman writer.

The American feminist Margaret Fuller met Lewes at a party at Thomas Carlyle's house and called him a "witty, French, flippant sort of man" who possessed a "sparkling shallowness." Most biographers have followed this line, slighting him as a bit of an adventurer and opportunist, as a facile but shallow and not entirely reliable writer.

The biographer Kathryn Hughes

persuasively takes a more appreciative view. Lewes, she writes, was witty and effervescent in a society that tended toward dour self-importance. He was knowledgeable about French and German life in a society that was often suspicious of anything that wasn't British. He had a genuine passion for ideas and for bringing neglected thinkers to public view. He was freethinking and romantic in a society that was in a stringent, buttoned-up Victorian phase.

Lewes was famously ugly (notoriously, the only major London figure who was even less attractive than George Eliot), but he could talk comfortably and sensitively with women, and this served him well. He married a beautiful young woman named Agnes when he was twenty-three and she was nineteen. They had a modern, freethinking marriage, mostly faithful for the first nine years and then mostly unfaithful after that. Agnes had a long-running affair with a man named Thornton Hunt. Lewes sanctioned this affair so long as she didn't have any children by Hunt. When she did, he adopted them as his own in order to spare them the disgrace of illegitimacy.

By the time he met Mary Anne, Lewes was living apart from Agnes (though he seems to have believed that someday he would move back, and their marriage would remain legally intact for the rest of his life). He was in what he regarded as a "very dreary wasted period of my life. I had given up all ambition whatever, lived from hand to mouth, and thought the evil of each day sufficient."[11]

Mary Anne, for her part, was also lonely, but maturing. She wrote to Cara Bray, "My troubles are purely psychical — self-dissatisfaction and despair of achieving anything worth doing." In her journal she embraced the sentiment that was first written by the feminist author Margeret Fuller: "I shall always reign through the intellect, but the life! The life! O my god! Shall that never be sweet?"[12]

But by this stage, in her midthirties, she was less frantic about herself: "When we are young we think our troubles a mighty business — that the world is spread out expressly as a stage for the particular drama of our lives and that we have a right to rant and foam at the mouth if we are crossed. I have done enough of that in my time. But we begin at last to understand that these things are important only to one's own consciousness, which is but as a globule of dew on a roseleaf that at midday there will be no trace of. This is no high flown sentimentality, but a simple reflection which I find useful to me every day."[13]

Lewes and Mary Anne met at a bookshop on October 6, 1851. By this time she had moved to London and had established herself as an anonymous contributor to (and eventually the editor of) the *Westminster Review*. They traveled in the same circles. They both had a close friendship with Herbert Spencer.

She was unimpressed at first, but before long she was writing to friends that she found Lewes "genial and amusing" and reporting that he has "quite won my liking, in spite of myself." On his part, Lewes seemed to understand the quality of the woman he was getting to know. Flitting and peripatetic in other spheres of life, Lewes was completely solid and dependable when it came to his service to the woman who would become George Eliot.

None of their letters to each other survive. That is in part because they didn't write very many (they were often together) and also because Eliot did not want later biographers raking over her private life and exposing the vulnerable heart that underlay the formidable novels. So we don't know exactly how their love grew. But we know that Lewes was gradually winning her over.

On April 16, 1853, she wrote to a friend, "Mr. Lewes, especially, is kind and attentive, and has quite won my regard, after having had a good deal of my vituperation. Like a few other people in the world, he is much better than he seems. A man of heart and conscience, wearing a mask of flippancy."

At some point Lewes would have told her about his broken marriage and his messy private life. This probably wouldn't have shocked Mary Anne, who was familiar with complex living arrangements. But they also would have talked a great deal about ideas. They were interested in the same authors: Spinoza, Comte, Goethe, Ludwig Feuerbach. Around this time Mary Anne was translating Feuerbach's *The Essence of Christianity.*

Feuerbach was arguing that even if the age had lost faith in Christianity, it was still possible to retain the essence of its morality and ethics, and this could be done through love. He maintained that through love and sex with someone you loved, human beings could achieve transcendence, and defeat the sinfulness in their own nature. He wrote:

Now by what means does man deliver himself from this state of disunion between himself and the perfect being, from the painful consciousness of sin, from the distracting sense of his own nothingness? How does he blunt the fatal sting of sin? Only by this; that he is conscious of love as the highest, the absolute power and truth, that he regards the Divine Being not only as a law, as a moral being of the understanding; but also as a loving tender even subjective human being (that is, having sympathy even with the individual man.)[14]

Mary Anne and Lewes fell in love over ideas. In the years before they met they had been drawn to the same writers, often at the same time. They composed essays on overlapping subjects. They both took the search for truth with the same earnest intensity, and both subscribed to the idea that human love and sympathy could serve as the basis for their own morality as a substitute for a Christianity they could not actually believe in.

INTELLECTUAL LOVE

We don't have access to the exact scene in which their hearts became inflamed with each other, but we do have access to the process by which similar sorts of people fell in love, and they give one the flavor of what

337

Mary Anne and Lewes must have felt. One famous passion of this sort occurred between the British philosopher Isaiah Berlin and the Russian poet Anna Akhmatova. Their meeting of the minds took on a special drama, because it happened all in one night.

The scene took place in Leningrad in 1945. Twenty years older than Berlin, Akhmatova had been a great prerevolutionary poet. Since 1925 the Soviets had allowed her to publish nothing. Her first husband had been executed on false charges in 1921. In 1938, her son was taken prisoner. For seventeen months, Akhmatova had stood outside his prison, vainly seeking news of him.

Berlin didn't know much about her, but he was visiting Leningrad and a friend offered to make an introduction. Berlin was taken to her apartment and met a woman still beautiful and powerful, but wounded by tyranny and war. At first their conversation was restrained. They talked about war experiences and British universities. Other visitors came and went.

By midnight they were alone, sitting on opposite ends of her room. She told him about her girlhood and marriage and her husband's execution. She began to recite

338

Byron's *Don Juan* with such passion that Berlin turned his face to the window to hide his emotion. She began reciting some of her own poems, breaking down as she described how they had led the Soviets to execute one of her colleagues.

By four in the morning they were talking about the greats. They agreed about Pushkin and Chekhov. Berlin liked the light intelligence of Turgenev, while Akhmatova preferred the dark intensity of Dostoyevsky.

Deeper and deeper they went, baring their souls. Akhmatova confessed her loneliness, expressed her passions, spoke about literature and art. Berlin had to go to the bathroom but didn't dare break the spell. They had read all the same things, knew what the other knew, understood each other's longings. That night, his biographer Michael Ignatieff writes, Berlin's life "came as close as it ever did to the still perfection of art." He finally pulled himself away and returned to his hotel. It was eleven o'clock in the morning. He flung himself on the bed and exclaimed, "I am in love, I am in love."[15]

The night Berlin and Akhmatova spent together stands as the beau ideal of a certain sort of communication. It's communication between people who think that the knowledge most worth attending to is found not in data but in the great works of culture, in humanity's inherited storehouse of moral, emotional, and existential wisdom. It's a communication in which intellectual compatibility turns into emotional fusion. Berlin and Akhmatova could experience that sort of life-altering conversation because they had done the reading. They believed you have to grapple with the big ideas and the big books that teach you how to experience life in all its richness and how to make subtle moral and emotional judgments. They were spiritually ambitious. They had the common language of literature written by geniuses who understand us better than we understand ourselves.

The night also stands as the beau ideal of a certain sort of bond. This sort of love depends on so many coincidences that it happens only once or twice in a lifetime, if ever. Berlin and Akhmatova felt all the pieces fitting amazingly into place. They were the same in many ways. There was such harmony that all the inner defenses fell down in one night.

If you read the poems Akhmatova wrote about that night, you get the impression that they slept together, but according to Ignatieff, they barely touched. Their communion was primarily intellectual, emotional, and spiritual, creating a combination of friendship and love. If friends famously confront the world side by side and lovers live face to face, Berlin and Akhmatova seemed somehow to embody both postures at once. They shared and also augmented each other's understanding.

For Berlin this night was the most important event of his life. Akhmatova was stuck in the Soviet Union, suffering under a regime of manipulation, fear, and lies. The regime decided that she had consorted with a British spy. She was expelled from the Writers' Union. Her son was in prison. She was desolated but remained grateful for Berlin's visit, speaking of him fervently and writing movingly about the numinous magic of that night.

The love Eliot felt for Lewes had some of that intellectual and emotional intensity. They, too, experienced love as a moral force that deepens a person, organizing human minds around other souls and lifting them so they are capable of great acts of service and devotion.

And indeed, if we look at love in its most passionate phase, we see that love often does several key things to reorient the soul. The first thing it does is humble us. It reminds us that we are not even in control of ourselves. In most cultures and civilizations, love is described in myth and story as an external force — a god or a demon — that comes in and colonizes a person, refashioning everything inside. It is Aphrodite or Cupid. Love is described as a delicious madness, a raging fire, a heavenly frenzy. We don't build love; we *fall* in love, out of control. It is both primordial and also something distinctly our own, thrilling and terrifying, this galvanic force that we cannot plan, schedule, or determine.

Love is like an invading army that reminds you that you are not master of your own house. It conquers you little by little, reorganizing your energy levels, reorganizing your sleep patterns, reorganizing your conversational topics, and, toward the end of the process, rearranging the objects of your sexual desire and even the focus of your attention. When you are in love, you can't stop thinking about your beloved. You walk through a crowd and think you see her in a vaguely familiar form every few yards. You flip from highs to lows and feel pain at slights that you know are probably trivial or illusory. Love is the strongest kind of army because it generates no resistance. When the invasion is only half complete, the person being invaded longs to be defeated, fearfully, but utterly and hopelessly.

Love is a surrender. You expose your deepest vulnerabilities and give up your illusions of self-mastery. This vulnerability and the desire for support can manifest itself in small ways. Eliot once wrote, "There is something strangely winning to most women in that offer of the firm arm; the help is not wanted physically at the moment, but the sense of help, the presence of strength that is outside them and yet theirs, meets a continual want of imagination."

Love depends on the willingness of each person to be vulnerable and it deepens that vulnerability. It works because each person exposes their nakedness and the other rushes to meet it. "You will be loved the day when you will be able to show your weakness without the person using it to assert his strength," the Italian novelist Cesar Pavese wrote.

Next, love decenters the self. Love leads you out of your natural state of self-love. Love makes other people more vivid to you than you are to yourself.

The person in love may think she is seeking personal happiness, but that's an illusion. She is really seeking fusion with another, and when fusion contradicts happiness, she will probably choose fusion. If the shallow person lives in the smallness of his own ego, a person in love finds that the ultimate riches are not inside, they are out there, in the beloved and in the sharing of a destiny with the beloved. A successful marriage is a fifty-year conversation getting ever closer to that melding of mind and heart. Love expresses itself in shared smiles and shared tears and ends with the statement, "Love you? I am you."

Many observers have noticed that love eliminates the distinction between giving and receiving. Since the selves of the two lovers are intermingled, scrambled, and fused, it feels more delicious to give to the beloved than to receive. Montaigne writes that the person in love who receives a gift is actually giving her lover the ultimate gift: the chance to experience the joy of giving to her. It doesn't make sense to say that a lover is generous or altruistic, because a lover in the frenzy of love who gives to her beloved is giving to a piece of herself.

In his famous essay on friendship, Montaigne described how a deep friendship or a love can rearrange the boundaries of self:

Such a friendship has no model but itself, and can only be compared to itself.

It was not one special consideration, nor two, nor three, nor four, nor a thousand; it was some mysterious quintessence of all this mixture which possessed itself of my will, and led it to plunge and lose itself in his, which possessed itself of his whole will, and led it, with a similar hunger and a like impulse, to plunge and lose itself in mine. I may truly say lose, for it left us with nothing that was our own, nothing that was either his or mine.

Next, love infuses people with a poetic temperament. Adam I wants to live according to a utilitarian calculus — to maximize pleasant experiences, to guard against pain and vulnerability, to maintain control. Adam I wants you to go through life as a self-contained unit, coolly weighing risks and rewards and looking out for your own interests. Adam I is strategizing and calculating costs and benefits. He wants you to keep the world at arm's length. But to be in love is to lose your mind a bit, to be elevated by magical thinking.

To be in love is to experience hundreds of small successive feelings that you never quite experienced in that way before, as if another half of life has been opened up to you for the first time: a frenzy of admiration, hope, doubt, possibility, fear, ecstasy, jealousy, hurt, and so on and so on.

Love is submission, not decision. Love demands that you make a poetic surrender to an inexplicable power without counting the cost. Love asks you to discard conditional thinking and to pour out your love in full force and not measure it by tablespoons. It crystallizes your vision so that, as Stendhal put it, your beloved shimmers like a sparkling jewel. To you she possesses magic that others don't see. To you the historic spots where love first bloomed take on a sacred meaning that others can't perceive. The dates on the calendar when the crucial first kisses and words were exchanged assume the aura of holy days. The emotions you feel cannot quite be captured in prose, but only in music and poetry, looks and touches. The words you exchange are so silly and overwrought that they have to be kept private. They would sound insane if they were bandied about with your friends in the daylight world.

You don't fall in love with the person who might be of most use to you — not the richest, most popular, most well-connected person, not the one with the best career prospects. Adam II falls for the distinct person, for no other reason than some inner harmony, inspiration, joy, and uplift, because he is he and she is she. Moreover, love doesn't seek the efficient path, the sure thing; for some perverse reason, love feeds on roadblocks and is not usually won by prudence. You might have tried to warn two people in love that they should be wary of marrying because their union will not be a happy one. But lovers caught up in magical thinking don't see what others see, and they probably wouldn't change their course even if they could because they would rather be unhappy together than happy apart. They are in love, not buying a stock, and the poetic temperament — part thinking, part brilliant emotion — guides their decisions. Love is a state of poetic need; it exists on both a higher and a lower plane than logic and calculation.

In this way, love opens up the facility for spiritual awareness. It is an altered state of consciousness that is intense and overwhelming but at the same time effervescent. In that state, many people are likely to have mystical moments when they feel an awareness of some wordless mystery beyond the human plane. Their love gives them little glimmerings of pure love, love detached from this or that particular person but emanating from some transcendent realm. These sensations come in fleeting moments. They are intense and effervescent mystical experiences, glimpses into an infinity beyond what can be known for sure.

In his masterpiece, *My Bright Abyss,* the poet Christian Wiman writes,

> In any true love — a mother's for her child, a husband's for his wife, a friend's for a friend — there is an excess energy that always wants to be in motion. Moreover, it seems to move not simply from one person to another but through them toward something else. ("All I know now / is the more he loved me the more I loved the world" — Spencer Reece.) That is why we can be so baffled and overwhelmed by such love (and I don't mean merely when we fall in love; in fact, I'm talking more of other, more durable relationships): it wants to be more than it is; it cries out inside of us to make it more than it is."[16]

For many people, religious and nonreligious, love provides a glimpse of some realm beyond the edge of what we know. It also in a more practical sense enlarges the heart. This act of yearning somehow makes the heart more open and more free. Love is like a plow that opens up hard ground and allows things to grow. It cracks open the crust that Adam I depends on and exposes the soft fertile soil of Adam II. We notice this phenomenon all the time: one love leads to another, one love magnifies the capacity for another.

Self-control is like a muscle. If you are called upon to exercise self-control often in the course of a day, you get tired and you don't have enough strength to exercise as much self-control in the evening. But love is the opposite. The more you love, the more you can love. A person who has one child does not love that child less when the second and third child come along. A person who loves his town does not love his country less. Love expands with use.

In this way love softens. We all know people who were brittle and armored up for life before they fell in love. But in the midst of that sweet and vulnerable state of motivation their manner changed. Behind their back we tell each other that they are aglow with love. The lobster shell has been peeled away, exposing flesh. This has made them more frightened, and more open to damage, but also kinder, more capable of living life as an offering. Shakespeare, the inevitable authority on this subject, wrote,

"The more I give to thee / The more I have, for both are infinite."[17]

And so, finally, love impels people to service. If love starts with a downward motion, burrowing into the vulnerability of self, exposing nakedness, it ends with an active upward motion. It arouses great energy and desire to serve. The person in love is buying little presents, fetching the glass from the next room, bringing a tissue when there's flu, driving through traffic to pick the beloved up at the airport. Love is waking up night after night to breastfeed, living year after year to nurture. It is risking and sacrificing your life for your buddy's in a battle. Love ennobles and transforms. In no other state do people so often live as we want them to live. In no other commitment are people so likely to slip beyond the logic of self-interest and unconditional commitments that manifest themselves in daily acts of care.

Occasionally you meet someone with a thousand-year heart. The person with the thousand-year heart has made the most of the passionate, tumultuous phase of love. Those months or years of passion have engraved a deep commitment in their mind. The person or thing they once loved hotly they now love warmly but steadily, happily, unshakably. They don't even think of loving their beloved because they want something back. They just naturally offer love as a matter of course. It is gift-love, not reciprocity-love.

This is the kind of love that George Lewes had for Mary Anne Evans. They were both transformed and ennobled by their love for each other, but Lewes's was in many ways the greater and more ennobling transformation. He celebrated her superior talent. He encouraged, elicited, and nurtured it. With a thousand letters and gestures, he put himself second and her uppermost in his mind.

THE DECISION

The decision to be together was a profound and life-altering one. Even though he and his wife were living in separate households and Agnes was bearing children by another man, Lewes was officially a married man. If Eliot and Lewes became a couple they would be committing brazen adultery in the eyes of the world. Polite society would be closed to them. Family would cut them off. They would be outcasts, especially Eliot. As Eliot's biographer Frederick R. Karl puts it, "The men who kept mistresses were called philanderers, but the women who were kept were called whores."[18]

And yet by the winter of 1852–53, Eliot seems to have recognized that Lewes was her soul mate. During the spring of 1853 they began to contemplate breaking with society to be with each other. In April, Lewes collapsed with dizziness, headaches, and ringing in the ears. Eliot spent these months translating Feuerbach. He argued that in its true definition, a marriage is not fundamentally a legal arrangement, it is a moral arrangement, and reading his thoughts on the subject would have helped Eliot conclude that the love she and Lewes shared was a truer and higher thing than the arrangement he had with his legal and separated wife.

Ultimately she had to make a decision about what sort of ties meant the most to her, and she decided that love must triumph over social connections. As she later wrote, "Light and easily broken ties are what I neither desire theoretically nor could live for practically. Women who are satisfied with such ties do not act as I have done."

With her genius for judging character, Eliot decided to put her faith in Lewes, even though at this point he had not fully committed himself to her. As she put it in a letter, "I have counted the cost of the step that

I have taken and am prepared to bear, without irritation or bitterness, renunciation by all my friends. I am not mistaken in the person to whom I have attached myself. He is worthy of the sacrifice I have incurred, and my only anxiety is that he should be rightly judged."

All love is narrowing. It is the renunciation of other possibilities for the sake of one choice. In a 2008 wedding toast to Cass Sunstein and Samantha Power, Leon Wieseltier put it about as well as possible:

> Brides and grooms are people who have discovered, by means of love, the local nature of happiness. Love is a revolution in scale, a revision of magnitudes; it is private and it is particular; its object is the specificity of this man and that woman, the distinctness of this spirit and that flesh. Love prefers deep to wide, and here to there; the grasp to the reach. . . . Love is, or should be, indifferent to history, immune to it — a soft and sturdy haven from it: when the day is done, and the lights are out, and there is only this other heart, this other mind, this other face, to assist in repelling one's demons or in greeting one's angels, it does not matter who the president is. When one consents to marry,

one consents to be truly known, which is an ominous prospect; and so one bets on love to correct for the ordinariness of the impression, and to call forth the forgiveness that is invariably required by an accurate perception of oneself. Marriages are exposures. We may be heroes to our spouses but we may not be idols.

Eliot's mind at that juncture seems to have been in a state of convulsive change. She was aware that her life was about to take an irreversible new form. She seems to have concluded that her life up to this moment had been based on a series of faulty choices and it was time to bet all on one true choice. She took the leap W. H. Auden described in his famous poem "Leap Before You Look":

The sense of danger must not disappear:
The way is certainly both short and steep,
However gradual it looks from here;
Look if you like, but you will have to leap.

Tough-minded men get mushy in their sleep
And break the by-laws any fool can keep;
It is not the convention but the fear
That has a tendency to disappear. . . .

The clothes that are considered right to
  wear
Will not be either sensible or cheap,
So long as we consent to live like sheep
And never mention those who
  disappear. . . .

A solitude ten thousand fathoms deep
Sustains the bed on which we lie, my dear:
Although I love you, you will have to leap;
Our dream of safety has to disappear.

On July 20, 1854, Eliot went to a dock
near the Tower of London and boarded a
ship, the *Ravensbourne,* bound for Antwerp.
She and Lewes would begin their life
together abroad. She wrote some letters to
a few friends informing them of her choice,
trying to soften the blow. They considered
this journey together something of a trial
cohabitation, but in reality they were about
to begin the rest of their lives. For both, it
was an amazing act of courage, and an
amazing commitment to mutual love.

LIFE TOGETHER
They chose well. The choice of each
redeemed both of their lives. They traveled
around Europe together, mostly in
Germany, where they were welcomed by the

leading writers and intellectuals of the day. Mary Anne loved living openly as Mrs. Lewes: "I am happier every day and find my domesticity more and more delightful and beneficial to me."[19]

Back in London, however, their relationship unleashed a storm of vituperation that would define Eliot's social life forever after. Some people took pleasure in thinking the worst of her, calling her a husband stealer, a homewrecker, and a sex maniac. Others understood that Lewes was effectively unmarried, understood the love that drew them together, but still could not sanction this relationship because it might loosen morals for others. One former acquaintance, who had conducted a phrenological examination of Eliot's head, declared, "We are deeply mortified and distressed; and I should like to know whether there is insanity in Miss Evans' family; for her conduct, with her brain, seems to me like a morbid mental aberration."[20]

Eliot was unwavering in her choice. She insisted on being known as Mrs. Lewes because even though her decision to be with Lewes had been an act of rebellion, she believed in the form and institution of traditional marriage. Circumstances had compelled her to do something extreme, but morally and philosophically she believed in the conventional path. They lived as traditional husband and wife. And they complemented each other. She could be gloomy, but he was a bright and funny social presence. They took walks together. They worked together. They read books together. They were exclusive, ardent, self-composed and self-completing. "What greater thing is there for two human souls," Eliot would later write in *Adam Bede*, "than to feel they are joined for life — to strengthen each other in all labor, to rest on each other in all sorrow, to minister to each other in all pain, to be one with each other in silent unspeakable memories at the moment of last parting."

Her bond with Lewes cost her many friendships. Her family renounced her, most painfully her brother, Isaac. But the scandal was also productive in furnishing them with deeper insights into themselves and the world. They were forever on edge, looking for signs of insult or affirmation. Because they were cutting against the grain of social convention, they had to pay extra attention to what they were doing, to exercise special care. The shock of public hostility served as a stimulant. It made them acutely conscious of how society functioned.

Eliot had always been a sensitive observer of other people's emotional lives. She had always devoured books, ideas, and people. People had always found her scarily perceptive — as if she was some sort of witch with magical powers. But now there was something more orderly about her thought processes. In the months after her scandalous departure with Lewes, she seems to have finally come to terms with her exceptional gifts. Everything was hardening into a distinct worldview, a settled way of seeing the world. Maybe it is simply that she could finally approach the world with a sense of self-confidence. After all her flailing about in life, Eliot had finally gotten the big thing right. She had taken a chance on Lewes. She had paid a fearsome price. She had endured a baptism of fire. But she was able slowly to come out the other side. The prize of a fulfilling love was worth the cost. As she put it in *Adam Bede*, "Doubtless a great anguish may do the work of years, and we may come out from that baptism of fire with a soul full of new awe and new pity."

NOVELIST

Lewes had long encouraged Eliot to write fiction. He wasn't sure she could come up with plots, but he knew she had a genius for description and characterization. Plus, fiction paid better than nonfiction, and the Lewes family was always hard up for cash. He urged her to just try her hand: "You must try to write a story." One morning in September 1856, she was fantasizing about writing fiction when a title popped into her head: *The Sad Fortunes of the Reverend Amos Barton.* Lewes was immediately enthusiastic. "Oh what a capital title!" he blurted.

A week later she read to him the first part of what she had written. He knew immediately that Eliot was a gifted writer. Eliot wrote in her journal, "We both cried over it, and then he came up to me and kissed me, saying, 'I think your pathos is better than your fun.' " They both realized that Mary Anne would be a successful novelist. She would be George Eliot, the name she took to hide (for a time) her scandalous identity. The skill that he doubted most — whether she could write dialogue — was actually the area where her talent was most obvious. Lewes still wondered if she could create action and movement in her tales, but he knew she had all the other tools.

Before long he was her consultant, agent, editor, publicist, psychotherapist, and general counselor. He understood quickly that her talent was vastly above his own, and he seems to have felt nothing but self-less delight in the way she was bound to overshadow him.

By 1861, her brief diary entries make it clear how intimately involved Lewes was in the development of her plots: She would write during the day and then read what she had written to Lewes. Judging by her letters and diary entries over the years, he was an encouraging audience: "I read the . . . opening scenes of my novel, and he expressed great delight in them. . . . After this record I read aloud what I had written of Part IX to George and he, to my surprise, entirely approved of it. . . . When I read aloud my manuscript to my dear, dear husband, he laughed and cried alternately and then rushed to me to kiss me. He is the prime blessing that has made all the rest possible to me, given me a response to everything I have written."

Lewes shopped her novels around, negotiating with different editors. In the early years, he lied about who the true author of the George Eliot novels was, claiming it was a clergyman friend who wished to remain anonymous. After the truth got out, he protected his wife from criticism. Even after she was celebrated as one of the greatest writers of her day, he would get to the newspapers first and cut out and discard any article that might mention her with anything but the most fulsome praise. Lewes's rule was simple: "Never tell her anything that other people say about her books, for good or evil. . . . Let her mind be as much as possible fixed on her art and not the public."

ARDUOUS HAPPINESS

George and Mary Anne continued to suffer from illnesses and bouts of depression, but they were generally happy together. The letters and diary entries they wrote during their years together bubble forth with assertions of joy and love. In 1859, Lewes wrote to a friend, "I owe Spencer another and deeper debt. It was through him that I learned to know Marian — to know her was to love her — and since then my life has been a new birth. To her I owe all my prosperity and my happiness. God bless her!"

Six years later Eliot wrote, "In each other we are happier than ever. I am more grateful to my dear husband for his perfect love, which helps me in all good and checks me in all evil — more conscious that in him I have the greatest of blessings."

Her masterpiece, *Middlemarch,* is mostly about unsuccessful marriages, but there are glimpses in her books of happy marriages, and marital friendship, such as she enjoyed. "I should never like scolding any one else so well; and that is a point to be thought of in a husband," one of her characters declares. She wrote in a letter to a friend, "I am happier every day, and find my domesticity more and more delightful and beneficial to me. Affection, respect and intellectual sympathy deepen, and for the first time in my life I can say to the moments, 'Let them last, they are so beautiful.' "

Eliot and Lewes were happy, but they were not content. In the first place, life did not cease happening. One of Lewes's sons from his earlier marriage came to them, terminally ill, and they nursed him until his death. Their frequent periods of ill health and depression were marked by migraines and dizzy spells. But through it all, they were impelled by their own need to cultivate themselves morally, to be deeper and wiser. Capturing this mixture of joy and ambition, Eliot wrote in 1857, "I am very happy — happy in the highest blessing life can give us, the perfect love and sympathy of a nature that stimulates my own healthy activity. I feel, too, that all the terrible pain I have gone through in past years, partly from the defects of my own nature, partly from outward things, has probably been a preparation for some special work that I may do before I die. That is a blessed hope, to be rejoiced in with trembling."

Eliot would write, "Adventure is not outside man; it is within."

As she aged, her affections grew stronger and were less perturbed by the egoism of youth. Writing for her remained an agonizing process. She fell into fits of anxiety and depression with each book. She despaired. Recovered hope. Then despaired again. Her genius as a writer derives from the fact that she was capable of the deepest feeling but also of the most discerning and disciplined thought. She had to feel and suffer through everything. She had to transform that feeling into meticulously thought-through observation. The books had to be pushed out of her like children, painfully and amid exhaustion. Like most people who write, she had to endure the basic imbalance of the enterprise. The writer shares that which is intimate and vulnerable, but the reader is far away, so all that comes back is silence.

She had no system. She was antisystem.

As she wrote in *The Mill on the Floss*, she despised "men of maxims," because the "complexity of our life is not to be embraced by maxims, and that to lace ourselves up in formulas of that sort is to repress all the divine promptings and inspirations that spring from growing insight and sympathy."

She didn't use her books to set forth an argument or make points so much as to create a world that readers could dip into at different times of life and derive different lessons each time. Rebecca Mead writes, "I think *Middlemarch* has disciplined my character. I know it has become part of my own experience and my own endurance. *Middlemarch* inspired me when I was young, and chafing to leave home; and now, in middle life, it suggests to me what else home might mean, beyond a place to grow up and grow out of."[21]

Eliot creates her own interior landscape. She was a realist. She was not concerned with the lofty and the heroic. She wrote about the workaday world. Her characters tend to err when they reject the grubby and complex circumstances of everyday life for abstract and radical notions. They thrive when they work within the rooted spot, the concrete habit, the particular reality of their town and family. Eliot herself believed that the beginning of wisdom was the faithful and attentive study of present reality, a thing itself, a person herself, unfiltered by abstract ideas, mists of feeling, leaps of imagination, or religious withdrawals into another realm.

In her early novel *Adam Bede,* she writes, "There are few prophets in the world; few sublimely beautiful women; few heroes. I can't afford to give all my love and reverence to such rarities: I want a great deal of those feelings for my every-day fellow-men, especially for the few in the foreground of the great multitude, whose faces I know, whose hands I touch, for whom I have to make way with kindly courtesy."

She ended her later and perhaps greatest novel, *Middlemarch,* with a flourish celebrating those who lead humble lives: "But the effect of her being on those around her was incalculably diffusive: for the growing good of the world is partly dependent on unhistoric acts; and that things are not so ill with you and me as they might have been, is half owing to the number who live faithfully a hidden life, and rest in unvisited tombs."

Sympathy lay at the heart of Eliot's moral vision. After a self-absorbed adolescence, she went on to develop an amazing capacity to enter the minds of others and observe them from different points of view and with sympathetic understanding. As she put it in *Middlemarch,* "There is no general doctrine which is not capable of eating out our morality if unchecked by a deep-seated habit of direct fellow-feeling with individual fellow-men."

She became, as she aged, an attentive listener. Because she registered other people with such emotional intensity, the facts and feelings of their lives lodged in her memory. She was one of those people on whom nothing is lost. Even though she was herself in a happy marriage, she wrote her greatest book about a series of unhappy marriages, and could describe them from the inside with concrete intensity.

"Every limit is a beginning as well as an ending," she writes in *Middlemarch.* She sympathizes with even her least sympathetic characters, such as Edward Casaubon, the dreary, narcissistic pedant whose talent isn't as great as he thinks it is and who slowly comes to realize this fact. Under her perceptive pen, the inability to sympathize and the inability to communicate, especially within families, is revealed as the great moral poison in many of her stories.

Eliot was a meliorist. She did not believe in big transformational change. She believed in the slow, steady, concrete march to make each day slightly better than the last. Character development, like historic progress, best happens imperceptibly, through daily effort.

Her books were aimed to have a slow and steady effect on the internal life of her readers, to enlarge their sympathies, to refine their ability to understand other people, to give them slightly wider experiences. In that sense her father, and the humble ideal he represented, lived in her all her life. In *Adam Bede,* she celebrated the local man:

> They make their way upward, rarely as geniuses, most commonly as painstaking, honest men, with the skill and conscience to do well the tasks that lie before them. Their lives have no discernible echo beyond the neighborhood where they dwelt, but you are almost sure to find some good piece of road, some building, some application of mineral produce, some improvement in farming practice, some reform of parish abuses, which their names are associated by one or two generations after them.

Many of her characters, and especially her magnetic character, Dorothea Brooke in *Middlemarch,* begin their adulthood with an ardent moral ambition. They want to achieve some great good, like a Saint Teresa, but they don't know what it is or what their vocation might be or just how to go about it. Their attention is fixed on some pure ideal, some distant horizon. Eliot was a Victorian; she believed in moral improvement. But she used her novels to critique such lofty and otherworldly moral goals. They are too abstract, and they can easily, as in Dorothea's case, be unrealistic and delusional. The best moral reform, she counters, is tied to the here and now, directed by honest feelings for this or that individual rather than for humanity as a whole. There's power in the particular and suspicion of the general. For Eliot, holiness isn't in the next world but is embedded in a mundane thing like a marriage, which ties one down but gives one concrete and daily opportunities for self-sacrifice and service. Holiness is inspired by work, the daily task of doing some job well. She takes moral imagination — the sense of duty, the need to serve, the ardent desire to quell selfishness — and she concretizes it and makes it useful.

There are limits, she teaches, in how much we can change other people or how quickly we can change ourselves. So much of life is lived in a state of tolerance — tolerating other people's weaknesses and our own sins, even as we try to have some slow, loving effect. "These fellow mortals, every one," she wrote in *Adam Bede,* "must be accepted as they are: you can neither straighten their noses nor brighten their wit nor rectify their dispositions; and it is these people — amongst whom your life is passed — that it is needful you should tolerate, pity, and love: it is these more or less ugly, stupid, inconsistent people whose movement of goodness you should be able to admire — for whom you should cherish all possible hopes, all possible patience." This posture is at the essence of her morality. It is easy to say but hard to enact. She sought to be tolerant and accepting, but also rigorous, earnest, and demanding. She loved but she also judged.

The word most associated with Eliot's work is "maturity." Hers is, as Virginia Woolf said, literature for grown-ups — seeing life from a perspective both more elevated and more immediate, both wiser and more generous. "People glorify all sorts of bravery except the bravery they might show on behalf of their nearest neighbor," she wrote — a mature sentiment if ever there was one.[22]

A woman named Bessie Rayner Parkes met Eliot when she was still a young woman. She wrote later to a friend saying that she didn't yet know if she would come to like this creature, still known then as Mary Anne Evans. "Whether you or I should ever love her, as a friend, I don't know at all. There is as yet no high moral purpose in the impression she makes, and it is that alone which commands love. I think she will alter. Large angels take a long time unfolding their wings, but when they do, soar out of sight. Miss Evans either has no wings, or which I think is the case, they are coming budding."[23]

Mary Anne Evans took a long road to become George Eliot. She had to grow out of self-centeredness into generous sympathy. But it was a satisfying maturation. She never overcame her fits of depression and her anxieties about the quality of her own writing, but she could think and feel her way into other people's minds and hearts to exercise what she called "the responsibility of tolerance." From disgrace she rose, by the end of her life, to be celebrated as a large angel.

The crucial event in that long journey was her love for George Lewes, which stabilized, lifted, and deepened her. The fruits of their love are embodied in the inscriptions she put in each of her works:

Adam Bede (1859): To my dear husband, George Henry Lewes, I give the MS of a work which would never have been written but for the happiness which his love has conferred on my life.

The Mill on the Floss (1860): To my beloved husband, George Henry Lewes, I give this MS of my third book, written in the sixth year of our life together.

Romola (1863): To the Husband whose perfect love has been the best source of her insight and strength, this manuscript is given by his devoted wife, the writer.

Felix Holt (1866): From George Eliot to her dear Husband, this thirteenth year of their united life, in which the deepening sense of her own imperfectness has the consolation of their deepening love.

The Spanish Gypsy (1868): To my dear — every day dearer — Husband.

Middlemarch (1872): To my dear Husband, George Henry Lewes, in this nineteenth year of our blessed union.

CHAPTER 8
ORDERED LOVE

Augustine was born in the year 354 in the town of Thagaste in what is now Algeria. He was born at the tail end of the Roman Empire, at a time when the empire was collapsing but still seemed eternal. His hometown was near the edge of that empire, two hundred miles from the coast, in a culture that was a messy mix of Roman paganism and fervent African Christianity. He lived, for the first half of his life, caught in the tension between his personal ambitions and his spiritual nature.

Augustine's father, Patricius, a minor town counselor and tax collector, headed a family that was somewhere in the upper end of the middle class. Patricius was materialistic and spiritually inert, and he hoped that his brilliant son would one day have the glittering career he had missed out on. One day he saw his pubescent son in the public baths and wounded Augustine with a lewd crack about his pubic hair or penis size or something. "He saw in me only hollow things," Augustine would write, dismissively.

Augustine's mother, Monica, has always riveted the attention of historians — and psychoanalysts. On the one hand, she was an earthy, unlettered woman, raised in a church that was dismissed, at the time, as primitive. She devoutly attended services each morning, ate meals on the tombs of the dead, and consulted her dreams as omens and guides. On the other hand, she had a strength of personality, and a relentlessness in her convictions about her views, that makes your jaw drop. She was a force in the community, a peacemaker, above gossip, formidable, and dignified. She was capable, as the magnificent biographer Peter Brown notes, of dismissing the unworthy with biting sarcasm.[1]

Monica ran the household. She corrected her husband's errors, waited out and rebuked his infidelities. Her love for her son, and her hunger to run his life, were voracious and at times greedy and unspiritual. Much more than most mothers, Augustine admitted, she longed to have him by her side and under her dominion. She warned him away from other women who might snare him into marriage. She organized her adult life around the care of his soul, doting on him when he tended toward her version of Christianity, weeping and exploding in a delirium of rage when he deviated. When Augustine joined a philosophic sect she disapproved of, she banished him from her presence.

At twenty-eight, when Augustine was already a successful adult, he had to trick her so he could get on a boat to leave Africa. He told her that he was going to the harbor to see a friend off and then slipped aboard a vessel with his mistress and son. As he sailed away, he saw her weeping and gesticulating on the shore, consumed, as he put it, by "a frenzy of grief." She followed him to Europe, of course, prayed for him, got rid of his mistress, and set up an arranged marriage with a ten-year-old heiress that she hoped would force Augustine to receive the rites of baptism.

Augustine understood the possessive nature of her love, but he could not dismiss her. He was a sensitive boy, terrified of her disapproval, but even in adulthood he was proud of her spirit and commonsense wisdom. He was delighted when he found she could keep conversational pace with scholars and philosophers. He understood that she suffered for him even more than he suffered for himself, or more than she could suffer for herself. "I have no words to express the love she had for me; and how much more anguish she was now suffering during the pangs of birth for my spiritual state than when she had given birth to me physically."[2] Through it all, she would love him fiercely and stalk his soul. For all her overbearing harshness, some of the sweetest moments of Augustine's life were moments of reconciliation and spiritual communion with his mother.

AMBITION

Augustine was a sickly child who grew seriously ill with chest pains at seven and looked prematurely old in middle age. As a schoolboy, he was brilliant and sensitive, but uncooperative. He was bored by the curriculum and detested the beatings that were a constant feature of school discipline. When possible, he skipped school to see the pagan bear fights and cockfights that were put on in the town arena.

Even as a young boy, Augustine was caught between the competing ideals of the classical world and the Judeo-Christian world. As Matthew Arnold writes in *Culture and Anarchy,* the primary idea of Hellenism is spontaneity of consciousness, while the governing idea of what he calls Hebraism is strictness of conscience.

That is to say, a person in a Hellenistic frame of mind wants to see things as they really are and explore the excellence and good she finds in the world. A person in this frame of mind approaches the world in a spirit of flexibility and playfulness. "To get rid of one's ignorance, to see things as they are, and by seeing them as they are to see them in their beauty, is the simple and attractive ideal which Hellenism holds out before human nature."[3] The Hellenistic mind has an "aerial ease, clearness and radiancy." It is filled with "sweetness and light."

Hebraism, by contrast, "seizes upon certain plain, capital intimations of the universal order, and rivets itself, one may say, with unequalled grandeur of earnestness and intensity on the study and observance of them."[4] So while the person in a Hellenistic frame of mind is afraid of missing any part of life and is really directing her own life, the person in a Hebraic frame of mind is focusing on the higher truth and is loyal to an immortal order: "Self-conquest, self-devotion, the following not of our own individual will, but the will of God, obedience, is the fundamental idea of this form."[5]

The person in the Hebraic frame of mind, unlike the Hellenist, is not at ease in this world. She is conscious of sin, the forces in herself that impede the passage to perfection. As Arnold puts it, "To a world stricken with moral enervation, Christianity offered the spectacle of an inspired self-sacrifice; to men who refused themselves nothing, it shows one who refused himself everything."[6]

Augustine lived nominally under the rule of the semidivine emperors, who had by then become remote, awe-inspiring figures and were celebrated by courtly sycophants as "Ever-Victorious" and "Restorers of the World."[7] He was taught the philosophy of the Stoics, with their ideal lives of calm, emotion-suppressing self-sufficiency. He memorized Virgil and Cicero. "My ears were inflamed for Pagan myths, and the more they were scratched the more they itched," he would later recall.[8]

By the time he hit his teenage years, Augustine seems to have established himself as something of a golden boy. "I was called a promising lad," he recalled. He attracted the attention of a local grandee, Romanianus, who agreed to sponsor the young man's education and send him away to centers of learning. Augustine hungered for recognition and admiration and hoped to fulfill the classical dream of living forever in the mouths of posterity.

At seventeen, Augustine went to Carthage to continue his studies. In his spiritual memoir, the *Confessions,* he makes it sound as if he was consumed by lust. "I came to Carthage," he says of his student days, "where the cauldron of illicit loves leapt and boiled about me." Augustine's presence didn't exactly calm things down. He describes himself as a tumultuous young man, his blood boiling with passions, lusts, jealousies, and desires:

> I was not yet in love, but I was in love with love, and from the depths of my need, I hated myself. . . . What I needed most was to love and to be loved, but most of all when I obtained the enjoyment of the body of the person who loved me . . . I rushed headlong into love, eager to be caught. . . . Happily I wrapped those painful bonds around me, and sure enough I would be lashed with red-hot iron rods of jealousy, by suspicion and fear, by bursts of anger and quarrels.

Augustine was apparently history's most

high-maintenance boyfriend. His language is precise. He is not in love with another human being, he is in love with the prospect of being loved. It's all about him. And in his memoir he describes how his disordered lusts fed on themselves. In book 8 of the *Confessions,* Augustine includes an almost clinical description of how his emotional neediness was an addiction:

> I was bound not by an iron imposed by anyone else but by the iron of my own choice. The enemy had a grip on my will and so made a chain for me to hold me prisoner. The consequence of a distorted will is passion. By servitude to passion, habit is formed, and habit to which there is no resistance becomes necessity. By these links . . . connected one to another . . . a harsh bondage held me under constraint.

Augustine was forced to confront, in a very direct way, the fact that he was divided against himself. Part of him sought the shallow pleasures of the world. Part of him disapproved of these desires. His desires were out of harmony with his other faculties. He can imagine a purer way of living, but can't get there. He was restless, unaligned.

In this most fevered writing, Augustine makes it sound like he was some sort of sex-obsessed Caligula. And throughout the centuries many people have read the *Confessions* and concluded that Augustine was really just writing about sex. In fact, it's not exactly clear how wild Augustine really was. If you look at what he accomplished during these years, he seems to have been a studious and responsible young man. He excelled at university. He became a teacher in Carthage and rose up the ladder from one good job to the next. Then he moved to Rome and eventually got a job in Milan, the real center of power, at the court of the emperor Valentinian II. He had a common-law wife, conventional in that day, for about fifteen years. He had one child by this woman and did not cheat on her. He studied Plato and Cicero. His sins, such as they were, seem to have consisted mostly of going to the theater to see plays, and occasionally checking out the women he saw at church. All in all, he seems like a contemporary version of a successful young Ivy Leaguer, a sort of normal meritocrat of the late Roman Empire. In Adam I career terms, Augustine's life was something of a model of upward mobility.

As a young man, Augustine belonged to a strict philosophic sect called the Manichees. This was a little like joining the Communist Party in Russia at the start of the twentieth century. It was joining a group of smart, committed young people who believed they had come into possession of an all-explaining truth.

Manichaeans believed the world is divided into a Kingdom of Light and a Kingdom of Darkness. They believed there is an eternal conflict between all that is good and all that is evil, and that in the course of this conflict, bits of good get trapped within the darkness. Pure spirit can be trapped in mortal flesh.

As a logical system, Manichaeism has several advantages. God, who is on the side of pure good, is protected from the faintest suspicion that he is responsible for evil.[9] Manichaeism also helps excuse individuals from the evils they perform: it wasn't me, I am essentially good, it was the Kingdom of Darkness working through me. As Augustine put it, "It gave joy to my pride to be above guilt, and when I did an evil deed, not to confess that I myself had done it." Finally, once you accepted its premises, Manichaeism was a very rigorous logical system. Everything in the universe could be explained through neat rational steps.

The Manichaeans found it easy to feel superior to everyone else. Plus, they had fun together. Augustine would remember "conversation and laughter and mutual deferrings; shared readings of sweetly phrased books, facetious alternating with serious, heated arguing, to spice our general agreement with dissent; teaching and being taught by turns; the sadness at anyone's absence, and the joy of return."[10] They also practiced asceticism to purify themselves of evil matter. They were celibate and ate only certain foods. They avoided contact with the flesh as much as possible and were served by "hearers" (including Augustine) who did soiling chores for them.

Classical culture placed great emphasis on winning debates, on demonstrations of rhetorical prowess. Augustine, living a life more of head than heart, found he could use Manichaean arguments to easily win debates: "I always used to win more arguments than was good for me, debating with unskilled Christians who had tried to stand up for their faith in argument."[11]

INNER CHAOS

All in all, Augustine was living the Roman dream. But Augustine was unhappy. Inside

382

he felt fragmented. His spiritual energies had nothing to attach to. They dissipated, evaporated. His Adam II life was a mess. "I was tossed to and fro," he writes in the *Confessions,* "I poured myself out, was made to flow away in all directions and boiled off."

At a phenomenally young age, he won the ultimate mark of success. He was given a chance to speak before the imperial court. He found that he was a mere peddler of empty words. He told lies and people loved him for it so long as the lies were well crafted. There was nothing in his life he could truly love, nothing that deserved the highest form of devotion: "I was famished within, deprived of inner food." His hunger for admiration enslaved him rather than delighting him. He was at the whim of other people's facile opinions, sensitive to the slightest criticism, always looking for the next rung on the golden ladder. This frantic pursuit of the glittering vices killed tranquillity.

Augustine's feeling of fragmentation has its modern corollary in the way many contemporary young people are plagued by a frantic fear of missing out. The world has provided them with a superabundance of neat things to do. Naturally, they hunger to seize every opportunity and taste every experience. They want to grab all the goodies in front of them. They want to say yes to every product in the grocery store. They are terrified of missing out on anything that looks exciting. But by not renouncing any of them they spread themselves thin. What's worse, they turn themselves into goodie seekers, greedy for every experience and exclusively focused on self. If you live in this way, you turn into a shrewd tactician, making a series of cautious semicommitments without really surrendering to some larger purpose. You lose the ability to say a hundred noes for the sake of one overwhelming and fulfilling yes.

Augustine found himself feeling increasingly isolated. If you organize your life around your own wants, other people become objects for the satisfaction of your own desires. Everything is coldly instrumental. Just as a prostitute is rendered into an object for the satisfaction of orgasm, so a professional colleague is rendered into an object for the purpose of career networking, a stranger is rendered into an object for the sake of making a sale, a spouse is turned into an object for the purpose of providing you with love.

We use the word "lust" to refer to sexual

desire, but a broader, better meaning is selfish desire. A true lover delights to serve his beloved. But lust is all incoming. The person in lust has a void he needs filled by others. Because he is unwilling to actually serve others and build a full reciprocal relationship, he never fills the emotional emptiness inside. Lust begins with a void and ends with a void.

At one point Augustine called his fifteen-year relationship with his lower-class common-law wife "a mere bargain of lustful love." Still, their relationship could not have been entirely empty. It is hard to imagine a person who lived at Augustine's intense emotional register taking a fifteen-year intimate relationship lightly. He loved the child they had together. He indirectly celebrated his wife's steadfastness in a tract titled "What Is Good in Marriage." When Monica intervened and got rid of the woman so Augustine could marry a rich girl of an appropriate social class, he seems to have suffered: "She was an obstacle to my marriage, the woman I lived with for so long was torn out of my side. My heart, to which she had been grafted, was lacerated, wounded, shedding blood."

Augustine sacrificed this woman for his social standing. The unnamed woman was sent back to Africa without her son, where we are told she vowed to remain celibate the rest of her life. The person chosen to be Augustine's official wife was just ten years old, two years below the legal age of marriage, so Augustine took another concubine to satisfy his cravings in the interim. This is what he was doing in all phases of his life at this point: shedding sacrificial commitments in favor of status and success.

One day, while walking in Milan, he observed a beggar who had clearly just finished a good meal and had a few drinks. The man was joking and joyful. Augustine realized that though he himself toiled and worked all day, fraught with anxieties, the beggar, who did none of these things, was happier than he was. Maybe he was suffering because he was shooting for higher goals, he considered. No, not really, he was seeking the same earthly pleasures as that beggar, but he was finding none of them.

By his late twenties Augustine had become thoroughly alienated. Here he was living an arduous life and it was providing him with none of the nourishment he needed. He had desires that didn't lead to happiness and yet he still followed his desires. What on earth was going on?

Augustine responded to this crisis by looking within himself. You'd think that somebody who has become appalled by his own self-centeredness would immediately head in the direction of self-forgetfulness. His advice would be simple: ignore yourself, pay attention to other people. But Augustine's first step was to undertake an almost scientific expedition into his own mind. It is hard to think of another character in Western history up to that time who did such a thorough excavation of his own psyche.

Looking in, he saw a vast universe beyond his own control. He sees himself with a depth and complexity almost no one had observed before: "Who can map out the various forces at play in one soul, the different kinds of love. . . . Man is a great depth, O Lord; you number his hairs . . . but the hairs of his head are easier by far to count than his feelings, the movements of his heart." The vast internal world is dappled and ever-changing. He perceives the dance of small perceptions and senses great depths below the level of awareness.

Augustine was fascinated, for example, by memory. Sometimes painful memories pop into the mind unbidden. He was amazed by the mind's ability to transcend time and space. "Even while I dwell in darkness and silence, in my memory I can produce colors if I will. . . . Yea, I discern the breath of the lilies from violets, though smelling nothing. . . ."[12] The very scope of a person's memories amazed him:

Great is the force of memory, excessive great, O my God; a large and boundless chamber; whoever sounded the bottom thereof? Yet is this a power of mine and belongs to my nature; nor do I myself comprehend all that I am. Therefore is the mind too straight to contain itself. And where should that be, which containeth not itself? Is it without it and not within? And how then does it not comprehend itself? A wonderful admiration surprises me, amazement seizes me upon this.

At least two great conclusions arose from this internal expedition. First, Augustine came to realize that though people are born with magnificent qualities, original sin had perverted their desires. Up until this point in his life Augustine had fervently desired certain things, like fame and status. These things didn't make him happy. And yet he kept on desiring them.

Left to ourselves, we often desire the wrong things. Whether it's around the dessert tray or in the late-night bar, we know we should choose one thing but end up choosing another. As the Bible says in Romans, "For the good that I would I do not: but the evil which I would not, that I do."

What sort of mysterious creature is a human being, Augustine mused, who can't carry out his own will, who knows his long-term interest but pursues short-term pleasure, who does so much to screw up his own life? This led to the conclusion that people are a problem to themselves. We should regard ourselves with distrust: "I greatly fear my hidden parts,"[13] he wrote.

SMALL AND PETTY CORRUPTIONS

In the *Confessions,* Augustine used an idle teenage prank from his own past to illustrate this phenomenon. One boring evening when he was sixteen, Augustine was hanging out with his buddies and they decided to steal some pears from a nearby orchard. They didn't need the pears. They weren't hungry. They weren't particularly nice pears. They just stole them wantonly and threw them to some pigs for sport.

Looking back, Augustine was astounded

by the pointlessness and the tawdriness of the act. "I lusted to thieve, and did it, compelled by no hunger, nor poverty, but through a cloyedness of well-doing, and pamperedness of iniquity. . . . It was foul, and I loved it; I loved to perish, I loved mine own fault, not that for which I was faulty, but my fault itself. Foul soul, falling from Thy firmament to utter destruction; not seeking aught through the shame, but the shame itself."

Casual readers of the *Confessions* have always wondered why Augustine got so worked up over a childhood prank. I used to think that the theft of the pears was a stand-in for some more heinous crime the teenage boys committed that night, like molesting a girl or some such thing. But for Augustine, the very small purposelessness of the crime is part of its rotten normality. We commit such small perversities all the time, as part of the complacent order of life.

His larger point is that the tropism toward wrong love, toward sin, is at the center of the human personality. People not only sin, we have a weird fascination with sin. If we hear that some celebrity has committed some outrageous scandal, we're kind of disappointed when it turns out the rumor isn't really true. If you leave sweet children to their own devices with nothing to do, before long they will find a way to get into trouble. (The British writer G. K. Chesterton once observed that the reality of sin can be seen on a lovely Sunday afternoon when bored and restless children start torturing the cat.)

Even sweet institutions, like camaraderie and friendship, can be distorted if they are unattached to a higher calling. The story of the stealing of the pears is also the story of a rotten friendship. Augustine realizes he probably wouldn't have done it if he had been alone. It was the desire for camaraderie, for mutual admiration, that egged the boys on into doing what they did. We so fear exclusion from the group that we are willing to do things that we would find unconscionable in other circumstances. When unattached to the right ends, communities can be more barbarous than individuals.

GOD'S PRESENCE

The second large observation that flows from Augustine's internal excavation is that the human mind does not contain itself, but stretches out toward infinity. It's not only rottenness Augustine finds within, but also intimations of perfection, sensations of transcendence, emotions and thoughts and feelings that extend beyond the finite and into another realm. If you wanted to capture Augustine's attitude here, you might say that his thoughts enter and embrace the material world, but then fly up and surpass it.

As Reinhold Niebuhr put it, Augustine's study of memory led him to the "understanding that the human spirit in its depth and heights reaches into eternity and that this vertical dimension is more important for the understanding of man than merely his rational capacity for forming general concepts."[14]

The path inward leads upward. A person goes into himself but finds himself directed toward God's infinity. He senses the nature of God and his eternal creation even in his own mind, a small piece of creation. Centuries later, C. S. Lewis would make a related observation: "In deepest solitude there is a road right out of the self, a commerce with something which, by refusing to identify itself with any object of the senses, or anything whereof we have biological or social need, or anything imagined, or any state of our minds, proclaims itself purely objective." We are all formed within that eternal objective order. Our lives cannot be understood individually, abstracted from it. Sin — the desire to steal the pears — seems to flow from the past through human nature and each individual. At the same time, the longing for holiness, the striving upward, the desire to live a life of goodness and meaning, are also universal.

The result is that people can understand themselves only by looking at forces that transcend themselves. Human life points beyond itself. Augustine looks inside himself and makes contact with certain universal moral sentiments. He is simultaneously aware that he can conceive of perfection, but it is also far beyond his powers to attain. There must be a higher power, an eternal moral order.

As Niebuhr put it, "man is an individual but he is not self-sufficing. The law of his nature is love, a harmonious relation of life to life in obedience to the divine center and source of his life. This law is violated when man seeks to make himself the center and source of his own life."

REFORM

Augustine began to reform his life. His first step was to quit the Manichees. It no longer seemed true to him that the world was neatly divided into forces of pure good and pure evil. Instead, each virtue comes with its own vice — self-confidence with pride, honesty with brutality, courage with recklessness, and so on. The ethicist and theologian Lewis Smedes, expressing an Augustinian thought, describes the mottled nature of our inner world:

> Our inner lives are not partitioned like day and night, with pure light on one side of us and total darkness on the other. Mostly, our souls are shadowed places; we live at the border where our dark sides block our light and throw a shadow over our interior places. . . . We cannot always tell where our light ends and our shadow begins or where our shadow ends and our darkness begins.[15]

Augustine also came to believe that the Manichees were infected with pride. Having a closed, all-explaining model of reality appealed to their vanity; it gave them the illusion that they had intellectually mastered all things. But it made them cold to mystery and unable to humble themselves before the complexities and emotions that, as Augustine put it, "make the heart deep." They possessed reason, but no wisdom.

Augustine hung between worlds. He

wanted to live a truthful life. But he wasn't ready to give up his career, or sex, or some of his worldly pursuits. He wanted to use the old methods to achieve better outcomes. That is to say, he was going to start with the core assumption that had always been the basis for his ambitious meritocratic life: that you are the prime driver of your life. The world is malleable enough to be shaped by you. To lead a better life you just have to work harder, or use more willpower, or make better decisions.

This is more or less how many people try to rearrange their life today. They attack it like a homework assignment or a school project. They step back, they read self-help books like *The Seven Habits of Highly Effective People*. They learn the techniques for greater self-control. They even establish a relationship with God in the same way they would go after a promotion or an advanced degree — by conquest: by reading certain books, attending services regularly, practicing spiritual disciplines such as regular prayer, doing their spiritual homework.

PRIDE

But eventually Augustine came to believe that you can't gradually reform yourself. He concluded that you can't really lead a good life by using old methods. That's because the method is the problem. The crucial flaw in his old life was the belief that he could be the driver of his own journey. So long as you believe that you are the captain of your own life, you will be drifting farther and farther from the truth.

You can't lead a good life by steering yourself, in the first place, because you do not have the capacity to do so. The mind is such a vast, unknown cosmos you can never even know yourself by yourself. Your emotions are so changeable and complex you can't order your emotional life by yourself. Your appetites are so infinite you can never satisfy them on your own. The powers of self-deception are so profound you are rarely fully honest with yourself.

Furthermore, the world is so complex, and fate so uncertain, that you can never really control other people or the environment effectively enough to be master of your own destiny. Reason is not powerful enough to build intellectual systems or models to allow you to accurately understand the world around you or anticipate what is to come. Your willpower is not strong enough to successfully police your desires. If you really did have that kind of power, then New Year's resolutions would work. Diets would work. The bookstores wouldn't be full of self-help books. You'd need just one and that would do the trick. You'd follow its advice, solve the problems of living, and the rest of the genre would become obsolete. The existence of more and more self-help books is proof that they rarely work.

The problem, Augustine came to believe, is that if you think you can organize your own salvation you are magnifying the very sin that keeps you from it. To believe that you can be captain of your own life is to suffer the sin of pride.

What is pride? These days the word "pride" has positive connotations. It means feeling good about yourself and the things associated with you. When we use it negatively, we think of the arrogant person, someone who is puffed up and egotistical, boasting and strutting about. But that is not really the core of pride. That is just one way the disease of pride presents itself.

By another definition, pride is building your happiness around your accomplishments, using your work as the measure of your worth. It is believing that you can arrive at fulfillment on your own, driven by your own individual efforts.

Pride can come in bloated form. This is the puffed-up Donald Trump style of pride.

This person wants people to see visible proof of his superiority. He wants to be on the VIP list. In conversation, he boasts, he brags. He needs to see his superiority reflected in other people's eyes. He believes that this feeling of superiority will eventually bring him peace.

That version is familiar. But there are other proud people who have low self-esteem. They feel they haven't lived up to their potential. They feel unworthy. They want to hide and disappear, to fade into the background and nurse their own hurts. We don't associate them with pride, but they are still, at root, suffering from the same disease. They are still yoking happiness to accomplishment; it's just that they are giving themselves a D− rather than an A+. They tend to be just as solipsistic, and in their own way as self-centered, only in a self-pitying and isolating way rather than in an assertive and bragging way.

One key paradox of pride is that it often combines extreme self-confidence with extreme anxiety. The proud person often appears self-sufficient and egotistical but is really touchy and unstable. The proud person tries to establish self-worth by winning a great reputation, but of course this makes him utterly dependent on the gossipy and unstable crowd for his own identity. The proud person is competitive. But there are always other people who might do better. The most ruthlessly competitive person in the contest sets the standard that all else must meet or get left behind. Everybody else has to be just as monomaniacally driven to success. One can never be secure. As Dante put it, the "ardor to outshine / Burned in my bosom with a kind of rage."

Hungry for exaltation, the proud person has a tendency to make himself ridiculous. Proud people have an amazing tendency to turn themselves into buffoons, with a combover that fools nobody, with golden bathroom fixtures that impress nobody, with name-dropping stories that inspire nobody. Every proud man, Augustine writes, "heeds himself, and he who pleases himself seems great to himself. But he who pleases himself pleases a fool, for he himself is a fool when he is pleasing himself."[16]

Pride, the minister and writer Tim Keller has observed, is unstable because other people are absentmindedly or intentionally treating the proud man's ego with less reverence than he thinks it deserves. He continually finds that his feelings are hurt. He is perpetually putting up a front. The self-cultivator spends more energy trying to display the fact that he is happy — posting highlight reel Facebook photos and all the rest — than he does actually being happy.

Augustine suddenly came to realize that the solution to his problem would come only after a transformation more fundamental than any he had previously entertained, a renunciation of the very idea that he could be the source of his own solution.

ELEVATION

Augustine later wrote that God sprinkled bitterness and discontent over his life to draw him toward God. "The greater I got in age, the worse I got in emptiness, as I could not conceive of any substance except the kind I saw with these eyes." Or, as he most famously put it, "our hearts are restless until we rest in Thee."

Augustine's pain during his years of ambition, at least as he describes it later, is not just the pain of someone who is self-centered and unstable. It is the pain of someone who is self-centered and unstable but who has a deep sensation that there is a better way to live, if only he could figure out what it is. As other converts have put it, they are so rooted in God that even when they haven't found God they feel the lack.

They are aware of a divine absence, which picks at them from the inside, and that absence is evidence of a presence. Augustine had an inkling of what he needed in order to feel peace, but still, perversely, was unmotivated to actually travel there.

To move from a fragmentary life to a cohesive one, from an opportunistic life to a committed life, it is necessary to close off certain possibilities. Augustine, like most of us in this situation, didn't want to close his options and renounce the things that made him feel good. His natural inclination was to think his anxieties could be solved if he got more of what he desired, not less. So he hung on an emotional precipice between a religious life he was afraid to sacrifice for and a secular one he detested but would not renounce. He commanded himself to decenter himself and put God at the center of his life. But he refused to obey himself.

He worried about his reputation. He worried he'd have to give up sex, sensing that for him, celibacy would be a necessary part of a religiously devoted life. "This controversy in my heart was self against self only." Looking back, he recalled, "I was in love with the idea of the happy life, but I feared to find it in its true place and I sought for it by running away from it."

His general solution was to delay. Make me virtuous — but not yet.

In the *Confessions,* Augustine paints the scene when the delay finally ended. He was sitting in a garden talking with a friend, Alypius, who told him some stories about monks in Egypt who gave up everything to serve God. Augustine was amazed. The people who were not part of the elite educational system were out doing amazing things while the graduates of that system lived for themselves. "What ails us?" Augustine cried. "The unlearned start up and take heaven by force and we, with this our learning, but without heart, wallow in flesh and blood."

In this fever of doubt and self-reproach, Augustine stood up and strode away while Alypius gazed on in stunned silence. Augustine began pacing around the garden, and Alypius got up and followed him. Augustine felt his bones crying out to end this self-divided life, to stop turning and tossing this way and that. He tore at his hair, beat his forehead, locked his fingers and hunched over, clasping his knee. It seemed as if God was beating on his insides, inflicting a "severe mercy," redoubling the lashes of fear and shame that afflicted him. "Be it done now, be it done now," he cried to himself.

But his worldly desires would not give up so easily. Thoughts jumped into his head. It was as if they were plucking at his garments. "Are you going to cast us off? You'll never experience our pleasures ever again?" Augustine hesitated, wondering, "Do I really think I can live without these pleasures?"

Then there appeared in his mind a thought, the ideal of dignified chastity and self-control. In the *Confessions,* he dresses up this thought in metaphorical terms, as a vision of a woman, Lady Continence. He does not describe her as an ascetic, puritanical goddess. On the contrary, she is an earthy, fecund woman. She's not renouncing joy and sensuality; she's offering better versions. She describes all the young men and women who have already renounced the pleasures of the world for the pleasures of the faith. "Can't you do what they did?" she asks. "Why are you standing apart in yourself?"

Augustine blushed, still undecided. "There arose a mighty storm, bringing a mighty shower of tears." He got up and walked away from Alypius again, wanting to be alone with his weeping. This time Alypius didn't follow but let Augustine go.

Augustine cast himself down under a fig tree, giving way to his tears. Then he heard a voice, which sounded like the voice of a boy or a girl from another house neighboring the garden. It said, "Take up and read. Take up and read." Augustine felt a sense of immediate resolve. He opened up a nearby Bible and read the first passage on which his eyes fell: "Not in rioting and drunkenness, not in chambering and wantonness, not in strife and envying; but put ye in the Lord Jesus Christ, and make not provision for the flesh, in concupiscence."

Augustine had no need to read any further. He felt a light flooding his heart and erasing every shadow. He felt a sudden turning of his will, a sudden desire to renounce worldly, finite pleasures and to live for Christ. It felt all the sweeter to be without shallow sweet things. What he had once been so terrified of losing was now a delight to dismiss.

Naturally, he went to Monica straightaway and told her what had happened. We can imagine her screams of joy, her praises to God for answering a lifetime of prayers. As Augustine put it, "thou had convertest me unto Thyself. . . . And Thou didst convert her mourning into joy, much more plentiful than she had desired, and in a much more precious and purer way than she required, by having grandchildren of my body."

The scene in the garden is not really a conversion scene. Augustine was already a Christian of a sort. After the garden he does not immediately have a fully formed view of what a life in Christ means. The scene in the garden is an elevation scene. Augustine says no to one set of desires and pleasures and rises to a higher set of joys and pleasures.

AGENCY

This elevation is not only a renunciation of sex — though in Augustine's case it seemed to involve that. It's a renunciation of the whole ethos of self-cultivation. The basic formula of the Adam I world is that effort produces reward. If you work hard, play by the rules, and take care of things yourself, you can be the cause of your own good life.

Augustine came to conclude that this all was incomplete. He didn't withdraw from the world. He spent the rest of his life as a politically active bishop, engaging in brutal and sometimes vicious public controversies. But his public work and effort was nestled in a total surrender. He came to conclude that the way to inner joy is not through agency and action, it's through surrender and receptivity to God. The point, according to this view, is to surrender, or at least suppress, your will, your ambition, your desire to achieve victory on your own. The point is to acknowledge that God is the chief driver here and that he already has a plan for you. God already has truths he wants you to live by.

What's more, God has already justified your existence. You may have the feeling that you are on trial in this life, that you have to work and achieve and make your mark to earn a good verdict. Some days you provide evidence for the defense that you are a worthwhile person. Some days you provide evidence for the prosecution that you are not. But as Tim Keller put it, in Christian thought, the trial is already over. The verdict came in before you even began your presentation. That's because Jesus stood trial for you. He took the condemnation that you deserve.

Imagine the person you love most in the world getting nailed to wood as penalty for the sins you yourself committed. Imagine the emotions that would go through your mind as you watched that. This is, in the Christian mind, just a miniature version of the sacrifice Jesus made for you. As Keller puts it, "God imputes Christ's perfect performance to us as if it were our own, and adopts us into His family."[17]

The problem with the willful mindset is, as Jennifer Herdt put it in her book *Putting On Virtue*, "God wants to give us a gift, and we want to buy it."[18] We continually want to earn salvation and meaning through work and achievement. But salvation and meaning are actually won, in this way of living, when you raise the white flag of surrender and allow grace to flood your soul.

The implied posture here is one of submission, arms high, wide open and outstretched, face tilted up, eyes gazing skyward, calm with patient but passionate waiting. Augustine wants you to adopt this sort of surrendered posture. That posture flows from an awareness of need, of one's own insufficiency. Only God has the power to order your inner world, not you. Only God has the power to orient your desires and reshape your emotions, not you.[19]

This posture of receptiveness, for Augustine and much Christian thought since, starts with the feeling of smallness and sinfulness one gets next to the awesome presence of God. Humility comes with daily reminders of your own brokenness. Humility relieves you of the awful stress of trying to be superior all the time. It inverts your attention and elevates the things we tend to look down on.

Throughout his early life, Augustine had been climbing upward, getting out of Thagaste, moving to Carthage, Rome, and Milan in search of more prestigious circles, more brilliant company. He lived, as we do today, in a thoroughly class-driven society, striving upward. But in Christianity, at least in its ideal form, the sublime is not in the prestigious and the lofty but in the everyday and the lowly. It is in the washing of feet, not in triumphal arches. Whoever exalts himself shall be humbled. Whoever humbles himself shall be exalted. One goes down in order to rise up. As Augustine put it, "Where there's humility, there's majesty; where there's weakness, there's might; where there's death, there's life. If you want to get these things, don't disdain those."[20]

The hero of this sort of humble life is not averse to the pleasures of praise, but the petty distinctions you earn for yourself do not really speak to your essential value as a human being. God possesses talents so all-encompassing that in relation to them, the difference between the most brilliant Nobel laureate and the dimmest nitwit are simply a matter of degree. Every soul is equal in the most important sense.

Augustinian Christianity demands a different tone of voice, not the peremptory command of the master to the servant but the posture of coming in under, coming to each relationship from below, and hoping to serve upward. It's not that worldly achievement and public acclaim are automatically bad, it's just that they are won on a planet that is just a resting place for the soul and not our final destination. Success here, acquired badly, can make ultimate success less likely, and that ultimate success is not achieved through competition with others.

It's not quite right to say that Augustine had a low view of human nature. He believed that each individual is made in God's image and possesses a dignity that merits the suffering and death of Jesus. It's more accurate to say that he believed human beings are incapable of living well on their own, as autonomous individuals — incapable of ordering their desires on their own. They can find that order, and that proper love, only by submitting their will to God's. It's not that human beings are pathetic; it's just that they will be restless until they rest in Him.

Augustine's thought, and much Christian teaching generally, challenges the code of the self-cultivator in one more crucial way. In Augustine's view, people do not get what they deserve; life would be hellish if they did. Instead people get much more than they deserve. God offers us grace, which is his unmerited love. God's protection and care comes precisely because you do not deserve it and cannot earn it. Grace doesn't come to you because you've performed well on your job or even made great sacrifices as a parent or as a friend. Grace comes to you as part of the gift of being created.

One of the things you have to do in order to receive grace is to renounce the idea that you can earn it. You have to renounce the meritocratic impulse that you can win a victory for God and get rewarded for your effort. Then you have to open up to it. You do not know when grace will come to you. But people who are open and sensitive to it testify that they have felt grace at the oddest and at the most needed times.

Paul Tillich puts it this way in his collection of essays, *Shaking the Foundations:*

> Grace strikes us when we are in great pain and restlessness. It strikes us when

we walk through the dark valley of a meaningless and empty life. . . . It strikes us when our disgust for our own being, our indifference, our weakness, our hostility, and our lack of direction and composure have become intolerable to us. It strikes us when, year after year, the longed-for perfection of life does not appear, when the old compulsions reign within us as they have for decades, when despair destroys all joy and courage. Sometimes at that moment a wave of light breaks into our darkness and it is as though a voice were saying: "You are accepted. *You are accepted,* accepted by that which is greater than you, and the name of which you do not know. Do not ask for the name now; perhaps you will find it later. Do not try to do anything now; perhaps later you will do much. Do not seek for anything; do not perform anything; do not intend anything. *Simply accept the fact that you are accepted.*" If that happens to us, we experience grace. After such an experience we may not be better than before and we may not believe more than before. But everything is transformed. In that moment, grace conquers sin, and reconciliation bridges the gulf of estrangement. And nothing is demanded of this experience, no religious or moral or intellectual presupposition, nothing but acceptance.[21]

Those of us in mainstream culture are used to the idea that people get loved because they are kind, or funny, or attractive, or smart, or attentive. It's surprisingly difficult to receive a love that feels unearned. But once you accept the fact that you are accepted, there is a great desire to go meet this love and reciprocate this gift.

If you are passionately in love with a person, you naturally seek to delight her all the time. You want to buy her presents. You want to stand outside her window singing ridiculous songs. This is a replica of the way those who feel touched by grace seek to delight God. They take pleasure in tasks that might please him. They work tirelessly at tasks that they think might glorify him. The desire to rise up and meet God's love can arouse mighty energies.

And as people rise up and seek to meet God, their desires slowly change. In prayer, people gradually reform their desires so that more and more they want the things they believe will delight God rather than the things they used to think would delight themselves.

The ultimate conquest of self, in this view, is not won by self-discipline, or an awful battle within self. It is won by going out of self, by establishing a communion with God and by doing the things that feel natural in order to return God's love.

This is the process that produces an inner transformation. One day you turn around and notice that everything inside has been realigned. The old loves no longer thrill. You love different things and are oriented in different directions. You have become a different sort of person. You didn't get this way simply by following this or that moral code, or adopting a drill sergeant's discipline or certain habits. You did it instead because you reordered your loves, and as Augustine says again and again, you become what you love.

HUMBLE AMBITION

We have arrived, therefore, at a different theory of motivation. To recapitulate the Augustinian process, it starts with the dive inside to see the vastness of the inner cosmos. The inward dive leads outward, toward an awareness of external truth and God. That leads to humility as one feels small in contrast to the almighty. That leads to a posture of surrender, of self-emptying, as one makes space for God. That opens the way for you to receive God's grace. That gift arouses an immense feeling of gratitude, a desire to love back, to give back and to delight. That in turn awakens vast energies. Over the centuries many people have been powerfully motivated to delight God. This motivation has been as powerful as the other great motivations, the desire for money, fame, and power.

The genius of this conception is that as people become more dependent on God, their capacity for ambition and action increases. Dependency doesn't breed passivity; it breeds energy and accomplishment.

THE OLD LOVES

After his "conversion" in the garden, Augustine did not live a tranquil, easy life. He enjoyed an initial burst of optimism, but then came the thudding realization that his own sinfulness was still there. His own false loves had not magically died away. As his biographer Peter Brown puts it, "The past can come very close: its powerful and complex emotions have only recently passed away; we can still feel their contours through the thin layer of new feeling that has grown over them."[22]

When Augustine writes the *Confessions,*

which is in some sense a memoir of his early manhood, he is not writing them as genial reminiscences. He is writing them as a necessary reassessment occasioned by hard times. As Brown writes, "He must base his future on a different view of himself: and how could he gain this view, except by reinterpreting just that part of his past, that had culminated in the conversion, on which he had until recently placed such high hopes?"[23]

Augustine is reminding believers that the center of their lives is not in themselves. The material world is beautiful and to be savored and enjoyed, but the pleasures of this world are most delicious when they are savored in the larger context of God's transcendent love. Augustine's prayers and meditations are filled with celebrations of the world that surpass the world. In one of his most beautiful meditations, for example, Augustine asks, "What do I love when I love my God?"

It is not physical beauty or temporal glory or the brightness of light dear to earthy eyes, or the sweet melodies of all kinds of songs, or the gentle odor of flowers and ointments and perfumes, or manna or honey, or limbs welcoming the embraces

415

of the flesh; it is not these I love when I love my God. Yet there is a light I love, and a food, and a kind of embrace when I love my God — a light, voice, odor, food, embrace of my innerness, where my soul is floodlit by light which space cannot contain, where there is sound that time cannot seize, where there is a perfume which no breeze disperses, where there is a taste for food no amount of eating can lessen, where there is a bond of union that no satiety can part. That's what I love when I love my God.

This is living life in a broader context. As the theologian Lisa Fullam has put it, "Humility is a virtue of self-understanding in context, acquired by the practice of other centeredness."

HUSH

After his renunciation in the garden, Augustine dragged himself through the end of the school term, teaching the rhetoric he no longer believed in. Then he, his mother, his son, and a group of friends went to stay for five months at the villa of a Milanese friend of theirs whose wife was Christian. The villa was in Cassiciacum, twenty miles north of Milan. The party engaged in a series of colloquia, which have the feel of a group of scholars meditating together on deep things. Augustine was delighted that Monica had enough native smarts to keep up with and even lead the conversations. Then Augustine decided to return home to Africa, where he could live a secluded life of prayer and contemplation with his mother.

The party headed south — over the same road, biographers remind us, that his mistress had traveled when she had been dispatched two years before. They hit a military blockade and made it only as far as the town of Ostia. One day in Ostia, Augustine was looking out a window that overlooked a garden (many events in his life take place in gardens), and he was talking with his mother. Monica clearly had a sense by this time that death was coming to her. She was fifty-six.

Augustine describes their conversation, saying that together they experienced "the very highest delight of the earthly senses, in the very purest material light . . . in respect of the sweetness of that light." But in the intimacy between mother and son, they began talking about God, and they "did by degrees pass through all things bodily, even the very heaven when sun and moon and stars shine upon the earth." From these material things "we came to our own minds and went beyond them into the realm of pure spirit."

In describing their talk, Augustine includes a long sentence that is hard to parse, but it includes, in some translations, the word "hushed" over and over — the tumult of the flesh was hushed, the waters and the air were hushed, all dreams and shallow visions were hushed, tongues were hushed, everything that passes away was hushed, the self was hushed in moving beyond the self into a sort of silence. Mother or son makes an exclamation: "We did not make ourselves, he who made us never passes away." But after saying this, that voice, too, is hushed. And "He who made them, He alone speaks, not through men or women, but by himself." And Augustine and Monica heard God's word "not through any tongue of flesh, or Angels' voices, not sound of thunder, nor in the dark riddle of similitude," but they heard "his very Self." And they sighed after a moment of pure understanding.

Augustine is describing here a perfect moment of elevation: hushed . . . hushed . . . hushed . . . hushed. All the clamors of the world slip into silence. Then a desire to praise the creator comes over them, but then even that praise is hushed amid the kenosis, the self-emptying. And then comes the infusing vision of eternal wisdom, what Augustine calls the "glad hidden depths." One imagines mother and son lost in joy in this climactic encounter. After the years of tears and anger, control and escape, rupture and reconciliation, pursuit and manipulation, friendship and fighting, they finally achieve some sort of outward-facing union. They come together and dissolve together in contemplation of what they both now love.

Monica tells him, "Son, for mine own part I have no further delight in any thing in this life. . . . One thing there was for which I desired to linger for a while in this life, that I might see thee a Catholic Christian before I died. My God has done this for me more than abundantly."

To be healed is to be broken open. The proper course is outward. C. S. Lewis observed that if you enter a party consciously trying to make a good impression, you probably won't end up making one. That happens only when you are thinking about the other people in the room. If you begin an art project by trying to be original, you probably won't be original.

And so it is with tranquillity. If you set out trying to achieve inner peace and a sense of holiness, you won't get it. That happens only obliquely, when your attention is a focused on something external. That happens only as a byproduct of a state of self-forgetfulness, when your energies are focused on something large.

For Augustine, that's the crucial change. Knowledge is not enough for tranquillity and goodness, because it doesn't contain the motivation to be good. Only love impels action. We don't become better because we acquire new information. We become better because we acquire better loves. We don't become what we know. Education is a process of love formation. When you go to a school, it should offer you new things to love.

A few days later, Monica came down with her fatal illness, which took only nine days to carry her off. She told Augustine that it was no longer important for her to be buried back in Africa, because no place was far from God. She told him that in all their tribulations she had never heard him utter a sharp word to her.

At the moment of her death, Augustine bent over and closed her eyes. "An innumerable sorrow flowed up into my heart and would have overflowed in tears." At that moment, Augustine, not even now fully renouncing classical Stoicism, felt he should exercise self-command and not give in to weeping. "But my eyes, under the mind's strong constraint, held back their flow and I stood dry-eyed. In that struggle it went very hard with me. . . . Because I had now lost the great comfort of her, my soul was wounded and my very life torn asunder, for it had been one life — made of hers and mine together."

Augustine's friends gathered around him, while he still tried to repress his grief: "For I was very much ashamed that these human emotions could have such power over me. . . . I felt a new grief at my grief and so was afflicted by a double sorrow."

Augustine went to take a bath and soothe his self-division, then fell asleep and awoke feeling better. "And then, little by little, I began to recover my former feeling about Your handmaid, remembering how loving and devout was her conversation with me, of which I was thus suddenly deprived. And I found solace in weeping in Your sight both about her and for her, about myself and for myself."

■ ■ ■ ■

Monica had entered a world in which the Roman Empire dominated Europe and a rationalist philosophy dominated thinking. In his writing, Augustine uses her as an example of faith against pure rationalism, of spiritual relentlessness against worldly ambition. He would spend the rest of his life as a bishop fighting and preaching and writing, fighting and arguing. He achieved the immortality he sought in his youth, but he did it in an unexpected way. He started with the belief that he could control his own life. He had to renounce that, to sink down into a posture of openness and surrender. Then, after that retreat, he was open enough to receive grace, to feel gratitude and rise upward. This is life with an advance-retreat-advance shape. Life, death, and resurrection. Moving down to dependence to gain immeasurable height.

CHAPTER 9
SELF-EXAMINATION

Samuel Johnson was born in Lichfield, England, in 1709. His father was an unsuccessful bookseller. His mother was an uneducated woman who nonetheless thought she had married beneath her. "My father and mother had not much happiness from each other," Johnson would remember. "They seldom conversed; for my father could not bear to talk of his affairs; and my mother, being unacquainted with books, could not talk of anything else. . . . Of business she had no distinct conception; and therefore her discourse was composed only of complaint, fear, and suspicion."[1]

Johnson was a frail infant who surprised everybody by living through the ordeal of birth. He was immediately handed over to a wet nurse whose milk infected him with tuberculosis of the lymph nodes, which made him permanently blind in one eye, with poor vision in the other, and deaf in one ear. He later developed smallpox, which left his face permanently scarred. His doctors, in an attempt to relieve his disease, made an incision, without anesthesia, in his left arm. They kept the wound open with horsehair for six years, periodically discharging the fluids they associated with disease. They also cut into his neck glands. The operation was botched and Johnson went through life with deep scars running down the left side of his face from his ear to his jaw. Physically, he was large, ugly, scarred, and ogrelike.

He fought vehemently against his maladies. One day, as a child, he was walking home from school but could not see the gutter in the street, and feared tripping on it. He got down on all fours and crawled along the street, peering closely at the curb so that he could measure his step. When a teacher offered to give him a hand, he became enraged and furiously beat her away.

All his life, Johnson was suspicious of the self-indulgence that he believed the chronically ill were prone to. "Disease produces much selfishness," he wrote toward the end of his life. "A man in pain is looking after ease." He responded to his illness, Walter Jackson Bate notes, with "a powerful sense of self demand, a feeling of complete personal responsibility. . . . What is of special interest to us now is how quickly as a small child — in discovering the physical differences between himself and others — he began groping his way to the independence and defiant disregard for physical limitations that he was always to maintain."[2]

Johnson's education was thorough and severe. He went to a school that trained him in the classical curriculum that was the core of Western education from the Renaissance until the twentieth century — Ovid, Virgil, Horace, the Athenians. He learned Latin and Greek. When he was lazy he was beaten. His teachers would have the boys lean over their chairs and then they'd swing at them with a rod. "And this I do to save you from the gallows," they'd say.[3] Later in life, Johnson would have some complaints about the beatings. But he believed the rod was still kinder than psychological pressure and emotional manipulation — the sort of suasion many parents use today.

Johnson's most important education was self-administered. Though he never warmed to his elderly father, he read through his father's stock of books, devouring travel books, romances, and histories, with a special taste for daring tales of chivalry. He read vividly. At age nine he was reading *Hamlet* when he came upon the ghost scene. He ran frantically out into the street, terrified and desperate to be reminded of the living world. His memory was tenacious. He could read a prayer once or twice and recite it for the rest of his life. He seems to have remembered everything he read, bringing obscure authors into conversations decades after encountering them. When he was a small boy, his father would parade him before dinner parties and force him to recite for the admiring crowd. Young Sam was disgusted by his father's vanity.

When Johnson was nineteen, his mother came into a small legacy, which was enough to pay for a single year at Oxford. Johnson promptly made the least of the opportunity. He came to Oxford fully aware of his ability, burning with ambition, panting, as he would later put it, for a name and the "pleasing hope of endless fame." But, accustomed to his independent autodidactic life and feeling financially and socially inferior to many of the students around him, he was incapable of playing by Oxford rules. Instead of submitting to the torpid system, he battled against it, reacting to the slightest touch of authority with rude aggression. "I was mad and violent," he would later recall. "It was bitterness which they mistook for frolic. I was miserably poor, and I thought to fight my way by my literature and my wit; so I disregarded all power and all authority."[4]

Johnson was recognized as a brilliant student, winning praise for his translation into Latin of a poem by Alexander Pope; Pope himself said he couldn't tell which was better, the Latin version or the original. But he was also rebellious, rude, and lazy. He told his tutor that he had neglected to attend lectures because he preferred to go sledding. He worked in a stop-and-start pattern that he would use all his life. He would sit in complete indolence for days, staring at a clock face but unable even to tell the time, and then he would rise to a feverish level of activity and fire off an assignment in a single masterful draft just before it was due.

Johnson became a Christian at Oxford, after a fashion. He sat down one day with the theological book by William Law titled *A Serious Call to a Devout and Holy Life,* expecting, he wrote, "to find it a dull book (as such books generally are) and perhaps to laugh at it. But I found Law quite an overmatch for me, and this was the first occasion of my thinking in earnest of religion, after I became capable of rational inquiry." Law's book, like Johnson's later moral writing, is concrete and practical. He invents characters to construct satirical portraits of types who neglect their spiritual interests. He emphasized that worldly pursuits fail to fill the heart. Christianity didn't really change Johnson, but it made him more of what he already was — extremely suspicious of self-indulgence, rigorous in his moral demands of himself.

Aware of his own mental abilities, he fixed his attention all his life on the biblical parable of the talents, and the lesson that the "wicked and slothful servant" who has not fully used the talents that have been bestowed upon him will be cast "into outer darkness, where there shall be weeping and gnashing of teeth." Johnson's God was a rigorous God more than a loving or healing God. Johnson would spend his life with a sense of being perpetually judged, aware of his inadequacy, fearing his own damnation.

After that one year at Oxford, Johnson's money ran out, and he returned to Lichfield in disgrace. He suffered what seems to have been a bout of severe depression. As his chronicler, James Boswell, would write, "He felt himself overwhelmed with a horrible hypochondria, with perpetual irritation, fretfulness, and impatience; and with a dejection, gloom and despair, which made existence misery."[5]

Johnson took thirty-two-mile hikes to occupy himself. He may have contemplated suicide. He seemed completely incapable of controlling his body movements. He developed a series of tics and gestures that look to many modern experts like Tourette's syndrome. He would twist his hands, rock back and forth, roll his head in a strange and compulsive manner. He would emit a bizarre whistling sound and display symptoms of obsessive compulsive disorder, tapping his cane in odd rhythms as he walked down the street, counting the number of steps it took him to enter a room and then reentering if the number wasn't right. To dine with him was a challenge. He ate like a wild animal, devouring huge quantities of food in messy haste, spewing it over his notoriously slovenly clothing. The novelist Fanny Burney would write, "[He] has a face most ugly, a person the most awkward, & manners the most singular that ever were, or ever can be seen. He has almost perpetual convulsive motions, either of his hands, lips, feet, knees and sometimes all together."[6] Strangers would see him in a tavern and mistake him for a village idiot, or somebody with a debilitating mental affliction. He would then astonish them by unfurling full paragraphs studded with erudition and classical allusion. He seemed to enjoy this effect.

Johnson's misery continued for years. He tried to teach, but a man with his tics was bound to generate more ridicule than respect from his students. The school he started, one historian noted, was "perhaps the most unsuccessful private school in the history of education." He married Elizabeth Porter when he was twenty-six and she was forty-six, in what many thought an odd pairing. Biographers have never known what to make of Porter, whom he called Tetty. Was she beautiful or haggard? Was she philosophical or frivolous? She, to her credit, saw a sign of the future greatness beneath the rough exterior, and he, to his credit, would remain loyal to her throughout his life. He was a very tender and grateful lover, with a great capacity for empathy and affection, but they spent many of those years apart, leading separate lives. It was her money that furnished the capital to start the school, and much of it was lost.

Until his late twenties, his life had been a steady calamity. On March 2, 1737, Johnson set off for London with his former pupil David Garrick (who would go on to become one of the most famous actors in British history). Johnson settled near Grub Street and began scratching out a living as a freelance writer. He wrote on any subject and across genres: poetry, drama, political essays, literary criticism, gossip items, casual essays, and on and on. The life of a Grub Street hack was hand-to-mouth, chaotic, disheveled, and frequently miserable. One poet, Samuel Boyse, pawned all his clothing and sat on his bed naked but for his blanket. He cut a hole in it large enough to stick his arm through and wrote poems on sheets of paper balanced on his knee. When he was writing a book, he would pawn the first few pages to raise money to pay for food so he could complete the next ones.[7] Johnson never quite sank to that low state, but much of the time, especially in the early years, he barely scraped by.

During this time, though, Johnson performed one of the most amazing feats in the history of journalism. In 1738, the House of Commons passed a law that it would be a "breach of privilege" to publish parliamentary speeches. *The Gentleman's Magazine* decided to publish thinly veiled fictional accounts of the speeches, to let the public know what was going on. For two and a half years, Johnson was the sole author, though he set foot in Parliament only once. A source would tell him who spoke and in what order, what general positions they took and the arguments they made. Johnson would then make up eloquent speeches, as they might have been given. These speeches were so well written that the speakers themselves did not disavow them. They were taken as authentic transcripts for at least the next twenty years. As late as 1899, they were still appearing in anthologies of the world's best oratory, credited to the alleged speakers and not to Johnson.[8] Once, overhearing the company at a dinner party raving over the brilliance of a speech by William Pitt the Elder, Johnson interrupted, "That speech I wrote in a garret in Exeter Street."[9]

Johnson was living a life, familiar to us now but more unusual in his own day, in which he was thrown continually back on himself. Without a settled trade, like farming or teaching, separated from the rootedness of extended family life, he was compelled to live as a sort of freelancer according to his wits. His entire destiny — his financial security, his standing in his community, his friendships, his opinions and meaning as a person — were determined by the ideas that flashed through his mind.

The Germans have a word for this condition: *Zerrissenheit* — loosely, "falling-to-pieces-ness." This is the loss of internal coherence that can come from living a multitasking, pulled-in-a-hundred-directions existence. This is what Kierkegaard called "the dizziness of freedom." When the external constraints are loosened, when a person can do what he wants, when there are a thousand choices and distractions, then life can lose coherence and direction if there isn't a strong internal structure.

Johnson's internal fragmentation was exacerbated by his own nature. "Everything about his character and manners was forcible and violent," Boswell observed — the way he spoke, ate, read, loved, and lived. Moreover, many of his qualities were at odds with one another. Plagued by tics and mannerisms, he could not fully control his own body. Plagued by depression and instability, he could not fully control his own mind. He was an intensely social person who warned all his life against the perils of solitude, but he was stuck in a literary profession that required long stretches of private time for composition. He effectively lived a bachelor's life, but he had an enormously strong sexual drive and struggled all his life with what he regarded as his "polluting thoughts." He had a short attention span. "I have read few books through," he confessed; "they are generally so repulsive I cannot."[10]

IMAGINATION

He was also plagued by his own imagination. We in post-romantic times tend to regard the imagination as an innocent, childlike faculty that provides us with creativity and sweet visions. Johnson saw the imagination as something to be feared as much as treasured. It was at its worst in the middle of the night. In those dark hours his imagination would plague him, introducing nighttime terrors, jealousies, feelings of worthlessness, and vain hopes and fantasies of superficial praise and admiration. The imagination, in Johnson's darker view, offers up ideal visions of experiences like marriage, which then leave us disappointed when the visions don't come true. It is responsible for hypochondria and the other anxieties that exist only in our heads. It invites us to make envious comparisons, imagining scenes in which we triumph over our rivals. The imagination simplifies our endless desires and causes us to fantasize that they can be fulfilled. It robs us of much of the enjoyment of our achievements by compelling us to think upon the things left undone. It distracts us from the pleasures of the moment by leaping forward to unattained future possibilities.

Johnson was always impressed, puzzled, and terrified by the runaway nature of the mind. We are all a bit like Don Quixote, he observed, fighting villains of our own imagining, living within ideas of our own concoction rather than in reality as it actually is. Johnson's brain was perpetually on the move, at odds with itself. As he wrote in one of his Adventurer essays, "We have less reason to be surprised or offended when we find others differ from us in opinions because we very often differ from ourselves."

Johnson did not just surrender to these mental demons; he fought them. He was combative, with others and with himself. When an editor accused him of wasting time, Johnson, a large and powerful man, pushed the man over and put his foot on his neck. "He was insolent and I beat him, and he was a blockhead and I told of it."

His diaries are rife with self-criticism and vows to organize his time better. From 1738: "Oh lord, enable me . . . in redeeming the time which I have spent in Sloth." From 1757: "Almighty God. Enable me to shake off sloth." From 1769: "I purpose to rise and hope to rise . . . at eight, and by degrees at six."[11]

At those moments when he succeeded in conquering indolence and put pen to paper, his output was torrential. He could produce twelve thousand words, or thirty book pages, in a sitting. In these bursts, he'd write eighteen hundred words an hour, or thirty words a minute.[12] Sometimes the copy boy would be standing at his elbow and would take each page to the printer as it was done so he could not go back and revise.

His modern biographer, Walter Jackson Bate, usefully reminds us that though Johnson's output as a freelancer astounds for its quantity and quality, for the first two decades not a single piece of it went out under his own name. This was partly his decision, and partly the rules of the Grub Street press at the time. Even into middle age, he had done nothing that he felt proud of, or that he thought made anything close to full use of his talents. He was little known and also anxiety-riddled and emotionally torn. His life, as he put it, had been "radically wretched."

The familiar picture we have of Johnson

comes from Boswell's magisterial *Life of Johnson*. Boswell was an epicurean and an acolyte and knew Johnson only in his old age. Boswell's Johnson is anything but wretched. He is joyful, witty, complete, and compelling. In Boswell's account we find a man who has achieved some integration. But this was a construction. Through writing and mental effort he constructed a coherent worldview. He brought himself to some coherence without simplification. He became trustworthy and dependable.

Johnson also used his writing to try to serve and elevate his readers. "It is always a writer's duty to make the world better," Johnson once wrote, and by maturity he had found a way.

HUMANISM

How did he do this? Well, he did not do it alone any more than any of us does. Much of our character talk today is individualistic, like all our talk, but character is formed in community. Johnson happened to come to maturity at a time when Britain was home to a phenomenally talented group of writers, painters, artists, and intellectuals, ranging from Adam Smith to Joshua Reynolds to Edmund Burke. Each raised the standards of excellence for the others.

These were humanists, their knowledge derived from their deep reading of the great canonical texts of Western civilization. They were heroic, but they practiced an intellectual form of heroism, not a military one. They tried to see the world clearly, resisting the self-deceptions caused by the vanity and perversities in their own nature. They sought a sort of practical, moral wisdom that would give them inner integrity and purpose.

Johnson was the ultimate representative of the type. Johnson, as biographer Jeffrey Meyers put it, was "a mass of contradictions: lazy and energetic, aggressive and tender, melancholic and humorous, commonsensical and irrational, comforted yet tormented by religion."[13] He fought these impulses within himself, as James Boswell put it, like a Roman gladiator in the Colosseum. He fought "the wild beasts of the Arena, ready to be let out upon him. After a conflict, he drove them back into their dens; but not killing them, they were still assailing him." All his life he combined the intellectual toughness of Achilles with the compassionate faith of a rabbi, priest, or mullah.

Johnson processed the world in the only way

he could: with his (barely functioning) eye, with his conversation, and with his pen. Writers are not exactly known for their superlative moral character, but Johnson more or less wrote himself to virtue.

He did his work in the tavern and café. Johnson — gross, disheveled, and ugly — was an astonishingly convivial man. He also thought by talking, uttering a relentless barrage of moral maxims and witticisms, a cross between Martin Luther and Oscar Wilde. "There is no arguing with Johnson," the novelist and playwright Oliver Goldsmith once said, "for when his pistol misses fire, he knocks you down with the butt end of it." Johnson would use whatever argument came to hand and often switched sides in a debate entirely if he thought it would make the controversy more enjoyable. Many of his most famous sayings feel as if they either emerged spontaneously during a tavern conversation or were polished to give the appearance of spontaneity: "Patriotism is the last refuge of a scoundrel. . . . A decent provision for the poor is the true test of civilization. . . . When a man knows he is to be hanged in a fortnight it concentrates his mind wonderfully. . . . When a man is tired of London he is tired of life."

His literary style had the to-and-fro structure of good conversation. He'd make a point, then balance it with a counterpoint, which in turn would be balanced by yet another counterpoint. The maxims above, which everybody quotes, give a false air of certainty to Johnson's views. His common conversational style was to raise a topic — say, card playing — list the virtues and vices associated with it, and then come down tentatively on one side. Writing of marriage, he displays his tendency to see every good linked with a bad: "I drew upon a page of my pocket book a scheme of all female virtues and vices, with the vices which border upon every virtue, and the virtues which are allied to every vice. I considered that wit was sarcastic, and magnanimity imperious; that avarice was economical and ignorance obsequious."

Johnson was a fervent dualist, believing that only tensions, paradoxes, and ironies could capture the complexity of real life. He was not a theorist, so he was comfortable with antitheses, things that didn't seem to go together but in fact do. As the literary critic Paul Fussell observed, the *but*s and *yet*s that dotted his prose became the substance of his writing, part of his sense that to grasp anything you have to look at it from many vantage points, seeing all its contradictory parts.[14]

One certainly gets the sense that he spent a lot of time just hanging out, engaging in the sort of stupid small adventures groups of friends get into when they are just passing the time. Told that someone had drowned in a certain stretch of river, Johnson proceeded to jump right into it to see if he could survive. Told that a gun could explode if loaded with too much shot, Johnson immediately put seven balls in the barrel of one and fired it into a wall.

He threw himself into London life. He interviewed prostitutes. He slept in parks with poets. He did not believe knowledge was best pursued as a solitary venture. He wrote, "Happiness is not found in self contemplation; it is perceived only when it is reflected from another." He sought self-knowledge obliquely, testing his observations against the reality of a world he could see concretely in front of him. "I look upon every day to be lost in which I do not make a new acquaintance," he observed. He dreaded solitude. He was always the last one to leave the pub, preferring walking the streets throughout the night with his dissolute friend Richard Savage to going home to the loneliness of his haunted chambers.

"The true state of every nation," he observed, "is the state of common life. The manners of a people are not to be found in schools of learning or the palaces of greatness." Johnson socialized with people at every level. Late in life he took vagabonds into his house. He also entertained and insulted lords. After Johnson had arduously completed his great dictionary, Lord Chesterfield belatedly tried to take credit as its patron. Johnson rebuked him with one of the greatest epistolary acts of revolt ever written, which climaxed with the passage:

> Is not a patron, my lord, one who looks with unconcern on a man struggling for life in the water, and, when he has reached ground, encumbers him with help? The notice which you have been pleased to take of my labors, had it been early, had been kind; but it has been delayed till I am indifferent, and cannot enjoy it; till I am solitary, and cannot impart it; till I am known, and do not want it.

ABSOLUTE HONESTY

Johnson did not believe that the primary human problems can be solved by politics or by rearranging social conditions. He is, after all, the author of the famous couplet

"How small, of all that human hearts endure, / That part which laws and kings can cause or cure." Nor was he a metaphysician or a philosopher. He liked science but thought it a secondary concern. He discounted those who led lives of pedantic research surrounded by "learned dust," and he had a deep distrust of intellectual systems that tried to explain all existence in one logical structure. He let his interests roam over the whole surface of life, wherever his natural interests took him, making connections as a generalist, from one field to another. Johnson endorsed the notion that "He who can talk only on one subject, or act only in one department, is seldom wanted, and perhaps never wished for, while the man of general knowledge can often benefit and always please."[15]

He was not mystical. He built his philosophy low to the ground, from reading history and literature and from direct observation — focusing relentlessly on what he would call "the living world." As Paul Fussell observed, he confuted all determinism. He rejected the notion that behavior is shaped by impersonal iron forces. He always focused with his searing eye on the particularity of each individual. Ralph Waldo Emerson would later observe that

"Souls are not saved in bundles."[16] Johnson fervently believed in each individual's mysterious complexity and inherent dignity.

He was, through it all, a moralist, in the best sense of that term. He believed that most problems are moral problems. "The happiness of society depends on virtue," he would write. For him, like other humanists of that age, the essential human act is the act of making strenuous moral decisions. He, like other humanists, believed that literature could be a serious force for moral improvement. Literature gives not only new information but new experiences. It can broaden the range of awareness and be an occasion for evaluation. Literature can also instruct through pleasure.

Today many writers see literature and art only in aesthetic terms, but Johnson saw them as moral enterprises. He hoped to be counted among those writers who give "ardor to virtue and confidence to truth." He added, "It is always a writer's duty to make the world better." As Fussell puts it, "Johnson, then, conceives of writing as something very like a Christian sacrament, defined in the Anglican catechism as 'an outward and visible sign of an inward and spiritual grace given to us.' "

Johnson lived in a world of hack writers,

but Johnson did not allow himself to write badly — even though he wrote quickly and for money. Instead, he pursued the ideal of absolute literary honesty. "The first step to greatness is to be honest" was one of Johnson's maxims.

He had a low but sympathetic view of human nature. It was said in Greek times that Demosthenes was not a great orator despite his stammer; he was a great orator *because* he stammered. The deficiency became an incentive to perfect the associated skill. The hero becomes strongest at his weakest point. Johnson was a great moralist because of his deficiencies. He came to understand that he would never defeat them. He came to understand that his story would not be the sort of virtue-conquers-vice story people like to tell. It would be, at best, a virtue-learns-to-live-with-vice story. He wrote that he did not seek cures for his failings, but palliatives. This awareness of permanent struggle made him sympathetic to others' failings. He was a moralist, but a tenderhearted one.

THE COMPASSION OF THE WOUNDED MAN

If you want to know what vices plagued Samuel Johnson, just look at the subjects of his essays: guilt, shame, frustration, boredom, and so on. As Bate observes, one fourth of his essays in the Rambler series concern envy. Johnson understood that he was particularly prone to resent other people's success: "The reigning error of mankind is that we are not content with the conditions on which the goods of life are granted."

Johnson's redeeming intellectual virtue was clarity of mind. It gave him his great facility for crystallizing and quotable observations. Most of these reveal a psychological shrewdness about human fallibility:

- A man of genius is but seldom ruined but by himself.
- If you are idle, be not solitary; if you are solitary, be not idle.
- There are people whom one should like very well to drop, but would not wish to be dropped by.
- All censure of self is oblique praise. It is in order to show how much he can spare.
- Man's chief merit consists in resisting the impulses of his nature.
- No place affords a more striking conviction of the vanity of human

hopes than a public library.

- Very few can boast of hearts which they dare lay open to themselves.
- Read over your compositions, and wherever you meet with a passage you think is particularly fine, strike it out.
- Every man naturally persuades himself he can keep his resolutions; nor is he convinced of his imbecility but by length of time and frequency of experiment.

Through his moral essays, Johnson was able to impose order on the world, to anchor his experiences in the stability of the truth. He had to still himself in order to achieve an objective perception of the world. When people are depressed, they often feel overcome by a comprehensive and yet hard to pin down sadness. But Johnson jumps directly into the pain, pins it down, dissects it, and partially disarms it. In his essay on sorrow he observes that most passions drive you to their own extinction. Hunger leads to eating and satiety, fear leads to flight, lust leads to sex. But sorrow is an exception. Sorrow doesn't direct you toward its own cure. Sorrow builds upon sorrow.

That's because sorrow is "that state of

mind in which our desires are fixed upon the past, without looking forward to the future, an incessant wish that something were otherwise than it has been, a tormenting and harassing want of some enjoyment or possession we have lost." Many try to avoid sorrow by living timid lives. Many try to relieve sorrow by forcing themselves to go to social events. Johnson does not approve of these stratagems. Instead, he advises, "The safe and general antidote against sorrow is employment. . . . Sorrow is a kind of rust of the soul, which every new idea contributes in its passage to scour away. It is the putrefaction of stagnant life and is remedied by exercise and motion."

Johnson also uses his essays as exercises in self-confrontation. "Life is combat to Johnson," Fussell writes, "and the combat is moral."[17] Johnson writes essays directly upon those topics that plague him: despair, pride, hunger for novelty, boredom, gluttony, guilt, and vanity. He is under no illusion that he can lecture himself to virtue. But he can plot and plan ways to train his will. For example, envy was indeed the besetting sin of his early adulthood. He understood his own talents, and also understood that others were succeeding while he failed.

He devised a strategy to defeat the envy in his heart. He said that in general he did not believe that one vice should be cured by another. But envy is such a malignant state of mind that the dominance of almost any other quality is to be preferred. So he chose pride. He told himself that to envy another is to admit one's inferiority, and that it is better to insist on one's superior merit than to succumb to envy. When tempted to envy another, he persuaded himself of his own superior position.

Then, turning in a more biblical direction, he preached charity and mercy. The world is so bursting with sin and sorrow that "there are none to be envied." Everyone has some deep trouble in their lives. Almost no one truly enjoys their own achievements, since their desires are always leaping forward and torturing them with visions of goods unpossessed.

THE STABILITY OF THE TRUTH

What Johnson said of the essayist Joseph Addison could be applied to himself: "He was a man in whose presence nothing reprehensible was out of danger; quick in observing whatever was wrong or ridiculous and not unwilling to expose it."

Through this process of strenuous

observation and examination, Johnson did transform his life. As a young man, he was sickly, depressed, and a failure. By late middle age, not only were his worldly accomplishments nationally admired, but he was acknowledged as a great-souled man. The biographer Percy Hazen Houston explained how a man of such a miserable and painful upbringing could look upon the world with judgments tempered with tolerance and mercy:

The iron had entered his soul, and he approached questions of human conduct in the light of a terrible experience, which enabled him to penetrate into human motives with sureness and understanding. Vividly conscious of the pettiness of our lives and the narrow limits of human knowledge, he was content to leave the mystery of final causes to power higher than his; for God's purposes are inscrutable, and man's aim in this early existence should be to seek laws by which he may prepare himself to meet divine mercy.[18]

Johnson thought hard and came to settled convictions about the complex and flawed world around him. He did it by disciplining himself in the effort to see things as they are. He did it through earnestness, self-criticism, and moral ardor.

MONTAIGNE

Johnson's method of self-formation through moral inquiry can be illuminated by contrast with another great essayist, the delightful sixteenth-century French writer Michel de Montaigne. As one of my students, Haley Adams, put it, Johnson is like an East Coast rapper — intense, earnest, combative. Montaigne is like a West Coast rapper — equally realistic but also relaxed, mellow, sun-drenched. Montaigne was a greater essayist than Johnson. His masterpieces created and defined the form. And in his way he was just as morally earnest, just as intent on finding a way to understand himself and pursue virtue. But they took different approaches. Johnson sought to reform himself through direct assault and earnest effort. Montaigne was more amused by himself and his foibles, and sought virtue through self-acceptance and sweet gestures of self-improvement.

Montaigne had an upbringing nothing like Johnson's. He grew up on an estate near Bordeaux as the treasured member of a wealthy, established family whose money was ample but not ancient. He was raised gently and nurturingly according to a humanist plan devised by the man he thought the best of all fathers, including being awoken sweetly each morning by the sound of a musical instrument. The upbringing was designed to make him educated, well-rounded, and gentle. He went to a prestigious boarding school and then served as a town counselor and member of the local *parlement*.

Montaigne's situation was comfortable, but his times were not. He was a public servant at a time of a series of religious civil wars, trying to play a mediating role in some of them. In his thirty-eighth year, he retired from public life. His goal was to return to his estate and lead a life of learned leisure. Johnson wrote in the teeming pub life of Grub Street; Montaigne wrote from the seclusion of his own tower library, in a large room decorated with Greek, Roman, and biblical maxims.

His initial goal was to study the ancients (Plutarch, Ovid, Tacitus) and learn from his church (at least in public, he was a Roman Catholic with orthodox views, although, with an earthy rather than an abstract slant of mind, he seemed to draw less wisdom from theology than from history). He thought he might write learned pieces on war and high policy.

But his mind did not allow that. Like Johnson, Montaigne had a midlife suspicion that he had been living wrongly in some fundamental way. Once he retired to a life of contemplation, he discovered that his own mind would not allow tranquillity. He found his mind was fragmented, liquid, and scattershot. He compared his thoughts to the shimmerings of light dancing on the ceiling when sunlight is reflected off a pool of water. His brain was constantly racing off in all directions. When he started to think about himself, all he found was some momentary perception, which was followed by some unrelated perception, which was then followed by another.

Montaigne fell into a depression, and in his suffering he became his own literary subject. "We are, I know not how, double within ourselves," he wrote. The imagination runs away. "I cannot fix my subject. He is always restless, and reels with a natural intoxication. . . . I do not portray being. I portray passing. . . . I must suit my story to the hour, for soon I may change."

Montaigne came to realize how hard it was to control one's own mind, or even one's body. He despaired over even his own penis, "which intrudes so tiresomely when we do not require it and fails us so annoyingly when we need it most." But the penis is not alone in its rebellion. "I ask you to consider whether there is a single part of our bodies that does not often refuse to work at our will, and does not often operate in defiance of it."

Writing, then, was an act of self-integration. Montaigne's theory was that much of the fanaticism and violence he saw around him was caused by the panic and uncertainty people feel because they can't grasp the elusiveness within themselves. The push for worldly splendor and eternal glory are futile efforts by people who are seeking external means to achieve internal tranquillity and friendship with themselves. As he put it, "Every man rushes elsewhere into the future, because no man has arrived at himself." Montaigne would use his essays to arrive at himself. He would, through writing, create a viewpoint and a prose style that would impose order and equanimity on the fragmented self inside.

Both Johnson and Montaigne were seeking deep self-awareness, but they went about it by different methods. Johnson described other people and the outer world, hoping to define himself obliquely.

Sometimes he would write a biography of someone else, but so many of his own traits peeped through that his portrait seems like an autobiography in disguise. Montaigne started from the other end. He described himself, and his responses to things, and through self-examination hoped to define the nature that all men and women share, observing, "Each man bears within himself the entire form of man's estate."

Johnson's essays sound authoritative, but Montaigne's are written in a style that is modest, provisional, and tentative. They were not organized formally. They do not follow a clear logical structure; they accrete. He would make a point, and if some related point came to him months later, he'd scrawl it in the margins for inclusion in the final edition. That haphazard method disguised the seriousness of his enterprise. He made it look easy, but he did not take his mission lightly. He understood how original his project was: completely honest self-revelation, and through that, a vision of the moral life. He understood he was trying to create a new method of character formation and implying a new type of hero, a hero of ruthlessly honest but sympathetic self-understanding. The manner was carefree, but the task was arduous: "We must really strain our soul to be aware of our own fallibility." The idea was not simply to expand his knowledge of himself, or to play around in his own mind, or to expose himself for the sake of fame or attention or success. His goal was to confront himself in order to lead a coherent and disciplined life: "Greatness of the soul is not so much pressing upward and forward as knowing how to set oneself in order and circumscribe oneself."

Montaigne sought to address his moral problems through self-knowledge and self-reform. He argued that this sort of self-confrontation imposes even harsher demands than those placed on an Alexander the Great or a Socrates. Those figures operate in public and are rewarded with glory and renown. The solitary seeker after honest self-knowledge works in private. Other people seek the approval of the crowd; Montaigne sought self-respect. "Every one can play his part in the farce, and act an honest role on the stage. But to be disciplined within, in one's own breast, where all is permissible and all is concealed. That is the point."

Montaigne cut short a successful career because he felt the struggle for internal depth and self-respect was more important. He did it by bravely facing the truth about himself. Even during the act of self-confrontation he created an attitude of equipoise that has charmed readers throughout the centuries since. He was willing to face unpleasant truths about himself without getting defensive or trying to rationalize them away. Most of the time his own deficiencies just made him smile.

He had, in the first place, a humble but secure view of himself. He admits that he is a small and uncharismatic man. If he rides around with his staff, people can't tell who is master and who is servant. If he has a poor memory, he will tell you. If he is bad at chess and other games, he will tell you. If he has a small penis, he will tell you. If he is decaying with age, he will tell you.

Like most people, he observes, he's a bit venal: "Let anyone search his heart and we will find that our inward wishes are for the most part born and nourished at the expense of others." He notes that most of the things we struggle for are ephemeral and fragile. A philosopher can cultivate the greatest mind in history, but one bite from a rabid dog could turn him into a raving idiot. Montaigne is the author of the take-you-down-a-peg saying that "on the loftiest throne in the world we are still only sitting on our own rump." He argues that "if others examined themselves attentively, as I do, they would find themselves, as I do, full of inanity and nonsense. Get rid of it I cannot without getting rid of myself. We are all steeped in it, one as much as another; but those who are aware of it are a little better off — though I don't know." As Sarah Bakewell observes in her superb book on the man, *How to Live,* that final coda "though I don't know" is pure Montaigne.

One day, one of his servants, who was riding behind him, took off at full gallop and crashed right into Montaigne and his horse. Montaigne was thrown ten paces behind his horse and lay unconscious, spread on the ground, as if dead. His terrified servants began carrying his lifeless form back to the castle. As they did, he began to come to. His servants later told him how he had behaved — gasping for air, scratching furiously at his chest, ripping at his clothes as if to free himself, apparently in agony. Inside, though, the mental scene was quite different. "I felt infinite sweetness and repose," he recalled, and took pleasure in "growing languid and letting myself go." He had the sensation of being gently carried aloft on a magic carpet.

What a difference, Montaigne later reflected, between the outward appearance and the inner experience. How astonishing. One sanguine lesson he drew is that nobody has to bother learning how to die: "If you don't know how to die, don't worry; Nature will tell you what to do on the spot, fully and adequately. She will do the job perfectly for you; don't bother your head about it."[19]

It's almost as if Montaigne's temperament could be reduced to an equation: a low but accurate view of one's own nature plus a capacity for wonder and astonishment at the bizarreness of creation equals a calming spirit of equipoise. He was, as Bakewell puts it, "liberated to lightheartedness."[20] He seemed to maintain an even keel, neither surrendering to exuberance when things were going well nor falling into despair when they weren't. He created a prose style that embodied graceful nonchalance and then tried to become as cool as his writing. "I seek only to grow indifferent and relaxed," he writes at one point, not entirely convincingly. "I avoid subjecting myself to obligation, he observes (or advises). In essay after essay you can practically see him trying to will himself into easy self-acceptance: "I may wish on the whole, to be otherwise; I may condemn my general character, and implore God to reform me throughout, and to excuse my natural weakness. But I should not, I think, give the name of repentance to this, any more than I should to my dissatisfaction at not being an angel or Cato. My actions are controlled and shaped to what I am and to my condition of life. I can do no better." He gave himself a moderating slogan: "I hold back."

He's a slow reader, so he focuses on just a few books. He's a little lazy, so he learns to relax. (Johnson gave himself fervent self-improvement sermons, but Montaigne would not. Johnson was filled with moral sternness; Montaigne was not.) Montaigne's mind naturally wanders, so he takes advantage and learns to see things from multiple perspectives. Every flaw comes with its own compensation.

The ardent and the self-demanding have never admired Montaigne. They find his emotional register too narrow, his aspirations too modest, his settledness too bland. They have trouble refuting him (he doesn't write in traditional logical structures, so it's hard to find the *there* there to refute), but they conclude that his pervasive skepticism and self-acceptance just lead to self-satisfaction, even a tinge of nihilism. They dismiss him as the master of emotional distance and conflict avoidance.

There's some truth to that view, as

Montaigne, of course, would have been the first to admit: "A painful notion takes hold of me; I find it quicker to change it than subdue it. I substitute a contrary one for it, or, if I cannot, at all events a different one. Variation always solaces, dissolves and dissipates. If I cannot combat it, I escape it; and in fleeing I dodge. I am tricky."

Montaigne's example teaches that if you have realistically low expectations, you'll end up pleased in most circumstances. But he is not merely a mellow fellow, a sixteenth-century beach bum with an estate. He sometimes pretends to nonchalance, and he often hides his earnest intent, but he does have a higher vision of the good life and the good society. It is not based on ultimate salvation or ultimate justice, as more ambitious souls would prefer, but on friendship.

His essay on friendship is one of the most moving pieces he produced. It was written to celebrate the bond he shared with his dear friend Étienne de la Boetie, who died about five years into their relationship. They were both writers and thinkers. As we would say nowadays, they were genuine soul mates.

Everything in such a friendship is held in common — will, thoughts, opinions, property, families, children, honor, life. "Our souls travelled so unitedly together, they felt so strong an affection for one another and with this same affection saw in the very depths of each other's hearts, that not only did I know his as well as my own, but I should certainly have trusted myself more freely to him than to myself." If you were to construct a perfect society, he concludes, this sort of friendship would be at its peak.

TWO STYLES OF GOODNESS

Both Montaigne and Johnson were brilliant essayists, masters of shifting perspective. Both were humanists in their way, heroically trying to use literature to find the great truths they believed the human mind is capable of comprehending but also doing so with a sense of humility, compassion, and charity. Both tried to pin down the chaos of existence in prose and create a sense of internal order and discipline. But Johnson is all emotional extremes; Montaigne is emotionally moderate. Johnson issues stern self-demands; Montaigne aims at nonchalance and ironic self-acceptance. Johnson is about struggle and suffering, Montaigne is a more genial character, wryly amused by the foibles of the world. Johnson investigated the world to become his desired self; Montaigne investigated himself to see the world. Johnson is a demanding moralist in a sensual, competitive city. He's trying to fire moral ardor and get ambitious bourgeois people to focus on ultimate truths. Montaigne is a calming presence in a country filled with civil war and religious zealotry. Johnson tried to lift people up to emulate heroes. Montaigne feared that those who try to rise above what is realistically human end up sinking into the subhuman. In search of purity they end up burning people at the stake.

We can each of us decide if we are a little more like Montaigne or a little more like Johnson, or which master we can learn from on which occasion. For my part I'd say that Johnson, through arduous effort, built a superior greatness. He was more a creature of the active world. Montaigne's equipoise grew in part from the fact that he grew up rich, with a secure title, and could retire from the messiness of history to the comfort of his estate. Most important, Johnson understood that it takes some hard pressure to sculpt a character. The material is resistant. There has to be some pushing, some sharp cutting, and hacking. It has to be done in confrontation with the intense events of the real world, not in retreat from them. Montaigne had such a genial nature, maybe he could be shaped through gentle observation. Most of us will end up mediocre and self-forgiving if we try to do that.

INDUSTRY

In 1746, Johnson signed a contract to create an English dictionary. Just as he was slowly bringing order to his own internal life, he would also bring order to his language. The French Academy had embarked on a similar project in the previous century. It had taken forty scholars fifty-five years to complete the task. Johnson and six clerks completed their task in eight. He defined 42,000 words and included roughly 116,000 illustrative quotations to show how the words were used. He culled an additional hundred thousand quotations that he ended up not using.

Johnson would pore over all the English literature he could get his hands on, marking the word usage and the usable quotations. He would have these copied onto slips of paper and then collate them in a vast organizational structure. The work was tedious, but Johnson saw a virtue in the tedium. He thought the dictionary would be good for the country and calming to himself. He entered the work, he wrote, "with the pleasing hope that, if it was low, it likewise would be safe. I was drawn forward with the prospect of employment, which, though not splendid, would be useful, and which, though it could not make my life envied, would keep it innocent; which would awaken no passion, engage me in no contention, nor throw in my way any temptation to disturb the quiet of others by censure, or my own by flattery."[21]

While Johnson was working on the dictionary, his wife, Tetty, died. She had suffered from poor health and she drank more and more as the years went by. One day she was upstairs sick in bed when there was a knock on the door. A maid answered and told the visitor that Tetty was ill. It turned out the man was Tetty's grown son from her first marriage. He had become estranged from her when she married Johnson and had not seen her in all the years since. When Tetty heard a few moments later that her son had been at the door, she threw on some clothes and rushed down to find him. But he had left, and she would never see him again.

Johnson was hit hard by her passing. His journals are filled with vows to honor her memory in one way or another. "Enable me to begin and perfect that reformation which

I promised her. . . . I kept this day as the anniversary of my Tetty's death with prayer & tears. . . . Resolved . . . to consult my resolves on Tetty's coffin. . . . Thought on Tetty, dear poor Tetty, with my eyes full."

The dictionary made Johnson famous and, if never rich, at least financially secure. He emerged as one of the great figures of British literary life. He spent his days, as usual, in cafés and taverns. He was in the Club, a group of men who met together regularly to dine and discuss. It was probably the single greatest collection of intellectual and artistic friends in British history, and maybe beyond. Its members included not only Johnson but the statesman Edmund Burke, the economist Adam Smith, the painter Joshua Reynolds, the actor (and Johnson's former pupil) David Garrick, the novelist and playwright Oliver Goldsmith, and the historian Edward Gibbon.

Johnson socialized with the lords and intellectuals but spent his domestic life with the down and out. His home was perpetually occupied by a strange collection of indigents and the marginalized. A former slave lived with him, as did an impoverished doctor and a blind poetess. One night he found a prostitute lying ill and exhausted on the street. He put her on his back, brought her home, and gave her a place to live. The beneficiaries of his mercy fought with each other and with him, and they made the home a crowded, fractious place, but Johnson was loath to turn them out.

He also did amazing amounts of writing for friends. The man who said "no man but a blockhead ever wrote except for money" composed thousands of pages for free. An eighty-two-year-old former physician had spent years trying to come up with a more accurate way to determine longitude while at sea. He was now dying, his work having come to nothing. Johnson, feeling compassion for the man, studied up on navigation and the man's theories on it and wrote a book, which he put out under the man's name, titled *An Account of an Attempt to Ascertain the Longitude of the Sea,* just to give him the sense at the end of his life that his ideas would live on. Another friend, a twenty-nine-year-old man named Robert Chambers, was elected to a professorship of law at Oxford. Chambers, sadly, was neither a noted legal mind nor a good writer. Johnson agreed to help him out by ghostwriting his law lectures. Johnson wrote sixty separate lectures for him stretching over sixteen hundred pages.

Johnson worked feverishly nearly until his

death. Between the ages of sixty-eight and seventy-two he wrote his *Lives of the Poets,* fifty-two biographies covering 378,000 words, at a time when age seventy really was elderly. He never achieved the equanimity that seems to have marked Montaigne's mature years, or the calmness and reserve he admired in others. He lived all his life with periodic feelings of despair, depression, shame, masochism, and guilt. In old age he asked a friend to hold a padlock for him that could be used if he should go insane and require physical restraint.

Nonetheless, there is an unmistakable largeness to Johnson's character in his final few years. Late in life, with his companion and biographer Boswell, he became one of the most famous conversationalists of all time. He could unfurl long paragraphs of repartee on almost any subject and for almost any occasion. These observations didn't just arise spontaneously. They were the product of a lifetime of mental labor.

He also built a consistent point of view. It began with an awareness of the constant presence of egotism, self-centeredness, and self-deception. But it was fueled by his own rebel spirit. From childhood and university days up through adult life he had a deep instinct to revolt against authority. He turned that rebellious spirit against his own nature. He turned it against evil, interior and exterior. He used it as fuel to propel him into self-combat.

Self-combat was his path to redemption. He defined a different type of courage, the courage of honesty (Montaigne had it, too). He believed that the expressive powers of literature, if used with utter moral sincerity, could conquer demons. Truth was his bondage breaker. As Bate puts it, "Johnson time and again walks up to almost every anxiety and fear the human heart can feel. As he puts his hands directly upon it and looks at it closely, the lion's skin falls off, and we often find beneath it only a donkey, maybe only a frame of wood. That is why we so often find ourselves laughing as we read what he has to say. We laugh partly through sheer relief."[22]

Everything was a moral contest for Johnson, a chance to improve, to degrade or repent. His conversation, even when uproarious, was meant to be improving. When he was an old man he recalled an episode in his youth. His father had asked him to man the family bookstall in the market square of a town called Uttoxeter. Johnson, feeling superior to his father, had refused. Now elderly, feeling the lingering shame, he made a special trip to the market square of Uttoxeter and stood on the spot where his father's stall had been. As he later recalled:

> Pride was the source of that refusal, and the remembrance of it was painful. A few years ago I desired to atone for this fault. I went to Uttoxeter in very bad weather and stood for a considerable time bareheaded in the rain. . . . In contrition I stood, and I hope that the penance was expiatory.

Johnson never triumphed, but he integrated, he built a more stable whole than would have seemed possible from his fragmented nature. As Adam Gopnick wrote in *The New Yorker* in 2012, "He was his own whale, and brought himself home."

Finally, when Johnson was seventy-five, death approached. He had a powerful fear of damnation. He put a text on his watch, "The night cometh," to remind himself to commit no sins that would lead to a bad final judgment. Nonetheless it hung passionately upon his mind. Boswell records an exchange with a friend:

> Johnson: I am afraid I may be one of those who shall be damned (looking

dismally).

Dr. Adams: What do you mean by damned?

Johnson: (passionately and loudly). Sent to Hell, Sir, and punished everlastingly.

In his final week his doctor told him he would surely die soon. He asked to be taken off the opium so he would not meet God "in a state of idiocy." When his doctor made some incisions in his legs to drain fluid, Johnson cried out, "Deeper, deeper; I want length of life, and you are afraid to give me pain, which I do not value." Later Johnson got some scissors and plunged them into his own legs in a further attempt to drain them. His pronouncement in the face of death was of a piece with his manner in life: "I will be conquered; I will not capitulate."

Johnson stands now as an example of humane wisdom. From his scattered youth, his diverse faculties cohered into a single faculty — a mode of seeing and judging the world that was as much emotional as intellectual. Especially toward the end of his life, it becomes hard to categorize his writing. His journalism rose to the level of literature; his biographies contained ethics; his theology was filled with practical advice. He became a universal thinker.

The foundation of it all was his tremendous capacity for sympathy. His life story begins with physical suffering. As a teenager and young man he was one of the world's outcasts, disfigured by fate. He seems never to have shaken that vulnerability, but he succeeded in turning his handicaps and limitations into advantages through sheer hard work. For a man who continually castigated himself for his sloth, his capacity for labor was enormous.

He wrestled, really wrestled with matters that were of real importance, matters of his very being. "To strive with difficulties, and to conquer them, is the highest human felicity," he wrote in one of his essays. "The next is to strive and deserve to conquer; but he whose life has passed without contest, and who can boast neither success nor merit can survey himself only as a useless filler of existence."

That wrestling was undertaken on behalf of an unblinking honesty. The Victorian writer John Ruskin wrote, "The more I think of it I find this conclusion more impressed upon me — that the greatest thing a human soul ever does in this world is to *see* something, and tell what it *saw* in a plain way. Hundreds of people can talk for one who can think, but thousands can think for one who can see."

Johnson's genius for epigram and for pithy observation emerged also out of his extraordinary sensitivity to the world around him. It was nurtured, too, by his skepticism about himself — his ability to doubt his motives, see through his rationalizations, laugh at his vanities, and understand that he was just as foolish as others were.

After his death, the nation mourned. A reaction from William Gerard Hamilton is the most often quoted and most accurately captures the achievement of the man and the void his death created: "He has made a chasm, which not only nothing can fill up, but which nothing has a tendency to fill up. Johnson is dead. Let us go with the next best: There is nobody; no man can be said to put you in mind of Johnson."

CHAPTER 10
THE BIG ME

In January 1969, two great quarterbacks faced each other from opposite sidelines in Super Bowl III. Both Johnny Unitas and Joe Namath were raised in the steel towns of western Pennsylvania. But they had grown up a decade apart and lived in different moral cultures.

Unitas grew up in the old culture of self-effacement and self-defeat. His father died when he was five and his mother took over the family coal delivery business, supervising its one driver. Unitas went to a strict Catholic school in the old tradition. The teachers were morally demanding and could be harsh and cruel. The domineering Father Barry would hand out report cards personally, flipping them at one boy after another, remarking cruelly, "You'll make a good truck driver some day. You'll be digging ditches." The prophecies terrified the boys.[1]

Football players in Western Pennsylvania

gloried in their ability to endure pain.[2] Unitas weighed 145 pounds while playing quarterback for his high school team, and he took a beating during every game. He went to church before every game, deferred to the authority of his coaches, and lived a football-obsessed life.[3] Turned down by Notre Dame, Unitas then played quarterback at a basketball school, the University of Louisville. He had a brief tryout with the Pittsburgh Steelers but was cut. He was back working on a construction gang, playing semipro football, when he got a long-shot call from the Baltimore Colts. He made the team and spent many of his early years with the Colts steadily losing.

Unitas was not an overnight sensation in the NFL, but he was steadily ripening, honing his skills and making his teammates better. When his pro career looked secure, he bought a split-level house in Towson, Maryland, and also took a job with the Columbia Container Corporation that paid him $125 a week throughout the year.[4] He was a deliberately unglamorous figure with his black high-top sneakers, bowed legs, stooped shoulders, and a crew cut above his rough face. If you look at photos of him traveling with the team you see a guy who looks like a 1950s insurance salesman, with his white short-sleeved button-down shirt and narrow black tie. He and his buddies would sit on the buses and planes, dressed almost exactly the same, haircuts the same, playing bridge.

He was unflamboyant and understated. "I always figured being a little dull was part of being a pro. Win or lose, I never walked off a football field without first thinking of something boring to say to [the press]," he would say later. He was loyal to his organization and to his teammates. In the huddle he'd rip into his receivers for screwing up plays and running the wrong routes. "I'll never throw to you again if you don't learn the plays," he'd bark. Then, after the game, he'd lie to the reporter: "My fault, I overthrew him" was his standard line.

Unitas was confident in his football abilities but unprepossessing in the way he went about his job. Steve Sabol of NFL Films captured some of his manner: "It's always been my job to glorify the game. I'm such a romantic anyway. I've always looked at football in dramaturgical terms. It wasn't the score; it was the struggle, and what kind of music could we use? But when I met Unitas I realized he was the antithesis of all that. Football to him was no different than a plumber putting in a pipe. He was an honest workman doing an honest job. Everything was a shrug of the shoulders. He was so unromantic that he was romantic, in the end."[5] Unitas, like Joe DiMaggio in baseball, came to embody a particular way of being a sports hero in the age of self-effacement.

Namath, who grew up in the same area but a half generation later, lived in a different moral universe. Joe Namath was the flamboyant star, with white shoes and flowing hair, brashly guaranteeing victory. Broadway Joe was outrageously entertaining and fun to be around. He made himself the center of attention, a spectacle off the field as much as on it, with $5,000 fur coats, long sideburns, and playboy manners. He didn't care what others thought of him, or at least said he didn't. "Some people don't like this image I got myself, being a swinger," Namath told Jimmy Breslin in a famous 1969 piece, "Namath All Night," for *New York* magazine. "But I'm not institutional. I swing. If it's good or bad, I don't know, but it's what I like."

Namath grew up in Unitas's shadow in poor Western Pennsylvania, but into a different way of being. His parents divorced when he was seven and he rebelled against his immigrant family by being cool, hanging around the pool hall and adopting a James Dean leather-jacketed swagger.

Namath's football talents were flamboyantly obvious. He was one of the most highly recruited players in the country that year. He wanted to go to college in Maryland, thinking it was in the South, but his SATs weren't high enough. So he went to the University of Alabama, where he went on to become one of the nation's best collegiate quarterbacks. He was given a gigantic signing bonus to play with the New York Jets and was immediately making much more than any of his teammates.

He cultivated a personal brand that was bigger than the team. He was not just a football star but a lifestyle star. He paid a fine so he could wear a Fu Manchu mustache on the field. He starred in pantyhose commercials, challenging old-fashioned notions of masculinity. He famously had six-inch shag carpets in his bachelor pad, and he popularized the use of the word "foxes" for women. He wrote an autobiography titled *I Can't Wait Until Tomorrow 'Cause I Get Better Looking Every Day.* This is not a title Johnny Unitas would have chosen.

Namath came to stardom at a time when New Journalism was breaking the mold of the old reporting. Namath was the perfect subject. Without a reticent bone in his body, he'd bring reporters along as he worked his way through bottles of scotch the night before games. He openly bragged about what a great athlete he was, how good-looking he was. He cultivated a brashly honest style. "Joe! Joe! You're the most beautiful thing in the world!" he shouted to himself in the bathroom mirror of the Copacabana one night in 1966, as a reporter from *The Saturday Evening Post* tagged along.[6]

Fiercely independent, he did not want to make a deep commitment to any woman. He created an early version of what we would now call the hook-up culture. "I don't like to date so much as I just like to kind of, you know, run into something, man," he told a reporter for *Sports Illustrated* in 1966. He embodied the autonomy ethos that was beginning to sweep through the country. "I believe in letting a guy live the way he wants to if he doesn't hurt anyone. I feel that everything I do is okay for me and doesn't affect anybody else, including the girls I go out with. Look, man, I live and let live. I like everybody."[7]

Namath heralded a new mode for being a professional athlete — a mode of personal branding, lavish endorsements, in which the star expressed his own vibrant personality and outshone the team.

CULTURAL CHANGE

Cultures change in ways that are both superficial and profound. When the essayist Joseph Epstein was young, he observed that when you went into the drugstore the cigarettes were in the open shelves and the condoms were behind the counter. But now when you go to the drugstore, the condoms are in the open shelves and the cigarettes are behind the counter.

The conventional view of the shift from the humility of Unitas to the brash flamboyance of Namath is that it happened in the late 1960s. The conventional story goes something like this. First there was the Greatest Generation, whose members were self-sacrificing, self-effacing, and community-minded. Then along came the 1960s and the Baby Boomers, who were narcissistic, self-expressive, selfish, and morally lax.

But this story doesn't fit the facts. What really happened goes like this: Starting in biblical times there was a tradition of moral realism, the "crooked-timber" school of humanity. This tradition, or worldview, put tremendous emphasis on sin and human weakness. This view of humanity was captured in the figure of Moses, the meekest of men who nonetheless led a people, and by biblical figures like David, who were great heroes, but deeply flawed. This biblical metaphysic was later expressed by Christian thinkers such as Augustine, with his emphasis on sin, his rejection of worldly success, his belief in the necessity of grace, of surrendering oneself to God's unmerited love. This moral realism then found expression in humanists like Samuel Johnson, Michel de Montaigne, and George Eliot, who emphasized how little we can know, how hard it is to know ourselves, and how hard we have to work on the long road to virtue. "We are all of us born in moral stupidity, taking the world as an udder to feed our supreme selves," Eliot wrote.[8] It was also embodied, in different ways and at different times, in the thought of Dante, Hume, Burke, Reinhold Niebuhr, and Isaiah Berlin. All of these thinkers take a limited view of our individual powers of reason. They are suspicious of abstract thinking and pride. They emphasize the limitations in our individual natures.

Some of these limitations are epistemological: reason is weak and the world is complex. We cannot really grasp the complexity of the world or the full truth about ourselves. Some of these limitations are moral: There are bugs in our souls that lead us toward selfishness and pride, that tempt us to put lower loves over higher loves. Some of the limitations are psychological: We are divided within ourselves, and many of the most urgent motions of our minds are unconscious and only dimly recognized by ourselves. Some of them are social: We are not self-completing creatures. To thrive we have to throw ourselves into a state of dependence — on others, on institutions, on the divine. The place that limitation occupies in the "crooked timber" school is immense.

Around the eighteenth century, moral realism found a rival in moral romanticism. While moral realists placed emphasis on inner weakness, moral romantics like Jean-Jacques Rousseau placed emphasis on our inner goodness. The realists distrusted the self and trusted institutions and customs outside the self; the romantics trusted the self and distrusted the conventions of the outer world. The realists believed in cultivation, civilization, and artifice; the romanticists believed in nature, the individual, and sincerity.

For a while, these two traditions lived side

by side in society, in creative tension and conversation. Except in artistic circles, realism had the upper hand. If you grew up in early twentieth century America, you grew up with the vocabulary and categories of moral realism, translated into a practical secular or religious idiom. Perkins grew up with the vocabulary of vocation, the need to suppress parts of yourself so you can be an instrument in a larger cause. Eisenhower grew up with the vocabulary of self-defeat. Day learned as a young woman the vocabulary of simplicity, poverty, and surrender. Marshall learned institutional thinking, the need to give oneself to organizations that transcend a lifetime. Randolph and Rustin learned reticence and the logic of self-discipline, the need to distrust oneself even while waging a noble crusade. These people didn't know they were exemplifying parts of the realist tradition. This ethos was just in the air they breathed and the way they were raised.

But then moral realism collapsed. Its vocabulary and ways of thinking were forgotten or shoved off into the margins of society. Realism and romanticism slipped out of balance. A moral vocabulary was lost, and along with it a methodology for the formation of souls. This shift did not happen during the 1960s and 1970s, though that period was a great romantic flowering. It happened earlier, in the late 1940s and 1950s. It was the Greatest Generation that abandoned realism.

By the fall of 1945, people around the world had endured sixteen years of deprivation — first during the Depression, then during the war. They were ready to let loose, to relax, to enjoy. Consumption and advertising took off as people rushed to the stores to buy things that would make life easier and more fun. People in the postwar years wanted to escape from the shackles of self-restraint and all those gloomy subjects like sin and depravity. They were ready to put the horrors of the Holocaust and the war behind them.

People right after the war were ready to read any book that offered a more upbeat and positive vision of life and its possibilities. In 1946, Rabbi Joshua L. Liebman published a book titled *Peace of Mind* that urged people to engrave a new morality on their hearts, one based on setting aside the idea that you should repress any part of yourself. Instead, thou shalt "love thyself properly . . . thou shalt not be afraid of thy hidden impulses . . . respect thyself . . . trust thyself." Liebman had an infinite faith in the infinite goodness of men and women. "I believe that man is infinitely potential, and that given the proper guidance there is hardly a task he cannot perform or a degree of mastery in work and love he cannot attain."[9] He struck a chord. His book remained on the top of the New York Times bestseller list for an astounding fifty-eight weeks.

That same year, Benjamin Spock came out with his famous baby book. That book was complex and is often unfairly maligned, but it did, especially in early editions, express a notably rosy view of human nature. Spock said that if your child steals something, you should give him as a present something similar to the item that he stole. That will show that you care for your child and that "he should have his heart's desire if it is reasonable."[10]

In 1949, Harry Overstreet published a wildly popular book titled The Mature Mind, which pushed the point a little further. Overstreet argued that those like Saint Augustine who emphasized human sinfulness had "denied to our species the healthy blessing of self-respect."[11] This emphasis on internal weakness encouraged people to "distrust himself and malign himself."

Then, in 1952, Norman Vincent Peale

came out with the mother of all optimistic books, *The Power of Positive Thinking*, urging readers to cast negative thoughts from mind and pep-talk themselves into greatness. That book rested atop the *Times* list for an astounding ninety-eight weeks.

Then came humanistic psychology led by people like Carl Rogers, the most influential psychologist of the twentieth century. The humanistic psychologists shifted away from Freud's darker conception of the unconscious and promoted a sky-high estimation of human nature. The primary psychological problem, he argued, is that people don't love themselves enough, and so therapists unleashed a great wave of self-loving. "Man's behavior is exquisitely rational," Rogers wrote, "moving with subtle and ordered complexity toward the goal his organism is endeavoring to achieve."[12] The words that best describe human nature, he continued, are "positive, forward moving, constructive, realistic and trustworthy." People don't need to combat themselves, they only need to open up, to liberate their inner selves, so that their internalized drive to self-actualize can take over. Self-love, self-praise, and self-acceptance are the paths to happiness. To the extent that a person "can be freely in touch with his valuing process in himself, he will behave in ways that are self-enhancing."[13]

Humanistic psychology has shaped nearly every school, nearly every curriculum, nearly every HR department, nearly every self-help book. Soon there were "IALAC" posters on school walls everywhere — I AM LOVABLE AND CAPABLE. The self-esteem movement was born. Our modern conversation lives in this romantic vision.

THE AGE OF SELF-ESTEEM

The shift from one moral culture to another is not a crude story of decline, from noble restraint to self-indulgent decadence. Each moral climate is a collective response to the problems of the moment. People in the Victorian era were faced with a decline in religious faith and adopted a strict character morality as a way to compensate. People in the 1950s and 1960s confronted a different set of problems. When people shift from one moral ecology to another, they are making a trade-off in response to changing circumstances. Since legitimate truths sit in tension with one another, one moral climate will put more emphasis here and less emphasis there, for better or worse. Certain virtues are cultivated, certain beliefs go too far, and certain important truths and moral virtues are accidentally forgotten.

The shift in the 1950s and 1960s to a culture that put more emphasis on pride and self-esteem had many positive effects; it helped correct some deep social injustices. Up until those years, many social groups, notably women, minorities, and the poor, had received messages of inferiority and humiliation. They were taught to think too lowly of themselves. The culture of self-esteem encouraged members of these oppressed groups to believe in themselves, to raise their sights and aspirations.

For example, many women had been taught to lead lives so committed to subservience and service that it led to self-abnegation. Katharine Meyer Graham's life illustrates why so many people embraced the shift from self-effacement to self-expression.

Katharine Meyer grew up in a wealthy publishing family in Washington, D.C. She attended the Madeira School, a progressive but genteel private school in which young ladies were raised amid mottoes such as "Function in disaster. Finish in style." At home, she was thoroughly dominated by a father who was awkward and distant and by a mother who demanded Stepford Wife perfection: "I think we all felt we somehow hadn't lived up to what she expected or wanted of us, and the insecurities and lack of self-confidence she bred were long lasting," she would write years later in her superb memoir.[14]

Girls were expected to be quiet, reserved, and correct, and Katharine grew up painfully self-conscious. "Had I said the right thing? Had I worn the right clothes? Was I attractive? These questions were unsettling and self-absorbing, even overwhelming at times."

In 1940, Katharine married a charming, witty, mercurial man named Philip Graham, who had a subtle or not so subtle way of belittling her views and abilities. "I increasingly saw my role as the tail to his kite — and the more I felt overshadowed, the more it became a reality."[15] Graham had a series of affairs, which Katharine discovered and was devastated by.

Graham, who suffered from depression, committed suicide on August 3, 1963. Six weeks later, Katharine was elected president of the Washington Post Company. At first she saw herself as a bridge between her dead husband and her children who would eventually inherit it. But she shut her eyes, took a step as manager, took another step, and found she could do the job.

Over the next few decades the surrounding culture encouraged Katharine to assert herself and to develop the full use of her capacities. The year she took over the *Post,* Betty Friedan published *The Feminine Mystique,* which embraced Carl Rogers's humanistic psychology. Gloria Steinem later wrote a bestselling book, *Revolution from Within: A Book of Self-Esteem.* Dr. Joyce Brothers, a prominent advice columnist at the time, put the ethos bluntly: "Put yourself first — at least some of the time. Society has brainwashed women into believing that their husbands' and children's needs should always be given priority over their own. Society has never impressed on women as it has on men the human necessity of putting yourself first. I am not advocating selfishness. I'm talking about the basics of life. You have to decide how many children you want, what kind of friends you want, what kind of relationships you want with your family."[16]

The emphasis on self-actualization and self-esteem gave millions of women a language to articulate and cultivate self-assertion, strength, and identity. Graham eventually became one of the most admired and powerful publishing executives in the world. She built the *Post* into a major and highly profitable national newspaper. She stood up to the Nixon White House and storm of abuse during the Watergate crisis, maintaining steadfast support for Bob Woodward, Carl Bernstein, and the rest of the journalists who broke that story. She never fully overcame her insecurities, but she did learn to project a formidable image. Her memoir is a masterwork, understated but also honest and authoritative, without a hint of self-pity or false sentiment.

Katharine Graham, like many women and members of minority groups, needed a higher and more accurate self-image — needed to move from Little Me to Big Me.

AUTHENTICITY

The underlying assumptions about human nature and the shape of human life were altered by this shift to the Big Me. If you were born at any time over the last sixty years, you were probably born into what the philosopher Charles Taylor has called "the culture of authenticity." This mindset is based on the romantic idea that each of us has a Golden Figure in the core of our self. There is an innately good True Self, which can be trusted, consulted, and gotten in touch with. Your personal feelings are the best guide for what is right and wrong.

In this ethos, the self is to be trusted, not doubted. Your desires are like inner oracles for what is right and true. You know you are doing the right thing when you feel good inside. The valid rules of life are those you make or accept for yourself and that feel right to you.

"Our moral salvation," Taylor writes, describing this culture, "comes from recovering authentic moral contact with ourselves." It is important to stay true to that pure inner voice and not follow the conformities of a corrupting world. As Taylor puts it, "There is a certain way of being that is my way. I am called to live my life in this way and not in imitation of anyone else's. . . . If I am not, I miss the point of my life. I miss what being human is for me."[17]

From an older tradition of self-combat we move to self-liberation and self-expression. Moral authority is no longer found in some external objective good; it is found in each person's unique original self. Greater emphasis is put on personal feelings as a guide to what is right and wrong. I know I am doing right because I feel harmonious inside. Something is going wrong, on the other hand, when I feel my autonomy is being threatened, when I feel I am not being true to myself.

In this ethos, sin is not found in your individual self; it is found in the external structures of society — in racism, inequality, and oppression. To improve yourself, you have to be taught to love yourself, to be true to yourself, not to doubt yourself and struggle against yourself. As one of the characters in one of the *High School Musical* movies sings, "The answers are all inside of me / All I've got to do is believe."

STATUS UPDATES

This intellectual and cultural shift toward the Big Me was reinforced by economic and technological changes. All of us today live in a technological culture. I'm not a big believer that social media have had a ruinous effect on the culture, as many technophobes fear. There is no evidence to support the idea that technology has induced people to live in a fake online world while renouncing the real one. But information technology has had three effects on the moral ecology that have inflated the Big Me Adam I side of our natures and diminished the humbler Adam II.

First, communications have become faster and busier. It is harder to attend to the soft, still voices that come from the depths.

Throughout human history, people have found that they are most aware of their depths when they are on retreats, during moments of separation and stillness, during moments of quiet communion. They have found that they need time, long periods of stillness, before the external Adam quiets and the internal Adam can be heard. These moments of stillness and quiet are just more rare today. We reach for the smartphone.

Second, social media allow a more self-referential information environment. People have more tools and occasions to construct a culture, a mental environment tailored specifically for themselves. Modern information technology allows families to sit together in a room, each absorbed in a different show, movie, or game in the privacy of their own screen. Instead of being a peripheral star in the mass-media world of the Ed Sullivan show, each individual can be the sun at the center of his or her own media solar system, creating a network of programs, apps, and pages oriented around their own needs. A Yahoo advertising campaign vowed, "Now the Internet has a personality — It's You!" Earthlink's slogan was "Earthlink revolves around you."

Third, social media encourages a broadcasting personality. Our natural bent is to seek social approval and fear exclusion. Social networking technology allows us to spend our time engaged in a hypercompetitive struggle for attention, for victories in the currency of "likes." People are given more occasions to be self-promoters, to embrace the characteristics of celebrity, to manage their own image, to Snapchat out their selfies in ways that they hope will impress and please the world. This technology creates a culture in which people turn into little brand managers, using Facebook, Twitter, text messages, and Instagram to create a falsely upbeat, slightly overexuberant, external self that can be famous first in a small sphere and then, with luck, in a large one. The manager of this self measures success by the flow of responses it gets. The social media maven spends his or her time creating a self-caricature, a much happier and more photogenic version of real life. People subtly start comparing themselves to other people's highlight reels, and of course they feel inferior.

THE SOUL OF MAN UNDER MERITOCRACY

The purification of the meritocracy has also reinforced the idea that each of us is wonderful inside. It has also encouraged self-aggrandizing tendencies. If you have lived through the last sixty or seventy years, you are the product of a more competitive meritocracy. You have, like me, spent your life trying to make something of yourself, trying to have an impact, trying to be reasonably successful in this world. That's meant a lot of competition and a lot of emphasis on individual achievement — doing reasonably well in school, getting into the right college, landing the right job, moving toward success and status.

This competitive pressure meant that we all have to spend more time, energy, and attention on the external Adam I climb toward success and we have less time, energy, and attention to devote to the internal world of Adam II.

I've found in myself, and I think I've observed in others, a certain meritocratic mentality, which is based on the self-trusting, self-puffing insights of the romantic tradition, but which is also depoeticized and despiritualized. If moral realists saw the self as a wilderness to be tamed, and if people in the new Age 1970s saw the self as an Eden to be actualized, people living in a high-pressure meritocracy are more likely to see the self as a resource base to be cultivated. The self is less likely to be seen as the seat of the soul, or as the repository of some transcendent spirit. Instead, the self is a vessel of human capital. It is a series of talents to be cultivated efficiently and prudently. The self is defined by its tasks and accomplishments. The self is about talent, not character.

This meritocratic mentality was beautifully captured in Dr. Seuss's 1990 book *Oh, the Places You'll Go!,* the fifth-biggest bestseller in the history of the *New York Times* list and still a popular graduation present.

The book is about a boy who is reminded that he has all these amazing talents and gifts, and ultimate freedom to choose his life: "You have brains in your head. You have feet in your shoes. You can steer yourself any direction you choose." The boy is reminded that his life is about fulfilling his own desires. "You're on your own. And you know what you know. And You are the guy who'll decide where to go." The challenges the boy faces in life are mostly external. And the life goals he pursues are all Adam I life goals. "Fame! You'll be famous as famous can be, / With the whole wide world watching you win on TV." The ultimate goal in this life is success, to have an impact on the external world. "And will you succeed? / Yes! You will indeed / 98 and 3/4 percent guaranteed."[18] And the main character in this success story is You. That little word appears in this very short book ninety times.

In this book, the boy is completely autonomous. He is free to choose exactly as he individually wishes. He is reminded how wonderful he is. He is not weighted down by any internal weakness. He proves his merit through work and ascent.

The meritocracy liberates enormous energies, and ranks people in ways good and bad. But it also has a subtle effect on character, culture, and values. Any hypercompetitive system built upon merit is going to encourage people to think a lot about themselves and the cultivation of their own skills. Work becomes the defining feature of a life, especially as you begin to get social invitations because you happen to inhabit a certain job. Subtly, softly, but pervasively, this system instills a certain utilitarian calculus in us all. The meritocracy subtly encourages an instrumental ethos in which each occasion — a party, a dinner — and each acquaintance becomes an opportunity to advance your status and professional life project. People are more likely to think in commercial categories — to speak about opportunity costs, scalability, human capital, cost-benefit analysis, even when it comes to how they spend their private time.

The meaning of the word "character" changes. It is used less to describe traits like selflessness, generosity, self-sacrifice, and other qualities that sometimes make worldly success less likely. It is instead used to describe traits like self-control, grit, resilience, and tenacity, qualities that make worldly success more likely.

The meritocratic system wants you to be big about yourself — to puff yourself, to be completely sure of yourself, to believe that you deserve a lot and to get what you think you deserve (so long as it is good). The meritocracy wants you to assert and advertise yourself. It wants you to display and exaggerate your achievements. The achievement machine rewards you if you can demonstrate superiority — if with a thousand little gestures, conversational types, and styles of dress you can demonstrate that you are a bit smarter, hipper, more accomplished, sophisticated, famous, plugged in, and fashion-forward than the people around you. It encourages narrowing. It encourages you to become a shrewd animal.

The shrewd animal has streamlined his inner humanity to make his ascent more aerodynamic. He carefully manages his time and his emotional commitments. Things once done in a poetic frame of mind, such as going to college, meeting a potential lover, or bonding with an employer, are now done in a more professional frame of mind. Is this person, opportunity, or experience of use to me? There just isn't time to get carried away by love and passion. There is a cost to making a soul-deep commitment to one mission or one love. If you commit to one big thing you will close off options toward other big things. You will be plagued by a Fear of Missing Out.

The shift from the Little Me culture to the Big Me culture was not illegitimate, but it went too far. The realist tradition that emphasized limitation and moral struggle was inadvertently marginalized and left by the side of the road, first by the romantic flowering of positive psychology, then by the self-branding ethos of social media, finally by the competitive pressures of the meritocracy. We are left with a moral ecology that builds up the exterior Adam I muscles but ignores the internal Adam II ones, and that creates an imbalance. It's a culture in which people are defined by their external abilities and achievements, in which a cult of busyness develops as everybody frantically tells each other how overcommitted they are. As my student Andrew Reeves once put it, it cultivates an unrealistic expectation that life will happen on a linear progression, a natural upward slope toward success. It encourages people to "satisfice," to get by on talent and just enough commitment to get the job done on time, without full soul commitment to any task.

This tradition tells you *how* to do the things that will propel you to the top, but it doesn't encourage you to ask yourself *why* you are doing them. It offers little guidance on how to choose among different career paths and different vocations, how to determine which will be morally highest and best. It encourages people to become approval-seeking machines, to measure their lives by external praise — if people like you and accord you status, then you must be doing something right. The meritocracy contains its own cultural contradictions. It encourages people to make the most of their capacities, but it leads to the shriveling of the moral faculties that are necessary if you are going to figure out how to point your life in a meaningful direction.

CONDITIONAL LOVE

Let me just describe one way the meritocracy's utilitiarian, instrumentalist mindset can, in some cases, distort a sacred bond: parenthood.

There are two great defining features of child rearing today. First, children are now praised to an unprecedented degree. Dorothy Parker quipped that American children aren't raised, they are incited — they are given food, shelter, and applause. That's much more true today. Children are incessantly told how special they are. In 1966, only about 19 percent of high school students graduated with an A or A− average. By 2013, 53 percent of students graduated with that average, according to UCLA surveys of incoming college freshmen. Young people are surrounded by so much praise that they develop sky-high aspirations for themselves. According to an Ernst & Young survey, 65 percent of college students expect to become millionaires.[19]

The second defining feature is that children are honed to an unprecedented degree. Parents, at least in the more educated, affluent classes, spend much more time than in past generations grooming their children, investing in their skills, and driving them to practices and rehearsals. As

Richard Murnane of Harvard found, parents with college degrees invest $5,700 more per year per child on out-of-school enrichment activities than they did in 1978.[20]

These two great trends — greater praise and greater honing — combine in interesting ways. Children are bathed in love, but it is often directional love. Parents shower their kids with affection, but it is not simple affection, it is meritocratic affection — it is intermingled with the desire to help their children achieve worldly success.

Some parents unconsciously shape their expressions of love to steer their children toward behavior they think will lead to achievement and happiness. Parents glow with extra fervor when their child studies hard, practices hard, wins first place, gets into a prestigious college, or joins the honor society (in today's schools, the word "honor" means earning top grades). Parental love becomes merit-based. It is not simply "I love you." It is "I love you when you stay on my balance beam. I shower you with praise and care when you're on my beam."

Parents in the 1950s were much more likely to say they expected their children to be obedient than parents today, who tell pollsters they want their children to think for themselves. But this desire for obedience hasn't vanished, it's just gone underground — from the straightforward system of rules and lectures, reward and punishment, to the semihidden world of approval or disapproval.

Lurking in the shadows of merit-based love is the possibility that it may be withdrawn if the child disappoints. Parents would deny this, but the wolf of conditional love is lurking here. This shadowy presence of conditional love produces fear, the fear that there is no utterly safe love; there is no completely secure place where young people can be utterly honest and themselves.

On the one hand, relationships between parents and children may be closer than ever before. Parents and children, even college-age children, communicate constantly. With only quiet qualms young people have accepted the vast achievement system that surrounds them. They submit to it because they long for the approval they get from the adults they love.

But the whole situation is more fraught than it appears at first glance. Some children assume that this merit-tangled love is the natural order of the universe. The tiny blips of approval and disapproval are built into the fabric of communication so deep that it is below the level of awareness. Enormous internal pressure is generated by the growing assumption that it is necessary to behave in a certain way to be worthy of another's love. Underneath, the children are terrified that the deepest relationship they know will be lost.

Some parents unconsciously regard their children as something like an art project, to be crafted through mental and emotional engineering. There is some parental narcissism here, the insistence that your children go to colleges and lead lives that will give the parents status and pleasure. Children who are uncertain of their parents' love develop a voracious hunger for it. This conditional love is like acid that dissolves children's internal criteria, their capacity to make their own decisions about their own interests, careers, marriages, and life in general.

The parental relationship is supposed to be built upon unconditional love — a gift that cannot be bought and cannot be earned. It sits outside the logic of meritocracy and is the closest humans come to grace. But in these cases the pressure to succeed in the Adam I world has infected a relationship that should be operating by a different logic, the moral logic of Adam II. The result is holes in the hearts of many children across this society.

THE AGE OF THE SELFIE

This cultural, technological, and meritocratic environment hasn't made us a race of depraved barbarians. But it has made us less morally articulate. Many of us have instincts about right and wrong, about how goodness and character are built, but everything is fuzzy. Many of us have no clear idea how to build character, no rigorous way to think about such things. We are clear about external, professional things but unclear about internal, moral ones. What the Victorians were to sex, we are to morality: everything is covered in euphemism.

This shift in culture has changed us. In the first place, it has made us a bit more materialistic. College students now say they put more value on money and career success. Every year, researchers from UCLA survey a nationwide sample of college freshmen to gauge their values and what they want out of life. In 1966, 80 percent of freshmen said that they were strongly motivated to develop a meaningful philosophy of life. Today, less than half of them say that. In 1966, 42 percent said that becoming rich was an important life goal. By 1990, 74 percent agreed with that statement. Financial security, once seen as a middling value, is now tied as students' top goal. In 1966, in other words, students felt it was important to at least present themselves as philosophical and meaning-driven people. By 1990, they no longer felt the need to present themselves that way. They felt it perfectly acceptable to say they were primarily interested in money.[21]

We live in a more individualistic society. If you humbly believe that you are not individually strong enough to defeat your own weaknesses, then you know you must be dependent on redemptive assistance from outside. But if you proudly believe the truest answers can be found in the real you, the voice inside, then you are less likely to become engaged with others. Sure enough, there has been a steady decline in intimacy. Decades ago, people typically told pollsters that they had four or five close friends, people to whom they could tell everything. Now the common answer is two or three, and the number of people with no confidants has doubled. Thirty-five percent of older adults report being chronically lonely, up from 20 percent a decade ago.[22] At the same time, social trust has declined.

Surveys ask, "Generally speaking, would you say that most people can be trusted or that you can't be too careful in dealing with people?" In the early 1960s, significant majorities said that people can generally be trusted. But in the 1990s the distrusters had a 20-percentage-point margin over the trusters, and those margins have increased in the years since.[23]

People have become less empathetic — or at least they display less empathy in how they describe themselves. A University of Michigan study found that today's college students score 40 percent lower than their predecessors in the 1970s in their ability to understand what another person is feeling. The biggest drop came in the years after 2000.[24]

Public language has also become demoralized. Google ngrams measure word usage across media. Google scans the contents of books and publications going back decades. You can type in a word and see, over the years, which words have been used more frequently and which less frequently. Over the past few decades there has been a sharp rise in the usage of individualist words and phrases like "self" and "personalized," "I come first" and "I can do it myself," and a sharp decline in community words like "community," "share," "united," and "common good."[25] The use of words having to do with economics and business has increased, while the language of morality and character building is in decline.[26] Usage of words like "character," "conscience," and "virtue" all declined over the course of the twentieth century.[27] Usage of the word "bravery" has declined by 66 percent over the course of the twentieth century. "Gratitude" is down 49 percent. "Humbleness" is down 52 percent and "kindness" is down 56 percent.

This dwindling of the Adam II lexicon has further contributed to moral inarticulateness. In this age of moral autonomy, each individual is told to come up with his or her own worldview. If your name is Aristotle, maybe you can do that. But if it isn't, you probably can't. For his 2011 book *Lost in Transition,* Christian Smith of Notre Dame studied the moral lives of American college students. He asked them to describe a moral dilemma they had recently faced. Two thirds of the young people either couldn't describe a moral problem or described problems that are not moral at all. For example, one said his most recent moral dilemma arose when he pulled in to a parking space and didn't have enough quarters for the meter.

"Not many of them have previously given much or any thought to many of the kinds of questions about morality that we asked," Smith and his coauthors wrote. They didn't understand that a moral dilemma arises when two legitimate moral values clash. Their default position was that moral choices are just a question of what feels right inside, whether it arouses a comfortable emotion. One student uttered this typical response: "I mean, I guess what makes something right is how I feel about it. But different people feel different ways, so I couldn't speak on behalf of anyone else as to what's right and wrong."[28]

If you believe that the ultimate oracle is the True Self inside, then of course you become emotivist — you make moral judgments on the basis of the feelings that burble up. Of course you become a relativist. One True Self has no basis to judge or argue with another True Self. Of course you become an individualist, since the ultimate arbiter is the authentic self within and not any community standard or external horizon of significance without. Of course you lose contact with the moral vocabulary that is needed to think about these questions. Of course the inner life becomes more level — instead of inspiring peaks and despairing abysses, ethical decision making is just gentle rolling foothills, nothing to get too hepped up about.

The mental space that was once occupied by moral struggle has gradually become occupied by the struggle to achieve. Morality has been displaced by utility. Adam II has been displaced by Adam I.

THE WRONG LIFE

In 1886, Leo Tolstoy published his famous novella *The Death of Ivan Ilyich*. The central character is a successful lawyer and magistrate who one day is hanging curtains in his fancy new house when he falls awkwardly on his side. He thinks nothing of it at first, but then he develops an odd taste in his mouth and grows ill. Eventually he realizes that at age forty-five he is dying.

Ilyich had lived a productive upwardly mobile life. Tolstoy tells us he was "capable, cheerful, good-natured and sociable, though strict in the fulfillment of what he considered to be his duty: and he considered his duty to be what was so considered by those in authority."[29] In other words, he was a successful product of the moral ecology and social status system of his time. He had a good job and a fine reputation. His marriage was cold, but he spent less time with his family and regarded this as normal.

Ilyich tries to go back to his former way of thinking, but the onrushing presence of death thrusts new thoughts into his head. He thinks back on his childhood with special fondness, but the more he thinks about his adulthood, the less satisfactory it seems. He had rushed into marriage almost as an accident. He had been preoccupied with money year after year. His career triumphs now seem trivial. "Maybe I did not live as I ought to have done?" he suddenly asks himself.[30]

The whole story plays with notions of up and down. The higher he goes externally, the farther he sinks internally. He begins to experience the life he had led as "a stone falling downward with increasing velocity."[31]

It occurs to him that he had felt small, scarcely noticeable impulses to struggle against what was thought good and proper by society. But he had not really attended to them. He now realizes that "his professional duties and the whole arrangement of his life and of his family and all his social and official interests, might all have been false. He tried to defend those things to himself and suddenly felt the weakness of what he was defending. There was nothing to defend."[32]

Tolstoy probably goes overboard in renouncing Ivan's Adam I life. It had not all been false and worthless. But he starkly paints the portrait of a man without an inner world until the occasion of his death. In those final hours the man finally gets a glimpse of what he should have known all along: "He fell through the hole and there at the bottom was a light. . . . At that very moment Ivan Ilyich fell through and caught sight of the light, and it was revealed to him that though his life had not been what it should have been, this could still be rectified. He asked himself, 'What is the right thing?' and grew still, listening."

Many of us are in Ivan Ilyich's position, recognizing that the social system we are part of pushes us to live out one sort of insufficient external life. But we have what Ilyich did not have: time to rectify it. The question is how.

The answer must be to stand against, at least in part, the prevailing winds of culture. The answer must be to join a counterculture. To live a decent life, to build up the soul, it's probably necessary to declare that the forces that encourage the Big Me, while necessary and liberating in many ways, have gone too far. We are out of balance. It's probably necessary to have one foot in the world of achievement but another foot in a counterculture that is in tension with the achievement ethos. It's probably necessary to reassert a balance between Adam I and Adam II and to understand that if anything, Adam II is more important than Adam I.

THE HUMILITY CODE

Each society creates its own moral ecology. A moral ecology is a set of norms, assumptions, beliefs, and habits of behavior and an institutionalized set of moral demands that emerge organically. Our moral ecology encourages us to be a certain sort of person. When you behave consistently with your society's moral ecology, people smile at you, and you are encouraged to continue acting in that way. The moral ecology of a given moment is never unanimous; there are always rebels, critics, and outsiders. But each moral climate is a collective response to the problems of the moment and it shapes the people who live within it.

Over the past several decades we have built a moral ecology around the Big Me, around the belief in a golden figure inside. This has led to a rise in narcissism and self-aggrandizement. This has encouraged us to focus on the external Adam I side of our natures and ignore the inner world of Adam II.

To restore the balance, to rediscover Adam II, to cultivate the eulogy virtues, it's probably necessary to revive and follow what we accidentally left behind: the counter-tradition of moral realism, or what I've been calling the crooked-timber school. It's probably necessary to build a moral ecology based on the ideas of this school, to follow its answers to the most important questions: Toward what should I orient my life? Who am I and what is my nature? How do I mold my nature to make it gradually better day by day? What virtues are the most important to cultivate and what weaknesses should I fear the most? How can I raise my children with a true sense of who they are and a practical set of ideas about how to travel the long road to character?

So far the propositions that define the crooked-timber tradition have been scattered across the many chapters that make up this book. I thought it might be useful to draw them together and recapitulate them here in one list, even if presenting them in numbered-list form does tend to simplify them and make them seem cruder than they are. Together these propositions form a

Humility Code, a coherent image of what to live for and how to live. These are the general propositions that form this Humility Code:

1. We don't live for happiness, we live for holiness. Day to day we seek out pleasure, but deep down, human beings are endowed with moral imagination. All human beings seek to lead lives not just of pleasure, but of purpose, righteousness, and virtue. As John Stuart Mill put it, people have a responsibility to become more moral over time. The best life is oriented around the increasing excellence of the soul and is nourished by moral joy, the quiet sense of gratitude and tranquillity that comes as a byproduct of successful moral struggle. The meaningful life is the same eternal thing, the combination of some set of ideals and some man or woman's struggle for those ideals. Life is essentially a moral drama, not a hedonistic one.

2. Proposition one defines the goal of life. The long road to character begins with an accurate understand-

ing of our nature, and the core of that understanding is that we are flawed creatures. We have an innate tendency toward selfishness and overconfidence. We have a tendency to see ourselves as the center of the universe, as if everything revolves around us. We resolve to do one thing but end up doing the opposite. We know what is deep and important in life, but we still pursue the things that are shallow and vain. Furthermore, we overestimate our own strength and rationalize our own failures. We know less than we think we do. We give in to short-term desires even when we know we shouldn't. We imagine that spiritual and moral needs can be solved through status and material things.

3. Although we are flawed creatures, we are also splendidly endowed. We are divided within ourselves, both fearfully and wonderfully made. We do sin, but we also have the capacity to recognize sin, to feel ashamed of sin, and to overcome sin. We are both weak and strong, bound and free, blind and far-seeing. We thus have the capacity to struggle with

ourselves. There is something heroic about a person in struggle with herself, strained on the rack of conscience, suffering torments, yet staying alive and growing stronger, sacrificing a worldly success for the sake of an inner victory.

4. In the struggle against your own weakness, humility is the greatest virtue. Humility is having an accurate assessment of your own nature and your own place in the cosmos. Humility is awareness that you are an underdog in the struggle against your own weakness. Humility is an awareness that your individual talents alone are inadequate to the tasks that have been assigned to you. Humility reminds you that you are not the center of the universe, but you serve a larger order.

5. Pride is the central vice. Pride is a problem in the sensory apparatus. Pride blinds us to the reality of our divided nature. Pride blinds us to our own weaknesses and misleads us into thinking we are better than we are. Pride makes us more certain and closed-minded than we should

be. Pride makes it hard for us to be vulnerable before those whose love we need. Pride makes coldheartedness and cruelty possible. Because of pride we try to prove we are better than those around us. Pride deludes us into thinking that we are the authors of our own lives.

6. Once the necessities for survival are satisfied, the struggle against sin and for virtue is the central drama of life. No external conflict is as consequential or as dramatic as the inner campaign against our own deficiencies. This struggle against, say, selfishness or prejudice or insecurity gives meaning and shape to life. It is more important than the external journey up the ladder of success. This struggle against sin is the great challenge, so that life is not futile or absurd. It is possible to fight this battle well or badly, humorlessly or with cheerful spirit. Contending with weakness often means choosing what parts of yourself to develop and what parts not to develop. The purpose of the struggle against sin and weakness is not to "win," because that is not

possible; it is to get better at waging it. It doesn't matter if you work at a hedge fund or a charity serving the poor. There are heroes and schmucks in both worlds. The most important thing is whether you are willing to engage in this struggle.

7. Character is built in the course of your inner confrontation. Character is a set of dispositions, desires, and habits that are slowly engraved during the struggle against your own weakness. You become more disciplined, considerate, and loving through a thousand small acts of self-control, sharing, service, friendship, and refined enjoyment. If you make disciplined, caring choices, you are slowly engraving certain tendencies into your mind. You are making it more likely that you will desire the right things and execute the right actions. If you make selfish, cruel, or disorganized choices, then you are slowly turning this core thing inside yourself into something that is degraded, inconstant, or fragmented. You can do harm to this core thing with nothing more than ignoble

thoughts, even if you are not harming anyone else. You can elevate this core thing with an act of restraint nobody sees. If you don't develop a coherent character in this way, life will fall to pieces sooner or later. You will become a slave to your passions. But if you do behave with habitual self-discipline, you will become constant and dependable.

8. The things that lead us astray are short term — lust, fear, vanity, gluttony. The things we call character endure over the long term — courage, honesty, humility. People with character are capable of a long obedience in the same direction, of staying attached to people and causes and callings consistently through thick and thin. People with character also have scope. They are not infinitely flexible, free-floating, and solitary. They are anchored by permanent attachments to important things. In the realm of the intellect, they have a set of permanent convictions about fundamental truths. In the realm of emotion, they are enmeshed in a web of unconditional loves. In the

realm of action, they have a permanent commitment to tasks that cannot be completed in a single lifetime.

9. No person can achieve self-mastery on his or her own. Individual will, reason, compassion, and character are not strong enough to consistently defeat selfishness, pride, greed, and self-deception. Everybody needs redemptive assistance from outside — from God, family, friends, ancestors, rules, traditions, institutions, and exemplars. If you are to prosper in the confrontation with yourself, you have to put yourself in a state of affection. You have to draw on something outside yourself to cope with the forces inside yourself. You have to draw from a cultural tradition that educates the heart, that encourages certain values, that teaches us what to feel in certain circumstances. We wage our struggles in conjunction with others waging theirs, and the boundaries between us are indistinct.

10. We are all ultimately saved by grace. The struggle against weakness often

has a U shape. You are living your life and then you get knocked off course — either by an overwhelming love, or by failure, illness, loss of employment, or twist of fate. The shape is advance-retreat-advance. In retreat, you admit your need and surrender your crown. You open up space that others might fill. And grace floods in. It may come in the form of love from friends and family, in the assistance of an unexpected stranger, or from God. But the message is the same. You are accepted. You don't flail about in desperation, because hands are holding you up. You don't have to struggle for a place, because you are embraced and accepted. You just have to accept the fact that you are accepted. Gratitude fills the soul, and with it the desire to serve and give back.

11. Defeating weakness often means quieting the self. Only by quieting the self, by muting the sound of your own ego, can you see the world clearly. Only by quieting the self can you be open to the external sources of strengths you will need. Only by

stilling the sensitive ego can you react with equipoise to the ups and downs of the campaign. The struggle against weakness thus requires the habits of self-effacement — reticence, modesty, obedience to some larger thing — and a capacity for reverence and admiration.

12. Wisdom starts with epistemological modesty. The world is immeasurably complex and the private stock of reason is small. We are generally not capable of understanding the complex web of causes that drive events. We are not even capable of grasping the unconscious depths of our own minds. We should be skeptical of abstract reasoning or of trying to apply universal rules across different contexts. But over the centuries, our ancestors built up a general bank of practical wisdom, traditions, habits, manners, moral sentiments, and practices. The humble person thus has an acute historical consciousness. She is the grateful inheritor of the tacit wisdom of her kind, the grammar of conduct and the store

of untaught feelings that are ready for use in case of emergency, that offer practical tips on how to behave in different situations, and that encourage habits that cohere into virtues. The humble person understands that experience is a better teacher than pure reason. He understands that wisdom is not knowledge. Wisdom emerges out of a collection of intellectual virtues. It is knowing how to behave when perfect knowledge is lacking.

13. No good life is possible unless it is organized around a vocation. If you try to use your work to serve yourself, you'll find your ambitions and expectations will forever run ahead and you'll never be satisfied. If you try to serve the community, you'll always wonder if people appreciate you enough. But if you serve work that is intrinsically compelling and focus just on being excellent at that, you will wind up serving yourself and the community obliquely. A vocation is not found by looking within and finding your passion. It is found by looking without and asking what life is ask-

ing of us. What problem is addressed by an activity you intrinsically enjoy?

14. The best leader tries to lead along the grain of human nature rather than go against it. He realizes that he, like the people he leads, is likely to be sometimes selfish, narrow-minded, and self-deceiving. Therefore he prefers arrangements that are low and steady to those that are lofty and heroic. As long as the foundations of an institution are sound, he prefers change that is constant, gradual, and incremental to change that is radical and sudden. He understands that public life is a contest between partial truths and legitimate contesting interests. The goal of leadership is to find a just balance between competing values and competing goals. He seeks to be a trimmer, to shift weight one way or another as circumstances change, in order to keep the boat moving steadily forward on an even keel. He understands that in politics and business the lows are lower than the highs are high. The downside risk

caused by bad decisions is larger than the upside benefits that accrue from good ones. Therefore the wise leader is a steward for his organization and tries to pass it along in slightly better condition than he found it.

15. The person who successfully struggles against weakness and sin may or may not become rich and famous, but that person will become mature. Maturity is not based on talent or any of the mental or physical gifts that help you ace an IQ test or run fast or move gracefully. It is not comparative. It is earned not by being better than other people at something, but by being better than you used to be. It is earned by being dependable in times of testing, straight in times of temptation. Maturity does not glitter. It is not built on the traits that make people celebrities. A mature person possesses a settled unity of purpose. The mature person has moved from fragmentation to centeredness, has achieved a state in which the restlessness is over, the confusion about the meaning and

purpose of life is calmed. The mature person can make decisions without relying on the negative and positive reactions from admirers or detractors because the mature person has steady criteria to determine what is right. That person has said a multitude of noes for the sake of a few overwhelming yeses.

MODES OF LIVING

The characters in this book followed many different courses and had many different traits. Some, like Augustine and Johnson, were quite introspective. Others, like Eisenhower and Randolph, were not. Some, like Perkins, were willing to soil their hands in politics in order to get things done. Others, like Day, wanted not only to do good but to be good, to live a life that was as pure as possible. Some of these figures, like Johnson and Day, were very hard on themselves. They felt the need to arduously attack their own weaknesses. Others, like Montaigne, accepted themselves and had a lighter and more relaxed attitude toward life, trusting in nature to take care of life's essential problems. Some, like Ida Eisenhower, Philip Randolph, and Perkins, were private people, a little detached and emotionally reticent.

Others, like Augustine and Rustin, exposed themselves emotionally. Some, like Day, were saved by religion, while others, like Eliot, were harmed by religion or were, like Marshall, not religious. Some, like Augustine, surrendered agency and let grace flood in. Others, like Johnson, took control of life and built their soul through effort.

Even within the tradition of moral realism, there are many differences of temperament, technique, tactics, and taste. Two people who both subscribe to the "crooked timber" view may approach specific questions in different ways. Should you stay in your suffering or move on from it as soon as possible? Should you keep a journal to maximize self-awareness, or does that just lead to paralyzing self-consciousness and self-indulgence? Should you be reticent or expressive? Should you take control of your own life or surrender it to God's grace?

Even within the same moral ecology, there's a lot of room for each person to chart a unique path. But each of the lives in this book started with a deep vulnerability, and undertook a lifelong effort to transcend that vulnerability. Johnson was fragmented and storm-tossed. Rustin was hollow and promiscuous. Marshall was a fearful boy. Eliot was desperate for affection. And yet each person was redeemed by that weakness. Each person struggled against that weakness and used that problem to grow a beautiful strength. Each person traveled down into the valley of humility in order to ascend to the heights of tranquillity and self-respect.

STUMBLERS

The good news of this book is that it is okay to be flawed, since everyone is. Sin and limitation are woven through our lives. We are all stumblers, and the beauty and meaning of life are in the stumbling — in recognizing the stumbling and trying to become more graceful as the years go by.

The stumbler scuffs through life, a little off balance here and there, sometimes lurching, sometimes falling to her knees. But the stumbler faces her imperfect nature, her mistakes and weaknesses, with unvarnished honesty, with the opposite of squeamishness. She is sometimes ashamed of the perversities in her nature — the selfishness, the self-deceit, the occasional desire to put lower loves above higher ones.

But humility offers self-understanding. When we acknowledge that we screw up, and feel the gravity of our limitations, we find ourselves challenged and stretched with a serious foe to overcome and transcend.

The stumbler is made whole by this struggle. Each weakness becomes a chance to wage a campaign that organizes and gives meaning to life and makes you a better person. We lean on each other as we struggle against sin. We depend on each other for the forgiveness of sin. The stumbler has an outstretched arm, ready to receive and offer care. He is vulnerable enough to need affection and is generous enough to give affection at full volume. If we were without sin, we could be solitary Atlases, but the stumbler requires a community. His friends are there with conversation and advice. His ancestors have left him diverse models that he can emulate and measure himself by.

From the smallness of her own life, the stumbler commits herself to ideas and faiths that are nobler than any individual ever could be. She doesn't always live up to her convictions or follow her resolutions. But she repents and is redeemed and tries again, a process that gives dignity to her failing. The victories follow the same arc: from defeat to recognition to redemption. Down into the valley of vision and then up into the highlands of attachment. The humble path to the beautiful life.

Each struggle leaves a residue. A person

who has gone through these struggles seems more substantial and deep. And by a magic alchemy these victories turn weakness into joy. The stumbler doesn't aim for joy. Joy is a byproduct experienced by people who are aiming for something else. But it comes.

There's joy in a life filled with interdependence with others, in a life filled with gratitude, reverence, and admiration. There's joy in freely chosen obedience to people, ideas, and commitments greater than oneself. There's joy in that feeling of acceptance, the knowledge that though you don't deserve their love, others do love you; they have admitted you into their lives. There's an aesthetic joy we feel in morally good action, which makes all other joys seem paltry and easy to forsake.

People do get better at living, at least if they are willing to humble themselves and learn. Over time they stumble less, and eventually they achieve moments of catharsis when outer ambition comes into balance with inner aspiration, when there is a unity of effort between Adam I and Adam II, when there is that ultimate tranquillity and that feeling of flow — when moral nature and external skills are united in one defining effort.

Joy is not produced because others praise

you. Joy emanates unbidden and unforced. Joy comes as a gift when you least expect it. At those fleeting moments you know why you were put here and what truth you serve. You may not feel giddy at those moments, you may not hear the orchestra's delirious swell or see flashes of crimson and gold, but you will feel a satisfaction, a silence, a peace — a hush. Those moments are the blessings and the signs of a beautiful life.

ACKNOWLEDGMENTS

Anne C. Snyder was there when this book was born and walked with me through the first three years of its writing. This was first conceived as a book about cognition and decision making. Under Anne's influence, it became a book about morality and inner life. She led dozens of discussions about the material, assigned me reading from her own bank of knowledge, challenged the superficiality of my thinking in memo after memo, and transformed the project. While I was never able to match the lyricism of her prose, or the sensitivity of her observations, I have certainly stolen many of her ideas and admired the gracious and morally rigorous way she lives her life. If there are any important points in this book, they probably come from Anne.

April Lawson came in for the final eighteen months of this effort. She is the editor of my newspaper column and brought that same astounding judgment to this manuscript. I may come to understand many things about life, but I will never understand how one so young can possess so much mature and considered wisdom, can understand so much about other people's lives, and can offer such bold and useful suggestions.

Campbell Schnebly-Swanson was a student of mine at Yale who helped with the final research, fact checking, and thinking. She is a tornado of insights, judgments, and enthusiasms. Her reactions sharpened this text, and her research infuses these pages. I wait with a sort of awed anticipation to see what kind of mark she leaves on the world.

For three years, I have taught a course at Yale University loosely based on some of the ideas here. My students there have wrestled with this topic alongside of me, and offered immeasurable insights, both in the classroom and at the bar of The Study Hotel. They've made the first two days of every week unbelievably fun. I'd especially like to thank my Yale colleagues Jim Levinsohn, John Gaddis, Charles Hill, and Paul Kennedy for welcoming me into their midst. Another Yale professor, Bryan Garsten, read a large chunk of the manuscript and helped clarify and deepen the thinking here. Large faculty groups at Yale and at Wheaton College heard me out and offered feedback and advice.

Will Murphy and I have worked on two books now for Random House. He is as supportive an editor as it is possible to imagine. I am the rare author who has nothing but good things to say about his publishing house. I've been fortunate to be writing for an enthusiastic, professional, and supportive team, especially London King, this book's lead publicist, who is as good at her job as anyone I've worked with. Cheryl Miller helped me early on to conceive the project and select the characters. Catherine Katz and Lauren Davis filled in with vital research and advice.

Many friends deserve my gratitude, acknowledgment, and devotion. Blair Miller read through everything, hunted for a less-than-awful title, encouraged me when that was needed, and offered advice and wisdom, large and small. Blair is an astonishing judge and connector of people and ideas. She did her best to help me tie the larger moral issues to the problems people face in the real world every day. In her own work, Blair serves the world, and the poorest people in the world, in a way that is practical and also idealistic, dignified but also joyful. She encouraged me to try to make this book of use to people, to make it not just a philosophical or sociological ramble, but an act of service.

My parents, Michael and Lois Brooks, are still my best and toughest editors. Pete Wehner tirelessly offered counsel and advice. Yuval Levin is much younger than me but has become an intellectual mentor. Kirsten Powers read crucial parts and provided moral and emotional support throughout. Carol Quillen, the president of Davidson College, has helped me understand Augustine, and much else, much better. An ecumenical group of clergy and lay people helped carry me through a crucial time in my life, including: Stuart and Celia McAlpine, David Wolpe, Meir Soloveichik, Tim Keller, and Jerry Root. My agents, Glen Hartley and Lynn Chu, have been friends since college and will remain so through life.

Life has its vicissitudes and unexpected turns. My ex-wife, Sarah, has done and continues to do an amazing job raising our three children. Those children, Joshua, Naomi, and Aaron, are now spread around the globe, and exemplify the traits of character that any parent dreams of: courage, creativity, honesty, fortitude, and loving kindness. They don't really need this book, but I hope they profit from it.

NOTES

Chapter 1: The Shift

1. Wilfred M. McClay, *The Masterless: Self and Society in Modern America* (University of North Carolina Press, 1993), 226.
2. Alonzo L. Hamby, "A Wartime Consigliere," review of David L. Roll, *The Hopkins Touch: Harry Hopkins and the Forging of the Alliance to Defeat Hitler* (Oxford University Press, 2012), *Wall Street Journal*, December 29, 2012.
3. David Frum, *How We Got Here: The 70's, the Decade That Brought You Modern Life (for Better or Worse)* (Basic Books, 2000), 103.
4. Jean M. Twenge and W. Keith Campbell, *The Narcissism Epidemic: Living in the Age of Entitlement* (Simon & Schuster, 2009), 13.
5. "How Young People View Their Lives, Futures and Politics: A Portrait of

'Generation Next.' " The Pew Research Center For The People & The Press (January 9, 2007).

6. Elizabeth Gilbert, *Eat, Pray, Love: One Woman's Search for Everything* (Penguin, 2006), 64.

7. James Davison Hunter, *The Death of Character: Moral Education in an Age Without Good or Evil* (Basic Books, 2000), 103.

8. Twenge and Campbell, *Narcissism,* 248.

9. C. J. Mahaney, *Humility: True Greatness* (Multnomah, 2005), 70.

10. Daniel Kahneman, *Thinking, Fast and Slow* (Farrar, Straus and Giroux, 2011), 201.

11. Harry Emerson Fosdick, *On Being a Real Person* (Harper and Brothers, 1943), 25.

12. Thomas Merton, *The Seven Storey Mountain* (Harcourt, 1998), 92.

13. Henry Fairlie, *The Seven Deadly Sins Today* (New Republic Books, 1978), 30.

Chapter 2: The Summoned Self

1. David Von Drehle, *Triangle: The Fire That Changed America* (Atlantic Monthly Press, 2003), 195.

2. Frances Perkins, "The Triangle Factory

Fire," lecture, Cornell University online archives. http://trianglefire.ilr.cornell.edu/primary/lectures/francesperkinslecture.html.

3. Von Drehle, *Triangle,* 158.

4. George Martin, *Madam Secretary: Frances Perkins; A Biography of America's First Woman Cabinet Member* (Houghton Mifflin, 1976), 85.

5. Von Drehle, *Triangle,* 138.

6. Von Drehle, *Triangle,* 130.

7. Von Drehle, *Triangle,* 152.

8. Von Drehle, *Triangle,* 146.

9. Perkins, "Triangle Fire" lecture.

10. Naomi Pasachoff, *Frances Perkins: Champion of the New Deal* (Oxford University Press, 1999), 30.

11. Viktor Frankl, *Man's Search for Meaning* (Beacon, 1992), 85.

12. Frankl, *Man's Search for Meaning,* 99.

13. Frankl, *Man's Search for Meaning,* 104.

14. Frankl, *Man's Search for Meaning,* 98.

15. Mark R. Schwehn and Dorothy C. Bass, eds., *Leading Lives That Matter: What We Should Do and Who We Should Be* (Eerdmans, 2006), 35.

16. Kirstin Downey, *The Woman Behind the New Deal: The Life of Frances Perkins, FDR's Secretary of Labor and His Moral*

Conscience (Nan Talese, 2008), 8.

17. Downey, *Woman Behind the New Deal,* 5.

18. Martin, *Madam Secretary,* 50.

19. David Hackett Fischer, *Albion's Seed: Four British Folkways in America* (Oxford, 1989), 895.

20. Lillian G. Paschal, "Hazing in Girls' Colleges," *Household Ledger,* 1905.

21. Martin, *Madam Secretary,* 46.

22. Russell Lord, "Madam Secretary," *New Yorker,* September 2, 1933.

23. Mary E. Woolley, "Values of College Training for Women," *Harper's Bazaar,* September 1904.

24. Martin, *Madam Secretary,* 51.

25. Jane Addams, *Twenty Years at Hull House: With Autobiographical Notes* (University of Illinois, 1990), 71.

26. Addams, *Twenty Years at Hull House,* 94.

27. Frances Perkins, "My Recollections of Florence Kelley," *Social Service Review,* vol. 28, no. 1 (March 1954), 12.

28. Martin, *Madam Secretary,* 146.

29. Downey, *Woman Behind the New Deal,* 42.

30. Downey, *Woman Behind the New Deal,* 42.

31. Martin, *Madam Secretary,* 98.

32. Downey, *Woman Behind the New Deal,* 56.

33. Martin, *Madam Secretary,* 125.

34. Downey, *Woman Behind the New Deal,* 66.

35. Martin, *Madam Secretary,* 232.

36. Martin, *Madam Secretary,* 136.

37. Downey, *Woman Behind the New Deal,* 317.

38. Frances Perkins, *The Roosevelt I Knew* (Penguin, 2011), 29.

39. Perkins, "Roosevelt I Knew," 45.

40. Martin, *Madam Secretary,* 206.

41. Martin, *Madam Secretary,* 206.

42. Martin, *Madam Secretary,* 236.

43. Martin, *Madam Secretary,* 237.

44. Perkins, *Roosevelt I Knew,* 156.

45. Downey, *Woman Behind the New Deal,* 284.

46. Downey, *Woman Behind the New Deal,* 279.

47. Martin, *Madam Secretary,* 281.

48. Downey, *Woman Behind the New Deal,* 384.

49. Christopher Breiseth, "The Frances Perkins I Knew," essay, Franklin D. Roosevelt American Heritage Center Museum (Worcester, MA).

50. Martin, *Madam Secretary,* 485.

51. Reinhold Niebuhr, *The Irony of American*

History (University of Chicago Press, 2008), 63.

Chapter 3: Self-Conquest

1. *The Eisenhower Legacy: Discussions of Presidential Leadership* (Bartleby Press, 1992), 21.
2. Jean Edward Smith, *Eisenhower in War and Peace* (New York: Random House, 2012), 7.
3. Smith, *Eisenhower in War and Peace,* 8.
4. Mark Perry, *Partners in Command: George Marshall and Dwight Eisenhower in War and Peace* (Penguin, 2007), 68.
5. Dwight D. Eisenhower, *At Ease: Stories I Tell to Friends* (Doubleday, 1967), 76.
6. Eisenhower, *At Ease,* 31.
7. Smith, *Eisenhower in War and Peace,* 59.
8. Eisenhower, *At Ease,* 52.
9. Anthony T. Kronman, *The Lost Lawyer: Failing Ideals of the Legal Profession* (Harvard University Press, 1995), 16.
10. Smith, *Eisenhower in War and Peace,* 59.
11. Evan Thomas, *Ike's Bluff: President Eisenhower's Secret Battle to Save the World* (Little, Brown, 2012), 27.
12. Thomas, *Ike's Bluff,* 27.
13. Paul F. Boller, Jr., *Presidential Anecdotes*

(Oxford University Press, 1996), 292; Robert J. Donovan, *Eisenhower: The Inside Story* (New York: Harper and Brothers, 1956), 7.

14. Thomas, *Ike's Bluff,* 33.
15. State of the Union message, Washington, D.C., January 10, 1957.
16. Thomas, *Ike's Bluff,* 30.
17. Fred Greenstein, *The Presidential Difference: Leadership Style from Roosevelt to Clinton* (Free Press, 2000), 49.
18. Stephen E. Ambrose, *Eisenhower: Soldier and President* (Simon and Schuster, 1990), 65.
19. Smith, *Eisenhower in War and Peace,* 19.
20. Smith, *Eisenhower in War and Peace,* 48.
21. Eisenhower, *At Ease,* 155.
22. Eisenhower, *At Ease,* 135
23. William Lee Miller, *Two Americans: Truman, Eisenhower, and a Dangerous World* (Vintage, 2012), 78.
24. Thomas, *Ike's Bluff,* 26; John S. D. Eisenhower, *Strictly Personal* (Doubleday, 1974), 292.
25. Smith, *Eisenhower in War and Peace,* 61.

26. Smith, *Eisenhower in War and Peace*, 65.

27. Dwight D. Eisenhower, *Ike's Letters to a Friend, 1941–1958* (University Press of Kansas, 1984), 4.

28. Eisenhower, *At Ease*, 193.

29. Boller, *Presidential Anecdotes*, 290.

30. Eisenhower, *At Ease*, 213.

31. Eisenhower, *At Ease*, 214.

32. Eisenhower, *At Ease*, 228.

33. Smith, *Eisenhower in War and Peace*, 147.

34. Smith, *Eisenhower in War and Peace*, 443.

35. Ambrose, *Eisenhower: Soldier and President*, 440.

36. Thomas, *Ike's Bluff*, 153.

37. Thomas, *Ike's Bluff*, 29.

38. Quoted in Steven J. Rubenzer and Thomas R. Faschingbauer, *Personality, Character, and Leadership in the White House: Psychologists Assess the Presidents* (Potomac Books, 2004), 147.

39. Thomas, *Ike's Bluff*, introduction, 17.

40. Thomas, *Ike's Bluff*, 161.

41. Thomas, *Ike's Bluff*, 161.

42. Smith, *Eisenhower in War and Peace*, 766.

43. Eisenhower, *Ike's Letters to a Friend*, 189, July 22, 1957.

Chapter 4: Struggle

1. Dorothy Day, *The Long Loneliness: The Autobiography of the Legendary Catholic Social Activist* (Harper, 1952), 20.
2. Day, *Long Loneliness,* 21.
3. Paul Elie, *The Life You Save May Be Your Own: An American Pilgrimage* (Farrar, Straus and Giroux, 2003), 4.
4. Elie, *Life You Save,* 4.
5. Day, *Long Loneliness,* 24.
6. Day, *Long Loneliness,* 35.
7. Elie, *Life You Save,* 16.
8. Day, *Long Loneliness,* 87.
9. Jim Forest, *All Is Grace: A Biography of Dorothy Day* (Orbis Books, 2011), 47.
10. Elie, *Life You Save,* 31.
11. Forest, *All Is Grace,* 48.
12. Forest, *All Is Grace,* 50.
13. Deborah Kent, *Dorothy Day: Friend to the Forgotten* (Eerdmans Books, 2004), 35.
14. Day, *Long Loneliness,* 79.
15. Day, *Long Loneliness,* 79.
16. Elie, *Life You Save,* 38.
17. Day, *Long Loneliness,* 60.
18. Robert Coles, *Dorothy Day: A Radical Devotion* (Da Capo Press, 1989), 6.
19. Elie, *Life You Save,* 45.
20. Nancy Roberts, *Dorothy Day and the*

Catholic Worker (State University of New York Press, 1985), 26.

21. Forest, *All Is Grace,* 62.
22. Day, *Long Loneliness,* 141.
23. Coles, *Radical Devotion,* 52.
24. Coles, *Radical Devotion,* 53.
25. Robert Elsberg, ed., *All the Way to Heaven: The Selected Letters of Dorothy Day* (Marquette University Press, 2010), 23.
26. Roberts, *Dorothy Day,* 26.
27. Day, *Long Loneliness,* 133.
28. William Miller, *Dorothy Day: A Biography* (Harper & Row, 1982), 196.
29. Day, *Long Loneliness,* 165.
30. Forest, *All Is Grace,* 61.
31. Dorothy Day, *The Duty of Delight: The Diaries of Dorothy Day* (Marquette University, 2011), 519.
32. Day, *Long Loneliness,* 182.
33. Day, *Long Loneliness,* 214.
34. Day, *Duty of Delight,* 68.
35. Schwehn and Bass, eds., *Leading Lives That Matter,* 34.
36. Day, *Duty of Delight,* 42.
37. Coles, *Radical Devotion,* 115.
38. Coles, *Radical Devotion,* 120.
39. Day, *Long Loneliness,* 236.
40. Forest, *All Is Grace,* 168.
41. Forest, *All Is Grace,* 178.

42. Forest, *All Is Grace*, 118.
43. Day, *Long Loneliness*, 243.
44. Day, *Long Loneliness*, 285.
45. Day, *Duty of Delight*, 9.
46. Rosalie Riegle Troester, *Voices from the Catholic Worker* (Temple University Press, 1993), 69.
47. Troester, *Voices*, 93.
48. Day, *Duty of Delight*, 287.
49. Day, *Duty of Delight*, 295.
50. Coles, *Radical Devotion*, 16.

Chapter 5: Self-Mastery

1. Forrest C. Pogue, *George C. Marshall*, 4 vols. (Viking Press, 1964), vol. 1, *Education of a General, 1880–1939*, 35.
2. Ed Cray, *General of the Army: George C. Marshall, Soldier and Statesman* (W. W. Norton, 1990), 20.
3. Cray, *General of the Army*, 25.
4. William Frye, *Marshall: Citizen Soldier* (Bobbs-Merrill, 1947), 32–65.
5. Pogue, *Marshall*, 63.
6. Pogue, *Marshall*, 63.
7. Richard Livingstone, *On Education: The Future in Education and Education for a World Adrift* (Cambridge, 1954), 153.
8. James Davison Hunter, *The Death of Character: Moral Education in an Age*

Without Good or Evil (Basic Books, 2000), 19.

9. Leonard Mosley, *Marshall: Hero for Our Times* (Hearst Books, 1982), 13.

10. Mosley, *Hero for Our Times,* 14.

11. Mosley, *Hero for Our Times,* 15.

12. Frye, *Citizen Soldier,* 49.

13. David Hein, "In War for Peace: General George C. Marshall's Core Convictions & Ethical Leadership," *Touchstone,* March, 2013.

14. Mosley, *Hero for Our Times,* Introduction, xiv.

15. Mosley, *Hero for Our Times,* 19.

16. Cray, *General of the Army,* 64.

17. Quoted in Major James R. Hill, "A Comparative Analysis of the Military Leadership Styles of Ernest J. King and Chester W. Nimitz," published master's thesis, General Staff College, Fort Leavenworth, KS, 2008.

18. Mosley, *Hero for Our Times,* 64.

19. Pogue, *Marshall,* 79.

20. Pogue, *Marshall,* 246; Mosley, *Hero for Our Times,* 93.

21. André Comte-Sponville, *A Small Treatise on the Great Virtues: The Uses of Philosophy in Everyday Life* (Macmillan, 2002), 10.

22. Frye, *Citizen Soldier,* 85.

23. Cray, *General of the Army,* 276.

24. Mark Perry, *Partners in Command: George Marshall and Dwight Eisenhower in War and Peace* (Penguin, 2007), 15.

25. Cray, *General of the Army,* 278.

26. Cray, *General of the Army,* 297.

27. Mosley, *Hero for Our Times,* 211.

28. Mosley, *Hero for Our Times,* 292.

29. Dwight D. Eisenhower, *Crusade in Europe* (Doubleday, 1948), 197.

30. Perry, *Partners in Command,* 238.

31. Pogue, *George C. Marshall* (Viking, 1973), vol. 3, *Organizer of Victory, 1943–1945,* 321.

32. Perry, *Partners in Command,* 240.

33. John S. D. Eisenhower, *General Ike: A Personal Reminiscence* (Simon and Schuster, 2003), 99, reproduced in Dwight D. Eisenhower, *Crusade in Europe,* 208.

34. John Eisenhower, *General Ike,* 103.

35. Mosley, *Hero for Our Times,* 341.

36. Mosley, *Hero for Our Times,* prologue, xxi.

37. Frye, *Citizen Soldier,* 372.

38. Robert Faulkner, *The Case for Greatness: Honorable Ambition and Its Critics* (Yale University Press, 2007), 39.

39. Faulkner, *Case for Greatness,* 40.

40. Aristotle, *Nichomachean Ethics* (Focus Publishing, 2002), 70; Faulkner, *Case for Greatness,* 43.
41. Mosley, *Hero for Our Times,* 434.
42. Mosley, *Hero for Our Times,* 522.
43. Mosley, *Hero for Our Times,* 523.
44. Mosley, *Hero for Our Times,* 523.

Chapter 6: Dignity

1. Cynthia Taylor, *A. Philip Randolph: The Religious Journey of an African American Labor Leader* (New York University Press, 2006), 13.
2. Jervis Anderson, *A. Philip Randolph: A Biographical Portrait* (University of California Press, 1973), 43.
3. Anderson, *Biographical Portrait,* 9.
4. Anderson, *Biographical Portrait,* 10.
5. Anderson, *Biographical Portrait,* 272.
6. Anderson, *Biographical Portrait,* 339.
7. Aaron Wildavsky, *Moses as Political Leader* (Shalem Press, 2005), 45.
8. Irving Kristol, *The Neoconservative Persuasion: Selected Essays, 1942–2009,* edited by Gertrude Himmelfarb (Basic Books, 2011), 71.
9. Murray Kempton, "A. Philip Randolph: The Choice, Mr. President," *New Republic,* July 6, 1963.

10. Anderson, *Biographical Portrait,* 176.

11. Larry Tye, *Rising from the Rails: Pullman Porters and the Making of the Black Middle Class* (Owl Books, 2005), 154.

12. Doris Kearns Goodwin, *No Ordinary Time: Franklin and Eleanor Roosevelt: The Home Front in World War II* (Simon & Schuster, 2013), 251.

13. Paula F. Pfeffer, *A. Philip Randolph: Pioneer of the Civil Rights Movement* (Louisiana State University Press, 1996), 66.

14. Pfeffer, *Pioneer,* 58.

15. John D'Emilio, *Lost Prophet: The Life and Times of Bayard Rustin* (Simon and Schuster, 2003), 11.

16. D'Emilio, *Lost Prophet,* 16

17. D'Emilio, *Lost Prophet,* 19.

18. Rachel Moston, "Bayard Rustin on His Own Terms," *Haverford Journal,* 2005, 82.

19. Michael G. Long, ed., *I Must Resist: Bayard Rustin's Life in Letters* (City Lights, 2012), 228.

20. Moston, "Bayard Rustin on His Own Terms," 91.

21. D'Emilio, *Lost Prophet,* 77.

22. Long, *I Must Resist,* 50.

23. D'Emilio, *Lost Prophet,* 172.

24. Long, *I Must Resist,* 49.

25. Long, *I Must Resist,* 51.
26. Long, *I Must Resist,* 65.
27. D'Emilio, *Lost Prophet,* 112.
28. D'Emilio, *Lost Prophet,* 159.
29. David L. Chappell, *A Stone of Hope: Prophetic Religion and the Death of Jim Crow* (University of North Carolina Press, 2004), 48.
30. Chappell, *Stone of Hope,* 54.
31. Chappell, *Stone of Hope,* 179.
32. Chappell, *Stone of Hope,* 55.
33. Chappell, *Stone of Hope,* 56.
34. D'Emilio, *Lost Prophet,* 150.
35. Chappell, *Stone of Hope,* 50.
36. Reinhold Niebuhr, *The Irony of American History* (University of Chicago Press, 2008), 5.
37. Niebuhr, *Irony of American History,* 23.
38. D'Emilio, *Lost Prophet,* 349.
39. D'Emilio, *Lost Prophet,* 352.
40. Anderson, *Biographical Portrait,* 332.

Chapter 7: Love

1. George Eliot, *Daniel Deronda* (Wordsworth, 2003), 15.
2. Kathryn Hughes, *George Eliot: The Last Victorian* (Cooper Square Press, 2001), 16.
3. Hughes, *Last Victorian,* 18.

4. Frederick R. Karl, *George Eliot: Voice of a Century; A Biography* (W. W. Norton, 1995), 36.
5. Karl, *George Eliot: Voice of a Century,* 36.
6. Rebecca Mead, *My Life in Middlemarch* (Crown, 2013), 28.
7. Hughes, *Last Victorian,* 47.
8. Mead, *My Life in Middlemarch,* 66.
9. Mead, *My Life in Middlemarch,* 125.
10. Karl, *Voice of a Century,* 146.
11. Gordon S. Haight, *George Eliot: A Biography* (Oxford University Press, 1968), 133.
12. Brenda Maddox, *George Eliot in Love* (Palgrave Macmillan, 2010), 59.
13. Haight, *George Eliot,* 144.
14. Karl, *Voice of a Century,* 167.
15. Michael Ignatieff, *Isaiah Berlin: A Life* (Henry Holt, 1999), 161.
16. Christian Wiman, *My Bright Abyss: Meditation of a Modern Believer* (Farrar, Straus and Giroux, 2013), 23.
17. William Shakespeare, *Romeo and Juliet,* Act II, Scene I.
18. Karl, *Voice of a Century,* 178.
19. Karl, *Voice of a Century,* 157.
20. Hughes, *Last Victorian,* 186.
21. Mead, *My Life in Middlemarch,* 266.
22. Virginia Woolf, "George Eliot," *The*

Times Literary Supplement, November 20, 1919.

23. Barbara Hardy, *George Eliot: A Critic's Biography* (Continuum, 2006), 122.

Chapter 8: Ordered Love

1. Peter Brown, *Augustine of Hippo: A Biography* (University of California Press, 2000), 17.
2. Brown, *Augustine of Hippo,* 18.
3. Matthew Arnold, *Culture and Anarchy* (Cambridge University Press, 1993), 130.
4. Arnold, *Culture and Anarchy,* 128.
5. Arnold, *Culture and Anarchy,* 128.
6. Arnold, *Culture and Anarchy,* 132.
7. Brown, *Augustine of Hippo,* 13.
8. Garry Wills, *Saint Augustine* (Penguin, 1999), 7.
9. Brown, *Augustine of Hippo,* 36.
10. Wills, *Saint Augustine,* 26.
11. Brown, *Augustine of Hippo,* 37.
12. Reinhold Niebuhr, *The Nature and Destiny of Man: A Christian Interpretation: Human Nature,* vol. I (Scribner's, 1996), 155.
13. Brown, *Augustine of Hippo,* 173; Augustine, *Confessions,* book 10, section 37.

14. Niebuhr, *Nature and Destiny of Man,* 157.

15. Lewis B. Smedes, *Shame and Grace: Healing the Shame We Don't Deserve* (Random House, 1994), 116.

16. Augustine, *Psalm 122: God Is True Wealth;* Mary Clark, *Augustine of Hippo: Selected Writings* (Paulist Press, 1984), 250.

17. Timothy Keller, *Freedom of Self Forgetfulness* (10Publishing, 2013), 40.

18. Jennifer A. Herdt, *Putting On Virtue: The Legacy of the Splendid Vices* (University of Chicago Press, 2008), 176.

19. Herdt, *Putting On Virtue,* 57.

20. Augustine, *The Works of Saint Augustine: A Translation for the 21st Century* (New City Press, 1992), 131.

21. Paul Tillich, *The Essential Tillich* (Scribner, 1999), 131.

22. Brown, *Augustine of Hippo,* 157.

23. Brown, *Augustine of Hippo,* 157.

Chapter 9: Self-Examination

1. Jeffrey Meyers, *Samuel Johnson: The Struggle* (Basic Books, 2008), 6.

2. W. Jackson Bate, *Samuel Johnson: A Biography* (Counterpoint, 2009), 8.

3. Bate, *Samuel Johnson,* 31.

4. John Wain, *Samuel Johnson* (Macmillan, 1980), 49.

5. Boswell, *Boswell's Life of Johnson* (Harper, 1889), 74.

6. Meyers, *Samuel Johnson: The Struggle*, 50.

7. Bate, *Samuel Johnson*, 211.

8. Meyers, *Samuel Johnson: The Struggle*, 205.

9. Bate, *Samuel Johnson*, 204.

10. Paul Fussell, *Samuel Johnson and the Life of Writing* (Norton, 1986), 236.

11. Bate, *Samuel Johnson*, 218.

12. Meyers, *Samuel Johnson: The Struggle*, 114.

13. Meyers, *Samuel Johnson: The Struggle*, 2.

14. Fussell, *Johnson and the Life of Writing*, 163.

15. Fussell, *Johnson and the Life of Writing*, 51.

16. Ralph Waldo Emerson, *The Spiritual Emerson: Essential Writings* (Beacon, 2004), 216.

17. Fussell, *Johnson and the Life of Writing*, 147.

18. Percy Hazen Houston, *Doctor Johnson: A Study in Eighteenth Century Humanism* (Cambridge University Press, 1923), 195.

19. Sarah Bakewell, *How to Live: Or a Life of*

Montaigne in One Question and Twenty Attempts at an Answer (Other Press, 2010), 21.

20. Bakewell, *How to Live,* 14.
21. Fussell, *Johnson and the Life of Writing,* 185.
22. Bate, *Samuel Johnson,* 4.

Chapter 10: The Big Me

1. Tom Callahan, *Johnny U: The Life and Times of John Unitas* (Random House, 2007), 16.
2. Michael Novak, *The Joy of Sports: Endzones, Bases, Baskets, Balls, and the Consecration of the American Spirit* (Madison Books, 1976), 241.
3. Callahan, *Johnny U,* 20.
4. Jimmy Breslin, "The Passer Nobody Wanted," *Saturday Evening Post,* November 1, 1958.
5. Callahan, *Johnny U,* 243.
6. John Skow, "Joe, Joe, You're the Most Beautiful Thing in the World," *Saturday Evening Post,* December 3, 1966.
7. Dan Jenkins, "The Sweet Life of Swinging Joe," *Sports Illustrated,* October 17, 1966.
8. George Eliot, *Middlemarch* (Penguin, 2003), 211.

9. Joshua L. Liebman, *Peace of Mind: Insights on Human Nature That Can Change Your Life* (Simon and Schuster, 1946), 56.

10. Benjamin Spock, *The Pocket Book of Baby and Child Care* (Duell, Sloan and Pearce, 1946), 309.

11. Harry A. Overstreet, *The Mature Mind* (Norton, 1949), 261.

12. Carl Ransom Rogers, *On Becoming a Person: A Therapist's View of Psychotherapy* (Harcourt, 1995), 194.

13. Carl Ransom Rogers, *The Carl Rogers Reader* (Houghton Mifflin, 1989), 185.

14. Katharine Graham, *Personal History* (Random House, 1997), 51.

15. Graham, *Personal History,* 231.

16. Eva Illouz, *Saving the Modern Soul: Therapy, Emotions, and the Culture of Self-Help* (University of California Press, 2008), 117.

17. Charles Taylor, *Multiculturalism: Examining the Politics of Recognition* (Princeton University Press, 1994), 30.

18. Dr. Seuss, *Oh, the Places You'll Go!* (Random House, 1990).

19. Ernst & Young Survey, "Sixty-five Per Cent of College Students Think They Will Become Millionaires" (Canada, 2001).

20. Greg Duncan and Richard Murnane,

Whither Opportunity? Rising Inequality, Schools, and Children's Life Chances (Russell Sage Foundation, 2011), 11.

21. "The American Freshman" Thirty Year Trends, 1966–1996. By Alexander W. Astin, Sarah A. Parrott, William S. Korn, Linda J. Sax. Higher Education Research Institute Graduate School of Education & Information Studies. University of California, Los Angeles. February, 1997.

22. Gretchen Anderson, "Loneliness Among Older Adults: A National Survey of Adults 45+" (AARP Research and Strategic Analysis, 2010).

23. Francis Fukuyama, *The Great Disruption: Human Nature and the Reconstitution of Social Order* (Profile, 1999), 50.

24. Sara Konrath, "Changes in Dispositional Empathy in American College Students Over Time: A Meta-Analysis" (University of Michigan, 2011).

25. Jean M. Twenge, W. Keith Campbell, and Brittany Gentile, "Increases in Individualistic Words and Phrases in American Books, 1960–2008" (2012), PLoS ONE 7(7): e40181, doi:10.1371/journal.pone.0040181.

26. David Brooks, "What Our Words Tell Us," *New York Times,* May 20, 2013.

27. Pelin Kesebir and Selin Kesebir, "The

Cultural Salience of Moral Character and Virtue Declined in Twentieth Century America," *Journal of Positive Psychology*, 2012.

28. Christian Smith, Kari Christoffersen, Hilary Davidson, *Lost in Transition: The Dark Side of Emerging Adulthood* (Oxford University Press, 2011), 22.

29. Leo Tolstoy, *The Death of Ivan Ilyich* (White Crow Books, 2010), 20.

30. Tolstoy, *The Death of Ivan Ilyich*, 66.

31. Tolstoy, *The Death of Ivan Ilyich*, 68.

32. Tolstoy, *The Death of Ivan Ilyich*, 71.

PERMISSION CREDITS

INDEX

resisting, 513–14

today's moral ecology and, 514

Blanck, Max, 52

Bloom, Allan, 105

Boetie, Étienne de la, 461

Boswell, James, 428–29, 433, 437, 468, 470–71

Boyse, Samuel, 431

Brabant, Dr. Robert, 326

Brancusi, Constantin, 91

Bray, Cara, 316–17, 334

Bray, Charles, 316–17

Brenman, Joseph, 54

Breslin, Jimmy, 477

Bridges, Harry, 100

Brothers, Dr. Joyce, 490

Brothers Karamazov, The (Dostoyevsky), 169

Brown, Peter, 373, 414

Brown, Tina, 239

Bucelli, Mary, 53

Buechner, Frederick, 59

Burke, Edmund, 466, 481

Burney, Fanny, 429

Bush, George H. W., 29

Call, The (newspaper), 167

career, 9–15, 122, 346, 506, 511

  Augustine and Adam I, 380

  increased importance of, 506

meritocracy and, 498, 501
the shrewd animal and, 12–15, 499
vocation vs., 55–57, 63
Carlyle, Thomas, 332
Case for Greatness, The (Faulkner),
    262–63
Catholic Worker, The, 189, 204, 205
Chambers, Robert, 467
Chapman, John, 327
Chappell, David L., 296–99
character, 125–31. *See also* humility; life;
    moral struggle; sin; *specific individuals*
Adam II and, 9–15, 40–41, 42, 46–47,
    118, 218, 496, 500, 514, 532
as built, not innate, 40
characteristics of people with, 521
as community-formed, 437
conquering the soul and, 118
"crooked timber" tradition for building,
    15–16, 18, 39, 46, 480, 482, 514–28,
    529
crucible moments and, 43, 45
everyday building of, 45
exemplars for, 16, 223–26
the humble path, 33–42, 532
Humility Code for, 514–28
Hunter on, 225
as internal (inner life), 78
Kierkegaard on, 225
Kronman's definition, 127

Reece, Spencer, 348
Reed, Jack, 81–82
Reeves, Andrew, 501
religion. *See also* Augustine of Hippo, St.
  Day and, 186
  Eliot and, 312–15
  Johnson and, 427–28
  Soloveitchik on, 186–88
  social gospel movement and, 75
renunciation, 73, 175, 181, 225, 270, 282, 313
  Augustine and, 400, 404, 416
  love and, 353
resilience, 116, 499
reticence, 19, 27
  Marshall and, 244, 246, 250, 257
  Perkins and, 82–92, 107
  Randolph and, 271, 483
  Rustin and, 308, 483
  vice of aloofness and, 92
Revolution from Within (Steinem), 490
Reynolds, Joshua, 466
River Brethren, 111
Road, The (London), 167
Rogers, Carl, 486
Roman Catholicism, 180–83, 202–10, 213.
      See also Augustine of Hippo, St.;
      Day, Dorothy
    Oxford Movement, 313
Romola (Eliot), 371

Schweitzer and, 193–94
social gospel movement and, 75
Seuss, Dr. (Theodor Seuss Geisel), 497
Sevareid, Eric, 252
Shakespeare, William, 349–50
Shaking the Foundations (Tillich), 410–12
shame, 54–57, 145, 287, 293, 517, 530
  Augustine and, 390, 402, 421
  Day and, 171, 173, 175
  Johnson and, 445–46, 468, 469–70
  suffering and, 198
Sibert, Gen. William, 235
Sibree, John, 326
Simons, Rayna, 167
sin (human weaknesses), 10, 16, 18,
    119–25, 519–20. *See also* moral
    struggle; *specific types*
  as abandoned concept, 119
  Abilene, Kansas and, 124
  Augustine and, 391
  awareness and, 18, 26, 35–36, 40, 46, 75
  building character and, 42, 122–23, 520
  as communal, 121
  "crooked timber" tradition and, 38–39,
    46, 480, 515, 529
  daily review of, 40
  Day and, 164, 170
  dual nature of man and, 119, 120–21,
    132, 517
  Eisenhower and, 132–33

transcendence and, 336
types of, 124
U shape of struggle, 522–23
vices as short-term, 519
Sinclair, Upton, 167
Smedes, Lewis, 394
Smith, Adam, 466
Smith, Al, 83, 92
Smith, Christian, 509
Smith, Jean Edward, 112, 139
Snyder, Howard, 132
social activism, 42, 107
social gospel movement, 75, 189
social media, 493–95, 500
society, 239. *See also* culture
  change (*see* civil rights movement; Day,
    Dorothy; Perkins, Frances)
  cultural change and, 487–91
  Eliot and handling public hostility, 357
  Eliot's beliefs about, 323
  Fear of Missing Out and, 384, 500
  moral ecology of, 514
Soloveitchik, Rabbi Joseph, 10, 11, 186
Solzhenitsyn, Aleksandr, 20, 65
soul, 120
  Augustinian thought on, 394
  crucible moments and, 45
  dappled, 122
  Eliot and, 328
  equality of souls, 408

ABOUT THE AUTHOR

David Brooks writes an op-ed column for *The New York Times*, teaches at Yale University, and appears regularly on *PBS NewsHour*, NPR's *All Things Considered*, and NBC's *Meet the Press*. Previously, he has been a senior editor at *The Weekly Standard*, a contributing editor at *Newsweek* and *The Atlantic Monthly*, and an op-ed editor at *The Wall Street Journal*. He is the author of *Bobos in Paradise: The New Upper Class and How They Got There*; *On Paradise Drive: How We Live Now (And Always Have) in the Future Tense*; and *The Social Animal: The Hidden Sources of Love, Character, and Achievement*. His articles have appeared in *The New Yorker*, *The New York Times Magazine*, *Forbes*, *The Washington Post*, *The Times Literary Supplement*, *Commentary*, *The Public Interest*, and many other magazines. David Brooks lives in Maryland.

"I don't intend to let you just walk out of my life."

Tod's voice was throaty. "We have to try and work something out."

Gina licked painfully dry lips. "You can't *enjoy* keeping someone against her will...."

"No," he agreed. "I'd far rather you stayed willingly. Will you stay, Gina?"

"No," she croaked, "I can't—I—"

"You're afraid to admit that you *want* to stay," he accused. "You still want me, Gina. Why not admit what your body tells me?"

If it were only her body, Gina thought miserably, but heart and mind were too closely involved with what her body felt.

"You said we'd come here to talk business," she whispered.

"I brought you here," Tod said, "because I wanted to make love to you. Because I'm going to make love to you...."

ANNABEL MURRAY has pursued many hobbies. She helped found an arts group in Liverpool, England, where she lives with her husband and two daughters. She loves drama: she appeared in many stage productions and went on to write an award-winning historical play. She uses all her experiences—holidays being no exception—to flesh out her character's backgrounds and create believable settings for her romance novels.

Books by Annabel Murray

HARLEQUIN PRESENTS
933—LAND OF THUNDER

HARLEQUIN ROMANCE
2549—ROOTS OF HEAVEN
2558—KEEGAN'S KINGDOM
2596—THE CHRYSANTHEMUM AND THE SWORD
2612—VILLA OF VENGEANCE
2625—DEAR GREEN ISLE
2717—THE COTSWOLD LION
2782—THE PLUMED SERPENT
2819—WILD FOR TO HOLD

ANNABEL MURRAY

fantasy woman

Harlequin Books

TORONTO • NEW YORK • LONDON
AMSTERDAM • PARIS • SYDNEY • HAMBURG
STOCKHOLM • ATHENS • TOKYO • MILAN

Harlequin Presents first edition April 1987
ISBN 0-373-10972-5

Original hardcover edition published in 1986
by Mills & Boon Limited

CHAPTER ONE

'COME on! *Come on!* Damn you!'

It was an old saw that a watched kettle never boiled and it certainly seemed that the more constantly you looked at a clock, the slower its hands moved. Irritatingly, the clock in Tod Fallon's hotel suite was no exception.

He could have gone for a walk to pass away the time, but London was in one of its wet, cold, grey moods. So instead, for the last hour, he had been pacing up and down from bedroom to sitting-room, with a monotonous, regular tread that might have inflicted serious damage on a less expensive carpet. His rawly masculine features wore an expression of intense irritation at the tedious waiting; irritation also with himself, at his nervous, anticipatory mood, the necessity for expending his valuable time. Marcha would be furious if she knew what he was up to, but though, for the past six months, it had been his habit to indulge Marcha in every way, this time she must bend to *his* will.

He was unaccustomed to waiting; efficient aides, secretaries and household staff saw to that. But not even a man of his wealth, power and influence could hasten time, even though, to him, time was money and time was something that was running short, thanks to Marcha's procrastination.

During his pacing he had thrown off the jacket of his impeccably tailored grey suit, wrenched loose the knot of his tie and discarded it, too, the violence of the act also serving to undo the top buttons of his blue silk shirt, revealing that the smooth bronze of his facial skin extended down the hard, firmly corded throat to his chest. His thick, dark, vibrant hair, liberally sprinkled with grey, had been disarrayed by the impatient, forceful thrusting of strong hands.

Tall and broad, physically dominating his surroundings, the energy and ill-suppressed eagerness exuding from him made even the generous proportions of his suite seem small and confining.

He picked up, for perhaps the twentieth time, the printed programme provided by the management; for all the suites in this luxury building boasted a television set. Though he could have recited its contents by heart, he re-read the blurb outlining the show he intended to watch. 'An extravaganza, produced in association with TLM Enterprises.' He studied intently the adjacent photograph of the presenter, a poor reproduction which did little to answer the numerous questions that exercised his mind. It was hard to believe she would be suitable, yet he had his secretary's firm assurance. Strange, though, that Marcha should be so against the idea.

An exasperated glance showed him that the hands of the clock had still barely moved and he threw aside the magazine, reaching for the television's remote control switch. Even the advertisements would be preferable to riding out this uncharacteristic tension.

Tod Fallon was accustomed to getting what he wanted. It was disconcerting to realise that this time he could not be one hundred per cent certain of attaining his objective. As the last of the adverts faded away and the music, the opening credits, of the next programme began, Tod found himself leaning forward, poised on the edge of his seat, and with an exclamation of annoyance he forced himself to relax. Damn it! He shouldn't have any doubts. If his own findings confirmed what his secretary had told him, his eventual object would be achieved. After all, he was in a position to pull several influential strings.

Only a fool would turn down the proposal he intended to make.

An anonymous voice, overlaid with dramatic emphasis made the announcement,

'Every week, millions of viewers tune in to this station to see her, the lady to whom no request is an impossibility. Ladies and gentlemen, viewers everywhere, your presenter, Fantasy Woman!'

To studio applause, she appeared, walking down, around the turn of a spiralling staircase, and this time Tod was unaware of his own forward inclination as his intelligent dark eyes scanned and assessed the star of the show. What age would she be? About twenty-five? Was that too old for what he had in mind? Television could be deceptive, but he guessed she was the right height, around five-seven, five-eight, long-legged, and frankly curvaceous, with firm, splendid breasts emphasised by the cut and drape of the sparkling evening gown she wore. Thick, almost straight hair, the colour of a red setter's coat, framed all that he could see of her face. If only the damned woman didn't have to wear that half mask. But his secretary had warned him about that ridiculous gimmick.

So far, she was just what he'd been led to expect. Her figure would have done justice to a Miss World candidate. Despite the mask, he could discern that her face was square, with a chin as uncompromisingly determined as his own—a little too strong perhaps for someone whom he intended to manipulate—and that below the lower edge of the black square her mouth was wide and generously proportioned.

The programme planners had certainly spared no expense, either on the lavish set or on her glamorous outfit; and the same applied to the stunts, the fulfilment of wishes. A young girl wanted to meet a favourite pop star. Others were more bizarre, such as the ninety-year-old woman who had always wanted to ride a camel.

There were the wildly extravagant, the comic; some
were even looking for the excitement of danger. As he
watched, Tod's eyebrows, a thick dark line, came down
heavily above brooding eyes and he nodded decisively.
This woman he had to meet, and if she was any
good . . .

Gina Darcy lowered her long, graceful length into the
only comfortable chair in her dressing-room and peeled
off the black mask which, with her make-up and the
perspiration caused by strong studio lights, had adhered
unpleasantly to her face. She was always glad to be rid
of the wretched thing, wished she need not wear it, but
her sponsors were adamant. It was part of her image, of
the anonymity behind which she hid, the apparently all-
powerful Fantasy Woman.

That was a joke! If only people knew it. Not that she
didn't enjoy her role, but sometimes she wished it had
greater depth of involvement; wished that the fame, the
nationwide acclaim, could be for Gina Darcy and not
for her *alter ego*; two minor adjustments to her role
which the sponsors had always refused to consider.

There was one advantage: no one from her old life
was likely to recognise her. The most likely people to
guess her identity from her voice and general
appearance, her parents, were living abroad. Even
Keith was unlikely to see, in her glamorous new
identity, the old Gina. In one sense that was a source of
dissatisfaction. She would *like* Keith to see her, to
realise that she had made a success of her life, despite
and without him. But her real name was never printed
in the programme and thus far, following instructions,
she had managed to evade and baffle the press. Still, she
thought, stretching her body in a movement as
languorous and graceful as a cat's, apart from the
frustrated ambition to be famous in her own right, as
Marcha had become, she had a lot to be thankful for:

her career in television and, discreetly in the background, a thriving business of her own, to which she could return if this life ever palled.

Not that she thought it would. She was busy, fulfilled, mistress of her own destiny, with no one other than her producer to interfere or to criticise her, no man to make demands of her; and if that was selfish, well, Gina considered she had earned her right to be so. She'd been self-sacrificing once and all that had brought was unhappiness and disillusionment.

A knock on her dressing-room door, the insertion of a glaringly ginger head and a pleasant, freckled face, heralded the arrival of Jimmy Riley, originator and executive producer of *Fantasy Woman*. Only he and the programme's sponsors were aware of Gina's true identity; there was Marcha, of course, but she'd been sworn to secrecy.

'Superb performance as ever, darling!' His voice was affectionate, his lean face full of enthusiasm. Precariously, he perched his long, wiry frame on a stool, too alight with nervous energy and excitement to take up any more permanent position.

'Yes, thank goodness!' The words, spoken in a warm, husky voice, were heartfelt. 'I'd much prefer it if the programme was all prerecorded items. When we go out live, you can never be sure something won't go wrong.'

'Hmm!' Jimmy did not sound convinced. 'On the other hand, our viewers like the live shows, the element of chance. Keeps them on the edge of their seats. Which reminds me ...' He pulled a sheet of paper from his jacket pocket. 'Thought you might like to see next week's schedule.'

As Gina perused the list, Jimmy watched her intently, studying her reactions. Her square, vivid face was so tellingly expressive, he thought, as always feeling himself deeply stirred by her attraction. Beautiful woman! Pity they had to disguise half the potential of those lovely features.

Gina had a large following. Fan mail arrived for her daily by the sackful, and the programme was inundated with requests from people wanting to be on her show. Not surprisingly, there was a high ratio of requests from curious men, but *they* were flogging a dead horse. Stage door Johnnies weren't encouraged, and, under the terms of Gina's contract, personal involvement with any of her guests was strictly forbidden. Not that there was any danger of Gina flouting the rule. As far as Jimmy could see, Gina didn't go in for personal relationships of any kind. He had never heard her mention her family or any women friends, and her reactions to men were all too clear.

He had particular reason to know that much. Strongly attracted to Gina, he had once tried to push their relationship beyond the bounds of producer and presenter, but only once. Gina had been perfectly polite but, nevertheless, she had made it quite clear that she was not interested. It was nothing personal, she'd explained, her tone coolly remote, simply that she had no intention of becoming involved with any man. She had her future mapped out. First and last, she intended to remain a career woman.

So chilly had been the barriers she erected that Jimmy had not even dared to ask why, for he guessed there must be some other reason besides ambition. He didn't believe for one moment that she was frigid. It was his theory that, at some time in the past, Gina had been badly hurt by a man and that she didn't intend to risk a similar occurrence.

But what a waste! She was a woman formed for love, and he wasn't just thinking of the physical side. She was a thoroughly nice person, caring and compassionate. She really enjoyed making people happy, especially kids. She would have made a wonderful mother.

Her smooth brow had furrowed into creases and he could guess why. He'd known she wasn't going to like one of the items on that list, but there was nothing he could do. The sponsors' word was law.

'This motor-cycle scramble, the fifteen-year-old girl who wants to compete against the boys . . .'

'I know what you're going to say, Gina, but it's no use. It's in. The girl's been contacted, so have the organisers of the rally. All *you* have to do is to *be* there, introduce the item, congratulate her or console her afterwards as the case may be and hand over the "Fantasy" memento.'

'It could be dangerous for the kid,' Gina began.

Jimmy sighed. With variations of theme, they had this same argument almost weekly.

'Nowhere near as risky as some of the stunts we used to pull. We do weed out the really dangerous ones nowadays. At the worst, the kid'll get a few bumps and bruises and a sore behind. The sponsors . . .'

'To hell with the sponsors!' she interrupted impatiently. 'They think they're little tin gods, but they're just damned irresponsible. It won't be one of them that gets the blame, or the pain, if there's an accident. If that kid gets injured, perhaps for life, it will be the programme that gets the bad publicity and I'll carry the can, too. I've never forgotten . . .' She shuddered, not finishing her sentence.

'Yes, well,' Jimmy put in hastily, 'the incident you're thinking of had its effect even on the sponsors. They won't permit anything like that again and'—as she looked to be on the point of arguing further—'you know it's no good your standing out against them. They reserve the power to hire and fire. What's the point in risking losing your job? You still enjoy it, don't you?' And *he* didn't want to lose her, he thought painfully.

'You know I still enjoy it and I don't want to lose it;

and I know I'm not irreplaceable. That damned mask
sees to that. I'm not the first to wear it and I know, if I
were to quit or get fired, I wouldn't be the last. The
name Fantasy Woman will fit anyone with a reasonable
figure and red hair. But Jimmy, if only they'd let me try
out some of the stunts, test them before these kids risk
their necks. And I'm getting tired of being an
anonymous figure. One of these days, I want to be a
show-business personality in my own right, as me, Gina
Darcy. I want to show the public that I'm more than
just a body, a figure-head.'

Jimmy shrugged. He wasn't complaining about the
figure she presented, but, if she only knew it, with her
looks and bubbling personality she had the potential to
go a long way. She had more than looks, a kind of
sparkle; but to himself he could admit that, in part, he
was responsible for holding her back, that her
anonymity suited him. He had a selfish desire to keep
Gina to himself. He hadn't given up hope that some
day he'd persuade her to ... Aloud, he said, not
unaware of hypocrisy,

'As a friend, as well as your producer, I'd advise
against any change at present, not while you're still so
popular in this role, while the show's still going down
well. Some day, maybe, hmm?'

'You mean when I start getting old and wrinkled?
When they decide to replace me with someone
younger? Then you'll have me playing old-lady
character parts? No thanks! Rather than wait for that
to happen, I'll go back and carry on running my
business.'

'I meant,' he interrupted hastily, 'when you're
established enough for the public to want to see you in
other roles.'

'How are they supposed to express their wishes,' she
demanded sarcastically, 'when they don't even know
what I look like? I could be as ugly as sin.'

'There's no guarantee that you'd be a success in other fields.'

'And there's always the fact that this show is your baby,' Gina retorted. Then, penitently, 'Sorry, Jimmy, that was uncalled for. I know your advice is well-meant, but sometimes I get so frustrated. I know I have it in me to do better things.'

'And you know, too,' he added drily, 'that if I had my way, you'd never work at all. I can well afford to support a wife and . . .'

'Jimmy, please!' she said hurriedly. Not that well-worn track again. She'd heard those words so often before, interminably. 'Don't start. Don't ruin our friendship. Nowadays you're the only man I've any respect for.'

His pleasure mingling with guilt, he shrugged himself off the stool.

'I suppose that's something,' he conceded wryly. Then, consulting his watch, 'Well, the fans should have given up by now. Time to go home.'

Gina always waited for an hour after the studio audience had left. Only once had she tried to leave immediately and she had run the gamut of a curious, sensation-seeking crowd. One man had even tried to snatch off her mask. These days she left the TV centre dressed shabbily, a scarf tightly obscuring the giveaway cascade of red hair, Jimmy driving her back to her flat in a deliberately unostentatious car. Now, the only other time she wore the mask was on location, when she was surrounded by the protective posse of cameramen and the production team.

'Any chance of a coffee?' Jimmy enquired, as they pulled up outside the block of flats near Regents Park which housed her bachelor apartment.

Amused, for it was a regular request which he already knew would not be granted, she shook her head.

'Fantasy Woman,' he quoted grumblingly, 'never

says no! Never says impossible. Except to poor old Jimmy Riley.'

Laughter faded from her lovely face as she slid from the passenger seat.

'Now you know that's not true, Jimmy, not in my private life. No one has seen the inside of my little flat except my cleaning lady, and to her, I'm just "Miss Darcy" who's "something in the City"!'

'You can't blame a chap for trying!' Jimmy said glumly and her amusement returned.

'And *you* can't blame a girl for being consistent! 'Night, Jimmy!'

'Little flat' was a purposely inadequate description of her four-room apartment. Like her past and her private life, she chose to keep her surroundings strictly to herself, a place where she could be herself, with no one else making their mark upon it, leaving memories to destroy the peaceful atmosphere she had created and which closed about her in a reassuring cocoon every time she came home.

With a sigh of relief she closed the apartment door behind her, shutting out the world, shutting out fantasy. What, she wondered, would her fans think if they ever discovered how different was the woman from the public image? She suspected that most of the people she interviewed found her daunting, thought of her as the kind of woman who would always have everything under control. Because, in her name, their fantasies were fulfilled, they probably believed her infallible where her own life was concerned. They were wrong; at least, they were wrong about the past.

But that mistake was behind her, never to be repeated. For the future all her energies and emotions would be wrapped up in her career. Only once had she let her heart rule her head, dropping ambition for what she had mistakenly expected to be personal happiness.

There would be no more Keiths to dispute her right to her individuality and independence and then, finally, worst blow of all, to destroy her confidence in herself as a woman.

She wandered into the modern, functional kitchen, walls, units and ceiling in stainless steel, and collected the items she needed to make herself a snack. Did her former husband ever think of her these days? Did he ever speak of her to Frances, making comparisons that would not be in Gina's favour? She'd met Frances just once; an insignificant little woman, the type who would fulfil Keith's notion of a 'proper wife': placid, domesticated and, perhaps even more important in view of his nature, unlikely to attract admiring notice from other men.

Ironically, now that she was not forced into a domestic role, Gina enjoyed her free time, experimenting with recipes in her streamlined kitchen; doing her own decorating; looking after her enormous collection of plants, which, growing in a variety of exotic pots, stood on a raised semi-circular dais under the living-room window.

She was entitled to enjoy her leisure! She worked hard, five days a week, researching, rehearsing and, quite often, filming on location, as she would have to at the motor-cycle rally.

She gave an irritated exclamation. She tried not to bring working problems home with her, but this one worried her, nearly as much as that other incident which had had near-fatal results.

She took her snack supper into the luxurious sitting-room, feeling her usual sense of satisfaction at its sybaritic comfort. Decorated in harmonising shades of green, it had a sunken central square of cushions; the shelving around the wall held valuable antiques. She sat down among the cushions, in her favourite place, the position from which she could best admire her small,

but precious, collection of Impressionist paintings.
When she'd been seventeen, she reflected wryly,
weekend evenings had been for dating. Staying in had
been a tragedy, not having a date a social stigma. But
all those agonies were gone. Supper for one in front of
the television was a pleasure nowadays, not a pain.
Who needed men?

'Gina, you are incredible!' Jimmy said, one morning a
few days later, as she joined him in the rain-sodden
field, the mud already churned ankle deep by the
spinning wheels of motor cycles.

'Ssh!' Anxiously, automatically, she looked about
her, seeking possible eavesdroppers. It was customary
for her to be addressed only as Fantasy Woman.
Satisfied that no one was within earshot, she asked,
'What do you mean?'

'I mean that only you could contrive to look both
sexy and mysterious in the middle of a muddy field,
wearing blue waterproofs, red wellingtons and *that hat*!'

She laughed aloud.

'What you forget, Jimmy, is that, basically, I *am* the
outdoor type!'

Her delighted laughter, throaty, husky, had carried
clearly on the damp morning air, and Tod Fallon,
already alerted to her arrival by the cavalcade of cars
and vans, the swivelling of cameras, the anticipatory
murmurs that had run through the watching crowd,
edged his way imperceptibly closer. She seemed to be on
good terms with the ginger-headed fellow at her elbow.
Boyfriend? Unlikely from what he'd heard about her.
Probably part of the production team. Whoever he was,
Tod decided, he wasn't man enough to handle *that*
redheaded package of dynamite.

There was even less of her visible today, he thought,
with a return of his irritation. Muffled up in a
voluminous blue cagoule, the top half of her face

obscured by the mask and the black, waterproof
sombrero, all that showed was the laughing mouth: a
wide, generous sweep of full lips, exposing white, even
teeth.

In view of the weather, he had expected feminine
petulance, moodiness, from the star of the show, but
she looked and sounded remarkably cheerful. Still, she
could afford to be cheerful. He had been pulling those
confidential strings and he now had some idea of just
how much she earned from this series and from the by-
products of her personality cult; her earnings reached a
figure that some people would find hard to match. But
not Tod Fallon. Finance presented no problem to him.
Besides, everyone had their price, and he had the best of
incentives to bid high ... Marcha!

In spite of the steady drizzle, which had seemed to
reduce everything and everyone to the same uniform
grey, Gina had noticed Tod Fallon. He would be a
difficult man to overlook. Even in casual, weatherproof
clothes, his height made him stand out in this motley
crowd; he was totally unlike the usual run of sensation
seekers. He looked too cultured, too sophisticated
somehow, to be interested in her or her show, or even in
today's events. Unless, of course, he was the bored but
indulgent parent of one of the young participants. Most
of these motor-cycle-mad kids had families who could
afford to buy them the best, the latest model of bike.
There must be at least a dozen of the machines here
today, a kaleidoscope of varying metallic colours,
circling and recircling the assembly point, practising
'wheelies', churning up the mud, the drone of high
revving engines monotonous to the ear, wearing on the
nerves.

Oh, let's get on with it, she thought suddenly, get it
safely over. She felt the usual butterflies churn in the pit
of her stomach. She hated this waiting. Would she

never forget the stunt that had gone so tragically wrong? No! Impossible! Not even if she were to neglect her self-imposed, regular reminder of it.

Inevitably there was a lot of waiting around on location shots, waiting for cameramen to decide on angles; and today they would wait while one or two of the regular kids were filmed going over the course, just to show how tricky it really was, wheels spinning helplessly on muddy inclines, bunny hopping over logs, easing their way beneath tricky limbos. Then it would be the 'victim's' turn. Despite the waterproof, some of the damp chill must have got through to her, for she shivered a little. Physically fearless herself, she would far rather be waiting to undergo the ordeal than to see if someone else, particularly a youngster, came safely through it.

Her curious gaze returned several times to Tod Fallon's strong, compelling face, as she speculated on who and what he was, why he was here. For some reason he interested her; in a purely academic way, of course. Because she shunned male company for herself, it didn't mean she couldn't appreciate a man's appearance, feel curiosity about his character and occupation.

This one was a little too spectacular-looking for her taste, with his splendid physique and those dark good looks, enhanced rather than marred by the generous scattering of grey hair. Such men, she'd always found, were arrogantly aware of their own masculine attractions. He looked a tough character, too, with those rugged features and that assertive chin. Not the sort you'd care to tangle with. The heavy black bar of eyebrows that just met across the straight, forthright nose, hinted at an intolerant nature, a hasty temper that it would be unwise to arouse.

Suddenly she realised that the prolonged analysis had not been one-way. *He* was watching *her*, his study more covert than her own, as though to avoid detection. But now she had discovered his ploy, he met her eyes openly, almost challengingly. No doubt he was accustomed to women giving him more than a second glance, was probably complacent and conceited about the fact. She too was accustomed to appreciation, male appreciation, which these days she shrugged aside. But why did she have the feeling that this man was not just admiring, that there was more to his assessment than that?

As his piercing eyes continued to hold hers, she realised that he was moving slowly but surely towards her, that, despite a supreme effort of will, she could not break the tenuous link between them. She felt more than just a slight unease now. He must have taken her idle curiosity for interest, invitation even?

'Jimmy,' she murmured, 'that man; he's getting too close.' But for once Jimmy was out of earshot. 'That's far enough,' she told the man, politely but coldly, so that there should be no mistaking the fact that she meant what she said.

'Surely there can be no objection to my paying homage to ... a celebrity?' The pause before the final words was mocking. Why on earth should a total stranger speak to her in this way?

'No objection,' she conceded coolly, 'but if you have anything to say, you can say it from where you are.'

'Right!' To her relief, he seemed to accept her dictum. 'First off, what's the purpose of the mask?' Tod asked bluntly. He knew the purpose very well, but he wanted to gauge her reaction to provocation. 'Are you disfigured?'

'No I'm not!' Energetically, Gina refuted the suggestion. But just suppose she had been? What a totally unfeeling brute of a man he must be!

'Then why?' he persisted.

'I thought everyone knew that by now,' she retorted

scornfully. 'It's to preserve Fantasy Woman's anonymity.'

'I've been out of the country for a while,' Tod said. 'Last week was only the first time I've watched your programme. It's not,' he added drily, 'my normal taste in viewing.'

I bet, Gina thought. He was probably an intellectual snob. The news and heavy documentaries would be about his only concession to the popular medium. But all levels had to be catered for and her programme provided a service to those who liked their entertainment light.

'I don't see the need for such a ridiculous charade,' Tod continued. 'Other presenters don't seem to find it necessary and there *are* very similar programmes.'

'Exactly!' she said triumphantly. 'So we need something different, a gimmick.' What was she doing, she wondered in amazement, defending the particular aspect of the show that she herself most disliked? It must be that this man made her hackles rise. She felt she would have taken issue with him on any subject.

'A feeble reason,' the big man retorted. 'Now, if you were afraid of being recognised outside the studio, that I *could* understand.'

'Why should I be afraid?' Gina challenged him.

'Oh, I don't know. Let's say something went wrong on your show? Wouldn't people blame you for any accidents? Threaten you even? The public can be very fickle where their idols are concerned. Just suppose this kid today breaks a leg or something?'

'Are you a reporter?' Gina asked suspiciously. 'Because if so, I don't give interviews.' It was a little late to make a stand on that principle, she thought, furious with herself. He'd already elicited enough information from her to write an article, embroidering it, misquoting her.

'I'm not a reporter and you haven't answered my question.'

'I don't have to answer your question, but just to put the record straight I'll tell you what you want to know and then perhaps you'll kindly stop pestering me. Things very rarely do go wrong. Stunts are always supervised by experts.'

'But there have been incidents?' Tod persisted, 'Injuries?'

'One or two, nothing serious, not since I . . .'

'OK, Fantasy Woman!' One of the cameramen sang out. 'We're ready to take the opening shots.'

Relieved, Gina turned away from her inquisitor. Briefly, she filled Jimmy in on the incident.

'Where were you when I needed you?' she reproached. 'I wonder who he is and why he was asking all those questions? He sounded as if he disapproved of the show, of me.'

'He'll be press of some kind, whatever he says. Forget him! It's time for the introduction. We'll have you sitting on one of these bikes, I think.'

'Why not have her carry out the stunt herself? Just to show how safe and easy it is?'

Gina swung around with a gasp of stupefaction, every sense suddenly wary and alert. The tall man had followed them, was at her elbow, only inches separating them. She felt herself tauten and quiver, almost as if he had touched her, unwelcomely conscious of the strong aura of masculinity that had been apparent even at a distance. She felt overpowered. She was tall, but he was taller. To her suddenly vibrating nerves, it seemed he exuded a kind of subtle menace.

'Will you please keep your distance, sir!' Jimmy was annoyed.

'Has your Fantasy Woman ever tried out any of the things she expects her guests to do?' Tod persisted, quite undeterred apparently by their joint hostile reaction.

'I don't expect people to do anything,' Gina snapped,

before Jimmy could answer. 'They ask me to arrange something. After that it's up to them.'

'So you don't care if they injure themselves?'

'Of course I'd care if someone was hurt.' Gina felt uncharacteristically close to tears, and she hadn't wept since . . . Oh, why did he have to set her nerves jangling just at this moment, when she was already tense?

'But you're too chicken to try the stunts yourself?'

'No! No! No! Will you stop pestering me? I'm not scared of anything! But the terms of my contract don't permit me to . . . Oh, go away! I've got a show to do.'

Determined that this arrogant, pushy man should not witness the distress he was causing her, she swung away, then felt her feet in their bright wellingtons slip from under her so that she sprawled her length in the cycle-churned mud. Before Jimmy could move to help her, the tall man had done so, his hands closing about her upper arms, hauling her unceremoniously to her feet. Gina felt like screaming with frustration. Her bright blue cagoule was soiled and, although she wasn't hurt physically, her pride was severely damaged. She'd made a fool of herself in front of all these people. It would be in every paper tomorrow, unless someone more important had an equally ridiculous accident. It was all this man's fault, she fumed. If he hadn't been so annoyingly persistent, made her angry, she wouldn't have moved so carelessly.

The heat of fury banished the tears that had threatened and she looked up, intent upon scorching him both verbally and with her eyes. Lips parted, the stream of invective she had planned was silenced by the mirth in his hitherto serious face. He was silently laughing at her! How dared he! Then, to add insult to injury, he gave vent to his amusement in a great shout, plainly audible to every bystander.

'Fantasy Woman!' he spluttered, scarcely able to articulate. 'Whatever happened to that air of dignified mystery? Right at this moment, you look more like a disreputable Paddington Bear!'

Gina gasped with outrage, but then the aptness, the ludicrous truth of his statement struck her and against her will her own sense of the ridiculous surfaced. She felt her mouth begin to quirk with the beginnings of a smile, a smile swiftly banished by his next words.

'That's better. At least it proves you're human, that you can laugh at your own misfortunes as well as those of others. Now, if I could only see what you look like, without that mask . . .'

But she backed away hastily, carefully this time, and to her relief he did not pursue her any further. But Gina was aware of his dark eyes watching the filming from the distance Jimmy insisted on for all members of the public, and annoyingly she found his words rankling with her.

At school and in her teens, she'd been a splendid athlete, horsewoman and swimmer; and she'd always kept herself fit. Recently, she had even been attending judo classes. She knew she was capable of feats of physical endurance, so why couldn't that dimension be added to the show?

As for the stranger's accusation that she laughed at the failures of others, she was frankly puzzled. It was something she wouldn't dream of doing, however comical such an incident might be. Like most people, she possessed the banana-skin sense of humour, but to give vent to it at the expense of her guests would be most unprofessional. It puzzled her, too, why this man seemed so set on annoying her.

Automatically, she went through the typical introductory script. The young motor cyclists performed. The girl who had made the request to compete against the boys did so and acquitted herself reasonably well. The shots were in the can and the episode would be one of many shown on the next programme. Nothing

further untoward occurred. The large man would have
to eat his words, admit that safety was a major factor of
their undertakings.

But there was no sign of him and, where she should
have felt relieved, Gina felt unreasonably disappointed.
It would have been pleasant to have given him a
triumphant 'I told you so' look. It would at least have
redressed some of the indignity of her own mishap.

CHAPTER TWO

THAT evening, she found her mind returning over and over again to the stranger's suggestion, a suggestion that, had he but known it, matched strongly with her own inclinations.

Without much hope, once again, she had broached the subject with Jimmy, and as usual he had been frankly horrified.

'Sorry, it's not on. The sponsors wouldn't allow it. If you started performing stunts, we'd have a totally different programme concept. And if it's that fellow that accosted you this morning, forget him. There's no reason for you to worry what he thinks. Is there?' he added suspiciously.

Gina sighed with exasperation. She was letting work intrude on her free time yet again, and this time it was the fault of that annoying man. Hoping to divert her thoughts, she switched on the television. At this time of night, there was usually something purely escapist, a laughable rather than spine-chilling horror film, or some corny soap opera.

It was the latter, set in a totally unbelievable hospital. None of the incidents shown could possibly happen in real life, would never have been permitted to happen in the hospital where she had once worked.

For, originally, Gina had intended to be a nurse. She'd just completed her first year, when she met Keith Taylor. A journalist, he'd come to the hospital to cover a heart transplant operation and Gina had been the only person passing through reception. He'd delayed his appointment with the hospital secretary just long enough to fix his image upon the impressionable

nineteen-year-old she'd been then, and had managed to
intercept her once more on his way out, to ask her for a
date.

It had been a whirlwind romance and, against all
advice, she had married Keith within six weeks of
their first encounter. Too late she'd realised that
married life was not all that she had anticipated.
Things had started to go wrong, even on their
honeymoon.

Following almost immediately upon Gina's disillusionment with married life, there had been drastic cuts
in the health service and she and many of her fellow
students had found themselves unemployed.

Keith had been delighted; now she would be totally
dependent on him. During their brief courtship, he'd
managed to disguise certain traits which, since
marriage, had come unpleasantly to the fore. He was
possessive and almost dangerously jealous. Not only
had he been jealous; he hadn't been satisfied with her as
she was, the girl he professed to love, but had tried to
mould her into his conception of a wife. Perhaps all
men had this desire for dominance, the need to change
the status quo? That man at the rally! Hadn't he been
suggesting change and hadn't she disliked his attitude
towards herself? She resented male scorn, the
assumption of male superiority.

The video of the girl motor cyclist was popular with the
following week's studio audience. It was usual to have
one live item and the rest of the events were
prerecorded. The show was going successfully and yet,
somehow, Gina felt dissatisfied.

She knew she was looking more than usually
stunning tonight. Apart from the fact that she had no
time for false modesty, other eyes besides her own had
told her so—those of the cameramen; the indrawn
breath of the audience had been complimentary; and

earlier, in her dressing-room, Jimmy had been lavish with his praise.

Her new outfit, a sensational, sparkling gold two-piece, fitted her like a second skin that echoed every movement of her voluptuous figure. Dolman sleeved, it had a plunging V-back top. Dramatic, high-heeled black shoes and daring black-seamed stockings completed the outfit. Yes, she looked good.

Yet all the time she laughed and joked with her guests, introduced their particular fantasies, another part of her mind held itself aloof, trying to analyse her dissatisfaction. There had been no mishaps so far and there were not likely to be; the mixture was as before. 'As before.' That was it! The show was becoming boringly predictable! It was time to inject a new dimension, but she was the only one who seemed to feel this way. Everyone else seemed happy, the guests, the audience, the production team. Out of camera shot, she could just see Jimmy's freckled face, set in complacent lines. Was she the only one to notice something lacking?

Then the penny dropped. It was all the fault of that damned man at the motor-cycle rally. That crack of his about her being too cowardly to try the stunts herself, the implication, with which secretly she had agreed, that she could make much more of her role. But to be honest, it wasn't entirely his fault she felt this way. She'd already begun to think along similar lines with her urge to shed her anonymity.

'And now,' the voice of the unseen announcer broke in upon her thoughts, 'a slight variation from our usual routine, a request that even Fantasy Woman herself knows nothing about.'

Gina jerked to attention; illogically her first reaction was one of indignation. How dared they spring something on her for which she was unprepared? And who had arranged for the gratification of the request, whatever it was? It was unprecedented; she'd never had to cope with the unexpected. Could she do it when she had no idea what was wanted of her?

Then the stubborn chin came into prominence. Of course she could. Besides, Jimmy would have arranged things. He wouldn't really have left everything to chance. Feeling about her as he did, he wouldn't permit anyone to make her look foolish.

So she donned a smile of sweet unconcern for the cameras; but, outwardly calm, inwardly she was in a turmoil of curiosity.

The introduction continued.

'People ask many things of Fantasy Woman: the simple, the outrageous, the ordinary, the bizarre, cheap or expensive. But no guest has ever asked for anything so easy to bestow and yet, he obviously thinks, and you the audience will surely agree, beyond price.'

The build up was making Gina uneasy and when the 'guest' came into sight, her unease grew. It was *that man*. A superstitious shudder cooled her spine. It was almost as if she'd conjured him up.

He was within inches of her now, broad, brown, powerfully built, exuding masculine virility, his slacks and shirt deceptively casual. He hadn't bought them in any chain store, or off the peg!

As she renewed her acquaintance with that square-cut jaw, looked once more into those glinting dark eyes, Gina felt again that almost primitive surge of fear. She wanted to turn and run. Instead she forced herself to remember who and where she was, parted her lips in a stiff parody of her usual welcoming smile and, with only an instant's hesitation, extended her slim hand.

'Good evening, Mr . . .?' So far had they deviated from the norm, she didn't even know her guest's name.

He smiled and Gina, fascinated against her will, saw that only one corner of his mouth curved upwards, a crooked, tantalisingly attractive smile.

'You're not the only one who prefers anonymity.' His deep voice had a mocking note. 'Call me Mr X.'

He watched her work that one out, amused at her annoyance which was obvious from her physical reactions, a straightening of the spine, an upward surge of that chin, rather than from any facial expression, which was camouflaged by the mask. How would she respond? Had she the spirit to retaliate in public? If she incurred the censure of her sponsors it could make *his* job rather easier. But it didn't really matter. Things would go his way in the end. They always did.

If he wanted to play it this way, it was OK by Gina. She had no wish to know anything further about him. By force of will, she kept the pleasant expression pinned to her face.

'And what can we do for you, *Mr X*?' She laid sarcastic stress on his pseudonym, to let him know she ridiculed his pretension.

'What *you* can do for *me* . . .' he paused for effect, 'is to give me just one kiss.'

To a man, the audience drew an anticipatory breath, but an aghast Gina acted instinctively. She stepped backwards. The cameras followed her movement. So did he.

'A very simple request, surely?' he suggested, undertones in his dark, resonant voice that made her shudder. His whole aura had suddenly become one of brooding sensuality, and she knew she would give almost anything not to have to agree to his demand. Why had he made it? What did a kiss from her mean to him?

'An unusual request,' she parried. If it had been any other man, she would have been totally unconcerned; his request would have been granted by now, the kiss casually bestowed, the incident over, herself unaffected by it. But within Gina, something screamed a warning. She didn't want this man to kiss her. For she knew instinctively that she wouldn't be the one doing the kissing. This man was one hundred per cent male, very much the type to take the initiative.

Tod waited. He knew she wanted to refuse. Dared she? It didn't matter to him either way; it was merely a preliminary to getting under her guard, getting to know more about her, discovering whether she was as suitable as his secretary had suggested; and he paid his staff to be right, to give him reliable information. He frowned slightly. Marcha wouldn't approve of what he was doing. But what was one kiss bestowed in the interests of research, in Marcha's interests if only she would accept the fact? Suddenly he longed to have her back from her protracted holiday, this business concluded, to get on with the real purpose of his life.

'Well?' he challenged. 'What are you afraid of? Have you never kissed a man before?'

The audience tittered.

As he'd guessed, Gina wanted to refuse. But she couldn't. Fantasy Woman never denied a request. They were going out live, millions of viewers waiting expectantly to see her perform. If she turned down something so simple, her popularity, the show's popularity, would plummet, the viewing ratings would drop, the sponsors would be furious and the newspapers would have a field day, leaping upon the unprecedented incident with delight.

She gave one desperate look towards the side of the set, at Jimmy. He was also making frantic 'winding up' signals. They were running out of time. It was now or never.

Drawing a shaky breath, she moved in, placed her hands on the tall man's shoulders, looked up at him enquiringly.

For a second, Tod stared into the apprehensive eyes, shadowed by the mask. He could not discern their colour. He smiled and once more Gina felt the goose steps traverse her spine. Then the smile was blotted out, as his dark head swooped down towards her and hard, muscled arms clamped about her with a relentless pressure, so that her breasts were painfully entrapped against his ribcage. She was aware of many things in that moment, of the soft appreciative murmurs of the audience, the heat of the studio lights, the pleasant, tangy smell of male aftershave as his hand traced the silky skin that covered her spine. Then his mouth captured hers, hard, possessive, inescapable, the kiss burning in its intensity.

Shockwave after shockwave jerked her body in a totally unexpected, spasmodic response to the eroticism of his kiss, of his body moulded to hers. Being pressed so tightly against him was evocative of past sensations she'd believed banished, forgotten. But the ache in her loins was unmistakably familiar. Familiar, yet different. Keith had never made her feel like this ... abandoned. She felt shame that such sensations could be aroused by a total stranger.

She was not the only one surprised by the effect of that kiss. Tod had gone into this embrace in a spirit of cynicism, it being his belief that a woman was more easily won over to a cause by an appeal, not to reason, on which most women were short, but to her sensuality. It wouldn't trouble him unduly if Gina Darcy responded favourably to the proposal he intended to put to her, just because she was attracted to him, rather than to the proposition. He'd been the victor in many such encounters and it was easy enough, after the battle was won, to depress any pretensions the woman might have. So it was with incredulity that he found himself strangely affected by the feel of Gina in his arms, the warmth and scent of her, the sudden, pliant softness of her body, as, against her will, she responded to him. Unexpectedly, he felt his body stir and, instinctively, he drew her closer, deepening the kiss.

Dimly, Gina heard the whistles and catcalls from the audience, realised that the kiss had gone on far too long, was becoming too intense. The theme music was playing. They were no longer on camera. Somehow she tore herself free of him and wondered that her legs should hold her, so limp and lifeless they felt.

'You swine!' she whispered. 'How *dare* you take advantage of me like that with the whole country watching?'

Tod was swifter to recover his composure. Thank God Marcha was abroad and not likely to be of that number. She certainly wouldn't have appreciated the little scene. And she'd been wrong about one thing; Gina Darcy certainly wasn't frigid.

'Really?' he drawled. 'You do rate your popularity high!'

Unable to utter another syllable, she swept past him, making for the sanctuary of her dressing-room. She passed Jimmy without even a look. He was to blame, too. He had known. He could have warned her. He was as bad as the rest of them. All he thought about was ratings, his wretched show. God, how she despised all men, especially this one! 'Mr X' was trouble! It didn't occur to her to wonder why her reaction to this particular man was so violent, why she had so arbitrarily assessed his character.

Later, at home, after a shower and a meal, she had calmed down a little, could look at the incident more rationally. She had taken out most of her anger on Jimmy during the drive home, but now that anger had evaporated, she felt curiously empty, drained.

'He went too far!' she'd raged. 'It was like being publicly raped.'

Jimmy had done his best to placate her. The item was by special request of the sponsors, he'd said, and he hadn't seen any real harm in it. After all, what was a kiss? Though even while he spoke the words, he knew he could almost hate the self-styled Mr X; would have given anything to be himself the recipient of Gina's kiss.

'OK. So he did make a meal of it,' he soothed, 'but, as a red-blooded male myself, I can't say I blame him, and maybe he didn't know the cameras had stopped rolling.'

'Oh, he knew,' Gina seethed. *'He knew!'*

What was a kiss, Jimmy had said. Before tonight, Gina would have answered, 'absolutely nothing', that a man's kiss was as unmoving as that of a maiden aunt. But she couldn't claim that now. Mr X was a past master of sensuality. She prayed the cameras had stopped filming before that moment when he'd used his tongue as a weapon to pierce her lips, probing, inciting her to unwilling response. She prayed the camera hadn't picked up the instinctive movements of her body, the heat which had flushed her face and throat, as she knew, for the first time in over a year, the wild compulsion of physical desire.

She couldn't fathom his motive, but she hoped to goodness he was satisfied, that she need never encounter him again; and yet, all evening, she found her thoughts returning to the incident, as a tongue returns to worry an aching tooth, her body reacting to the mental stimulus.

It was a week or two before Gina could relax, convince herself that Mr X was not going to make any further unheralded appearances; and then, annoyingly, she found herself wondering why he had abandoned his campaign of irritation, just as much as she wondered why he had ever begun it. Life, though peaceful once more, seemed suddenly ordinary, the programme even more lifeless and mundane.

She was relaxing in bed one Sunday evening, when the telephone shrilled.

'Gina?' It was Jimmy. No one else had her private number, which was only to be used in case of emergency. 'Gina, I'm sorry to disturb you, but I've just had a call from one of the sponsors. It seems they're calling a special meeting, tomorrow, early. I wanted to make sure you'd be on time.'

Gina felt unreasonable irritation; he should know she was always punctual for briefings. She had been a businesswoman before she'd become a television personality and, in business, time was money.

'Of course I'll be there,' she said. 'What's it all about?'

'I don't know.' Jimmy sounded uneasy. 'But somehow I sense the winds of change.'

'Change?' Her tone became sharper. 'You don't mean they're thinking of taking the show off or replacing me in the series?' It wouldn't be disaster financially speaking, but it would be a blow to her self-esteem, her belief in her popularity, a setback to ambition.

'I honestly don't know.' Jimmy sounded unhappy. 'I wish I did. But whatever it is, I'll be there, rooting for you.'

'Thanks, and thanks for warning me.' Slowly she replaced the receiver and sank back against frilled, pastel-blue pillowcases. Her mind furiously active, she went over the past two or three shows, seeking for flaws which could have made the sponsors dissatisfied with her. Her fan mail was as steady as ever. The press had been favourable. Was there any significance in the fact that she'd been presenting the show for exactly six months? The current series was ended, and her predecessor had only just completed six months when Gina replaced her ... though *she* had retired voluntarily. The public knew nothing of this. The two girls were sufficiently alike in colouring and stature for the substitution to remain unnoticed. Was there another tall, statuesque redhead somewhere, waiting to step into

Gina's shoes? Ever practical, she bagan to plan ahead
for this contingency. Her own business still awaited her,
ably run by a deputy. She could always go back and
take up the reins once more. Business had proved to be
a panacea before . . .

Unable to return to nursing, Gina had told her
husband she intended to look for another job, but it
had been difficult to find something sufficiently
interesting and stimulating. Then, one day, waiting
patiently in a shop while a foreigner was being served,
the idea was presented to her. Mechanically, she had
noted the price of the item the man bought, simply
because she was about to ask for the same thing. She
was surprised when the figure asked of her was so much
less.

'Surely there must be some mistake?' she'd said, to
find her query treated with callous amusement.

'They've got plenty of money, their sort,' the assistant
told her. 'They can afford to pay more. They don't
quibble.'

'No,' Gina had retorted, unable to contain her
disgust and indignation. 'Because they don't realise
they're being ripped off.'

The more she brooded, the more she disliked this
attitude that overseas visitors were fair game for
overcharging. Out of this sense of indignation grew the
idea of an advisory service for foreigners, whether with
or without a fortune to spend, but with no way of
knowing if they were getting true value. What both
kinds needed was an agent to see they were not cheated.

With the money an elderly aunt had left her and a
personal loan from the bank, Gina had rented a
modest, but centrally situated office. A lot of money
went in advertising, but it paid dividends. Soon it
became known that the GD Agency would get you an
honest deal, would do its best to satisfy any request,
however bizarre. 'We don't claim to perform miracles,

just the next best thing,' was Gina's slogan and it wasn't long before she'd moved to larger premises, taken on several assistants upon whom she impressed her own strict standards of honesty.

Yes, if her television career was about to take a downward swoop, she could always return to business, she thought, as, true to her promise, she arrived promptly at the Television Centre. She had risen early to take more than usual care with her appearance, since there was always the chance that she might be fighting for her job.

Briefly, she took in the presence of several opulent-looking limousines that distinguished the car park by their presence. The 'Big Three' were here. Jimmy's small office was cramped still further by the presence of the three men who were the programme's sponsors. Three? This morning there were four formally suited figures; and, with a sense of outrage, Gina recognised the fourth; her persecutor, Mr X. With a gesture that was instinctive, she threw up her hands to protect her unmasked face, demanding,

'What the hell are *you* doing here?'

There was a pregnant silence, during which she heard the uneasy clearing of throats, and then one of the sponsors, a white-haired, elderly man, was reproving her.

'Miss Darcy! That's no way to address Mr Fallon.'

Fallon? It meant nothing to her. A week or two ago he had been merely another guest on her show. How had he conned his way into the select circle of those who knew her real name?

'Mr Tod Fallon is a new shareholder in TLM Enterprises, a *considerable* shareholder,' he emphasised. 'And since he has never met you, I suggested that he attend this meeting. He has a few questions to ask.'

Oh, yes, Gina thought ironically, Mr Benson might

think the suggestion was his, but she knew who had brainwashed him into making it.

'Actually, Mr Fallon and I *have* met before,' she said coldly. 'Twice. On both occasions, he made a considerable nuisance of himself and made some very insulting suggestions. If Mr Fallon had a financial interest in me, why couldn't he have said so instead of subjecting me to a third degree, just before an important filming session; instead of infiltrating his way on to the show? Doesn't he realise just how long a waiting list there is to appear with Fantasy Woman? And yet he uses his influence to take up a place. Besides, his questions could just as easily have been answered by any of you.' She looked around at the three men and was disconcerted to see that they all looked uneasy.

'I don't think you quite understand, Miss Darcy.' Mr Benson seemed to have elected himself as spokesman. 'Mr Fallon is now the principal shareholder in our firm and as such he has the right to make policy decisions. It's some of these decisions he wants to discuss with you.'

Gina was aghast. For the last year, the trio of elderly men had been content to accept Jimmy's advice, her own suggestions, on the way the programme should develop. She knew there was no way Tod Fallon was going to be so complacent. Fear fluttered in her stomach, a fear she would not show and that made the thrust of her chin more belligerent.

'Well, bully for Mr Fallon,' she said. 'Perhaps he's looking for a new presenter, since he's obviously dissatisfied with the way things are.'

For the first time since her arrival, Tod Fallon spoke. 'Let's say I have certain plans for you, Miss Darcy.'

'What plans?' she demanded. 'Do I have any say in what I'm asked to do?'

'You will be consulted.'

And any objections she might have would be overridden, Gina thought angrily. So far she had remained standing, her body tense with anger. Now she perched herself on the arm of Jimmy's chair, a study in casually insolent indifference, as she consulted her wristwatch.

'Shall we get to the point then?'

Disconcertingly, he was shaking his head.

'My ideas are far too complex for a brief session. Besides, I wish to speak to you alone. I suggest we take a working lunch and then spend the rest of the day discussing the future. *Fantasy Woman* will be off the screen for a while, until certain other plans have been put into execution.'

Gina was stunned, but she was not going to let this man see the extent of her reaction.

'In that case,' she said, 'I think it would be better if you hold this discussion with Mr Riley. He can keep me advised of your "plans".'

'I don't wish to deal with your producer, Miss Darcy.' His icy politeness matched her own. 'I wish to deal with you. Mr Riley accepts that fact and so, I'm afraid, must you.'

Looking with an appeal at Jimmy, she saw the regretful nod of his ginger head, the helpless spread of his hands.

'Very well.' She sought to hide her angry frustration. 'Then I want Jimmy present at our discussion.'

But Tod Fallon was inflexible. He wanted everything his way, she seethed, as she saw the negative movement of the dark head.

'Just you and me, Miss Darcy. Oh, don't worry. Mr Riley won't be adversely affected. It's accepted that he's to remain the producer of the show in any event.'

'Oh, and suppose I refuse to accept your ideas? I'm not just a puppet that you can manipulate.' There had never before been any unpleasantness in her discussions

with the sponsors and she could feel the charged
surprise of the three elderly men, who had never known
her to be anything but charmingly co-operative.

'We'll deal with that problem if and when it arises,'
Tod told her. He shot his cuff, consulting the expensive
Rolex watch that banded his strong wrist. 'It's too early
for lunch, so I suggest we begin over a coffee. I have a
premonition that this discussion is going to take longer
than I anticipated.'

He sounded edgy, impatient, as though he were not
accustomed to having to negotiate. In whatever field he
operated, he was probably surrounded by 'yes' men. He
was probably used to women, too, deferring to his
lightest word, totally bowled over by his male charisma.
Well he would find *her* a very different proposition!

Tod had already come to the same conclusion, even
before this meeting. This was no auburn-haired
equivalent of the dumb blonde. His first glimpse of that
strong chin had reinforced Marcha's warning. But he
felt only reluctant admiration for her fiery, independent
temperament stir within him; and a man would have to
be lacking in some way not to appreciate her
appearance, which, this morning, was singularly
dramatic. He was pretty sure she knew just how
effective her outfit was against the cream of her skin,
the red glow of her hair. A fine striped, black wool
jumpsuit, worn with a red leather belt and red shoes. A
red pigskin clutch bag and a stylish black fedora hat,
tilted at a defiantly rakish angle, completed the picture.
Yes, she was quite something. This was definitely not a
woman who could be domineered, and she would
require more subtle handling than he had orginally
intended to employ. But whatever tactics he had to use,
he was determined that the result would be the same in
the end. She might be strong, but he was stronger and,
something he had not expected, he had a weapon

against which, he had already discovered, she was not, after all, immune. Marcha need never know what methods he had employed; the means justified the end, which would be to her benefit.

Gina had been well aware of his scrutiny and she wondered what thoughts were passing through that well-shaped head. Some sixth sense warned her they were thoughts which, in some way, boded her no good.

Suddenly the brief consultation with the other sponsors was over and Gina found herself, Tod's large hand at her elbow, being urged towards the door. Over her shoulder, she cast a glance at Jimmy. His features were drawn into angry lines, but there was also a worried expression in his eyes. By nature, Jimmy was an optimist and that he should so openly show his anxiety added to Gina's own sense of unease. Just what had Tod Fallon got in mind that was going to take so long to discuss? Would she be forced into taking a stand or was there the remotest possibility that his suggestions would be acceptable to her? Bemused by the rapidity of events, she allowed him to usher her into the gleaming, chauffeur-driven Rolls Royce.

An expensive car, and he was expensively dressed. From the corner of her eye, she was conscious of muscular thighs in taut, well-cut dark trousers; the Gucci shoes. His shirt was undoubtedly of pure silk, his tie a discreet statement in slate blue. Her mental catalogue ended as her eyes lifted further, to his face, and met a brooding black gaze intent upon her. He had been fully aware of her comprehensive assessment. Unconsciously, her chin lifted.

'Where are we going?'

'My hotel.'

'Oh! I thought you had an office. Isn't a hotel rather a public place?' Especially, she thought, since their discussion might well become acrimonious.

'I don't have an office in London. But I do have a suite at the hotel. I think that will ensure us complete privacy, if that's what you have in mind.' A quizzical, sideways glance caught her face creased into an expression of doubt. In the last year, the only man with whom she'd been completely alone was Jimmy Riley and he didn't present any threat to her composure, as she knew, from the other night, this man did.

'Unless you'd rather we went to your place? I assume *you* live in London?'

'No!' she snapped, then, 'I mean, yes, I do have a flat in London, but no, we're not going there.'

'Private love nest is it?' His deep, incisive voice mocked her.

'It's private,' she agreed levelly, 'but nothing else.'

'What?' He was openly incredulous. 'No "Mr Fantasy"?'

'Mr Fallon,' she said icily, 'I'm perfectly prepared to answer your questions where they concern my work. My private life is not for discussion.'

The laugh that greeted her remark was a short, cynical bark.

'That means no man! If there had been, you'd have been only too ready to claim his existence.'

'Why should I need, or want, to lie about a thing like that?'

'Pride?' he conjectured. 'No woman likes to admit that she hasn't got a man in tow.'

'But then, perhaps I'm different to the other women you know, Mr Fallon.'

His glance assessed her, very comprehensively.

'Oh no!' he drawled insinuatingly. 'I don't think so.'

She could feel the angry colour rising, was furious that she couldn't control or hide it. Though the width of the seat was between them, she was unwillingly aware of his overpowering virility and his look had been blatantly sexual in its implications.

Against her will, she was impressed by his suite; that he was used to such a lifestyle was evident in his casual ease, the way in which he summoned room service, ordered coffee and announced that his guest would be staying for lunch. Invited to sit down, Gina sank into the luxury of a settee upholstered in a soft pile, cream velvet, but wished she had chosen an armchair when he joined her.

'Tell me, Miss Darcy, are you totally satisfied with your screen image?'

'Not totally,' she admitted slowly. 'I love meeting people, satisfying their ambitions. That part's fine.'

'Then in what way *are* you dissatisfied?' He was watching her all the time he spoke, as if he were taking face and figure item by item, assessing all the component parts that made up Gina Darcy, and she turned her head aside, made half annoyed, half self-conscious by his scrutiny.

'I'm not keen on the mask, the loss of my identity.'

'Aah!' It was difficult to interpret the sound. 'Tell me more.' Was he trying to trap her into an expression of displeasure; looking for some reason to replace her?

'I'd rather you told me just what you have in mind,' Gina said, still deliberately not looking at him. 'That's why we're here.' But he was not to be diverted.

'It's part and parcel of the same thing. So, the mask?'

'All right! I don't go for the incognito approach, but the sponsors wanted it, so ... *I* want my face to be seen and recognised. I'm ambitious, Mr Fallon. I don't believe the show's popular *because* of my anonymity. It would be just as successful, perhaps more, if the viewers could see me. Like you,' she added resentfully, 'half of them probably think I'm disfigured.'

'Except that now *I* know that's not so, but very much the opposite.' To her alarm, a strong hand captured her chin and forced her to face him. For a moment his voice had been caressive, than it snapped back into

interrogative mood. 'So you want to be famous? Fame
can be a chancy thing.'

'It was pure chance that got me into television in the
first place, plus experience in providing people with what
they wanted.' She wasn't going to volunteer any further
information, matters which didn't concern Tod Fallon,
matters which included the failure of her marriage.

Tod watched as she brooded. He knew a fair bit
about her past, mainly from Marcha. By all accounts,
Gina Darcy was a hard-headed woman, selfish, not one
to take a back seat, which was going to make his task
that much harder—not initially, but later, when he had
to reveal the full extent of his plans.

'Drink your coffee,' he urged.

The coffee smelt delicious, but Gina was more
interested in the answer to certain questions.

'According to Mr Benson, you're the principal
shareholder in TLM Enterprises, so why have we never
met officially?' She flushed hectically as she recalled the
nature of their second informal encounter.

'I've only become a shareholder in the last month.
We may not have met "officially", but I've been
making a close study of you.'

'Why?' Gina asked suspiciously. 'Aren't you satisfied
with my work?'

'Not entirely.' This was blunt. Tod Fallon certainly
didn't believe in pulling his punches. But Gina wasn't
going to show him that this one had struck below the
belt. 'Certain changes will have to be made.'

She kept her voice level, purposely unconcerned.

'Does that include replacing me?'

CHAPTER THREE

'THAT depends on whether you're prepared to co-operate.' Tod was aware that he was bluffing. Suppose she called his bluff? Mentally, he crossed his fingers. If Gina proved recalcitrant, it could take him a long time to find another woman anywhere near as suitable.

'Co-operate?' she murmured non-committally.

'Don't sound so suspicious.' His dark eyes mocked her fears. Again he reached out one large, bronzed hand to grasp her chin, and she had to force herself to meet his gaze as he made an itemised study of her features.

'Great green cat's eyes,' he mused, '*and* red hair. An inflammable combination. Redheads are reputed to be quick-tempered, as are cats, and I think I've already seen the flash of your claws.' With interest, he watched the colour flood her lovely face.

'Could we confine our discussion to business?' she asked coldly, trying to ignore the feelings the warmth of his hand was producing. As he had intended, she had a sudden terrifying image of Tod Fallon making love to her on this sofa. What kind of subconscious tricks was her mind playing? Or *was* it her mind? She was a normal, healthy young woman; except for one thing, she thought bitterly, and for a long time she had been suppressing normal urges. No, that wasn't quite right. The urges hadn't been there. But now . . .

'Did you know that your nose has the most delightful sprinkling of freckles?' he continued, as if he hadn't heard her demand.

'I know my failings!' she snapped, very much afraid that soon, if he didn't release her, loss of control would be one of them.

'Failings?' He repeated the word thoughtfully. 'The freckles? Oh no, they give you a reassuring touch of humanity. Too much perfection can be rather frightening. But then,' he added softly, 'you're far from perfect, aren't you?'

'What do you mean?' Gina tried to jerk away from him, but Tod's fingers had a vice like hold of her. He couldn't possibly know about . . .

'Oh, I'm not referring to your physical attributes.' His dark eyes were bold as they swept downward from her face over other, more concealed, yet still apparent aspects of her femininity; and an outraged Gina could read his mind. It was quite beside the point that, a moment or two ago, she had been imagining much the same thing; but his words had broken the spell.

Tod, too, had been surprised at the trend of his own thoughts. Whatever kind of co-operation he hoped to wring from Gina Darcy, it wasn't that kind. His idea had been to flatter her, to seduce her into agreement with his plan; seduction of a metaphorical, not a literal nature. But, damn it, he was a man wasn't he? Just because he was committed to one woman it didn't mean he couldn't appreciate the rest of the species. Outwardly, Gina Darcy was something quite spectacular, even if he didn't much like what he'd been told about her character.

'Just what *are* you referring to?' she demanded.

He prevaricated. He had no wish for Gina to learn how much he knew about her. Not unnaturally she would be curious about his sources of information and that was something he was not yet ready to divulge.

'Whatever contributed to the break-up of your marriage. That would suggest failings of some kind. Your marriage didn't last very long.'

She gasped. Still, she shouldn't be surprised. Tod Fallon was the kind of man who would make it his business to know all about anyone on his payroll.

'That's past history,' she snapped. 'Something I prefer to forget.'

'Maybe. But it's all part of you, made you what you are. Tell me, why *did* you divorce your husband?'

'You mean,' sarcastically, 'there's something you don't know?'

'I've heard one version,' coolly, 'but I'd be curious to hear yours.'

'Well, you won't. It's none of your business.'

'Oh no, Miss Darcy. You're wrong! From now on, everything about you is my business.'

Their eyes met. His were so dark that the pupils were indistinguishable from the velvety irises; it was as if she were being drawn into the depths. Her expression must have changed, revealing her awareness of him, for he smiled slowly, that lop-sided, attractive smile which made such an alteration to his normally grave face. Something, somewhere deep inside her, leapt wildly. Oddly breathless, she gave him back look for look.

What on earth was the matter with her? She didn't like Tod Fallon. She didn't trust him. She'd known from the very beginning that there was an element of danger in his acquaintance. From their very first encounter he seemed to have gone out of his way, sometimes to taunt and insult her, sometimes to flatter, insinuatively, almost seductively. Why? And yet, against her will, there was something about him that drew her.

After Keith, she'd sworn that no man would ever have the chance to come near her, mentally or physically, to affect her pulse rate; but Tod seemed to have achieved all of these things, insidiously, but surely. Yet she felt certain he'd had no intention of doing so. He seemed to like her as little as she liked him; and that was another puzzle. Apart from their brief, previous clashes, she had done nothing to earn his censure. But it was almost as if he disapproved of her. Was it her work, or her personality?

'Were you ever in love with your husband?' His voice broke her trance-like state.

'Of course, when I married him,' she said curtly, still unwilling to discuss her private affairs. It seemed to her that the more knowledge he had of her, the more power he could exercise over her.

'And afterwards, before the divorce?'

'No. He'd succeeded by that time in killing every vestige of feeling I'd ever had for him.' She shivered as she remembered that claustrophobic possessiveness and jealousy, but most of all, how he had finally destroyed her.

Tod was surprised at the curiosity he felt about Gina and her husband. It had nothing to do with him, nor with their future association. Probably it was because she was such a damned attractive woman that he wanted to hear her deny what he'd been told, convince him that she had not been the one at fault.

'So you put all the blame on him, then?' His enquiring tone sounded derogatory, accusing, to Gina's over-sensitive ear.

'No!' she said and saw that she'd surprised him. 'I know my ambitions contributed to our break-up. Keith was bitterly jealous of my work, my friends. He wanted a *Hausfrau* running after him, feeding him, doing his washing and ironing, and it just wasn't me.'

'Is that all he required?' Tod asked in an insinuative tone that made her flush. 'Surely there were *some* fringe benefits?'

'There's more to love and marriage,' she retorted, 'than good sex and a few shared tastes. There has to be trust. If you want to hold someone, then you also have to know when to let go.' Then, with a return of her indignation, 'I don't know why I'm telling *you* all this.'

'Because I have my reasons for needing to know. And has there been anyone else since?' He went on inexorably with his catechism.

'No, Mr Fallon, there has not! And I don't intend
that there will be. I discovered that marriage and a
career don't mix, so I've settled for the career, freedom,
independence.'

'A very suitable frame of mind for what I intend for
you; no distracting relationships. But then, I wasn't
necessarily implying marriage when I asked if there was
anyone else.'

Her green eyes snapped at him, matching her tone of
voice.

'I don't know what standards *you* hold, Mr Fallon,
but *I* don't go in for "casual" relationships.'

Considering what he'd been told of her, Tod was
surprised at her total honesty. He'd expected her to
refute any faults on her own part, any responsibility for
the failure of her marriage. But then he was almost
constantly revising his preconceived ideas about
Fantasy Woman. As to a career versus marriage, he had
no doubt she meant what she said right at this moment.
But there was always the chance that some man would
persuade her otherwise.

He wondered, as he had done before, whether it
would be safer for his purposes to ensure her co-
operation by making her fall in love with *him*. He had
no doubt of his ability to do so, and it would serve to
bind her to him for the necessary length of time.

Yet, despite this deliberately cold calculation, he
knew that the physical attraction he felt towards her
was genuine. She was extraordinarily lovely; tall,
statuesque, no, almost Junoesque in her build. Both
body and face held a passionate promise of generosity
for any man who could penetrate the icy shell she had
constructed around her heart.

That her mouth could be ardent, he already knew. It
was a large mouth, and it should have been ugly. Yet,
because of its flawless shape, it wasn't. Unbidden there
came to him an acute physical remembrance of that

mouth's unwilling response. He'd seen the alarm in her eyes, too, wide set, a shade of green he didn't recall encountering before, when she'd thought he was about to touch her. So she hadn't forgotten, either, the chemistry that momentarily had flowed between them.

But might it not be dangerous for him to attempt to tamper with her affections? Could he risk personal involvement this time, now that he and Marcha ... Perhaps he would do better to stick to a straightforward business proposition, and in surroundings where the attraction he felt had to be disguised. Wiser, yes. But he still felt a sense of disappointment.

'I don't intend to renew your contract for *Fantasy Woman* just for the present,' he said, deliberately brisk.

She stared at him. His decision must already have been made, so why the pretence at discussion? Why wait until now, when her fears of just such an eventuality had begun to abate somewhat?

'Why?' It was ridiculous the way her voice quivered. 'Have you found someone to replace me?' Her thought processes were swift and her eyes narrowed. '*That's* why you've bought your way into TLM Enterprises, so you can keep some girlfriend of yours sweet.'

It was uncomfortably close to the truth, but, 'Not at all!' His manner was annoyingly laconic. She had hoped to see her shot go home, see anger stir his imperturbable surface. 'Correct me if I'm wrong, but I believe you did express a wish to test out the stunts performed on the show? Gina, it was Jimmy who held you back, not the sponsors. They're quite willing for you to take a more active part in the show, provided ...' He paused quite deliberately, as he studied her lovely face for its reaction; and it was there, the eager flicker of anticipation he'd hoped to see. 'Provided you put yourself entirely in my hands for the next six months.'

She quailed at the thought, but this time she was able to hide her feelings.

'And what happens to the show meanwhile?' she demanded.

'It goes on, of course, with a substitute.'

'I knew it!' She began to rise from the table. 'You *are* putting in some girlfriend . . .'

'Shut up! Sit down and listen. I've no idea *who* they'll use and frankly I don't give a damn. That's your Jimmy's problem.'

She regarded him steadily for a few moments. Maybe he was speaking the truth, maybe not.

'And what will *we* be doing during that six months?'

'*You*,' he emphasised, 'if you agree, will be putting in some pretty strict training to become a stunt girl. In fact, if you're the right material, by the time I've finished with you, you may not want to return to something as tame as *Fantasy Woman*.'

He watched as realisation flooded her lovely face, as incredulity, dawning hope, radiant excitement followed each other in quick succession.

'You really mean it?'

'Yes.'

'When do I start?'

'You're not afraid?'

'No way.'

'Right,' he said, unable to conceal his satisfaction. 'Can you be ready by Saturday?'

'Of course! But ready for what, and where?'

'In the first instance you'll come down to Mallions, my home. A great deal of your training can take place there and in the immediate neighbourhood. Most of the necessary facilities are available.'

'No!' Gina protested at once. 'I can't come and stay with you, just like that. What about my flat? I'd rather do my training nearer home.' Tod Fallon would have to accept that she had a mind and will of her own. Somehow the thought of several months on his territory, the advantage inevitably his, worried her.

'You can't.' He was inexorable. 'There are no comparable facilities. Besides, I intend to keep a personal eye on your training; and there are other reasons why I have to work from home.' He gave her no further chance to argue, but rose from his seat. 'Right! That's settled, I'll drive you home.'

'No!' she said again; then, catching his lowering expression, 'thank you, but I prefer to take a taxi.'

He said nothing for a moment as she met his eyes defiantly. She thought he was going to insist, but, instead, he shrugged and felt in his inside pocket for a pen.

'Then you'd better give me your address, so I know where to pick you up on Saturday.'

'I'm sorry. I don't give my address to anyone. If you'll set a time, I'll meet you here, or anywhere else convenient to you. Now, if you'll excuse me, I believe I saw a taxi rank outside?'

Tod fought his exasperation. He couldn't remember when he'd ever met a woman so stubbornly determined to go her own way, except Marcha, of course, but hers was a special case. Still, he had gained the initial advantage. Gina had accepted his challenge and once she was actually on his territory, he would reveal the further extent of his plans. There were other ways of discovering what he wanted to know right now.

'I'll see you to your taxi then. Can you be here by ten o'clock Saturday morning?'

'Of course.' She was so relieved by his easy acquiescence that she would have promised to be there at six, if he'd suggested it.

The taxi rank was only a hundred yards from the hotel, but Tod was punctilious in seeing Gina into the first vehicle. She had been careful, he noted with dry amusement, to refrain from giving the driver her direction before he pulled away from the kerb. Casually, Tod strolled back towards the next cab in line

and, before Gina's taxi was out of sight, he was offering
the driver double fare if he could succeed in following
her, unobserved.

Gina sank back into a chair. Thank heaven Todd had
not insisted on accompanying her home. What did she
really think of him? What really disconcerted her was
his habit of staring at her. One moment it was as if he
'fancied' her, the next as though his plans for her boded
no good. Which was the real Tod Fallon?

As the flat's soothing ambience closed around her,
Gina wondered whether she could bear to leave its
familiar security for a whole six months. Though she'd
agreed to the training Todd had suggested she had no
idea what particular skills he would ask of her, nor if
she would prove capable of mastering them. He hadn't
even enquired about her athletic prowess. She might
have been able to surprise him by her list of
accomplishments.

Nevertheless, she was grateful for Tod Fallon's
intervention at this stage in her career. With more skills
to offer, other areas of the media might open up to her,
fields requiring more than a pretty face and a desirable
body, which could not last forever. Right now, though,
that body was badly in need of the soothing relaxation
of warm water.

Later, wandering through to the bedroom, wrapped
toga-wise in a large bath sheet, she sat on the edge of
the bed and, from the bedside cabinet, took out a
photograph album. Flicking over the earlier years, she
paused to study herself as she had been at nineteen,
when she'd first met Keith. She was better looking now,
and her brain was more informed. But at twenty-five
she might be said to have reached her peak of
attraction. How much longer would she go on looking
like this? How much longer before she had to really
work at being attractive?

It was a relief to have these depressing thoughts interrupted, until she realised just what the source of the interruption was: the doorbell.

Damn! She'd hoped that none of her neighbours had witnessed her return. Without being uncivil, Gina had firmly discouraged casual droppings in; but there was one elderly woman who could not be dissuaded from borrowing the occasional half-pint of milk and as meticulously returning it.

Sighing resignedly, she discarded the bath sheet in favour of a silk wrap and headed for the source of the irritation. Obviously it was no use pretending she wasn't in.

Tod paid off his taxi, but with the success of his tailing operation, he lost his impetus. For a while he walked up and down outside the apartment block, imagining Gina's reaction when she opened the door and saw him. He had no doubts of his ability to gain entry. He would have the advantage of being prepared for the confrontation and he was physically stronger. It would be a confrontation. She would be furious, of course.

Hell! Was he afraid of her? With an impatient shrug, he swung in through the double front doors, pausing momentarily to study the names against the apartment numbers. His eyebrows rose as he saw she was on the top floor, in the penthouse, no less.

Why go any further, he wondered. He had her address; that was all he needed. He knew why. He was curious about Gina, the private woman, her background. He wanted to see her with her defences down. As the lift carried him upward, he felt the sudden unexpected warmth of sensuality engulf him at the thought of being alone with Gina in her apartment. Good God! What was he thinking of? What would Marcha think if she could read his mind at this moment?

Outside Gina's door, he took himself to task. It was weakness to let such emotions ride him. His use of his masculinity must be calculated, with no danger of serious involvement on his part.

She opened the door, recoiled, the polite smile freezing into a grimace of angry horror.

'What the hell are *you* doing here? How did you find out where I live?'

'Easy!' Tod crossed the threshold, brushing past her with as much nonchalance as if he had been invited to do so. 'I followed you.'

'Damn you! How dare you!' Gina's words drifted after Tod's back view, and she felt a sense of ridiculous anti-climax as he preceded her into her living-room, threw himself down on to *her* favourite seat.

'I thought,' he said, as he looked around him with a calm appraisal that infuriated her, 'in view of our new policy, your secretiveness about your address was a little outmoded.'

'Oh?' she snapped. 'And do you intend to publicise that? So that the world and his wife can swarm all over my doorstep, invade my privacy?'

'No,' he drawled. 'This is a privilege I intend to reserve for myself, assuming I am the first man to cross your hallowed threshold?'

She refused to give him the satisfaction of acknowledging or denying his words.

'Right! So you've got what you wanted. You know where I live. Now you can get out!' Dramatically, she pointed towards the door, the dignity of the gesture impaired as she realised that the silky, material belt had come unfastened, so that she was forced to grab the edges of her robe and clasp it more firmly about her slim waist.

Apart from a lop-sided smile that recognised her predicament, Tod made no indication of having heard her words. Instead he rose and strolled casually through the apartment, looking speculatively about him. He even had the colossal nerve, Gina seethed, to inspect her bedroom. What did he expect to learn from that? Was he looking for traces of male occupation? And what did that matter to him?

'Hmm! You have good taste, *expensive* taste.'

'I've worked damned hard for what I have,' she said defensively, and, seeing that he had no immediate intention of leaving, she shot into the hallway and slammed the apartment door.

'Not furnished on hefty alimony payments then?' His gesture encompassed the décor, the antiques, the Impressionist paintings.

'No!' she snapped. 'It isn't.'

When her marriage had finally broken up, she'd refused alimony; she wanted nothing from Keith. She didn't need his money. Her agency was prospering and there was no reason why it shouldn't go on doing so. But even if she'd been on the breadline, it would have sickened her to be dependent on Keith.

'You were the guilty party, perhaps?' Tod suggested.

'I most certainly was not!' Her green eyes blazed fire at him at the injustice of the remark.

'*He* was unfaithful to *you*?' Tod's incredulity stemmed from the thought that, if such were the case, her husband must have been all kinds of a damned fool not to know the treasure he'd had in his possession.

'Yes,' Gina confirmed dully. She sat down in the cushioned recess. Since Tod seemed unlikely to depart until he had finally satisfied his curiosity, she might as well be comfortable.

'Tell me,' Tod suggested, joining her uninvited, his proximity disturbingly unwelcome. Imperceptibly she tried to edge away.

She shook her auburn head. She had never related the exact details of that traumatic time to anyone.

'Perhaps your marriage was never consummated,' he

insinuated. 'If you behaved like this, like a frightened virgin, every time your husband came near you, I'm not surprised he looked elsewhere.'

'Never consummated!' She knew her voice sounded shrill, orchestrated by indignation, a sudden stab of pure physical frustration. How dared Tod Fallon, a total stranger until a few hours ago, make such an outrageous insinuation! Keith, far from being deprived, had had his cake *and* eaten it.

'Before I met you,' Todd informed her, 'someone told me your marriage failed, not only because you were highly ambitious, but also because you were frigid.'

'Then that "someone" is a liar!' She faced him squarely, her green eyes angry but steady. Who could have told him such a thing? She shook her head vehemently, the movement making the gleaming red hair swirl about her silk-clad shoulders, its perfume drifting to Tod's nostrils a heady enticement, and a wave of pure eroticism shafted through him as he felt himself wishing that he might be the one to put her to the test.

'Care to prove that to me?' he heard himself saying softly. His eyes held hers and hers were the first to drop.

'Get out!' she muttered. She was trembling with a sudden anguished desire that his words had aroused. It had been so long since she'd known a man's touch, the exploration of his hands upon her body, a man's lovemaking. She'd managed to quell the need for so long, but now it rose in a flood tide that threatened to engulf her, because she *knew* Tod Fallon was capable of assuaging that need. He was the only man who had managed to penetrate her reserve, to give new life to senses she'd believed permanently frozen, the only man to move her physically in a long, long time.

'I don't think you mean that.' He was too perceptive. He leant towards her, slowly, tantalisingly, and she seemed incapable of movement, of retreat.

CHAPTER FOUR

THERE was a brief second when his mouth was only a butterfly touch on hers, when there was still time for her to retreat. But she hesitated an instant too long. Then Tod's weight carried her back full-length upon the settee, his kiss deepening as the hardness of his chest crushed her soft breasts.

All along Gina had known instinctively that this man represented danger and she had realised the form that danger took. She should be fighting him off, she thought bemusedly, but her body, so long controlled, had betrayed her. Scarcely knowing what she did, she moved beneath him, a deep, primitive sound vibrating in her throat.

Without removing his lips from hers, he levered himself a little away, so that his hand might invade the scanty protection of her silken robe, might have access between their bodies to the fullness of her breasts. She couldn't move. She knew what he wanted to do, knew she wanted it, too. His hand found the smooth flesh he sought. He raised his head, so that his eyes could devour what he had discovered, the darkening aureole, the hardening tips of her breasts. He lowered his head again, not to her lips this time, but to those rosy tips, the movement of his tongue, his teeth, imparting an ecstasy part pleasure, part pain.

'Oh please, please, don't!' she heard herself saying, knew that while her mind was still coherent, her body was not.

'You don't mean that,' he murmured.

'I do . . . I don't want . . .'

'Nonsense! You told the truth, Gina. You're *not*

frigid. You're no unawakened virgin; you've been married. You're a mature, sexually attractive woman, and you've been starving yourself of love. You want me.'

Yes, she thought miserably, the first time in years I've allowed myself to want a man and it had to be *you*, a man I hardly know and dare not trust.

But even these thoughts could not stem the primitive flood of awareness surging through her as, against her will, her body responded to the proximity of his, its muscular hardness, its musky scent. She was coming dangerously close to forgetting her self-imposed tenets of behaviour where men were concerned.

He had succeeded now in sliding the robe from her shoulders and as it fell in a silken pool around her hips, she heard him exclaim beneath his breath, knew his wondering gaze was roaming lingeringly over her naked curves. An exploratory hand began to stroke her skin, the intimate lingering of his fingers triggering off sharp sensations deep within her.

'You're very lovely, Gina.' His voice was husky, shaken. He took her mouth again and this time she found her lips parting, responding willingly to his probing, moist invasion. His fingers tightened their grasp of her; his mouth trailed its burning route down the side of her neck, pausing tantalisingly at her nipples, to encompass, to stimulate, then on down the flat curve of her stomach to the indentation of her navel. The warmth of pleasure heated her loins and yet . . .

'Tod! Please!' Somewhere she found sufficient breath to make the protest she knew she ought to make.

'Please what? Please make love to you?'

'No! Ah! No!' She wanted him. How she wanted him! But not like this. She didn't know anything about him. If she were ever again to be intimate with a man, first she must know him through and through, be certain that he was worthy of her admiration and trust, as well as her love. Without that knowledge there could be no self-respect in her giving.

Frantically she pushed him away. Amazingly he did not resist. Instead he rose to stand over her, his eyes clouded, remote, as he watched her trembling fingers attempt to straighten the silk robe.

'Don't worry, Gina. I didn't intend to go all the way.'

'You never stood a chance of doing so!' she retorted, the shame at the liberties she had allowed now overwhelming her.

'No?' Despite his own self-disgust, he raised a satirical eyebrow. 'Allow me to differ.'

She jumped to her feet, the fiery temper that went with her hair aroused by his arrogant presumption.

'You can think what you like! You can't possibly know what I think or feel, so I'll tell you. I think you're despicable. Just because you've bought your way into TLM, into *Fantasy Woman*, doesn't mean you've bought me, too. If I agree to work with you ...'

'If?' he enquired sardonically, 'I seem to remember you leaping at my offer.'

'I can still change my mind!' she flared. 'And if there's any repetition of ... your ... your behaviour, I will change it. Just remember, *if* I still agree to work with you, that's the only kind of co-operation you can expect.'

But that was all he wanted, wasn't it, Tod asked himself as he, too, rose, making her a sardonic half-bow of acknowledgement. He already knew she was eager and willing to take part in his new venture, so why had he still thought it necessary to try the ploy of binding her closer to him by the mutual attraction he knew existed? Always honest with himself, at least, Tod knew that for those few minutes no such devious considerations had been in his mind. The plain fact of the matter was that he had desired her, desired her desperately. For God's sake, what had got into him? Usually clear

thinking, master of his own moods, Tod didn't relish
bewilderment at his own motives. He must be missing
Marcha, he decided. He'd been too long away from her.

'My humble apologies!' he said, aware that he
sounded far from humble, aware that he was inflaming
her irritation. 'I was under the impression that you
weren't averse to being kissed.'

'That's a typical male attitude!' She was scornful
now. 'To imagine that just because a woman doesn't
have some one currently dancing attendance, she'll be
pathetically grateful for any man's attention.'

Tod didn't like allowing a woman to have the last
word, but, prudently, he recognised that Gina was very
different from most women of his acquaintance. Having
secured her agreement to work with him, there was no
point in alienating her. He must keep his prime
objective to the forefront of his mind. He moved
towards the door.

'Until Saturday then,' he said, his tone now matter-
of-fact. Then, with a brief flash of mischievousness, 'I
presume there's no objection to my calling for you here,
now I've discovered your hideout?'

After his departure, Gina made no attempt to dress.
She didn't feel she had the strength. Instead, she sank
back on to the cushions that still bore the impression of
their combined weight.

She could scarcely believe in the happenings of the
last half hour. She realised that in some subtle way Tod
Fallon was not really interested in her as a woman, but
as a commodity. And why, when she'd resisted the
efforts of so many men, had she failed to resist Tod?
For, despite her wariness where he was concerned, she
couldn't deny her growing fascination.

But worse than the knowledge of her failure to
hold out against him, was the recognition of the
nature of the ache that had begun to grow within her,
like the thawing of some great glacier, not only in his

presence, but just at the thought of him; and it frightened her.

Despairingly, she looked around her, but for the first time the quiet peace of her flat did not appeal. Tod Fallon had only entered it once and yet he had left an indelible imprint. The old, cosy feeling of being in an impregnable haven, listening to the external, alien noises, had gone. Suddenly silence didn't appeal any more and she rose to put on a record. She felt lonely, a sensation she hadn't experienced in a long time, and angry with herself for feeling that way, and she had a strong suspicion as to the identity of the responsible catalyst.

Damn it! She was getting maudlin. Men, marriage, were not for her ever again. It was a long time since she'd taken out the failure of her marriage and really looked at it. That she'd done so lately was entirely Tod Fallon's fault. Until just recently she'd been so certain that personal freedom was preferable to the restrictions of a close relationship. But what if it hadn't been marriage itself that was at fault? Suppose it had been the participants. Not just Keith, but her, too. What if she had never really been in love, since so many little issues had annoyed her, including curtailment of her personal liberty.

Keith hadn't liked Gina's success. His pride demanded that he be the dominant partner, the breadwinner, whereas Gina's independent spirit needed equality. She wanted a loving relationship, but it must also allow her to retain originality of thought and action. Most of all Keith had disliked her work bringing her into contact with other attractive, wealthy men. His so-called love, his fear of losing her, had been suffocating. His moods, heralded by brooding, sullen preoccupation, could, at a moment's notice, flare into noisy, unreasonable accusation. He had believed her career to be a 'whim', that eventually she must and would conform to his ideas, but, on the contrary, her work had absorbed more and more of her time and energy. Yet she had genuinely believed she could cope with career and marriage.

Keith's work continually took *him* away from home and he didn't seem to consider that made him any less of an asset as a husband. Why should a career adversely affect her value as a wife? She'd tried every way she knew to cure him of his emotional jealousy, continually reassuring him of her constancy. She'd even begged him to go with her to a Marriage Guidance Councillor, or to see a psychiatrist, but in vain.

They'd been married two years when Keith presented his ultimatum. Either she settled down to being a full-time wife or their marriage was at an end. It forced her to sit down and take stock. Even if theirs wasn't a good relationship, she believed in the marriage vows she'd taken. But she did love her challenging career, was proud of the success she'd made of her agency. She suggested a compromise. She would do as he asked, employ a manager, if they could start a family. To her indignant amazement, Keith refused. He didn't want any encumbrances; to share her attention. It seemed to Gina that he wanted everything his own way.

A couple of months later, fate intervened. After a particularly lively New Year party, they had forgotten to take precautions. Gina was pregnant. Perhaps, she thought, Keith wouldn't mind too much. Her optimism was short-lived. He even refused to believe that the child was his.

It had never occurred to Gina that Keith's displays of jealousy had been a disguise for his own desire for outside sexual experience. His accusations that she was having an affair had been a cover for his own liaison. Gina might never have known of this if Frances hadn't come to see her. Keith didn't know of her visit, but

Gina must let him have a divorce, because she, Frances, was pregnant and Keith must marry her.

It was inevitable that Gina had begun to compare Tod with Keith. Had Keith ever made her feel the heat of sexual desire that she felt flooding through her now, as she remembered Tod's hands upon her naked breasts, his lips hot and seeking on hers? Would Tod really have called a halt if she had not?

From this point, her thoughts turned to the future, to her next encounter with Tod. How should she face him, with this recent incident lying between them? Coolly, that was the answer, on her guard at all times. He must never guess how much he had affected her. She must keep before him her determination that their relationship would be strictly that of business.

It was going to be difficult. If she hadn't wanted this opportunity to further her career, she would have taken the coward's way out and made sure they never met again.

'I imagine you're accustomed to flying? You'll have flown quite a bit on location work?'

Tod had been making most of the conversation since he'd picked Gina up at her flat; none of it, to her relief, of a personal nature.

'Actually, no. I've only been in a plane once in my life.' Gina hoped her face hadn't paled. She wasn't going to admit to Tod that there was anything that scared her, that he had picked on her Achilles' heel. But during the flight in question she had been literally paralysed with fear which, despite all her attempts at rationalisation, she had been unable to conquer. Since then, programmes that involved filming overseas had been made by the camera team and Gina had merely introduced them from the studio.

'Oh?' Tod sounded mildly surprised. 'It doesn't make any difference, except that I wondered if you were troubled by airsickness at all?'

'We'll be going abroad by plane?' If she had to spend any length of time in the air, with him at her side, there was no way she'd be able to hide her fears. *Not* a good recommendation for a stuntgirl! The answer to her question nearly destroyed her self-control.

'No. We're not going abroad. But one of the things you'll have to do is fly a small plane . . . solo!'

Gina felt her stomach flip, her throat close up. They hadn't discussed the nature of the stunts she would be expected to perform.

'Why?' she croaked, hastily turned the croak into a cough, as if something had irritated her throat.

'You'll find out,' was his maddeningly cryptic reply. He angled a glance at her set face. 'You have some objection?'

'N . . . no,' she managed. 'Wh . . . why should I?'

'No reason that I can think of. Good. Then a fortnight's intensive training should be sufficient for that particular incident.' He drove on towards their destination, which she now knew to be just north of Aylesbury in Buckinghamshire.

'Mallions!' Tod said about an hour later, an hour during which Gina had feigned sleep. But she hadn't slept. She'd spent the time in appalled contemplation of what was in store for her, a prospect as daunting as that of hiding her reactions to Tod himself, the ordeal she must face without revealing her abject terror. Hiding her fear was one thing, but how was she to overcome it? She could only hope that she would be lucky enough to get an instructor who would be understanding and able to reassure her.

She opened her eyes. The car had halted before massive iron gates set in a high wall that seemed to stretch for ever in either direction. The gates were locked and two formidably large men, whom Tod hailed as Greg and Andy, emerged from a gatehouse to allow the vehicle access.

Once through the gate, the car negotiated a slight bend in the drive, which straightened out to reveal a panoramic view of a Tudor house of stately home proportions, standing in what appeared to be a great many acres of land.

The instant the Rolls came to a halt before the house, figures appeared, as if from nowhere; one man to drive the car away, two more to carry suitcases, while an elderly woman stood in the doorway to greet them; Gina realised that she was not family, but the housekeeper.

'Welcome home, Mr Fallon. I hope you had a pleasant journey?' and, to Gina, 'Good afternoon, miss. Your room is ready, but perhaps you'd like some tea first?'

Gina nodded and smiled her acknowledgement.

'Tea in the library then, Mrs Bush,' Tod requested briskly. 'Then perhaps you'll be good enough to show Miss Darcy the general layout of the house. I have an important phone call to make.'

About to turn away, the housekeeper hesitated.

'Will you be wanting to see Miss Melanie just yet, sir?'

'No,' Tod said, a little brusquely Gina thought, wondering who Melanie was that she could be so lightly dismissed. 'Later will do.'

Tod ushered Gina into the library. From floor to ceiling, two walls were lined with exquisitely bound books. Gina wondered cynically whether Tod had ever read any of them, or whether they were just part of the décor. He didn't strike her as the kind of man who could ever sit still long enough to read a book.

The rest of the room was sparsely, though expensively, furnished. Two large leather chesterfields faced each other before a massive hearth and a large leather-topped desk was angled to the fourth wall. This was composed almost entirely of a large mullioned window, looking out over sweeping parkland to the rear of the house. Beyond and above a colourful shrubbery, Gina caught sight of an object, which rose and fell with the breeze. A windsock? She turned to Tod with a question on her lips.

'Yes. That's an airstrip. I have a small Cessna for my private use, the one you'll be learning to fly.'

An insidious suspicion crossed Gina's mind. 'Who's going to teach me?'

'I shall, of course!' His reply confirmed her uneasy conjecture.

The arrival of Mrs Bush with a tray interrupted this topic and, as she sipped her tea, Gina avoided any return to it by complimenting Tod on his house.

'Has it been in your family long?' she asked, as she studied a large oil painting hung above the fireplace. The work depicted a beruffed Elizabethan gentleman in doublet and hose.

Tod smiled, that brief flash of white teeth which lent his face such disconcerting charm.

'Sorry to disappoint you, but I can't claim any lengthy noble descent. I bought the place lock, stock and barrel, including the family portraits, about five years ago when the last member of the family died.' Again that glimmer of amusement. 'Now you're here, you'll find out a lot about me you didn't know. Perhaps,'—the gleam in his eye, its suspect implication, disconcerted her—'the reverse will apply and I'll be finding out more about you. What else would you like to know?'

'Nothing,' she said sharply, 'I wasn't prying.'

'Nonetheless, I'll give you a brief résumé; it will save explanations later. Tod Fallon, christened Theodore, which incidentally I hate! Age, thirty-three. Multi-millionaire by the time I was twenty-eight. Eighty per cent owner of a large group of companies, some of which are located overseas and one of which is a film company, based in this country. This house stands in two hundred acres of land, every boundary of which is humming with security precuations, controlled from the gatehouse we passed.'

He hadn't mentioned whether or not he was married, Gina noticed.

'Why the security precautions?'

'Various reasons. Among other things, this place is a treasure house of antiques.'

'And?'

'Excuse me,' he said abruptly, 'I must make the telephone call I spoke of. If you've finished your tea, ring the bell and Mrs Bush will show you round. I'll see you at dinner.'

The tour of the main areas of the house left Gina bewildered. Even then there was a whole wing and the attics left unexplored.

'How can one man possibly live in all this?' she asked the friendly housekeeper.

'Bless you, miss. It's never empty! Later on today it'll be swarming with people. It always is when Mr Tod is filming.'

'Filming? Here?'

'Bushie! Bushie! Is he home yet? *Is* he?'

A very diminutive person erupted from a room Gina had not entered, a little doll of a girl, with saucer-wide sapphire eyes and jet black hair that bubbled in natural curls. This unexpected apparition was followed by an apologetic young woman in a nursemaid's uniform.

'I'm so sorry, Mrs Bush. I did tell Miss Melanie she should wait until Mr Fallon sent for her. But she's been so excited . . .'

'Who are *you*?' The child was staring up at Gina. At first the blue eyes had been hostile, but now this was replaced by puzzlement. 'At first I thought it was *her*.

You're very like her, but I think you're prettier and I think I might like you. *She's* horrid!'

Gina wondered with some amusement which of the child's female acquaintances had warranted such rancour.

'That will do, Miss Melanie.' Mrs Bush spoke firmly, though her expression was indulgent. Gina guessed that the housekeeper sympathised with the child's feelings about the unknown. 'Miss Darcy doesn't want to be bothered with your nonsense just now.'

'Are you staying here?' The dark-haired mite was evidently aware of the housekeeper's partiality. 'Are you going to be in my daddy's films?'

Tod Fallon was this child's father? Gina knew just why her heart rose so sickeningly in her throat, preventing speech.

'*She*'s in his films,' Melanie continued.

'Melanie,' the nursemaid intervened, 'you heard what Mrs Bush said. Now back to the nursery for your tea. Miss Darcy will want to unpack and rest.'

'All right.' The child responded to the urging hand, but over her shoulder she had a parting word for Gina. 'Will you play with me sometimes, when you're not tired?'

Protests from housekeeper and nursemaid that Gina's presence at Mallions was not principally for Melanie's entertainment fell on unheeding ears, and the child fixed Gina with a penetrating stare which demanded an answer.

'I'd like that, Melanie,' she said truthfully, 'so long as your daddy doesn't object. I'm here to work, you see.'

With this the child appeared satisfied and allowed herself to be led away, but the encounter had given Gina more food for thought than she relished. Tod Fallon had a daughter and therefore, presumably, a wife. She was dismayed by the strong disappointment this conclusion engendered.

Dinner, she realised Mrs Bush was warning her, would be a formal affair.

'Mr Tod always says it would be a crime to own a house like this and not live in it in the style to which it's accustomed.'

Gina was grateful for the housekeeper's hint. 'Will there be many other people at dinner?'

'Bless you, yes. It's rarely Mr Tod sits down with less than twenty.'

'He must have a lot of friends.'

'Technicians mostly,' Mrs Bush returned, 'actors and actresses. He's choosy who he calls friends.'

Left alone in the white-walled, low-beamed, chintzy bedroom, Gina considered what she should wear for her first dinner party at Mallions. Thank goodness she had brought a large and varied selection from her wardrobe, even though Tod's eyes had risen a visible inch or two at the number of suitcases he'd been required to fit into the boot of the Rolls Royce.

The house, which earlier had seemed so vast and silent, was beginning to come alive. Gina could hear the movement of feet over the groaning boards of stairs and passageways; the sound of water tormenting the joints of ancient plumbing; men's and women's voices raised in conversation and laughter.

The minx! Tod thought, as Gina paused deliberately in the doorway, her gaze coolly sweeping the room. Did she realise the effectiveness of her late arrival? Of course she did. She was a consummate, natural actress. That damned Jimmy Riley had been hiding her light for too long.

She looked magnificent, her red hair lending a rich glow to the magnolia skin of face, neck and shoulders. The silky black bodice of her simple dress covered one shoulder only, leaving the other dramatically bare; the long full skirt with its matching tie belt was white, with enormous black polka dots. Her outfit was simplicity itself.

'This is Gina, everyone. Gina, let me introduce you to some of the people you'll be working with.'

There followed a succession of names and faces which, she was sure, would take her months to assimilate. She could not doubt the genuine warmth of her greeting from the men, but Gina, often intuitive, recognised the barely polite aloofness of the majority of the women.

At the table, she was seated between the two singularly large and muscular men, Greg and Andy. Stuntmen, she hazarded? The younger of the two, about her own age, was open in his admiration of her.

'Greg Gibson,' he introduced himself. 'We'd no idea old Tod was bringing along such a stunning addition to our number. He has a pretty taste in redheads.' Over a lull in the conversation, his voice carried quite clearly and Gina was aware of Tod's sudden frowning gaze upon them. 'Of course, it's obvious why he picked *you*,' Greg was continuing, when Tod interrupted him, his voice unusually harsh, even for Tod.

'I haven't explained our project to Gina yet and I'd prefer to do so myself.' It wasn't a request but a definite command, issued, not just to Greg, but generally. Gina sensed the surprise of those around her.

'Sure thing, Tod. You're the boss!' Greg said, but the puzzled look remained on his ruggedly handsome features for some time as he turned the conversation into other channels.

This interchange increased Gina's unease. She'd had the idea all along that there was some underlying motive for Tod's selection of her for special training. She had never really been able to believe in his dedication to improving *Fantasy Woman*. As he'd said on the occasion of their first meeting, it just wasn't his kind of television.

As she might have expected in Tod's home, the meal was superb, five courses following each other in smooth, efficient succession, and she enjoyed the food, despite her awareness of covert glances from the other women around her. Not one of them was a redhead. What had Greg meant?

Only a girl seated directly opposite seemed disposed to be friendly. 'I'm Debbie. Never mind the second name. It's bad enough having to remember first names when you're plunged into a whole crowd of people.'

At the end of the meal, there was a general movement to leave the dining-room.

'Gina!' Without a word of apology, Tod interrupted her conversation with Debbie. 'I'd like to see you in the library, now.' He didn't wait for her agreement, but turned on his heel, striding away as though he confidently expected her to follow him. Like a dog called to heel! she thought indignantly.

Determined that she was going to set the pattern for their future relationship, she lingered deliberately, pursuing the topic she and Debbie had been discussing. But all the while, she noticed the younger girl throwing anxious glances towards the door.

'If ... if Tod wants you, hadn't you better go?' Debbie said at last. 'He ... he doesn't like to be kept waiting.'

'Is that so?' Gina said. 'Then perhaps it's time someone *made* him wait.'

A tall, statuesque blonde nearby overheard their exchange.

'Perhaps Gina has a special dispensation, Deborah darling. After all, it does rather look as if he's traded in the old model for a new one, doesn't it? His last redhead fawned on him disgustingly.'

Debbie flushed scarlet.

'Shut up, Stephanie!' she muttered. 'You heard what Tod said. You know we weren't to ...'

'Gina!' Greg was at her elbow, apologetic, but determined. 'Tod sent me to get you.'

For a moment she contemplated prolonging her defiance, then decided that she'd made her point sufficiently clear.

'See you later,' she told Debbie, then accompanied Greg, her pace a deliberate stroll. He left her outside the library door.

Tod was seated behind the large desk, a script laid out in front of him. He was just in the act of banging down the telephone receiver and it was obvious that not all his irritation was caused by Gina's tardiness. Just as apparently, however, he intended to take it out on her.

'When I say I want to see you, I mean right away, not half an hour later!'

She was determined not to appear daunted by his manner, not to forsake the stand she had taken.

'If you'd asked me politely, I wouldn't have kept you waiting,' she said coolly, taking the chair his impatiently gesturing hand indicated, leaning back to indicate her complete ease. 'I'm accustomed to a certain amount of civility from my employers.'

'Then you'll have to get reaccustomed!' he snapped. 'Don't come the starlet with me. You may have been big time on TV, but here you're nobody until I make you somebody. I'm a busy man; I haven't time for pussy-footing around. When I say jump, that's just what people do.'

'Not me!' she retorted. Then, before he could make an angry answer, she leant forward in her chair, fixing him with a keen glance of her green eyes. 'You want my co-operation, Mr Fallon. For some reason you appear to want it very badly, or you wouldn't have gone to the lengths you have to secure it. If you're the kind of man you purport to be, you'd have given up on me long since, told me to get lost. I wonder why you didn't?' She leant back, crossing one shapely silk-clad leg over the other, aware that he was watching the movement, that he couldn't hide his interested reaction to it. 'You *need* my co-operation and you can have it, but on my terms; and you must admit they're not very onerous. Simple courtesy, the odd "please" and "thank you", won't cost you money.'

'You cool little bitch!' But there was a grudging admiration, rather than anger, in his tone. 'All right, thank you for deigning to answer my summons. And now,' his tone altered once again to impatient briskness, 'd'you mind if we get down to business?'

She knew it had been a sarcastic, rhetorical question, requiring no reply, but she answered, nevertheless.

'Not at all. In fact I'm dying to have the mystery solved. Why all the secrecy? Why weren't the others allowed to discuss it with me?'

'Briefly,' he told her, 'we're in the process of making a film, a fast-moving thriller, something on the lines of a James Bond except that the agent is a woman. But that doesn't mean there'll be any punches pulled. Anything a male agent can perform, this woman can equal.'

'Excepting in the sexual field, of course?' Gina asked, mock seriously. 'You won't be expecting her to pull birds?'

He missed her straight-faced humour.

'Use your head!' he snapped. 'Obviously it's the other way around. She's as ruthless in her use of men as Bond of his women. The whole point of this briefing is to warn you that the stunts aren't going to be easy. There'll be no faking, no trick photography. You'll be earning your salary, *if* you pass through your training successfully.'

'But what's any of this got to do with *Fantasy*

Woman?'

'Not a thing,' he startled her by admitting, but only confirming her earlier suspicions.

'But you said . . .'

'Good God, woman! Don't you realise you're being given an opportunity in a million, an opportunity to break away from that third-rate rubbish?'

'But why was it necessary to lie, to let me think . . . ?'

'Because you might have refused, out of some ridiculous sense of loyalty towards the programme, to Riley.'

'Jimmy doesn't know about this?'

'Of course!' Coldly, 'It was only fair to give him an opportunity to replace you.'

Gina leapt to her feet.

'You high-handed bastard! You might at least have given me the choice!'

'And what would that choice have been?'

Trapped, she stumbled over her reply.

'I . . . I . . .'

'You'd have chosen to move on. *You* know it; *I* know it. So don't let's have any hypocritical claptrap.'

The fact that the adjective was apt did nothing to improve Gina's mood, but she let it pass. His words so far had conjured up bright attractive images that she wanted to hear confirmed. If she were to train for all the skills necessary to Tod's dauntless heroine, this, by implication, must mean that she was to play the role. Surely stardom didn't come that easily? Her day-dreaming was interrupted.

'Don't you want to know any more about your duties?'

Duties? A strange way of putting it, but then this was an unfamiliar world.

'Yes, of course I do.'

'Right. I understand you swim and ride passably well. Anything else?'

He *was* well-informed.

'I've recently taken up judo.'

'Done any running?'

'At school, hundred-yard sprints, that sort of thing,' but he was shaking his head impatiently.

'This will call for stamina. Cross-country would have been more useful. Right.' He made a note on a pad in front of him. 'We'll put daily jogging on your schedule.'

Obviously, Gina though wryly, this job was to be no sinecure; but then she hadn't expected that it would be.

'You asked about swimming and riding?' she queried. 'Will they be of use?'

'Well. You'll be expected to scuba dive; to learn how to make a horse fall; how to fall from a horse yourself, without breaking your neck.'

'You must have a large staff of tutors.'

'Not at all,' he contradicted. 'Most of your training I'll undertake personally.'

'But ...' Gina couldn't hide the discomposure this intelligence caused her and he smiled his amusement.

'I wasn't born a director, you know. I started out as a stuntman and found that a stuntman must also be an actor. In fact I still act in my own films and I still perform my own stunts.'

'Are ... are you acting in *this* particular film?'

'Naturally!'

'As ... as what?'

'Since you're so interested, not that it will affect *you* much, as the man who finally outruns, outrides and generally tames the wild cat of a heroine.'

Why wouldn't it affect her? She'd have to act opposite him!

'I met your daughter before dinner!' Gina blurted out the words.

Tod's dark eyebrows rose.

'Oh? I fail to see what that has to do with our present discussion.'

'N-nothing really. I just remembered it. She ... she asked if I would play with her sometimes. I said I'd find out if that was all right with you.'

His face still bore a look of incredulity.

'You're not here as a nursemaid for my daughter. The one she has is perfectly adequate. Besides which,' his expression became sardonic, 'you'll have little time, or energy, left for playing games, of any kind.'

'And just what does that imply?' she asked, though his tone had carried an unmistakable hint of his meaning.

'That I don't encourage liaisons between members of my team while a film is in process. It distracts them, prevents them giving of their best. Stay away from the men, Gina! I've already noted your dramatic effect on Greg.'

'Have you?' she retorted. 'I accept that I'm here to work for you; and if you refuse to let me make friends with your daughter, I'll accept that, too, though I think it's a shame. She seems to lead a lonely life, shut up in the nursery, only seeing you when you condescend to summon her, as you do your employees. But I won't accept your right to dictate my other friendships.'

Tod's face darkened to a frightening intensity and, as he pushed back his chair and rose from behind the desk, Gina took a backward step towards the door.

'My daughter, though it's none of your business, leads a secluded life for a very good reason, a reason which also gives me the right to decide whose company she seeks. It's true I can't physically prevent you from making assignations with Greg, or with any other man here; but if anyone's work suffers, you'll be the one out on your ear. You may think you have me in a cleft stick, because I so obviously needed a redhead, but you're not unique. If I have to, I can afford to search the length and breadth of the world to find a replacement.'

'Then why didn't you?' she taunted. 'Why pick on me?'

'Oh, don't get any big ideas about your own talent; you haven't any until I drum it into you. You were simply available!'

Available? What exactly did he mean by that? She couldn't voice her suspicions, but she could put the record straight, subtly.

'You needn't worry!' She injected scorn into her voice. 'I'm not interested in Greg or any of the men here, you included. I came here to work. You'll get your money's worth!'

'Oh, I will!' he said with dauntingly grim assurance. Then, coming to tower over her, the closed door barring her escape, 'As for your other point, your total lack of interest in men, don't try to fool yourself, Gina! You forget,' he said softly, 'I've held you in my arms. I know just how little it takes to bring that body of yours flooding back to life. You may have had it in deep freeze for the last year or so, but it wouldn't take much to start a thaw. I've done it once. I can do it again.'

She gasped at his presumption, sought for words to deflate his pretensions, to cool the dark warmth she could see deepening in his eyes.

'Sorry to disappoint you,' she gibed, 'but instant coffee, instant snacks I've learnt to put up with; instant sex doesn't turn me on at all.'

It had been a mistake to provoke him, to issue what he must only see as a challenge. She realised that at once from the expression on his face. And simultaneously with her recognition of his intention his arm shot out, snaking around her waist, hauling her, tall as she was, clear of the floor and hard up against him. At once her violent trembling betrayed her own rising desire, which not even his triumphant words could quell.

'No? I think I've just disproved that.'

CHAPTER FIVE

His hand reached behind her for the key of the library door, turning it, securing the room against intrusion or escape.

'I warn you,' she said breathlessly against the bronzed flesh of his throat, 'I shall scream.'

He lowered his head, his breath fanning her temple, his mouth nuzzling the point of her cheekbone.

'Scream away! No one's going to come to your assistance.'

She tried to keep her tone light, sarcastic, tried to lean away from him.

'They'll think you're giving me my first acting lesson, I suppose?'

'Possibly,' he agreed drily. 'In any event,' he mumbled the words down the side of her neck, 'no one would dare to intrude.'

Frantically, Gina's fists pushed against his shoulders.

'Oh? Not even your wife? Isn't *she* curious about what you get up to with actresses, behind locked doors?'

'I should hardly thinks so, no, since she's been dead for some years.'

'Oh!' Gina gasped, shock almost deadening all other reactions to this intelligence. He was free then? But she didn't know whether or not she should express conventional sorrow. How could he speak so callously, so unfeelingly? Didn't he have any heart, any regrets for the mother of that lovely little girl upstairs? But she was given no opportunity to voice her opinion, to ask her question.

'Shall we get on with the experiment?' he asked

huskily. It wasn't a question, but a declaration of intent.

She began to struggle more violently, but he had her backed hard against the door.

'Let me go! Don't you dare!'

'Oh, but I *do* dare.' One arm was completely encircling her, holding her immobile, his free hand performing the same service for her chin, so that she was powerless to evade the dark, descending head, the threat of the firm, shapely mouth lowered to hers.

She gave a little moan in her throat as her lips parted to his ruthless invasion of them. Her head forced back against the hard panels of the door, kept there by the pressure of his mouth, left his hand free to go marauding over her body, caressing the shoulder bared by the sophisticated drape of her dress, revealing the other shoulder to match, then sliding the silky material to her waist, seeking the softness of her breasts, necessarily, because of the cut of the dress, unencumbered by a bra.

Hard, exploratory fingers brushed vulnerable peaks, played provocatively with them, until of themselves they seemed to strain against his hand, inviting further, tantalising caresses. She knew she was letting him prove his outrageous claim, but somehow there was nothing she could do about it; she didn't want him to stop, ever.

His mouth moved on now, descending to her breasts, then lower still, growing impatient of the remaining barrier caused by the folds of her dress. He fumbled for the zip, dealt competently with it, and Gina felt the material cascade down over hips and thighs to pool about her feet. Now only the scantiest triangle of lace protected her and as his hand sought to explore beneath it, she went curiously still, even the trembling of her body ceased, as, with a cold shock, sanity returned.

'All right, damn you! You've proved your point! But

that's as far as you go. Now let me get the hell out of here.'

He met her damp-eyed defiance with an implacable stare.

'Conceding victory so soon? And it was just getting interesting!'

But he released her and watched with what appeared to be clinical detachment as she bent to retrieve her dress with hands whose trembling she could not conceal, though she hoped he was not aware that her whole body vibrated with an unassuaged quivering; he seemed so cool, so unperturbed.

In reality, Tod was finding great difficulty holding himself in check. He had been on the point, he knew, of removing that final garment, of carrying her to one of the chesterfields, of taking his seduction scene to its ultimate conclusion. But something had prevented him. A belated sense of loyalty to the absent Marcha? Strangely, he didn't think so. True, there had been no other women in his life since he'd met Marcha. Physically she was all that a man could desire, always avid for his possession of her, a demanding, skilful lover. They were well matched, he and Marcha, but without any emotional complications, and that was all he wanted, wasn't it: the satisfaction of his natural needs?

Something else, something to which he couldn't put a name, had stopped him making love to Gina, and it hadn't been her belated show of resistance. That, he could have overcome, but suddenly he hadn't wanted to see her like this—an unwilling victim!

He unlocked the library door, holding it wide open for her.

'That will be all for the moment,' he said formally, for the benefit of anyone within earshot. 'It would be as well if you went to bed now. You've a long day ahead of you.'

'Sunday?' she said, protest in her voice, despite her

still uncontrollable shaking.

'In this house, Sunday is like any other day. Breakfast is served from seven-thirty. At eight-thirty you'll be out on the airstrip, suitably dressed for climbing in and out of an aircraft. Sleep well!'

He couldn't know what a mockery those last words were. How would she manage to sleep at all now? She'd known they would come some time, the flying lessons, but at least she'd believed herself to have one more day's grace in which to steel herself. She sidled past him, careful to avoid the slightest contact between their bodies, and made for the stairs.

But, honest with herself, she knew that it wasn't just the thought of tomorrow's lessons that kept her awake until the small hours, and, when she did sleep, her dreams were troubled and erotic.

Gina was glad to discover, next morning, that Tod had already breakfasted. At least he wasn't there to note and comment upon her lack of appetite, speculate as to its cause. As it was, the one piece of toast, which was all she dared eat, clung to the roof of her mouth with the consistency of blotting paper. Hastily, she washed it down with hot, strong coffee.

Inexorably, the hands of the clock crept nearer to eight-thirty and at last she could procrastinate no longer. The idly drifting windsock pointed out her direction and she was standing beside the aircraft hangar with exactly a minute to spare as Tod taxied out on to the runway.

She had been uncertain what to wear, settling finally for an emerald green track suit and tying back her tumbling red hair with a matching, silky ribbon.

Without any preliminaries, Tod ordered her into the plane, which looked extremely small and frail to Gina's nervous eyes. He told her to pay attention while he demonstrated first the bewildering array of controls and then innumerable take-offs and landings.

All the while, Gina remained rigid with fright. For her the next hour passed in a haze, her brain scarcely functioning as she struggled to give intelligent answers to his remarks, to take in what he was saying.

This procedure was repeated twice daily for a week and she received no kid-glove treatment from Tod. This was no hobby to be practised in idle moments, he emphasised. You persevered and if you couldn't take it, there was no point in continuing. Nor could you bluff your way through it.

'You can't fake an aptitude for flying. Either you can do it or, if you can't, you stick at it for hour after hour until you can.'

Once or twice during that week, to her horror, he demonstrated looping the loop.

'Not that you'll ever be called upon to perform one yourself, but it's as well to know the technique in case of accident, to know how to get out of one. Watch! You apply full opposite rudder, at the same time pushing the stick into forward position.'

However, by the end of the week, she was surprised to find that her mind was beginning to take in what it was all about, that she was beginning to conquer her fears. There came a morning when she was able to eat a hearty breakfast and set out for the airstrip full of enthusiasm and an intense curiosity to discover her own limitations, for that day she was to take the controls herself, with Tod at her side.

One thing lacking during the past few days, she realised with gratitude, had been any sense of embarrassment in his company. She'd been concentrating far too hard on conquering her fears to have time for indulging other emotions. And even though she felt more at ease in the little aircraft, there were new problems to contend with. Now the martinet at her side was informing her that, despite his presence, she was totally responsible for their safety.

It was hard physical work, too, she found, wrestling with a heavy plane; for, despite its deceptively fragile appearance, the Cessna was no featherweight to control by fingertip touch.

It was during the second week that she realised she was no longer afraid of actually being in the plane, that she was even enjoying herself, just so long as Tod was there to take care of any emergencies. But this euphoria was short-lived, for it dawned on her that the more she improved, the sooner he would make her go up alone. This thought actually impaired her progress for a couple of days, her blunders earning her bellows and harsh words from her inflexible instructor, bringing her almost, but not quite, to the verge of tears. She would *not* give way to such weakness before him! And his tactics worked where kindly patience might not have done, making Gina stubbornly determined to prove herself.

Then, one morning, after a series of practice take-offs and landings, Tod announced that he was getting out.

'Tod!' Panic-stricken she called after his departing figure. 'Please! Not yet! I'm not ready!'

He ignored her pleas and turned to gesture impatiently, indicating that she should take off.

Hands shaking, her lips muttering imprecations against the tyrant, she went through the motions. She had never been so scared in all her life. This was worse than her one flight in a commercial aircraft. How could she have been scared by that? At least then she had been in the competent hands of a qualified, experienced pilot. Now she was mistress of her own fate.

Unaware that she was doing so, she recited the take-off ritual aloud, only assimilating, some considerable time later, the fact that she was actually flying; the altimeter told her that she was at nine hundred feet above the ground; the realisation had a strange, heady effect upon her.

She'd done it! She was supposed to land now, but her new confidence, the exaltation she felt, made that seem too tame a proceeding. Far off to her right, her attention was caught by the sight of another plane. Its yellow body small against the vastness of the sky, it cavorted around, practising aerobatics. The pricklings of a crazy desire invaded her being, a desire as strong, as compulsive as that of sexual stimulation. Could she? *Dared* she?

Without giving herself time to think, she turned Tod's Cessna into a rather ragged barrel roll. What had he said? 'Opposite rudder, stick forward'? It worked like a dream! She repeated the performance again and again, until suddenly the loop was a perfect, graceful arc, the machine she flew an extension of her being in a satisfying oneness, like the coming together of man and woman.

Now she was content to come down to earth, making a perfect three-point landing, taxiing to within a few feet of where Tod stood, by the hangar.

She released her harness, sprang from the plane, ran towards him, her lovely features alight with jubilation.

'I did it! I did it! *I can fly!* Did you see me?'

'I saw you all right, you bloody little fool!' His face was grey, drawn into grim lines, as he grabbed her arm and dragged her into the hangar. 'What the hell did you think you were doing up there? You were supposed to take off, do a few bumps and circuits and then land, not behave like a bloody flying circus. You haven't had enough experience for that sort of thing. Suppose you'd crashed the plane?'

His anger, its violent expression, quelled her exuberance, and anti-climax took over as she realised he was right. In her excitement at her own achievement, her triumph over fear, she had become over-confident, foolhardy even. Her legs began to shake with reaction and tears trembled on her eyelashes as with a quivering voice she sought to take out her sudden sense of mortification on him.

'*If* I'd crashed, I suppose I'd have been killed and your precious aeroplane would have been a write-off. But that wouldn't have mattered so much, would it? You're rich! You could go out and buy another plane, like some people buy a bicycle. And as you said yourself, redheads are two a penny.'

But not this one, Tod thought savagely, as her legs finally gave under her and she would have fallen, if his arms had not gone around her in a steely hold. Unable to think, to feel beyond this moment, he lowered himself on to a pile of crumpled tarpaulins, taking her with him, kissing the salty tears from her eyelids, planting fierce little kisses all over her damp, pale cheeks.

'Don't ever do anything like that to me again!' he groaned, before his mouth took hers, hungrily, mercilessly.

She turned her head from side to side, trying to evade him, but to no purpose. His kiss was blistering her lips, his hands were seeking the lower edge of her track suit top, lifting it up so that he could curve his fingers about her breasts, exploring her body as though he would reassure himself that she had come to no physical harm.

Did he *care* that she had put herself into danger? She felt her body's involuntary surge against his, recognised their mutual arousal for what it was, an urgent, primitive response to the danger in which she had placed herself, a heady, frightening excitement, more powerful than any aphrodisiac.

He ripped the top off, over her head, burying his face between her breasts, his hands warm and proprietary upon her, hands that were beginning to move lower, gradually easing down the track suit trousers, stroking her stomach, shaping her hips.

With a little moan of pleasure she wound her arms

around his neck, holding his head tightly to her breasts, loving the feel of his crisp hair against her skin.

'Let's get rid of these damned trousers,' he murmured thickly, and she didn't argue. Scorching desire rode her; the last of the icy barrier she had constructed around her had melted away.

His body was crushing her and, greatly daring, she felt for the waistband of his trousers. The ache in the pit of her stomach was becoming intolerable.

'Tod! Oh, Tod!' she whispered. 'Help me! Please help me!' Frustratingly, her trembling fingers could not master the task she had set them.

But suddenly, all in one fluid movement, he rolled over, thrusting her away from him. Rising to his feet, he strode to the door of the hangar and stood there, staring out over the airstrip. In the sudden silence, Gina could hear the drone of the little yellow aircraft, still performing its aerobatics, and it seemed to her that this moment would be forever imprinted on her memory with that accompanying sound.

'Tod?' Her voice was barely above a whisper. 'Tod? What is it? What's wrong?'

He did not answer for a moment or two, but flexed his shoulders, as if they bore an intolerable burden, ran his hand through his hair, trying to restore some order to the devastation her fingers had created. Then he turned towards her, his voice harsh, barely under control.

'*I'm* wrong! That's what it is!'

'But why? Don't you ... don't you want me?' Still her voice was barely audible, but he heard her.

'Damn you, Gina!' His voice shook with anger. 'Of course I wanted you. I still do, confound it!'

'Then ... then why?' she repeated. She didn't care that all the defences she'd ever erected had come crashing down. For a few moments, she had been alive again, gloriously alive. She had wanted Tod and he had wanted her. Where was the problem? She couldn't believe that he hadn't made love to dozens of women, before and since his marriage.

'Because ... because ... Oh, to hell with it, just because! For God's sake, Gina, take that look off your face. Get up and get dressed. Go back to the house. If it's any consolation, you've passed your flying test with honours.'

'But I didn't pass *yours*? Is that it?' The tears began to pour down her cheeks and she made to run past him. But the sight of her tear-stained face and hurt eyes was too much for him and he barred her way, holding her, crushing her against him, his body still hard against hers in arousal.

'Gina, Gina, for God's sake, don't cry,' he groaned. 'I can't stand it. I'm only human!'

'You're not,' she gulped. 'You're ... you're inhuman, to be able to stop, just like that, to be so cruel ...'

'Damn it! Haven't you ever heard of being cruel to be kind? What would have happened, if I'd made love to you? Would that have been the last of it? You know it wouldn't. Women are all the same, with only a few exceptions. You'd have wanted some commitment from me and I can't give it.' But he buried his face in her neck and his body shook.

'I see!' In control of herself again now, desire effectively dampened by his words, she pulled free of him. 'Thank you for the flying instruction and,' bitterly, 'the *other* lesson. You're a good teacher in the school of hard knocks.'

She turned on her heel and marched away, head held high, shoulders back. Tod Fallon would never see her cry again. What a fool she had been to lower her guard, to let herself believe that there was something special about this man.

Half-way across the field, she halted, struck by a sudden thought. Surely it couldn't be anything to do with that ridiculous rule of his, no fraternising between the sexes during filming? Did he adhere to his own rules? No. She couldn't believe that. There had to be some stronger, more valid reason for his rejection of her. Another woman? That was more likely. She continued on her way.

Tod had watched her retreat, unbearably touching in its determined dignity. He had seen her pause. He held his breath. Did she mean to turn around, come back, make one last appeal? Almost he found himself hoping that she would. Knew that if she did, this time he would be unable to leash his desires, that he would have to make her his. But her pause was short-lived. She marched on as doggedly as ever, and he heard himself utter a single sigh, a mixture of disappointment and relief.

By the time he, too, returned to the house, he was fully in command of himself once more. Gina must continue her training; she must be ready by his deadline to commence filming. He wished now that he *could* hand her over to some other tutor, but, not given to false modesty, he knew he was the best tutor she could have.

He was not the only one to wish that her further training was in other hands. After dinner that evening, a cool, composed Gina sought him out in the library, standing poised in the open doorway, ready for instant departure should the need arise.

'Come in!' he growled. 'Shut the door! I don't bite!' Then his skin colour deepened beneath his tan at the unfortunate choice of words; for he *had* bitten her that morning, nibbling enticingly at her breasts, and they both remembered it.

'No thanks!' Her own face flushed, she remained where she was. 'I can say what I have to say from here.

I want a different trainer. I want you to let Greg or one of the others teach me my job.'

He gave a short laugh.

'If any of them were capable, I'd grant your request, believe me! But Greg's no stuntman. Nor are any of the others.'

'But . . . but he looks like . . .'

'Greg and Andy are here as bodyguards. You may not have noticed, but one or the other of them is always around. They're never off duty together.'

'Bodyguards? Who needs them? Not you surely?' she mocked disbelievingly.

'Not me,' he agreed. 'I can take care of myself. They're here to protect Melanie.'

'Your daughter? Why should *she* need protection, and from whom?'

His face was drawn into stern lines and she realised she was trespassing.

'That's a long story, an old, unhappy one; I've no wish to resurrect it. Besides, it doesn't concern you.'

'All right!' She turned on her heel. 'I get the message. Mind my own business. That will be easy. I'm not remotely interested in anything that concerns you.' It should have been a good exit, but,

'Gina!' His abrupt use of her name halted her in mid-stride. 'Wear riding clothes tomorrow.'

She swung around. Tomorrow! They'd only just completed a gruelling flying course. Was there to be no break, no relaxation? He caught her thoughts from her expression.

'We're working to a tight schedule. In another fortnight, we start the actual filming. If you thought learning to fly was tough, think again! The riding will take us all of that fortnight, maybe more. It depends on you. Think you can take it?'

'I can take it,' she told him confidently.

'You're not scared of horses I suppose?'

'Of course not!' Her eyes widened in surprise. 'Why should I be?'

'You were terrified of the Cessna at first,' he said bluntly.

'I ...' Her words of denial trailed away at the certainty in his face. 'How did you ...?'

'But you've got guts, Gina.' His tone was suddenly gentle, disarming, his voiced admiration genuine, she could swear. He took a step towards her. 'You were petrified, yet you never said a word. You went through with it, conquered your fear. How?'

She had retreated before his advance and despite his changed mood, or perhaps because of it, she was even more on the defensive.

'How?' Nervous tension lent a sharp edge to her voice. 'You need to ask me that, after all the cracks you made at me the very first time we met? I've a long memory. I swore I'd never give you a chance to call me a coward, ever again.'

'No,' he agreed, much to her amazement. 'I was wrong. You're not a coward, Gina, not in that way. It takes great courage to face and overcome physical fear.'

She was in physical fear now, but it stemmed from his increasing proximity. He had ably demonstrated his power to arouse her, yet each time he had demonstrated that he was only playing with her, that the undoubted chemistry between them meant nothing to him. She stepped backwards into the hallway.

'Good night!' she said, coldly formal. 'Will half-past-eight be suitable for the riding instruction?'

'Greg?' Gina came downstairs just as the security man was leaving the breakfast room. 'Can you spare me a moment?'

'Any number of them!' He grinned and followed her as she made a selection from the heavily laden sideboard. 'In fact I could spare you a few hours, if you'd only say the word. It's my evening off. How about it?'

Gina hesitated. Despite her defiant words to Tod about her right to choose her own friends, she didn't really want to go out with Greg.

'All right,' she said hesitantly and then, aware that it was hardly a gracious acceptance, 'thank you. I'd like that,' and she allowed her face to relax into the dazzling smile that had floored many men before Greg Gibson.

Tod, putting his head into the breakfast room to see if she was there, witnessed the smile. Grim-faced, he told her that he was ready when she was and withdrew. Oh dear. Obviously Tod thought she'd been chatting Greg up.

'That's great!' Greg said, his own grin widening. 'Say!' he halted in the doorway, 'you were going to ask me something?'

'Oh! Oh yes, but it wasn't that important. It can wait till tonight now, when we've more time. I daren't be late for my riding lesson.' She smiled wryly, jerking her head in the direction Tod had taken.

'Oh yeah!' His tone was disbelieving. 'You're the first woman we've had here who didn't jump whenever Tod cracked the whip. But by all means leave it till tonight. See you!' His complacent expression as he departed told Gina that he believed she'd waylaid him for a purpose, that all she'd been after was a date with him.

She gritted her teeth. Maybe she'd been too hasty in her agreement.

'You mean we're actually going outside the "Berlin Wall"?'

The Rolls Royce had swept around the perimeter of the house and crunched down the long gravelled drive towards the massive gates.

'We need the facilities of an indoor arena!' Tod's manner was brusque and Gina prepared to lapse into silence for the remainder of the journey. But to her surprise, he continued to speak, still in the same abrupt manner, and she sensed his reluctance even while he imparted the information. 'I suppose I can't blame you for your curiosity. It must seem a strange set-up we have here.'

'It is rather like a prisoner-of-war camp,' she returned lightly, as the gates clanged to behind them, 'but I've no desire to pry, provided *I'm* not a prisoner here. I *should* like a day off sometime!'

'You're free to come and go as you wish. As I told you last night, these precautions are for Melanie's sake. As to days off, we'll see!'

'I suppose,' Gina said slowly, feeling her way, 'that there are bound to be risks involved in being a rich man's child, being kidnapped, held to ransom?'

'Yes,' he acknowledged. 'It is kidnapping I fear; not for the sake of money, though, but of vendetta.'

'"Vendetta".' She repeated the word incredulously. 'It sounds like something out of an Italian gangster movie, the Mafia, family feuds.'

'Maria, my wife, was Italian. I met her when I was making a circus documentary in La Spezia, Italy. She was a trapeze artiste, part of a family act, the "Flying Mantalinis". To cut the story short,' there was pain in Tod's voice as if the telling hurt still, 'I saw a lot of Maria. We fell in love, Her family weren't pleased, because it broke up the act. But we married, came back to this country and, a year later, Melanie was born.'

'Did ... did Maria die in childbirth?' Gina asked gently.

'It might have been better if she had. At least that would have been one of life's natural hazards, an act of God. Then the Mantalinis might not have blamed me for her death.' They were travelling faster now, almost as if Tod sought to escape from the horrors of the past. 'Maria had been brought up to circus life. Danger was the breath of life to her. Without her family, she could no longer do trapeze work, so she pestered me to let her become one of my stuntwomen.'

'And did you let her?'

'Not at first. I wanted to keep her apart from my work. I wanted her to be my wife, Melanie's mother, to grace my home.'

His words held bitter memories for Gina, too, carrying as they did a recollection of Keith's feelings on the same subject.

'But performing was in her blood. She needed excitement, challenge. Finally I let her have her way, and lived to regret it. She was killed,' he concluded bluntly, 'performing aerobatics, as you might have been yesterday!'

Oh no! No wonder he had been so furious, so shaken. During her thoughtless stunting, he had been reliving his wife's death, expecting to see a re-enactment of the tragedy that had killed her. In his anger, in his relief, had it been Maria that he had taken in his arms? Had he wanted to make believe, just for a few moments, that it was his wife who had survived?

'But where do the Mantalinis come into this? Why the vendetta?'

'They blamed me, of course,' he said impatiently, 'for allowing Maria to fly.'

'But it was her idea!'

'In Italy,' Tod's tone was heavy, 'the women obey their fathers, their brothers and finally their husbands. Old Mantalini contends that I was no fit husband for his daughter and therefore no fit father for his granddaughter.'

'I think that's most unfair,' Gina said hotly. 'He let Maria risk her life on the trapeze.'

Tod shook his dark head sadly.

'There was little danger for Maria. Oh, some, I grant you. But surrounded by her father and six brothers,

who wouldn't have seen one hair of her head harmed
...? But I, her husband, let her go up, alone, in an
aeroplane. There's no safety net to catch you when you
fall from the sky.'

'And Melanie? The bodyguards?' Horror widened
Gina's beautiful eyes. 'Surely Mantalini wouldn't ...?
Oh he couldn't? Not a child?'

'He doesn't plan to kill her. She's his grandchild,
after all. No, he wants her with him. Twice he's very
nearly succeeded in snatching her, hence the precautions.'

'And what about you?' Gina's voice rose a nervous
octave. 'Would ... would he try to kill *you*?' How could
Tod continue to move about the world as he did,
knowing that at any moment he might be struck down
by an assassin's knife, or by gunshot? It was in that
moment of fear for him that Gina knew she loved Tod
Fallon, and the shock of realisation was so great that it
was only dimly she heard him say,

'No. Mantalini's no killer. His thugs only carry
weapons to frighten. But he does want his revenge, and
it would seem a fitting one to him to take away my
daughter, as I deprived him of his.'

'But you can't keep Melanie locked up forever!' Gina
protested, as Tod braked, skilfully easing the large car
into a narrow turning. 'What sort of life would that be
for a little girl? And what about when she grows up?'

'Mantalini can't live for ever. He's an old man now,
and I hope, when he goes, his sons will drop the
vendetta. I don't think they have the same heart for it.'

The road had brought them to some riding stables, a
long, pristinely white house, flanked by outbuildings
and a larger building which Tod told Gina was the
indoor arena. 'Theresa had it built so she can give
riding lessons all year round.'

As they got out of the car, Gina reflected ruefully
that she need not have accepted Greg's offer of a date

since, unexpectedly, Tod had provided her with all the
answers to her questions. Still, she couldn't back out
now. But she must make it clear to Greg that it was
only a friendly, social occasion, that she wanted no
complications, no involvements.

Because of that moment in the car, a moment of
mingled fear and revelation, she found herself looking
at Tod with new eyes as he strode across the
stableyard towards the owner's office. She could have
described him in detail with her eyes closed, so familiar
had that splendid physique become, topped by the dark
hair with its distinguished scattering of grey. Even
though his back was towards her, his features were
indelibly printed on her inner eye, the heavy brows
spanning dark eyes, the forthright nose and assertive
chin; and this, she marvelled, was the man with whom
she had fallen in love.

'Gina! Get a move on!' His impatient voice recalled
her wandering wits to the present and to the lowering
remembrance that *he* was not interested in her, other
than as a commodity. The morning's discoveries had
explained a lot. She had been right in fancying that
another woman lay between her and Tod; but the
woman was his dead wife. Tod was still in love with
Maria.

Theresa, who owned the stables, was a petite,
energetic blonde. Her admiration for Tod was patently
obvious, his manner towards her companionably
affectionate, and Gina felt a stab of envy. How long
had he known Theresa? The blonde girl had an
advantage that Gina did not. She lived not too far away
from Tod's home and it was obvious that their business
arrangement brought them together quite often. Gina
sighed. She had hoped that never again would she
experience the jealousy syndrome. Now she knew she
would resent any woman who came within Tod's
orbit.

Twenty minutes later, elbows, knees, shoulders and hips heavily padded, she had something else to occupy her mind; she was finding out just what Tod had meant when he'd said that flying an aeroplane was nothing when it came to the risks and discomforts of horse stunting.

Over and over again she must practise falling to the sawdust of the indoor arena, learning just how to part company with the horse and turn in the air to get into the correct position. The aim was to fall backwards and sideways so that the first impact with the ground was with forearm and heel; thus she would finish in a face down position.

'You won't just be falling off willy-nilly, anywhere you like,' Tod explained, during a rest break. 'You'll be given a set spot and moment in which to do it. So you'll need to know the disposition of every camera, how much of the frame you and the horse are filling, the whereabouts of other actors and props.'

By the end of that morning's session, despite the heavy padding, Gina felt that every bone in her body was jarred, that every inch of flesh was bruised.

'Still want to be a stunt girl?' Tod asked, as Gina eased herself gingerly into his car.

She leant back against the silver grey upholstery, her answer, though positive, coming out on a weary sigh.

'Yes!'

'You see now why it requires a high standard of general fitness?'

'You can say that again!' It was a sardonic riposte, but Tod chose to take it seriously.

'I *do* say it again, *and* again. It's a subject in which your only tools are experience and more experience. The knowhow can only be handed down from a trained stuntman to the novice, either by word of mouth, or by demonstration.'

And Tod had used both methods, Gina thought,

Get your fabulous gifts
ABSOLUTELY FREE!

MAIL THIS CARD TODAY.

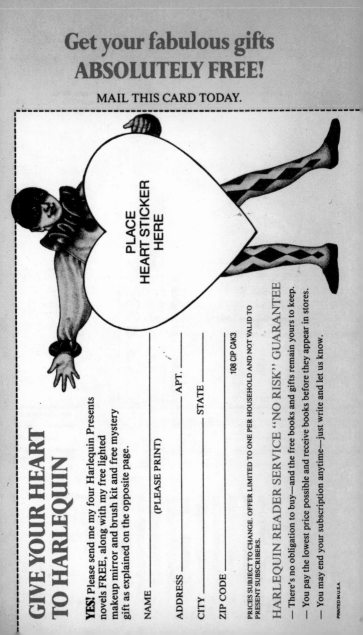

PLACE
HEART STICKER
HERE

GIVE YOUR HEART
TO HARLEQUIN

YES! Please send me my four Harlequin Presents novels FREE, along with my free lighted makeup mirror and brush kit and free mystery gift as explained on the opposite page.

NAME _____

(PLEASE PRINT)

ADDRESS _____ APT. _____

CITY _____ STATE _____

ZIP CODE _____

108 CIP CAK3

PRICES SUBJECT TO CHANGE. OFFER LIMITED TO ONE PER HOUSEHOLD AND NOT VALID TO PRESENT SUBSCRIBERS.

HARLEQUIN READER SERVICE "NO RISK" GUARANTEE

— There's no obligation to buy—and the free books and gifts remain yours to keep.
— You pay the lowest price possible and receive books before they appear in stores.
— You may end your subscription anytime—just write and let us know.

PRINTED IN U.S.A.

START YOUR
HARLEQUIN HONEYMOON TODAY.
JUST COMPLETE, DETACH AND MAIL YOUR
FREE OFFER CARD.

If offer card below is missing, write to: Harlequin Reader Service, 901 Fuhrmann Blvd.
P.O. Box 1394, Buffalo, NY, 14240-1394

BUSINESS REPLY CARD

First Class   Permit No. 717   Buffalo, NY

Postage will be paid by addressee

Harlequin Reader Service®
901 Fuhrmann Blvd.
P.O. Box 1394
Buffalo, NY 14240-9963

NO POSTAGE
NECESSARY
IF MAILED
IN THE
UNITED STATES

DETACH AND MAIL TODAY!

almost asleep with fatigue. He'd bellowed instructions at her from the side of the ring, making her repeat the actions over and over again, until she was bone weary and almost on the point of rebellion. But he had also proved that he was capable of practising what he preached. Several times he had taken over her patient mount and shown her, by example, what he wanted. Yet he seemed totally untroubled by the numerous aches and pains that beset her. He must be fantastically fit.

As the iron gates closed them in once more, Tod glanced at her, noting her drawn face and closed eyes.

'Straight into a hot bath, the moment you get in,' he advised. 'This afternoon, we'll have a session in the swimming-pool.'

As she climbed the stairs to her room, Gina emitted the groans she had not allowed to escape her in front of Tod. The man was superhuman, or inhuman as she'd told him yesterday. Did he honestly expect her to have the strength to go on working on top of this morning's gruelling session?

The bath however did a lot to alleviate her discomfort and she was in a reasonably philosophical mood as she went down to lunch. Maybe swimming wouldn't be such a bad idea after all. It might complete the loosening up process.

Like breakfast, lunch in Tod's home was an informal, staggered meal, everyone eating of the cold collation as and when they had the time or the inclination, so that Gina was not surprised to find the dining-room empty, except for one person.

Standing with her back to the room, looking out of the window, the tall girl looked familiar, with her long fall of red hair and her statuesque height, and when, at the sound of Gina's heels in the parquet floor, the other swung around, Gina gave a gasp of recognition. But the surprise was mutual.

'What the hell are you doing here, Gina?' Then, with shrill fury, 'The fool! The bloody fool! I told him not to ... But he just had to be right, as usual ... And of course you wouldn't take much talking into it. *You* wouldn't be able to resist ...'

Now Gina was able to speak, voicing her own shocked, bewildered surprise.

'Marcha! Why are *you* here?'

CHAPTER SIX

AFTER the break-up of Gina's marriage she'd thrown herself even more into her agency work, and through the agency had renewed her acquaintance with a distant cousin, whom she hadn't seen since childhood.

At that time, Marcha Durrant was a relative newcomer to the world of television, and a new programme had been conceived for her, a programme that would aim at gratifying people's private fantasies. Her producer had heard of the GD Agency and had suggested that she contact Gina, as the expert, for some ideas and advice.

'But I never dreamt it would be you!'

Marcha had wanted to talk about herself and her ambitions. It seemed that, as a relation, however distant, she expected Gina to help further her career. It was only some time later that Gina had been able to touch on her own life, to mention her marriage, its outcome, and that she had reverted to her maiden name. Even then Marcha's interest had been cursory, falsely sympathetic. Her manner implied that she, Marcha, would never have allowed her personal relationships to get into such a mess, nor would any man ever be permitted to thwart her will.

So, in the beginning, it had not been Gina who had worn the mask of Fantasy Woman, but Marcha. Despite the older girl's assiduous cultivation of her, Gina had not been deceived; she knew her cousin was working only towards her own ends and, as in childhood, she was unable to like or trust Marcha. Filled with a sense of her own importance at having a show of her own, Marcha displayed an unsympathetic, almost brusque manner towards her guests, especially when they failed abysmally at things they professed themselves eager to do; and while Gina, in the background, genuinely worried over the safety of others, Marcha had no reservations about the quite dangerous stunts ordinary people had, at first, been allowed to attempt.

'If the fools want to break their silly necks, why should I care?' was her standard retort, when, at planning meetings, Gina had essayed a protest. Gina had been right to fear that some day there would be a dreadful accident, but it was no consolation to her that the format of the show was moderated only after such an event had taken place.

When Marcha suddenly decided to abandon her television career for one in films, Gina had been startled, though flattered, when Jimmy Riley had offered her the vacant role.

'I've no experience of working in television.' Despite the irresistible temptation of a new challenge, she had felt impelled to be honest.

'All the better,' the producer had retorted, 'we can train *you* the way we want you to go. Besides, you've been adviser to the series for the past six months; you have some idea of what goes on; and you and Marcha are physically so alike that, with that mask on, no one will ever know there's been a change over.'

So, once more, she had put her advisory service into the capable hands of her deputy and, not without some trepidation, had assumed her new role. Despite the fatigue she often felt, she enjoyed the travelling to various locations, provided they were not abroad, revelled in the stir her arrival always caused.

Nevertheless, her strong streak of common sense had not allowed *her* coppery head to be turned. She knew that, like anyone in the public eye, she was constantly on trial, that she could not, for one instant, afford to

relax from her public image; and she worked
conscientiously at putting herself across, liking people,
wanting them to like her. It wasn't vanity, but part of
the job; and it was not vanity which told her that the
production team preferred her to Marcha. Gina was
friendly with everyone, unpretentious, grateful for help
and advice. She never played the 'star'.

'You mean you didn't *know* I'd be here?' Marcha
sounded haughtily disbelieving.

'I had no idea,' Gina admitted to her cousin; and, to
herself, that if she had known, she might not have been
so ready to agree to Tod's proposition. She wasn't sure
she relished having to work with Marcha again, if that
was why the other girl was here. She couldn't forget
her cousin's callous indifference, when . . .

'I can't think why Tod didn't tell you.' Marcha's eyes
narrowed speculatively. 'Since it was his idea that you
should train as my double.'

'As . . . as your double?' Gina's unease increased.

'Yes!' The other girl continued impatiently. 'What
did you think this was in aid of? Some wretched
secretary of his watches your programme every week,
noticed this family likeness of ours. I needed a stand-in
and she had to go and suggest you. I don't need to tell
you I objected . . . strongly.'

'Marcha! I haven't the least idea what you're talking
about.'

'You have, I presume, spent your time here training
as as stuntwoman?' And, as Gina nodded, 'Filming is
an expensive business. If a leading player falls ill, it
holds up the work of hundreds of people, adds
enormously to the cost. Illness can't be helped, but
injury can, by employing a double to do the
stuntwork.'

'I'm well aware of the function of doubles,' Gina
returned. 'But just what are you trying to tell me?'

'That you're *my* stand-in, of course. Much as I would have loved to do everything myself...'

'You?' Gina said ironically. 'Pull the other one! You're the world's worst coward. It's like you to want a stand-in. You don't care just *how* much other people are injured do you, Marcha? Young, innocent people, like...'

'Shut up! Shut up!' her cousin shouted furiously. 'Don't you dare to mention that incident here. Tod knows nothing about it. I don't want you here, Gina, and I shall tell Tod so. He'll have to get rid of you if he wants to keep me.'

Dismay mingled with the growth of Gina's inward anger. Tod had never actually said anything—oh, he'd been too clever for that—but he had allowed her to gain the impression that she was to star in his film.

'Of course there are other reasons, besides monetary ones, why Tod wants to protect me,' Marcha broke in on her cousin's thoughts. 'He couldn't bear to have me hurt. His first wife was killed performing a stunt.'

'His *first* wife?' Gina said carefully.

Marcha laughed complacently.

'A bit premature of me, a slip of the tongue. It's not generally known, but Tod and I will be getting married. Probably when this film is in the can.'

'I see,' Gina said, and she thought she did. Her former conclusions had been totally wrong. The barrier between her and Tod had not been the shadow of Maria Mantalini, but that of Marcha. No wonder Tod had gone too far at times; he'd been using her as a substitute for Marcha in more ways than one. What would Marcha think if she knew that, she reflected bitterly. But Gina would never stoop to tell her, whereas, if the positions had been reversed...

'You haven't eaten your lunch,' Marcha pointed out now.

'No... no, I haven't.' She pushed it away from her.

'Still it's just as well. I'm swimming this afternoon with Tod. It isn't wise to swim on a full stomach.'

'Oh I don't think you will be. Because I'm back a day earlier than he expected, Tod wants to run through the script with me. We play lovers in the film. Very appropriate, isn't it?' Marcha was smugly self-satisfied.

'Very appropriate!' Gina said drily, wondering if she had imagined the innuendo. Just how thoroughly would Tod and Marcha be following the script that afternoon? By all accounts they had been apart for a while. 'Since I seem to have some free time,' she continued, 'I think I'll make the most of it. Excuse me.'

She had reached the dining-room door, when Marcha recalled her, her tone acidly sweet.

'I suppose you didn't by any chance think you'd be playing this part?'

Gina's cheeks scorched.

'I see that you did!' Marcha wasn't speaking so sweetly now. 'But then dear Tod can be just a little unscrupulous in obtaining his ends. I shouldn't set your heart on any kind of part if I were you. Not after I've spoken to him.'

After her hectic morning, Gina had thought longingly of a restful afternoon. But now her wish was granted the empty hours no longer seemed desirable. Her mind was in a turmoil, varying emotions fighting to gain the upper hand. There was disappointment, downright chagrin in fact, that she was not to play the female agent in Tod's film. There was annoyance that Tod had not put her fully in the picture. Had he deliberately misled her, as Marcha had insinuated, or had it never occurred to him that she might make the wrong assumption? She wasn't really afraid, however, that Tod would dismiss her. By all accounts he'd known of Marcha's unwillingness to have her cousin as her stand-in, but he'd still gone ahead and hired her and she didn't think Tod was a man to see all his weeks of training go for nothing.

Uppermost was a dragging depression. Tod was going to marry Marcha. Despite the physical attraction that had flared between them, Gina stood no chance with him. The chemistry that she'd hoped might develop into something deeper was just that, chemistry. Tod *loved Marcha*. But Gina knew her cousin wasn't worthy of his love. Totally selfish, Marcha was incapable of making him happy. If only he knew about ... But she could never be the one to tell him.

In this frame of mind, Gina knew she would never be able to rest and, on a sudden impulse, she turned aside to knock at the nursery door. It opened a fraction to reveal the anxious face of Sally, the nursemaid. But when she saw Gina, she opened the door fully, smiling her relief.

'It's you, miss. I'm always afraid ...'

'That it might be kidnappers?' Gina followed the girl into the room. 'Were you working for Mr Fallon then?'

'When the second attempt was made, yes, miss. It was horrible. One man had a gun, and another had one of those horrible flick knives.'

'Where was this?'

'Out in the grounds, miss. I was walking Melanie in her baby buggy. She was smaller then, and it was before Mr Fallon had all those electric fences put round the walls.'

'What happened?'

'Luckily both Greg and Andy were around that day. They managed to disarm the men and throw them out, but it was a near thing.' The girl shuddered.

'Can I see Melanie?' Gina asked, glancing towards the closed door of an inner bedroom.

'Do you really want to be bothered, miss? You look rather tired if you don't mind me saying so. Melanie can be a real handful, very demanding.'

Gina smiled wryly. Melanie Fallon must have a lot of her father in her make up.

'Frankly, I'd welcome some sort of diversion,' she confessed. 'I'm a bit fed up right at this moment.'

'So's Melanie. That's why she's acting up. Ever since she heard that *she* was back.'

Gina didn't need to ask whom. That was obvious, since her encounter with Marcha.

The child was sitting in a window seat, looking down broodingly into the grounds. Here in the bedroom, as in the nursery, was every plaything a child might want; a rich man's child, yet the little figure was a pathetic one. She turned and, at the sight of Gina, her olive-complexioned face brightened and she beckoned imperiously.

'Come and sit here with me. I didn't think you'd *ever* come. No one else bothers, except Greg and Andy.'

'What about your father?' Gina tried to hide her disapproval. Didn't he ever make time to play with his small daughter?

'Sometimes,' Melanie admitted, 'but quite often he's too busy and when *she's* here, I don't want him to come, because *she* comes with him.'

Of course, as Tod's future wife, Marcha would need to get acquainted with his daughter. Gina frowned slightly. It was out of character. Normally Marcha had no time for children. In fact she had always claimed to detest them.

'Well, I'm not busy this afternoon,' she said in a deliberately cheerful tone. 'I'll play with you if you like. What shall we do?'

'What I'd *really* like,' Melanie said wistfully, 'is to go down there.' She pointed out into the grounds. 'Greg says the gardener's cat has kittens. Sally, do you think Daddy would let me have one, for my very own? It *would* be somebody to play with.'

Gina looked at Sally, her face expressing all that she

felt for the child's pathetic state of loneliness, and saw her sympathy reflected in the nursemaid's face.

'We'll ask him about the kitten,' Sally promised, 'but you know you're not allowed outside unless Greg or Andy goes with us.'

'Oh, well!' The child was philosophical for one so young; Gina would have expected tantrums. 'At least I've got you! What's your name?' Gina told her. 'I like that. It sounds Italian. I'm half-Italian,' she bragged as she slid from the window seat. 'Did you know that, and that my wicked grandpa wants to steal me?'

So Melanie knew that. Fancy allowing her to be troubled by such fears; how could she ever have a normal childhood?

'Don't worry,' Gina said comfortingly. 'Your daddy would never let that happen.'

'Oh, I wouldn't mind,' the child said surprisingly. 'I could go to Italy and meet all my relations. Then I'd have plenty of people to play with. I'd rather live with my grandpa, anyway, if Daddy's going to marry *her*.'

'You really will have to stop calling Miss Durrant that!' Sally remonstrated. 'When she's your step-mother . . .'

'I *shan't* call her Mummy *or* Aunt Marcha!' Melanie stamped one small foot. 'She's not my mummy or my aunt and she'll be a *wicked* stepmother, I know she will, much more wicked than my grandpa!' The childish lips set mulishly, but they had a tendency to tremble. Observing this Gina put an arm around the child's shoulders.

'I'm sure your daddy won't let anyone be unkind to you and we're not going to worry about it just now. You never know, he might not get married.' She was telling herself that as well as the child. The only trouble was that, whereas Melanie's face brightened, Gina could not believe so easily in her own optimism. 'Look, I can see Greg down there. Let's knock on the

window and ask him up. Perhaps he'll take us to see
the kittens.'

Greg's delight was all too evident and Gina had an
uncomfortable suspicion that most of his pleasure was
derived from the prospect of her company.

'You haven't forgotten we have a date tonight?' he
asked.

'I haven't forgotten,' Gina said, aware of Melanie's
interested stare.

The cat and her kittens were housed in an unused
wing of the stable block. Already the kittens were
mischievous, ready to leave their mother. There were six
of them in assorted colours.

'I shall have the black one,' Melanie announced.

The black kitten was a pathetic scrap, the smallest of
the litter. It was not as boisterous as its brothers and
sisters and Gina doubted whether it would thrive.

'Wouldn't you rather have one of the livelier,
healthier ones?' she asked. 'What about the pretty little
ginger one?'

But Melanie was stubborn, another trait which
seemed to be inherited equally from mother and father,
Gina reflected.

'No. This one's like me. He's lonely. The others don't
play with him. I want him.'

She sat in the straw with the kitten in her lap, quite
content to watch as the naughtier, more inquisitive ones
climbed all over Gina, sticking like burrs to her slacks
and sweater, licking her with tiny sandpaper tongues.

They were, all three of them, Melanie, Greg and
Gina, still sprawled in the straw, and Greg was
attempting to remove a stubborn kitten from the front
of Gina's sweater, when Todd looked over the half
door. They were all making so much noise with their
talk and laughter that they hadn't heard his light tread,
and Tod was able to stand, unobserved, for some
minutes, his dark eyes unconsciously wistful at first as

they surveyed the warm, attractive, almost domestic scene. His daughter, more dishevelled and grubby than he had ever seen her, yet also, somehow, happier, was clutching a kitten, while innumerable others seemed to be using Greg and Gina as an assault course.

Dishevelment suited Gina, he brooded. Her cheeks and eyes glowed with laughter. An emerald green sweater clung lovingly to her generous breasts and as Greg attempted to remove the kitten, his hand accidentally brushed against her lovely curves. Instantly, Tod felt within himself the stir of the other man's reaction, as he saw how Greg, his eyes involuntarily widening, movement arrested, looked at Gina.

She was not unaware either, he noticed. Her flushed face was in profile to Tod as she lifted her eyes to Greg's, and he saw her bite on her lip, a troubled little gesture. But then she was smiling again, pushing the other man's hands away.

'Better let me do that.'

'Gina!' Greg's husky voice carried to Tod's alert ears and his hands clenched at his sides. And, as Greg leant forward, his mouth seeking Gina's parted lips, Tod erupted into the loose-box.

'So there you are, Gina! I thought I made it quite clear that I wanted you down at the pool this afternoon. And after searching everywhere for you, what do I find? You, fraternising with one of my men; a man, furthermore,' he glared at Greg, 'who's supposed to be on duty; and I find my daughter, looking like a gutter brat.'

In one swift movement, he scooped Melanie from the straw, the kitten tumbling away. He thrust his daughter at Greg.

'Here! Get her back to the nursery. I'll talk to you and Sally later. As for you . . .' as Gina made to slip past him, 'I'll deal with *you* here and now.'

Greg's pleasant, rugged face was red with mingled

guilt and embarrassment, but Melanie proved more recalcitrant. She set up a heartbroken wailing.

'You've hurt my kitty. I want my kitty. *Gina* said I could have him.'

'I . . .' Gina began, then faltered into silence as she met Tod's glare.

'Be quiet, Melanie!' he roared. 'You're not having the damned thing. It's probably full of fleas. Greg, tell Sally that child's to have a bath immediately and her hair washed.'

'OK, Mr Fallon.' Greg paused in the doorway, his muscular arms easily restraining the threshing child. 'See you about seven then, Gina.'

'I'm looking forward to it!' she told him with deliberate enthusiasm.

Melanie's screams diminished into sobbing, and, as Greg departed with the child, there was silence in the stable, an ominous silence, broken only by the sound of breathing, Tod's deep and heavy with recent anger, Gina's fast and light with apprehension and indignation. Rather than wait for the predictable attack, she plunged into the offensive.

'You callous brute! There's nothing I hate worse than a man who's cruel to children and animals. Melanie was happy, really happy . . .'

'So was Greg, I noticed,' Tod snarled.

So that was what was eating him, because she'd defied his policy of non-fraternisation.

'We were *all* happy,' she retorted, 'until you came along.'

'I spend a fortune on two men's salaries just to see that my daughter comes to no harm and you . . .'

'She wasn't in any danger!' Gina snapped. 'Greg was here . . .'

'With his mind on other things.' The ginger kitten was still adhering to Gina's sweater and almost absently he reached out to pluck it away, but she retreated.

'Leave it alone and leave me alone.'

'I didn't hear you protesting so violently when Greg tried to come to your assistance.'

'No! Because he's my friend. You're only my employer and he hasn't tried to deceive me . . .'

'And *I* have?' Tod's heavy brows rose enquiringly.

'You know damned well you have! Oh, you were very clever. You never actually put it into words, but you must have known what I thought.'

'No,' sardonically, 'please enlighten me.'

'You didn't tell me I was just a stand in for Marcha Durrant, that I was to take all the risks, while she takes all the glory.'

'What touching family feeling. Marcha is your cousin.'

'Very distant, not distant enough for me.'

'Do I detect a note of female jealousy?'

'No, you do not! I wouldn't change places with Marcha if it meant my name in lights in Hollywood. She hasn't got a thing I want.' Except you, her heart mourned, but she kept her features strictly schooled.

'Yet you wouldn't have objected to her part in my film.' He had her there.

'I assumed, you led me to believe, it was my part.'

'Not at all,' he denied coolly. 'The subject was never discussed. I said nothing which could lead you to suppose anything so ridiculous. *You* play the lead in a major production? What acting experience have *you* had?'

It was an unanswerable question. He knew she had none. But she had a question for him.

'Why did you hire me when you knew Marcha objected so strongly? And now that she's back, do I get the sack?'

'Not at all,' he said calmly. 'Marcha is many things in my life, but she doesn't tell me how to make my films. And to return to the whole point of this conversation, why weren't you at the pool this afternoon?'

'Because,' she said witheringly, 'you were to be otherwise engaged.'

'Who said so?' he asked sharply.

'Marcha, of course.'

A look of palpable disbelief crossed his face.

'You've made it pretty clear that you've no natural affection for your cousin. Well, she told me you were a pretty cold fish. But don't you think it's rather despicable to lie about her, to blame *her* for your rebellious defiance?'

Gina opened her mouth, then closed it again. What was the use, she thought wearily. It was her word against Marcha's and it was pretty obvious who Tod was going to believe. But why had Marcha told Tod she, Gina, was cold? What was her cousin up to?

'Can I go now?' she asked.

'No! I haven't finished with you yet. I warned you, Gina, to stay away from the men in this outfit. Stay away from Greg Gibson! I want his mind on his job, not on your body ...' a husky note crept into his voice, 'delectable though it may be. And since you obviously have no sense of responsibility, stay away from my daughter as well.'

Swift as a lance, the answer came back.

'Is that why *you* stay away from her? Because you don't have any responsibility towards her, other than as a provider of expensive, useless toys, as a gaoler. What about being a natural father for once, noticing that a child needs affection, company of her own age, or, failing that, a pet to love? Something warm, something living, that she can call her own.'

'Ah!' He scowled. 'I wondered when we'd get around to the cat, mangy, flea-ridden ...'

'It is *not* mangy. Flea-ridden it may be, but fleas can be dealt with and Melanie loves it. Look at it, go on,

look at it.' She picked up the black kitten and thrust it
under his nose. 'Take notice for once of something
lovable, something that doesn't mean money.'

His eyes flickered briefly over the kitten, then
returned to her flushed, angry face, dropped to the
tumultuous heaving of her breasts.

'I'd rather look at you,' he said softly, 'but then you
know that, don't you? Did I say you couldn't act? I'm
beginning to wonder!' Suddenly his hands erupted from
his sides, clamped her upper arms and he shook her as
he spoke. 'Dammit, Gina! Just how devious are you?
Do you know, I wonder, just how effective your anger
is, how magnificent it makes you look? I think you do.
Can you assume it at will?'

'Anger? You think my anger's assumed?' she spat at
him. 'Don't be so damned patronising. I don't need to
pretend with you. You make me bloody, seething
furious, with your arrogance, your high-handed ways,
your inhumanity! And you had the neck to call *me* cold.
You're Mr Iceberg himself.'

Suddenly the atmosphere about them was charged
with an electricity that was not only that of anger, and
other tempestuous emotions made Gina tremble. But
this time she was determined she would not be
disarmed, become putty in his hands. Boldly, she
continued to outface him.

'Let go of me! I'm Marcha's stand-in, remember?
She's back now, so you don't need a substitute, you can
go and sate your sexual appetites on her!'

'While you do likewise with Greg, I suppose?' he
snarled. 'Oh, I noticed your reference to a date, made in
flagrant defiance of my orders.'

Once she would have denied vehemently that there
was anything between herself and Greg other than
mutual liking, but she knew that on Greg's side there
was more and, besides, she felt annoyed, contrary.

'As I told you before, who I date is my business. And

since we're on the subject of free time, I want a whole day off next week.'

'For what purpose?' he snapped.

'To go and see someone I usually visit regularly. I haven't been able to go since I've been here.'

'Another boyfriend?'

'You could say that.' After all, Rusty certainly wasn't female.

'Greg not enough for you?' he taunted. 'And you talk about my sexual appetites! And if I refuse permission?'

'I'll go anyway.' She elevated the square, stubborn chin. 'It's important to me.'

With one finally exasperated, bruising grip of his hands, he released her, stood frowning down at her, his expression, she noted gleefully, one of frustrated exasperation.

'Can I go now?' she asked again, coolly.

'Yes, go! Go your own damn fool, pig-headed way. And here,' as she was about to turn on her heel, 'take this thing with you.' With one fluid movement he bent and scooped up the black kitten. 'Tell Greg to have the local vet check it over and clean it up. Then Melanie can have the blasted thing!' His manner was suddenly the awkward, endearingly sulky one of a small boy trying to make amends.

Good Lord, the man had a streak of humanity in him after all, Gina marvelled as she received the fluffy scrap from his hands.

In doing so, their fingers accidentally brushed and static shock seemed to spark through her. Damn it, would nothing ever quell this man's irritating effect upon her senses? To hide her agitation, she turned away with no word of acknowledgment for his unexpected concession and almost ran across the stableyard in search of Greg.

For the first time that day, she was glad she had accepted the security man's invitation to go out with him. She needed something, someone, *anyone* to take her mind off Tod Fallon. Why wouldn't the message her brain imparted infiltrate the rest of her, quell turbulent heart and traitorous body? The message that he belonged to Marcha.

'Where are we going?' she asked Greg, as they left Mallions that evening.

'Somewhere local, I'm afraid. Even on my evening off I'm still on call.' He patted his breast pocket. The unobtrusive bulge, Gina knew by now, was a personal alarm. 'If this thing starts, I have to get to a phone, or back to Mallions at the double.'

'I don't mind,' Gina assured him, as the gates opened to let Greg's fast sports car through. 'I'd prefer somewhere quiet and relaxing. Life's been pretty hectic lately.'

'Tod been driving you, hmm? Well, I expect you've guessed the reason? No need for me to keep my mouth shut, now that his "star" is back from her holidays . . . two weeks late, I might add. No wonder he's been a bit testy. I for one don't blame him. I wouldn't trust that dame any further than I could kick her.'

'Oh?' Gina couldn't hide her curiosity.

'Proper little hot pants where men are concerned, our Marcha Durrant. At the moment she's satisfied with Tod, because he gave her her *entrée* into films. But if another, bigger director came along, I wouldn't give that,' Greg snapped his fingers, 'for Fallon's chances.'

'She gave me the impression,' Gina said, carefully casual—no one must ever know how it hurt—'that they'd be getting married after this film.'

'What!' Greg's sideways glance was sardonic. 'Haven't you figured Tod Fallon yet? No dame, however sexy, will ever get him to the altar again. Not after what happened to Maria. I reckon what passed for his heart was buried with that little Italian girl. No, he believes in loving 'em and leaving 'em. Marcha's lasted longer than most. By "love", I'm not referring to the emotion, you understand?'

'Oh, I understand all right!' Gina told him grimly.

'Made a pass at you, too, has he?' Greg sounded oddly fierce. 'First off we all reckoned you were the next in succession.'

Gina didn't want the conversation to take this personal turn. She directed her companion's thoughts back to her cousin.

'So you don't think his relationship with Marcha will last?'

'Not only that, we hope it won't. She's bad news. In fact, we all thought she'd walked out for good, but, like the bad penny she is, she's back.'

'Did they have a row?'

'Not exactly. Marcha's a dab hand at emotional blackmail. She can usually get her own way straight off. But Tod got pretty narked, when she refused to do her own stunting. He told her straight, more famous stars than she'll ever be managed without doubles. It was a near thing, I reckon, but she's got one advantage that she uses to good effect.'

'Oh?'

'Yeah! Her body. However mad Tod gets with her, one wiggle of that sexy little bottom and he's promising milady the earth; and this time it was her own stuntwoman.'

'I see.' Gina was silent, until the braking of the sports car disturbed the gravel frontage of a small, picturesque pub. So Marcha's hold on Tod was more precarious than her cousin had boasted. Not that it improved Gina's chances. She had no wish, anyway, to be one in a succession of short-lived affairs. She didn't like the picture Greg had painted for her of a man refusing ever again to be swayed by emotion, seeking only physical gratification, which swiftly palled.

'Hope you like pub food?' Greg asked, as he steered Gina into the bar.

The interior was in keeping with the exterior, white-walled and beamed. Twinkling brasses reflected subdued lamplight, pewter mugs hung above the bar and colourful Toby jugs were displayed at strategic points. They sat in a secluded corner on a padded bench semicircling an oak table.

The food was as good as a first-class restaurant. They chose succulent steaks with a side salad and Gina could not resist a generous slice of Black Forest gateau. As she deprecated her weakness, Greg smiled a disclaimer.

'You've no need to worry about your figure, Gina.' His gaze was openly admiring and his hand patted her thigh in a proprietary gesture, which she found she disliked. 'Not like Marcha. That one'll run to seed well before she's forty.' He broke off. 'Talk of the devil! Look who's here.'

Gina turned in her seat, dismayed to see Tod and Marcha entering the room, Tod helping Marcha to remove her coat. The bar room was too small for Greg and Gina to escape notice and in any case Greg was already lifting his hand in a lazy gesture of welcome. It was inevitable that the other couple should join them, though Marcha didn't look any more pleased than Gina felt.

'So you're back!' Greg observed to Marcha, as Tod went to the bar to order drinks. 'How was Italy?'

'Italy?' Marcha stared haughtily at him. 'What *are* you talking about? I was in France.'

'Funny.' Greg drawled. 'Steph and Debbie were in Italy a couple of weeks ago. They said they saw you.'

'Then they were mistaken,' Marcha said shortly.

Gina wondered if Marcha was lying. Had her extended holiday been connected with another man, another film director perhaps? Was Marcha two-timing Tod? Gina found herself hoping so, hoping Tod would find out. And what good would that do you, she asked herself cynically. You know you're not prepared to join the long line of 'has beens' in Tod's life.

Tod returned with their drinks and conversation became general, mostly about the film they would shortly be shooting.

'How's Gina shaping up?' Marcha asked Tod, as if Gina wasn't present. 'Is she fully trained?' Now she darted a sweet smile at Gina, a smile which Gina knew to be utterly false.

'No,' Tod was saying, 'but we can start work on the early stages of the film. Her tuition can go on concurrently. Making a horse fall won't present too much of a problem. Gina is an excellent horsewoman and Theresa already has a trained animal. It's just a matter of horse and rider practising together.'

Marcha's eyes had narrowed slightly at the mention of Theresa.

'You've been over to the stables while I've been away?'

Gina sensed her cousin's jealousy and suspicion. *Had* Theresa been one of Marcha's predecessors, or was the other girl afraid the stable owner might succeed her?

'Naturally we've been to Theresa's. You know she possesses the only suitable facilities.'

'Oh, Gina went with you?' The obvious relief in Marcha's tone wasn't very flattering. As if Marcha felt that Gina presented no competition.

'That was the purpose of the exercise.' Tod's manner was abrupt, almost absent. He didn't look at Marcha as he spoke. Instead, his eyes seemed to be fixed somewhere between Greg and Gina, or rather where the space between them should have been; for, their meal finished, Greg had moved closer on the leather bench-seat and now his arm was draped about her shoulders, his thigh pressed to hers; and Gina, though his proximity left her unmoved, permitted his touch, deliberately armouring herself against her vulnerability to Tod.

'Well, I guess we'll leave you folks to eat in peace,' Greg said, as a waitress brought the other couple's meal.

'Going straight back to Mallions?' Tod enquired casually.

'No. Thought we might take a drive around first,' Greg said. 'Gina hasn't had much chance to view the scenery. You've kept her nose pretty close to the grindstone since she's been here.'

'Actually I have been in Buckinghamshire before,' Gina said, 'but further south. I'd love a guided tour of this area.'

The countryside was quietly undulating, soft slopes of grass, woodland flung here and there in masses. Villages dotting the landscape added to the general peaceful aspect of the wide sweeps of green hills and valleys. They drove around for about an hour. Then, as it began to get too dark to appreciate the scenery, Greg turned the car for home.

'It's still early,' he said. 'Care for a nightcap?'

'A strictly non-alcoholic one then,' Gina said. 'I'm not a great drinker, except for the occasional glass of wine with a meal.'

'Whatever you like. You won't mind if I have a beer? I'm no toper. I wouldn't hold on to this job for long if I were. We have to be on the *qui vive* the whole time, but I do like the odd half pint.'

'Do you think Mantalini will try again?' Gina asked, as they sipped their drinks in Greg's comfortable sitting-room.

'Who knows? He's an old man now. Maria died three years ago. How long can you go on feeling anger, wanting revenge? It seems a pity for the kid to be deprived of her only grandparent and vice versa.' He put his beer mug down. 'But we didn't come here to talk about Tod's problems.'

'I didn't know the subject was taboo,' she said lightly, her intuition ahead of him in his next move.

'What I meant, as you very well know, is that we should be talking about us.' He came to sit on the side of her chair.

'Greg!' Gina thrust his arm away, speaking pleasantly but firmly. 'Don't get any ideas, please. Don't ruin a nice evening. There is no "us". We had a date, a friendly one, nothing more.'

'Aw, come on. You weren't so discouraging back there at the pub.'

'That was different. We were in public. I didn't want a scene. We're alone now and I can tell you, I don't play about, Greg.'

'Depends on what you call playing about.' Greg sounded annoyed now. 'I call it playing about to give a guy the "come on" in public and the cold shoulder in private.'

'I'm sorry if you've misunderstood me,' Gina said quietly. 'I never intended . . .'

'No?' Greg said, then, slowly, bitingly, 'no, you didn't intend to give *me* the wrong idea. It was Tod, wasn't it? I noticed the way he was watching us. Maybe you two have got a thing going, in spite of Marcha. Maybe you were trying to make him jealous.'

'Don't be ridiculous!' It was too near to the truth for comfort.

'No, Gina! I don't like to appear ridiculous, or to be made to look ridiculous.' There was a menacing undercurrent in Greg's voice now. The big amiable man had disappeared and in his place was one slighted ego. 'Which is why I intend to get out of the evening at least what I put into it.'

Threats of that kind left Gina unperturbed.

'I think you're confusing me with some other type of girl,' she told him. 'I don't "pay" for my entertainment "in kind".'

'Maybe you haven't in the past. But if you get involved with Fallon, you'll have to change your principles. And right now you're going to get some practice. And it's no use struggling,' as he grabbed her in a clumsy bear hug. 'You're no match for me.'

'Greg!' Desperately Gina twisted her face from side to side. 'Please don't do this. You'll be sorry when you're sober. I don't want to fall out with you. I'd much rather we stayed friends.'

'If you want to stay friends, then co-operate,' he growled. 'Don't forget, you angled for this date . . .'

'I didn't, I . . .'

But his mouth was grinding hers into silence and during that silence, Gina made up her mind. As he stopped to draw a shuddering breath, she warned him.

'Greg, if you don't like to appear ridiculous, let me go this instant, or that's just what's going to happen.'

'What could you possibly do? Come on now,' placatingly, 'we'll take it more slowly if you like . . .'

One minute he was standing straight, an arm holding her firmly, his free hand attempting to cup her breast, the next moment his head was lower than his heels on his way to lying flat on the floor. He shook his head, blinked, then made to get up.

'Stay there!' she told him.

Neither of them heard the door open just as Greg, ignoring her warning, rose and made a dive at her. One leg and one hand arrested his progress in such a way that he tripped and fell heavily once more. This time the breath was knocked from his body and he lay prone, gasping.

'Judo, by God! You play rough with your boy-friends!'

Gina whipped round to see Tod leaning in the doorway, his expression unfathomable.

'Fallon!' Greg had recovered himself somewhat. 'What the hell? This is a private room,' he growled as he crawled painfully to his feet.

'A private room for your own use, yes. But it is under my roof, I would remind you, and not a place to entertain your floosies!'

'How dare you call me a . . .' Gina began, but Tod cut in as if she hadn't spoken.

'You're fired, Gibson.'

'But . . .'

'You heard me. You're fired.' He turned on Gina. 'And you . . . get the hell out of here.'

'Are you firing me, too?' She held herself proudly erect.

'Don't tempt me! Is that what you want? To leave with Gibson?'

'N-no, of course not,' she faltered, 'I . . .'

'Then get out of here. Get to your own quarters.'

But in all fairness she couldn't leave without attempting to put things right. However annoyed she was with Greg, she'd had no reason to fear for her safety and she hadn't meant to lose him his job.

'Greg, I'm sorry. I wouldn't have had this happen . . .' Her words faltered away as the big man turned his back on her. Tod continued to stare at her implacably, threateningly. There was nothing she could do right now but obey him.

CHAPTER SEVEN

'TOD?' Gina studied his unapproachable profile as they drove out towards the riding stables next morning. She still felt guilty about Greg's dismissal, because she *had* been using the other man for her own ends.

He hadn't answered her and she tried again.

'Tod ... about Greg ...'

'*What* about him?' he snapped, with more ferocity than she had expected.

'Did you really have to fire him? I feel ...'

'Yes?' His profile was still granite-like. 'Just what *do* you feel for Greg, Gina? I'd be interested to know.'

She ignored his ill-humour and persevered.

'I feel you were too hard on him. He wasn't behaving any worse than ... than ...' She stopped abruptly, aware of treading on dangerous ground.

'Yes?' he enquired ominously. 'Go on!'

'All right! I will.' She reacted defiantly to his tone. 'His behaviour wasn't any worse than yours! At least he was only trying to kiss me. Whereas you ... you ...' Again she could not go on and swiftly she changed tack. 'When I first arrived, you said if my presence interfered with anyone else's work, it would be me that got fired. Why didn't you ...'

'Why didn't I fire you? Use your head! Do you think I want all your training to be wasted?'

'But surely that's less important than Melanie's safety?'

'Why should you worry about her? I didn't think you "career" women were overfond of children.'

Gina winced. His words had struck her a body blow. But then Tod couldn't know how she longed to have

122

children, couldn't know that happiness was forever denied her.

'I'm very fond of children,' she told him now, 'and Melanie is a darling. That's why I believe you should think again about firing Greg.'

'Don't worry.' He sounded almost weary. 'You're not losing your boyfriend. I've told him he can stay.'

Gina's face broke into a smile of relief, but to the man, glancing sideways at her, its apparent radiance held other connotations.

'Perhaps now,' he said brusquely, 'we could concentrate on business?' And Gina realised that, for the last five minutes, they had been parked in Theresa's stableyard and she hadn't even noticed, so intent had she been upon the subject of their discussion.

'Today you're going to meet The Clown. He's a horse.' A wry smile answered her look of surprised enquiry. 'Theresa christened him that when she found he was a "natural" at playing the fool, ideal material for a "falling" horse. Certain horses are kept for certain stunts, simply because they have an aptitude for them. The Clown is a "faller"!'

'The Clown has been taught to fall when required,' Tod explained, 'but even so, his rider has to learn to control him.'

'It seems rather cruel,' Gina said doubtfully, as they watched Theresa saddling up, preparatory to giving a demonstration.'

'Not at all. Such horses are valuable and treated with great care. Everything is taught by kindness. All you need is time, patience and plenty of sugar!'

Though he had proved an apt pupil from the first, Tod told Gina, the gelding's training had been very gradual. At first his foreleg had been bent and tied with a rope or bandage around the knee. The extra large saddle he wore was capable of taking a considerable weight of equipment and had a hole just below the pommel. During early training, a lunge rope passing through the hole had been attached to the right side of the bit, used in conjunction with a curb chain under the jaw.

'When the trainer pulls on the rope,' Tod told her, 'if the horse allows himself to fall easily to the left, then he's likely to make a good faller. First falls are made indoors, with the horse standing still and the floor covered in deep sawdust, so that there's no danger of injury.'

'Suppose a horse does hurt itself?'

'It would hold up his training for a considerable period of time because, for quite a while, he'd refuse to fall again. When the horse has taken to falling readily on the lunge rope, the rope is replaced by a rein, as now. Watch Theresa.'

The slight girl had mounted. She demonstrated The Clown's accomplishments, bringing her mount down from a walk, then a trot and finally at the canter.

'Now we come to your training,' Tod said. 'This particular stunt is very demanding. As his rider, you're responsible for the fall being made in exactly the right place, for giving him the correct signal at the correct moment. In effect, you're responsible for the horse's safety as well as your own.'

Gina was a little nervous at first, not so much for herself, but that she should not harm an obviously valuable animal. But Theresa was coolly competent and since Tod had wandered off, leaving the two girls together, she felt less pressure and by the end of the session was giving quite a good account of herself.

'Give her a week,' Theresa told Tod, when he returned, 'and she should be ready to go. Fortunately, you've picked yourself an excellent horsewoman.' She smiled at Gina in a friendly fashion and Gina found herself liking the other girl.

Next morning, Tod handed over the keys of his car.

'Think you can get yourself over to Theresa's for the rest of your lessons?'

'What will you be doing?' Gina felt a stab of disappointment. She had enjoyed her early morning drives with Tod, able to pretend for a while that he was hers.

'We start filming today. We'll work on Marcha's scenes, the close-ups, and then, when you're ready to go, we'll take the "stand-in" shots.'

In her absence, would they also be shooting the love scenes between Marcha and Tod? Gina hoped so. She hoped fervently that they would all be completed before she was expected to attend the filming sessions. She didn't want to actually see Marcha in Tod's arms; imagining it was bad enough.

For the rest of that week, she travelled alone, returning to Mallions each day, sore and weary, but with a growing sense of achievement. She was becoming more and more confident of her ability to do what was asked of her. She saw little of Tod or Marcha. If they were not filming, they seemed to be dining out. Greg was coldly civil whenever she encountered him and she was sorry their easy cameraderie was gone.

Thus, feeling a little lonely, Gina began spending her spare time in the nursery.

'I wonder,' Sally said one evening, rather diffidently, 'if you'd mind being on your own with Melanie. I have the offer of a date and I'd rather like to accept.'

'Of course you must go,' Gina said at once. 'I'd love to babysit.'

'Do you think we ought to ask Mr Fallon's permission first?'

'We can't. He's out himself. But in any case, I don't see why he should object, as long as there's someone with Melanie. Andy's on duty outside tonight, isn't he?'

So it was arranged, and Gina had the satisfaction of playing with the child, giving her her tea, bathing her

and reading a bedtime story until she fell asleep. She
turned the light down, barely a glimmer retained just in
case Melanie woke. There was no reason now why she
should not return to the outer room and read her own
book. But somehow it was very peaceful, sitting here in
the dim light, watching the child's lovely little face
tranquil in sleep, hearing the even tenor of her
breathing. Seated in a low chair beside the bed, Gina
leant over Melanie, her expression rapt, her eyes
wistful. How she would have loved a daughter just like
this.

So engrossed was she in her silent worship that she
did not hear the soft opening of the door that
communicated between nursery and bedroom. But then
awareness of another presence in the room made her
start. She knew at once who it was, every nerve end told
her. After Tod had assured himself of his daughter's
well-being, he beckoned Gina to follow him into the
outer room.

'What the hell,' he demanded, 'are you doing here?
Where's Sally?'

'She had the chance of an evening out, so I
volunteered to babysit.'

'I suppose,' he said sarcastically, 'that it never
occurred to either of you that, as Sally's employer, my
permission might be sought?'

'Yes, it occurred to us,' Gina said evenly, 'but since
you were out yourself, presumably with Marcha, it
wasn't possible to consult you. It seemed a pity for
Sally to miss her chance, just because you're always out
enjoying yourself. And I'm quite capable of looking
after Melanie.'

He moved to shut the door between the two rooms,
then returned, studying her appraisingly.

'You puzzle me,' he said at last.

'Oh?' she returned lightly. 'In what way?'

'This ... this "thing" you seem to have about your

cousin. Don't think I haven't noticed your subtle denigration of her. Yet she never has anything but good to say of you.'

Gina's lip curled. How easily men were deceived by a lovely face, and of course Marcha was a consummate actress, by profession and by nature.

'Except apparently, that I'm "frigid".'

'That,' he said drily, 'was in the nature of a recommendation as far as I was concerned. She knows my views on fraternisation and she said you'd hardly be a threat to any of my crew, since you'd turned violently against all men; that probably you should never have married in the first place, since you weren't the domesticated or the romantic type.'

'Well thank you, Marcha!' Gina exclaimed. 'As a recommendation that takes the biscuit. Or was it a recommendation? It sounds to me as if she was more afraid that your attention might wander in her absence. Obviously she's not blind to your weaknesses.'

To accuse a man like Tod of any weakness was a dangerous thing to do, a provocation to retaliation. Gina recognised the danger signals in the tightening of his lips, the hardening of his eyes.

'Are you blind to your weaknesses, Gina?' he asked softly. He moved to the outer door of the nursery and, scarcely believing her eyes, she saw him turn the key in the lock.

'W-what are you doing? I don't know what you mean.' Unfortunately, she did and the knowledge turned her knees to water.

'Oh, you know very well, Gina. It seems Marcha was mistaken. With your own sex you may be able to keep up your act, but not with a man, a real man. I don't know anything about your husband, whether or not he was capable of plumbing your depths, but I know I am. I've come very close to it once or twice and now I'm tempted to go all the way.'

'No! You . . . you won't. I shan't let you. I'll . . .'

'You'll what? Throw me over your shoulder as you did Greg? Now that puzzles me, too! You've had plenty of opportunities, Gina, but you didn't take them. Is it possible you didn't really want to discourage *me*? Why didn't you use your unarmed combat skills?'

'I . . . I didn't think it would be any use,' she improvised. 'You said you'd been a stuntman. I . . . I thought your skills would be far more advanced than mine.'

'They are, as it happens. But I still don't believe you. I know women, Gina. You're not as immune to me as you'd have me believe. It's there in the way you talk about your cousin in relation to me. I believe you're jealous, not just because she has the lead in my film but because . . .'

'Because she's your mistress? Never!' Gina said vehemently. 'I'll never lower myself to be that to any man. If ever I were to trust one of your sex again, which I doubt, it would be marriage or nothing. Marcha may have the morals of an alley cat, but they don't run in the family.'

'No?' he enquired softly. 'Then how would you describe your undoubtedly receptive reactions to my lovemaking?'

'Lovemaking? Is that what you call it? I'd call it good old-fashioned lust. Oh, I won't deny you know precisely how to arouse a woman's baser instincts to match your own, and I am only human.'

'Yes, I know how to arouse you, Gina, and it's a very pleasurable experience. But I wouldn't call your instincts base, just natural. Especially in view of your alleged long abstinence.'

It was a warm night, but she knew that was not responsible for the prickles of nervous perspiration bedewing her skin. His eyes were fixedly regarding her breasts and she knew that the thrust of them against the thin material of her summer dress was betraying her body's immediate reaction to him, to his words. Her instinct was to step backwards, but there was nowhere to retreat.

To relieve their nervous dryness, she licked her lips, tried to avoid his gaze, but his eyes held hers. His were amused, yet dark, too, with something else, something physically frightening yet, at the same time, infinitely exciting. Like a wild creature charmed by its predator, she was unable to move as he reached out and touched the soft creamy flesh exposed by the elasticated, boat-shaped neckline of her dress.

'You're warm, Gina,' he murmured, 'warm and living. What was it you said about everyone needing something warm and living to hold?'

'I was talking about Melanie and . . . and the kitten.' But she was helpless to push his hand away as it continued its investigation.

He moved closer, both of his hands now employed in stretching the neckline until it slid down, exposing her shoulders, the swell of her breasts. Slowly, so slowly, his head bent over her, then his mouth tasted and savoured her skin, sending tremors of sensation through her, arousing a desire to know more of his sensual expertise.

'I've found myself thinking about you a lot just lately, Gina,' he murmured, 'imagining what it would be like to make love to you fully.' His voice grew throatier. 'Not just once, but day after day.'

If he only knew it, her thoughts had paralleled his often, imagining such moments as this, moments, however, of genuine emotion, of commitment, which could be carried without shame to their natural conclusion. *This* could not, must not.

His fingers at the nape of her neck drew her nearer to him.

'Can you imagine it, Gina?' His voice was seductive, evocative of the picture he painted. 'I know you can.

You, naked, in my arms, both of us naked. It so nearly happened once, didn't it? I touched your body, felt it come alive, but then I drew back, fool that I was. For a while I had this crazy idea that I was wrong about you, that you were worthy of something better, that you weren't for me or for any man on a casual basis. But I should have known better, shouldn't I? You wanted me then, you would have let me possess you, and I threw away my opportunity. Can you imagine how many times I've regretted that? But I'm not going to throw away my chance this time. Why should I when there's been Greg! And then there's this man you want to visit. I can't speak for him, of course, but I know Greg. I think I can promise you I'd be more subtle, more sensitive.'

She shook her head. He was wrong, horribly wrong in his insinuations and yet, bemused, still she stared into his eyes, unaware how hers registered her conflicting emotions. The recent, searing contact of his mouth against her shoulders had brought all the sensuality of her own nature into leaping life. He took advantage of her immobility, covering her mouth with his, parting her lips with consummate ease, the pressure of his warm and firm, erotically evocative.

Unable to restrain herself from following instincts she had long wished to indulge, she allowed her hands to glide up over Tod's broad shoulders, then over his neck, until her fingers were lost in the crisp, dark hair, a delicious, tactile experience. Meanwhile, he plundered her mouth with an expertise that made her whole body tremble furiously.

When the kiss ceased, it was all she could do to remain standing. Indeed, if it had not been for the support of his arms, she doubted she would have done so. His voice was warm, seductive.

'You want me, Gina, don't you?'

Helplessly, she shook her head, made an attempt to

pull away, but it was a feeble effort at best. She felt limp, boneless, and she could sense his triumphant awareness of her pliancy.

This time the pressure of his lips was harder as he sought to force a verbal as well as a physical acknowledgment from her, and she knew this was serious. He wasn't playing with her. His body proclaimed all too surely its own arousal, evidence of a very powerful and unmistakable physical need, and for the first time she began to realise that he did intend to appease it.

Her body grew warmer still as the blood heated and flowed more rapidly in her veins, while pulses hammered a minor accompaniment to her heart. There was no resistance in her, her total concentration was upon her senses, their crying needs. Too often her body had awakened to Tod's, too often been denied. Now he had no need to force her lips apart. They opened to him willingly, her tongue duelling frantically with his. Her hands clasped vicelike about his neck, as if they would never release him, her body stirred and pressed against him in deliberate provocation, making its own plea for satisfaction.

In answer, he pushed her down upon the settee, his weight upon hers a glorious, temporary appeasement of her wanting, but not for long. It was not enough. As his lips, his hands made tormenting trails over her body, she tensed against him, small husky groans in her throat protesting against his procrastination, urging him to release the pent-up dam of their mutual longing. Never, not even with Tod himself, had she experienced such violent, such painful surges of desire, feelings so strong that they obliterated all reason, all promptings of common sense, so that nothing mattered but that they should reach the natural harmony of final consummation.

It was the squeak of the communicating door that

broke across what no other force could have destroyed. Melanie's bedroom door. This was no scene for a child to witness. Abruptly they were apart, each thankful for the temporary dazzlement in the child's eyes as she came from the half-light of her room into the brightness of the nursery.

'Gina, where's my kitten? I want him.'

'Sally took him down to the kitchen for his supper,' Gina explained gently. To Tod, *sotto voce*, she said, 'We thought you might not approve of him sleeping on her bed.'

'Oh.' He shrugged impatiently and she knew frustrated desire was still riding him, as it did her. 'If she wants the animal let her have it. I'll go down and get the damned thing.'

Gina guessed that he needed the excuse, time to bring himself under control. As for herself, she concentrated her attention on the child, drawing her into her arms, leaning her cheek against the dark, curly hair. If only this were her own child, she held . . . hers and Tod's, the outcome of their impassioned lovemaking. Such intensity of feeling as they had known here this evening would surely have resulted in . . . Then she remembered, remembered that such a thing could not be for her, ever, with any man. Her face crumpled suddenly and she felt the sting of bitter tears.

When Gina had realised how Keith had deceived her, the traumatic shock had precipitated a miscarriage, followed by the shattering intelligence that, for her, there were unlikely to be more pregnancies.

For a long while before and after her divorce, Gina had been low in health and spirits, too numb to care. Grief for the child that might have been brought its own, blessed, concomitant paralysis of thought. Only later, when her physical strength began to return, did she realise the depths of her hurt, the psychological damage caused by the loss of her most valuable

feminine attribute. She hadn't realised until then just
how much her confidence in her own femininity had
buoyed her up in her career. Now she felt only half a
woman, uncertain of her identity.

Returning, the kitten tucked under his arm, Tod
paused on the threshold, his breath catching in his
throat, all the measures he had taken to cool his
feverish wanting undone by the sight before him.

How lovely she was, how lovely and how desirable.
There was that family resemblance to Marcha and yet,
somehow, disturbingly, she wasn't like her. And she sat
there, holding his child, as if it were the most natural
thing in the world that she should do so ... his child!
He felt his breath exhale raggedly. What sort of
children would they produce, he and Gina, if ever ...
Then, as Gina had done, he crushed the thought. Never
again, he vowed, never again. Those who loved got
hurt. When Maria had died, he'd sworn always to keep
a part of himself to himself; any hurt, therefore, would
be minimal, easily shaken off. Never again would he
submit mind and heart, as well as body, to the toll love
took.

And now, here he was, almost wallowing in
unwanted sentimentality, just because a lovely woman,
whom he desired, nursed his child. He moved, cleared
his throat and the little tableau was disturbed; but as
Gina looked up, he caught the unmistakable glint of
tears on her cheeks and all his resolutions wavered. He
was beside her in an instant.

'What is it, Gina? Tell me, what is it?'

'N-nothing. At least ...' She could not quell the little
sob that rose in her throat. 'It was just that ... sitting
here with Melanie, it brought home to me all that I'm
missing ... a ... a child of my own.' Her throat closed
up. She could say no more. She couldn't find the words
to tell him of her deepest unhappiness, that she could
never bear a child.

So she was regretting the past, was she? Tod thought grimly. A few years ago, according to Marcha, she'd refused her husband's pleas that she lead a domesticated life, so he'd left her for a woman willing to bear his children. Yet despite this knowledge, Tod found himself unable to harden his heart against her. His arms encircled them both, Gina and the now sleeping child.

'Never mind, my love,' he whispered, 'it's not too late. You're still young.' He did not see the despairing shake of her head, the lips that shaped the word 'never' as he took Melanie from her arms and carried the child back to bed.

When he returned, he found Gina talking to Sally, her face as composed as if she had never shed those tears.

'Yes, thank you, miss,' Sally was saying. 'I had a lovely evening at the cinema at Aylesbury. Oh, Mr Fallon,' as she noticed him on the threshold of the two rooms, 'I hope you didn't mind, but . . .'

'Not a bit,' he said brusquely. 'I'm afraid we've all tended to take you for granted. I'm sure Miss Darcy will sit for you again?' He looked at Gina.

'Oh . . . oh yes,' she whispered, head suddenly downbent. But could she bear to do this again, expose her still vulnerable heart to the ecstatic agony of watching over another woman's child? But Melanie was also Tod's child; in holding Melanie, she held, too, a part of Tod, a very important part. She raised her head, eyes brilliant with yet more tears, but steadily fixed on his. 'I'd like that,' she said.

He steered her from the room and she went with him blindly, for the stupid tears would not let her see where she walked. On the darkened landing, he drew her into his arms again.

'I'll give you five minutes,' he whispered, his body trembling against hers, 'then I'll come to your room.'

Oh no. No. Give me the strength to resist, to refuse him, she pleaded inwardly.

'Gina?' His voice was questioning as he lifted her chin, endeavouring, in the gloom, to see her expression.

'No, Tod. Please. I . . . I'd rather you didn't.'

'Not tonight?' There was infinite tenderness in his voice, patience. 'Then some other night, darling, please?'

'Not tonight, not ever.' She tried to make her voice strong. 'I've told you before, I don't . . . don't . . .'

'This wouldn't be a casual affair, Gina.' His tone was sincere and she trembled anew. What was he trying to say? 'No one night stand. I swear to you, there'd be no other woman in my life but you.' It sounded like the prelude to a proposal of marriage and yet . . . Had he said those same words once to Marcha? 'Let me love you, Gina.'

'In what capacity?' she whispered.

He caught her to him anew. 'As my love, of course, my *dearest* love.'

'What the French call a *chère amie*, I suppose,' she said bitterly. 'No, Tod!' Sure now of her ground, she withdrew herself from his arms. 'I'm sorry, but no. Good night.' With an effort that cost all her will-power, she made herself turn and walk away from him towards her own room, head and shoulders erect. But she could not prevent herself turning briefly, her hand on the latch, to see him still standing there, watching her.

She saw him start eagerly towards her, as though he believed her to have relented, and with a swift movement she was inside her room, the door locked behind her. For a moment she stood listening, trembling, as his footsteps advanced, paused, were motionless for a long, long time. Then she heard a sigh, a deep-hearted one, as if it came from the very depths of his being, before he moved on.

Only then could she relax, sagging, almost tottering

to her bed where she threw herself face down, muffling the crying that felt as if her heart must break.

For Gina, her work began in earnest next day and she was glad of the tiring, sometimes actually painful activity that would render her body immune to all other sensations.

A grim-faced Tod greeted her, spoke to her as he did to any other member of his crew and, though she knew she ought to be relieved not to have any reminders of his softer moods, her heart was sore.

They were to begin making the linking shots, from where Marcha was seen mounting a horse, her expression of fear and distaste masked from the camera, until she was discovered, face down, supposedly having fallen with her horse. The ground over which Gina must gallop had been broken up and covered with shredded peat and other shock-absorbent materials on which the horse and rider would fall.

At first she had merely to take The Clown over the course he was to run, not only for the benefit of the director, Tod, and his cameramen, but also to rehearse the run for herself. The actual fall itself would not be practised, though Gina had been warned that she might have to do it several times with the cameras turning before Tod and his crew were satisfied with the result.

To Gina's surprise, Tod came over before the actual 'take' and uncertainly she wondered if the expression in his dark eyes was what it seemed to be, anxiety.

'All right?' he asked curtly. 'Not afraid?'

She shook her head, tightening her lips to quell their trembling. Not of fear; it was the light pressure of his hand on her back as she mounted which had been enough to disturb her hard-won equilibrium. For a moment her green eyes tried desperately to fathom the meaning of his.

It had taken Gina a while during training sessions to

get used to all the special equipment, the personal padding, the falling stirrups. These latter consisted of leather pouches, made so the rider's feet could be removed from them instantly without any risk of being dragged along the ground. Her elbows and knees were well protected. Her collarbones she must shield as she fell by folding her arms across them. Some riders wore close fitting jockey helmets, but in this case it was essential that her long, flowing red hair be visible.

'This time then?' he said, still looking up at her, and now there was no mistaking the agony in his eyes. *He was afraid, for her*, as she had been afraid in the past for so many others. Intuitively, from her own experience, she knew he would rather be up here, taking the risks himself, instead of watching her take them.

'I'll be all right,' she said quietly.

'OK, then. But for God's sake, watch your head when you fall. Cameras? Ready to follow? Take him away then.'

Gina urged The Clown forward. Faster and faster the gelding galloped as he approached the prepared stretch and Gina drew a deep breath, concentrating her mind totally on everything she had learned. One mistake now could spell disaster. As she reached the point of fall, she removed her left foot from the stirrup, at the same time thrusting her right leg out straight, and pulled hard on the right rein. As she felt The Clown beginning to fall to the left, she made sure *her* left leg was well clear of the horse's body and began her own fall towards the prepared ground.

As she lay there, slightly winded in spite of all her precautions, she heard pounding footsteps, then Tod was prone beside her on the ground, turning her over, his face inches from hers, his eyes anxiously scanning her face.

'Gina?' he asked urgently. 'Are you all right? When you didn't move, I thought . . .'

Bewildered, shaken by his proximity, his urgency, she stared into the bronzed features that meant so much to her.

'I thought I wasn't supposed to move,' she said, 'until . . .'

He swore then and a look of fury crossed his face.

'Did no one tell you we'd filmed the rest of that damned sequence, days ago? The cameras cut just now, as soon as you hit the ground. I thought . . . My God, I thought . . .'

For a moment she thought he would actually haul her into his arms, as he had done on the last occasion when he thought she'd been in danger, but then he seemed to recollect their surroundings, their audience. Instead, he hauled her to her feet and began walking her back.

'OK. Break for lunch,' Tod called, as they aproached the little group of technicians and actors. From the evidence of her pursed lips and flaring nostrils, Gina deduced that Marcha had not liked Tod's all too obvious concern for her stand-in. She heard her cousin's fluting voice deprecating people who couldn't remember the easiest instructions.

For the next two or three days, Gina was in constant demand. There were more riding scenes; swimming. Gina had to fly the little Cessna and this time she was aware of Tod's tension before she even took off. Something prompted her, an instinct which she swiftly regretted, to pass close to him en route to the aircraft and murmur,

'Don't worry, Tod. I'll be OK.'

He met her green compassionate gaze with an icy stare.

'No reason why you shouldn't be!' She felt chilled by his rebuff. Yet why shouldn't he rebuff her presumption? After all, if she did crash and kill herself, it would mean nothing to him except a temporary inconvenience, a delay in filming.

After five days of continuous stunting, Gina rebelled, demanding her day off, pointing out that she hadn't had one since she'd been at Mallions. At first she thought Tod was going to refuse.

'I suppose you want to visit this other, mysterious boyfriend of yours?' And, as she didn't answer, merely waited silently, 'Oh, do what you like! Take the Mini. I can't spare the Rolls today.'

As the vast gates of the estate opened and closed behind her, Gina had the sensation of one escaping from prison. It was as if a weight lifted from her; and yet she knew it was only a temporary reprieve from a life sentence. Under different circumstances she would be a voluntary inmate, if only Tod returned her love. She wouldn't mind spending the rest of her life behind iron gates and electrified fences with him and Melanie. But the invitation to do so would never be issued.

To banish these fruitless thoughts, she gave all her concentration to her driving and pressed on, her foot hard down, towards Aylesbury and beyond . . . to Stoke Mandeville.

'Hallo, Rusty!'

There was an instant's silence before the wheelchair turned on its axis, its occupant staring up at her with disbelieving eyes.

'Gina! It's really you! I thought you'd got fed up with visiting me. It's been simply ages.' The chair was propelled towards her and she bent to embrace and kiss its occupant.

'I'm sorry, Rusty darling. I should have written but, honestly, I thought I would have made it before this, especially as I'm living quite near here.'

'Living near here? Have you given up the flat? But that's marvellous!' the boy's freckled face lit up. 'Does that mean . . .'

'Perhaps living is a bit misleading. I should have said

working. But my job means living in, temporarily.' She pulled up a chair and sat close beside him, her arm about his shoulders.

'Aren't you running your agency any more?' Not even Rusty knew that Gina had taken over the role of Fantasy Woman and she doubted if he ever watched it any more. He would scarcely want to be reminded of the incident which had placed him in a hospital for spinal injuries.

'I still own the agency. But I'm working with a film company at the moment.' She hesitated, wondering whether she should tell him or not. But he would be bound to find out some time. 'Doing stunt work.'

As she had feared, his brown eyes clouded over and he ran his one good hand through the ginger hair that had given him his nickname.

'Oh no, Gina! I wish you wouldn't. Suppose something were to happen to you!'

'I'm very careful,' she promised him. 'We take every possible precaution.'

He grimaced. 'That's what they said about my ride with Mick and look what happened to us!'

'Miss Darcy?' A nurse was approaching down the ward. 'There's a gentleman asking for you. Is it all right if he comes in?'

'A gentle . . .?' Gina broke off as she recognised the tall, broad figure already striding purposefully in the nurse's wake. Tod Fallon! What was he doing here, she wondered resentfully? He must have followed her . . . again. Her cheeks began to burn angrily. Didn't he trust her out on her own? Her eyes narrowed. Or was it that he'd wanted to find out whom she was visiting? It was an unwarranted impertinence. It was no concern of his what she did with her free time.

'Do you intend to make a habit of following me?' she demanded irately, as soon as he was within earshot, but to her annoyance he totally ignored her remark, grinning in a friendly fashion at Rusty.

'Aren't you going to introduce me to your friend?' There was a gleam of humour in Tod's dark eyes. Oh, he could afford to look amused, now he knew her 'boyfriend' was a mere teenager. 'Or is he your brother?' He looked from Gina's auburn head to Rusty's ginger curls.

'Gosh!' Rusty exclaimed, 'I wish Gina were my sister. Then I could live with her. She'd have me like a shot if she could, but my sister can't be bothered. That's why I have to stay here.'

'But you know you like it here, Rusty,' Gina reminded him gently. 'They're very good to you and you're improving a lot under their care. You'd be awfully lonely in my flat all day, alone.' She turned to Tod, grudgingly making the introduction he'd requested. 'This is Peter, known to his friends as Rusty, for obvious reasons. Rusty, this is Mr Fallon, my employer. He's a film director.'

'Gosh!' Peter was obviously impressed. 'I've heard of you! You make super, exciting films. And Gina's actually starring in one of your films?'

'Hold on!' Gina darted Tod a sour look as she interrupted the enthusiastic boy. 'My face will never be seen. I'm just a stand-in for the real star.'

'Oh?' Rusty asked interestedly. 'Someone famous? Anyone I know?'

'No!' she said hastily.

'Mr Fallon?' Rusty looked up at Tod, his freckled face drawn into lines of worry. 'Stunting is awfully dangerous. You won't let anything happen to Gina, will you?' Despite a manful effort, his lip quivered. 'She's all the family I have now.'

'I thought you mentioned a sister?' Tod said gently.

The boy's face contorted with scorn.

'I don't count her. I don't care if I never see her again. But Mr Fallon,' doggedly he repeated his question, 'you won't let Gina get hurt?'

'I promise you, Rusty.' Tod squatted on his
haunches, his right hand outstretched. 'As one man to
another . . . we'll take the greatest care of her. She's
worth her weight in gold.'

Yes, Gina thought bitterly, as a fully trained stunter;
not as a woman, not so far as Tod was concerned.

Rusty's face relaxed.

'Oh good! I'd hate to have *this* happen to her.' He
indicated his wheelchair.

'What happened to you, old chap?'

'Can't we talk about something more cheerful?' Gina
intervened hastily.

'I don't mind telling people about it,' Rusty assured
her.

Rusty, as he preferred to be known, had in the early
days of *Fantasy Woman* written in with a request and,
since Fantasy Woman herself was an anonymous
figure, the sponsors saw no reason not to humour her
young relation's whim. For what Gina hoped the story
now being told would not reveal was that Rusty's full
name was Peter Durrant, that he was her cousin and
Marcha's stepbrother.

Too young to drive, Peter had an urge to be a
passenger in a fast car. It had been arranged for him to
ride with a stuntman in a hair-raising chase scene. At
the time, Gina, then only in an advisory capacity, had
protested that it was far too dangerous, influenced also
perhaps by the fact that her young step-cousin, unlike
his sister, was a firm favourite of hers. But Rusty had
been enthusiastically determined and Marcha had
pooh-poohed her fears, all in favour of any scheme that
would add panache to her programme. It didn't seem to
matter to her that the life at risk was that of her young
stepbrother.

It should have been a simple stunt, calling for the car
to be driven towards five other oncoming vehicles and

weave between them. Originally the plan had been that the car should travel at only thirty miles per hour and the resulting film speeded up. But for some reason, the film's director had decided that he wanted genuine faster action.

When things had started to go wrong the television camera crew had automatically gone on filming, but Gina knew that they had been as horrified and shaken as she by the subsequent tragedy. The speeding car, narrowly missing the first approaching vehicle, hit the next in an appalling smash-up. No one had ever found out exactly what caused the accident, though examination of the wreck had suggested possible failure of the steering system.

Rusty's retelling of the story resurrected the whole picture: the fear; the stench of spilled petrol, of burning rubber, of scorched and tortured metal; the chaos of revolving lights as police cars, fire engines and ambulances raced to the scene. Gina could hear quite plainly the sound of grinding metal as the firemen had cut away the buckled wreck, scarcely able to reach the man and the boy inside.

Then there were doctors swarming over the vehicle, giving painkillers, intravenous fluids; a pneumatic jack had been shoved between doorpost and dashboard of the wreck to wrench it apart. The mangled steering wheel had been a horrible sight. The impact with it had burst both of Mick's lungs; no wonder he hadn't survived. Rusty, thank God, had, but he had been badly injured, looked so vulnerable that Gina had scarcely known how to restrain her tears. For Rusty's sake she had controlled herself and, with her nursing training, she had been able to give the medical team valuable assistance. She had begged Marcha to stay and hold Rusty's hand while the men worked, and later to go with him in the ambulance, but Marcha had refused, running in a blind panic from the scene of blood and carnage.

'Mick, the driver,' Rusty was telling Tod, 'was killed, and I ended up like this. Paraplegic they call it.'

'I know, son,' Tod said and Gina could see that he was genuinely moved by the story. He turned to Gina. 'And this happened on your programme? How *could* you permit such a . . .'

'It wasn't Gina's fault!' Rusty interrupted indignantly. 'She was the programme adviser and she didn't want me to do it. I can tell you, I wish I'd taken her advice. No, it was . . .'

'Rusty,' Gina interrupted, 'we must try not to blame anyone. It was an accident.'

The boy gave her a rueful grin.

'You're too charitable, Gina. I believe you'd defend the devil himself.' He went on with his story. 'The pain was awful. I thought I was dying. I wanted to die. But Gina was marvellous. She stayed with me the whole time, holding my hand. And she's been marvellous ever since. She's visited me whenever she can, once a fortnight usually. But it's been simply ages this time,' he concluded reproachfully, 'because of *you.*'

'I admit it, old man, it is my fault,' Tod apologised. 'I've kept Gina pretty busy these past weeks. But then I didn't know about you, you see. If I'd known she had a young friend in hospital, so near to my home, I'd have seen to it that she visited once a week at least, and from now on, I promise you, she will.'

Gina could see that Tod was now totally involved with Rusty's tragedy and she rather wished he wasn't, since further revelations could well prove awkward.

'Rusty,' she said gently, 'perhaps Mr Fallon and I ought to be going. We mustn't tire you.'

But the boy complained vigorously. 'When do I ever get tired?' he scoffed. 'You know you always stay for lunch and tea and take me out.'

'Tell you what,' Tod suggested before Gina could think of anything to say, 'if you and Gina don't mind me butting in, why don't we all go out somewhere together? My car is a big comfortable one. We could even drive out to my home, show you how a film is made.'

And Marcha would be there!

'No!' Gina said hastily, 'I don't think that would be a good idea. Too tiring for one day.'

'OK,' Tod said good-naturedly. 'Perhaps just a short spin then ... and a pub lunch? Ever had a pub lunch, young man?'

Rusty was charmed and the outing was speedily arranged. But Gina was still on tenterhooks in case her young cousin should mention his relationship to Marcha. It was fortunate he didn't know his stepsister was involved in Tod's film. Though why Gina should feel any loyalty to Marcha ... It just wasn't in her nature, she decided with a sigh, to be bitchy, to use her knowledge to discredit Marcha in Tod's eyes. After all, even if it did shock him enough to cause a breakdown in his relationship with Marcha, what did she, Gina, stand to gain? Precisely nothing.

Over lunch, Rusty was only too willing to give further details of his stay in hospital, of the months of agonising physical therapy.

'I think I'd have given up long ago and just become a vegetable if it hadn't been for Gina,' he confided. 'She told me I would improve gradually, if I worked at it. She said, "You've got to keep saying to yourself, one day I'll walk again, even if it takes years. I won't let the damned thing lick me". Though,' he looked slyly under his stubby eyelashes at Gina and her heart melted, '*she* said "bloody".'

'Extremely suitable,' Tod commented gravely.

Gina thought how very nice he could be when it suited him. Rusty needed a man to talk to sometimes, other than those on the hospital staff. He hadn't known his own father for very long.

'Gina was there the day when I first moved my right hand.' In between talking Rusty was demonstrating, very thoroughly, his ability to use it as he shovelled food into his mouth. 'I absolutely shrieked, didn't I, Gina? I said, "Did you see it? Did you see it?" And do you know what?' Rusty's voice was filled with puzzlement. 'She did the darnedest thing. She started to cry. Aren't women odd?'

'I've been convinced of that for a long time,' Tod concurred and for a brief instant his large hand came out and covered Gina's where it lay on the table, his eyes meeting hers in warm understanding.

'So I can write and eat. I hated being fed, like a great baby. I can even stand a bit now, on crutches. I'm going to walk one day, just like Gina said.'

Tod nodded emphatically. 'That you will!'

Gina was glad she and Tod must return home in separate cars. It meant she would not be subjected immediately to his cross-questioning. She was well aware that there were areas of Rusty's story which left room for speculation.

As the Mini, followed by the Rolls, swept into the parking area behind the house, Marcha appeared, moving at a brisker pace than was usual for her indolent nature. The older girl stood, impatiently tapping a foot, until both Tod and Gina had emerged from their respective vehicles.

'Where the hell have you been all day?' Her usual veneer of charm where Tod was concerned had slipped badly. 'Have you been with her?'

Gina didn't want to be involved in an emotional scene and she turned to go, but as she walked towards the rear entrance of the house she heard Tod say,

'Yes. We've been to Stoke Mandeville, to visit a very interesting and courageous young man.'

Oh Lord! Gina's stride faltered. That'd torn it. Now Marcha would think ... The tap of high heels pursuing her over the uneven surface confirmed her conjecture. Marcha's hand on her shoulder arrested her progress and the older girl swung Gina round to face her.

Marcha's face was almost unrecognisable in its fury. Careful of her blandly smooth complexion, she usually avoided all strong expressions, the lines they brought in their wake. Now the lovely features were contorted with hatred ... and fear.

'You took him to see Rusty? Why, for God's sake?' she hissed. 'I suppose you've told him everything. I've seen through you, Gina. You want Tod for yourself. Don't think I can't recognise the signs, you ... you scheming little bitch. You stepped into my shoes once, but only because I let you, because I didn't want the rotten job any more. But you needn't think you're going to repeat the performance here. This film is mine and *Tod* is mine.'

'Marcha! For heaven's sake, calm down. I didn't tell Tod anything. He knows about Rusty's accident, but not who he is. Please don't credit me with having the same underhand methods as you! If the positions had been reversed, you'd have made damned sure Tod heard all the sordid details.'

Marcha's face flushed an unbecoming brick red.

'OK,' she said grudgingly, 'so you didn't tell him. See you don't, and keep him away from Rusty in future or it's bound to come out. That little brat's always had it in for me. I don't know why you bother with him. He's only half related to us.'

'I bother with him because he's a nice kid, because your stepmother was a nice woman, and, since she and your father were killed, we're all the family Rusty's got.'

'Count me out,' Marcha disclaimed. 'I don't want my career hampered by having to tow a crippled brat around with me. I never want to see him again and, remember, Tod's not to either.'

'He's not likely to,' Gina snapped, turning on her heel, unable to bear another second of her cousin's company, to listen to her unfeeling remarks.

But neither girl could control destiny, nor predict the actions of a man who was a law unto himself.

CHAPTER EIGHT

THERE seemed to be no logic in this film-making business. The story wasn't taken in chronological order. Later scenes were filmed before earlier ones and not until they were put together as a whole would it be possible to follow the plot in correct sequence.

So Gina discovered, when Tod told her they would now film the beginning of the story, at a point where hero and heroine were at odds, vying to outdo each other in their feats of daring, the heroine coming to grips with villainous men.

'I'll be needed then?' Gina asked.

'You certainly will!' Marcha told her, before Tod could answer. 'There's a lot of rough stuff involved and *I'm* not going to be slapped about,'—one slender hand caressed her own cheek—'I can't afford to have any bruises.' Gina was reminded of Marcha, in childhood, singing at a talent contest, 'My face is my fortune, sir, she said'. 'In fact,' Marcha concluded with an arch look at Tod which made Gina wince, 'apart from a couple of steamy love scenes, my work is finished.'

'Thinking of taking another holiday then?' the tall blonde Stephanie asked. 'Will it be Italy again? La Spezia, perhaps?'

'No!' Marcha snapped. 'And how many times do you need telling? It wasn't Italy. It was France . . . Nice.'

Gina had found herself a little disappointed in Tod lately. It was over a week since her visit to Rusty and, despite his promises, he hadn't once suggested that she take another day off to visit the boy. And when she had introduced the subject into conversation, he had adroitly changed its direction. He had seemed particularly remote and unapproachable for several days, not just to Gina, but to the whole of his workforce. The unit had seen very little of him; supervision of the shooting had been left to his assistant. Tod merely approved each day's rushes. Marcha had been showing distinct signs of petulance over his absences and Gina wondered if, like her, her cousin believed him to be seeing another woman, though Gina kept telling herself he would hardly neglect his work to do so.

But the early scenes he had mentioned required his presence. The script called for one of the gangsters to slap the heroine around, to actually connect with a punch, so that she was 'knocked out'. No wonder Marcha was only too pleased to let Gina do the scene. Tod, in his guise as the hero, would come to the heroine's rescue, defeating her opponent, assistance for which he would receive no thanks from the still prickly, independent heroine.

The scene was an indoor one, the confrontation taking place at the top of a wide sweeping, semicircle of stairs. After the blow, Gina must fall backwards and down the staircase.

'I don't envy you this one,' Stephanie told Gina, as they stood waiting for the action to commence. 'I've done something similar once or twice and the thought of it still scares me.'

'I must admit I don't feel too happy,' Gina confessed, 'but that's what I'm paid for!' She was aware of a smirking Marcha near at hand, waiting to see her fall, and she was determined not to let her cousin witness any reluctance on her part.

The fight scene went without a hitch, but just as the action reached the point where Gina must receive the knock-out blow, Tod called for a 'cut'.

Puzzled, Gina and her opposite number leant over the balustrade, watching, as Tod and his assistant went into a huddle. There seemed to be some disagreement between them, but finally the assistant director spread his hands in a gesture of defeat, nodded his head, then took the stairs two at a time to where Gina stood.

'The boss isn't keen about you doing this stunt. He says it's too risky for a novice. He's going to tell one of the men to put on a wig and . . .' He didn't get any further with his explanation, as Gina brushed him aside.

'Oh, no he's not!' she exploded. Her former nervousness forgotten in indignation, she ran down the stairs to where Tod stood, faced him, arms akimbo, green eyes flashing. 'If you're not satisfied with my work, at least have the decency to tell me so yourself. I've practised for this and I'm going to do it.'

'Not if I say you don't.'

They stood, almost toe to toe, glaring at each other, while an interested crew and cast waited for the outcome of the duel. Knowing their boss, most of them reckoned it was no contest. His word was law. He might have a weakness for a pretty face, a seductive body, but he was no woman's 'yes man'.

'You once accused me of cowardice,' Gina said, her voice low but fierce.

'Oh! *That!*' Tod said wearily. 'God God, girl, don't you know you've proved to me over and over again just what you're made of. I know you have the courage of a lioness, but you don't have to kill or maim yourself to . . .' As he spoke, his firm tones wavered. 'Do you want to end up like Rusty?' he demanded in a savage undertone.

'No, of course not, but I've trained for this,' she argued. 'Rusty hadn't, and besides, his injuries were an accident.'

'Were they? Or were they the result of callous indifference to safety measures?' There was a note of challenging enquiry in his voice. 'The way I hear it, it was the gross conceit and selfish unconcern of Fantasy

Woman that was responsible.' He watched her intently. What would her response be?

Gina was aware of the tension in him. It puzzled her. What was he expecting her to say? Just what had he learnt about that accident and from whom?'

'Who . . . who told you that?' she whispered. 'Rusty?' No, there'd been no opportunity.

'Marcha told me!' His tone was abrupt.

'Marcha?' Gina was taken aback. Was it possible she'd misjudged her cousin? Had Marcha found the moral fibre to confess her fault to Tod? Had they discussed Rusty during one of their intimate moments? Would they be bringing him to live at Mallions after they were married? If so, Gina should be rejoicing for the sake of the lovable teenager. But it wasn't joy that brought her heart sickeningly into her throat.

'Don't forget,' Tod was continuing, 'it was Marcha who told me her cousin was the famous Fantasy Woman when I suggested you as her double, because of your likeness to each other.'

'Marcha told you I was to blame?'

'Yes!' He was still watching her reactions closely.

'I see!' Cheeks flaming, eyes blazing, Gina hissed her retort at him. 'If that's what you believe, then there's all the more reason for me to perform this stunt. If it does go wrong and I do end up by crippling myself, it would only be justice in your eyes.' Before he could make any reply or further protest, she strode for the stairs, calling over her shoulder for the benefit of the waiting, wondering watchers. 'I'm not standing down for this stunt. I've worked for this and I'll damned well do it!'

'Right then!' Tod roared, his own temper obviously at flashpoint. 'Get on with it then, get it over, damn your eyes!'

God, but she was stubborn, he thought with reluctant admiration. His fingernails made deep impressions in the palms of his clenched hands. His anger with her stemmed from fear for her safety. He knew that. The possibility of Gina injured stirred primitive urges within him, even while he tried to tell himself he would feel equal concern for anyone performing so risky a stunt.

Gina mounted the stairs with every appearance of determination, hoping her legs didn't look as tremulous as they felt. It wasn't fear of the fall she was about to make that weakened her legs, but the awful despairing knowledge she had just gained. Tod didn't know Marcha had been Gina's predecessor in the role of Fantasy Woman. Marcha knew Gina too well, knew the younger girl would never stoop to defend herself by revealing Marcha's culpability. It was with almost a sense of fatalism that she launched herself into the fight scene once more.

As the contest moved towards its destined climax, Gina tried to think coolly and calmly of all the advice she had received during training. She must let herself go as fast as possible, yet remain relaxed and detached from the job. A pity, she thought wryly, that she couldn't approach her task in the boneless condition of intoxication. Falling drunks rarely harmed themselves.

The blow slammed home. It was a 'pulled' punch, but even so it carried enough impact to be painful. But there was no time to dwell on pain. She was falling, rolling, toppling. It was a horrible sensation, one to which she felt she would never become accustomed, never be able to approach with real sang-froid. But this was what she had wanted, worked for: personal involvement, even though she would still remain an anonymous figure. There would be no star billing for her, not even a credit. Everyone, except a few professionals, seeing the finished product would think Marcha had done all her own stuntwork, as Mary Pickford and Helen Gibson had done in the early days of filming.

'Gina?' Tod was bending over her, holding out a

hand to pull her to her feet. 'You OK?' And, as she nodded rather shakily, 'Sure? If you're in any doubt, any pain whatsoever, we'll have the doc check you over right away.'

Tod always made a point of having a doctor present during the filming of dangerous scenes and his concern, she reminded herself, would have been just as great for any other member of his team.

'Surely you're not satisfied with *that* take?' Marcha drawled. 'I thought it an extremely clumsy effort. It ought to be done again.' For heaven's sake! Did Marcha want her to break her neck, Gina wondered groggily! 'After all,' her cousin was continuing, 'it is my image that's at stake.'

Gina was not the only one taken aback by the sudden savage fury in Tod's face and voice as he turned on Marcha.

'I'm totally satisfied!' he snapped. 'Gina knows her job. You should consider yourself fortunate I didn't insist on you doing your own stuntwork.'

The stunned expression on Marcha's face should have been funny, and indeed there was no doubt that the film crew found it so. Marcha was not popular and there were subdued and not so subdued titters of laughter, at which Marcha flounced angrily away to the edge of the crowd. But Gina knew the incident had only increased Marcha's enmity towards her; while the cousins had never been friends, at least until Tod had brought them together there had existed an unarmed hostility, an unspoken agreement to differ.

The fight sequence completed, Gina's work on the film was finished. Over the preceding weeks she hadn't wanted to look ahead to the end of this period in her life. While it had not been exactly happy, her emotions were too torn for that, it had been eventful, stimulating. She had enjoyed knowing and being known by a large group of people. To her surprise, she found she had no desire to return to the peaceful isolation of her flat and now she realised that she had no idea what was to happen next. Would she be retained for further stuntwork, or was this it, a one-off? Was she expected to leave now, go back to television? Unfortunately, in view of her reluctance to confront Tod, there was only one way to find out: to ask him. And that involved choosing just the right moment since she didn't want to raise the subject before the rest of the team. But on the other hand she was reluctant to seek Tod out on his own.

In the event, the decision of when to tackle him was taken out of her hands by Tod himself.

That same evening she had been sitting with Melanie again, while Sally kept what had now become a regular date with one of the cameramen. Much of Gina's time had been spent in brooding on the uncertainty of her future, even more on the hopelessness of her love for Tod. Feeling somewhat depressed, she emerged from the nursery suite to find him waiting for her.

'After the day you've had, you shouldn't be sitting up so late,' he growled, taking her arm in a fierce grip, which, while it hurt, sent a thrill of ecstasy, far more agonising, darting throughout her entire being.

'There'll be plenty of time for rest, now the film's over,' Gina told him. But her voice was shaky and she felt stupid tears blur her eyes. She wished she did not have to encounter Tod right now. It was fatigue of course. In the morning she would be better able to face the knowledge that the time had come for her to leave Mallions. She wasn't needed here any more, not in any capacity.

Tod was drawing her along a passageway into a wing of the house she had not yet seen, but which she knew housed his private quarters.

'That's what I want us to talk about,' he told her.

'Your future plans. We may as well discuss them in comfort, over a drink.'

A heavy door opened into a sitting-room, whose occupancy was so obviously male that it seemed an extension of Tod's personality. Comfortable, but purely functional, it had none of the little personal touches a woman would have added. If there had been any reminders that once Maria had shared these rooms, they had been removed.

'Do they really concern you?' Gina asked wearily as she refused the drink. 'I thought my agreement with you was only for the duration of this film. If your "star" needs a double in your next production, count me out.'

'You're contracted to TLM Enterprises,' he reminded her, as he indicated by gesture that she should be seated, 'and, technically, I now *am* TLM Enterprises.'

Which was clear enough for anyone to understand. She was bound to him. Of course she could ask to be released from her contract. She told him so.

His answering smile was hawkish, making her uneasy, an unease which proved to be valid.

'You should have read the small print more closely. Our agreement binds you to me for three years and, while I *could* release you if I felt so inclined, I must warn you, I don't intend to do so.'

'I could break the contract, just walk out!' she said, a touch of her normal spirit in her tone.

'In which case I could sue you. But if you prove difficult, there's a much easier way. Remember the security precautions? They can keep people in as well as out.'

She stared at him, green eyes wide with disbelief. This was pure melodrama.

'You mean you'd actually go so far as to ... to ...'

'Yes,' he said simply.

She was still near to tears. He couldn't do it, could he? It was illegal, immoral. She was entitled to *personal*

freedom even if she were tightly bound by her contract
to work for him. And what about her visits to Rusty?
Suppose she were immured here indefinitely, unable to
see him, the boy would think she, too, had abandoned
him.

'That's ... that's ...'

'Blackmail,' Tod said unexpectedly. She wouldn't
have expected him to admit it. 'You see, Gina ...' He
joined her on the settee, placing himself so close to her
that they touched at shoulder, hip and thigh, and the
heat his body exuded seemed to penetrate the very
fabric of the wrap she wore. 'You see, I don't intend to
let you just walk out of my life. It would be impossible,
now.' He reached out for her and, as he pulled her into
his arms, she felt a weakening warmth engulf her body.
Her eyes seemed unable to drag their mesmerised gaze
from that attractive mouth now smiling crookedly at
her. 'We have to try and work something out.' His
voice was throaty and she recognised the fire of passion
that leapt dangerously in his dark eyes.

'Tod ... I ...' She licked painfully dry lips. 'You
can't *enjoy* keeping someone against their will ...'

'No,' he agreed. 'I'd far rather you stayed willingly.
Will you stay, Gina?'

'No,' she croaked, 'I can't ... I ...'

'You're afraid,' he accused, 'afraid to admit the truth,
that you *want* to stay. You still want me, Gina. Oh,
you've tried to pretend. You even tried to make me
think you were interested in Gibson, but I soon saw
through that. Why do you have to be so damnably
proud? Why not admit what your body tells me?'

If it were *only* her body, Gina thought miserably,
perhaps she could bring herself to have a casual affair
with him. But heart and mind were too closely involved
with what her body felt, and all three would be broken
on the wheel of despair if she gave herself to him on his
terms.

'Please let me go,' she whispered. 'You ... you said we'd come here to talk business.'

'I brought you here,' Tod said, his voice raw with undisguised emotion, 'because I wanted to make love to you. Because I'm going to make love to you.'

'No! No, damn you! Oh, why can't you be satisfied with Marcha?' It was a cry of despair. 'Or does it turn you on because I'm so like her? Well, we're not alike, not under the surface.'

'No, you most certainly are not,' he agreed obscurely. 'This has nothing to do with Marcha. *This* is you, Gina, you and me.'

She had taken a bath earlier, to ease some of the bruises gained during filming, and, since she was only going to sit with Melanie, she hadn't bothered to dress again, slipping along to the child's rooms in nightdress and robe. She had never expected to encounter Tod, believing him to be out as usual, with Marcha, or at whatever mysterious rendezvous he'd been keeping of late.

Now his hands were dexterously parting the front edges of her dressing-gown, had it open before she could prevent him. In fact, one hand trapped both of hers, while with his free one he continued to reveal the warm, curvaceous swell of her breasts, their contours outlined by the soft, smooth silk crossover front of her nightdress.

Common sense, pride, told her she should repulse him; use feet and legs, since her hands were captive; but her body seemed independent of her brain, her breasts hardening against the soft fabric, a shudder of fierce, breathtaking pleasure destroying all will-power as his dark head bent and his mouth pushed aside the flimsy barriers, until he found the scented shadowy cleft between her breasts.

'Tod! Please! Don't!' Mingled pain and pleasure drew the tortured plea from her. But it was only a token protest and they both knew it, for he freed her hands which had ceased to struggle in his clasp, his whole attention centred now on holding, cupping her breasts, while his tongue wrote moist, burning messages of desire against the creamy flesh, igniting a thousand aching, answering fires within her.

As her arms went about his neck, he gathered her up and rose, all in one easy movement, carrying her towards a door which led into an adjoining bedroom.

Her heart was drumming so loudly, it deafened her to the words he was muttering against her throat, her temples, her mouth. He dealt swiftly, competently, with the removal of her dressing-gown and nightdress, before setting her down in the centre of his bed. She was past all protesting now, with no time to be shy or embarrassed by her nakedness. He knelt over her, his mouth moving lingeringly over her from throat to breast, down over her ribcage, the silken smoothness of her stomach, his tongue making sudden erotic, tormenting little forays that left her gasping, half senseless with the urgent need for fulfilment.

Tod knew there was no need for tentativeness on his part as if Gina had been an untutored virgin, but made an assured, sensuous progression towards what he knew they both desired. She was already a woman, a woman starved, ripe and hungry to know a man's possession once more, but above all, *his* possession. Despite all her dissembling, to an experienced man all the signs were there, plainly to be seen. He wanted her, wanted her more than he had ever desired any other woman, since Maria; and he realised with a sense of wonder that the pain of that loss had become less in these last few weeks, knew that the miracle had been achieved by the presence of Gina in his life, in his home. It wasn't, as Gina had accused him, because of her superficial resemblance to Marcha. Since he had met Gina, seeing her, knowing her, was like possessing the print of a photograph after having only seen the negative. He knew she had penetrated the armour he had grown slowly and painfully during the years since Maria.

Gina's fingers fumbled frantically with the buttons of his shirt, with the waistband of his trousers.

'Help me, please help me.' She muttered the words against the slightly rough texture of his jaw and throat, a sensual stimulus that increased the intensity of the sensations riding her.

Together they removed his shirt, sliding it from his muscular body, the roughness of his chest hair brushing her breasts in erotic tantalisation. Desperately she whispered his name, her hands spanning his back, her gripping fingers raising weals on his naked flesh, causing him to cry out in husky pleasure as his mouth covered hers, his tongue plunging again and again in simulated possession.

'Tod, love me ... oh, love me!' Her whispered plea was almost lost against the warm, sweat-bedewed dampness of his shoulder.

'I will ... I do ...' came his fervent reply.

Somehow he had discarded his trousers and now, as he lowered himself against her, the hirsute flatness of his stomach, the thrust of his desire against her, the acute sensation, brought a sobbing breath from her throat.

His hands shaped her hips, curved around beneath her, lifting her towards him. In the light that filtered through from the room beyond, she could just make out his features, knew he was watching her face, waiting for her reaction.

'Was it ever like this with your husband?' he demanded suddenly, the words accompanied by an increasing pressure of his body upon hers that forbade her to answer in the affirmative. He need not have feared. There was no comparison. She had never loved before, not like this.

'No ...' She could scarcely speak. Speech was the last thing she wanted of him now; all she wanted was for him to fill this empty, aching cavern within her.

'Tonight I'm going to make you forget there ever was another man in your life,' he promised huskily.

Molten heat built between her thighs, her body craved that final union and she moved against him, an involuntary convulsion of fluttering nerves. Then there was no more delay, only a series of movements, mounting in their intensity. Again her hands contoured his back, traced his spine, caressed the sensitive spot at its base, feeling the unmistakable shudder of response that ran through him. She felt those shudders grow in intensity as she arched into him.

'I've wanted this for so long,' he groaned huskily, 'wanted you for so long.'

Desperately she pressed kisses against his jaw, the corner of his mouth, the closed lids of his eyes. It was heaven to feel and taste the salty flavour of his male body, to know the increasing intimacy with it. She didn't know how much longer she could bear this feverish insanity of longing. Then, as though in answer to her unspoken cry for mercy, he was between her thighs, his arms locking her to him as he moved into the rhythm of possession.

Something seemed to snap within her, all the months of pent-up emotions, of self-denial, the belief that love was not for her ever again, and she cried out her satisfaction at the same moment that Tod uttered her name; it was a sound of awed jubilation.

For a moment or two there was nothing but sweet release, the aftermath of lethargy. Then she began to realise what she had done. Despite all her vows to the contrary, she had become one of Tod's women. What she had felt for him had been love, a need to give of that love, freely, generously; but in spite of that there had been no sign, no indication from him, other than that of physcial need.

In a sudden access of self-loathing, she wrenched herself away from the heavy encircling arm, the hand that still covered one love-swollen breast.

'Gina? What is it? What's wrong?' Instantly his senses were alert and he half raised himself to look at her.

'You know what's wrong, damn you!' she whispered, as she scrabbled on the floor, looking for her robe. 'Damn you for . . . for making me . . .'

'For making you want me?' he challenged softly. His eyes, warm with remembered satisfaction, were also gently laughing at her. 'I didn't have to do anything about that. You've wanted me for a long time, Gina. All I did was to help you cast aside your inhibitions, make you admit it.'

'And what good has that done me?' she demanded as she dragged the belt of her robe, jerking it in a tight, double knot, a belated precaution. 'It seems to me you're the one who's benefited, by a build-up to your already inflated ego, by having your sexual appetite appeased. Did you have to have me as well as Marcha?'

'No!' he said softly, eyes and voice caressing her. 'Instead of!'

'Instead . . .' She gasped, then broke off, speculation rife within her. Marcha, it seemed, had fallen into the same trap as her predecessors; she had begun to be too possessive and Tod was retreating to his defensive position; and what better defence than to install another woman in Marcha's place? Only Gina wasn't going to be used like that. 'Sorry Tod,' she said, trying to steady her voice as she retreated towards the door. 'But you'll have to look elsewhere for your substitute. Tonight was . . . was . . .'

'A glorious experience for both of us, and you know it.' The sensuousness in his voice sent shudders racing along her spine.

'I was going to say it was a mistake,' she continued more firmly. 'You took an unfair advantage, caught me tired and off guard. But it won't happen again.'

He made no move, but his voice was husky, mocking as he said,

'Oh, yes it will, Gina. You'll see. Now that you know how it can be between us, you'll crave it, like a drug, every time we're together.'

And, God help her, she knew he was right; that was why they mustn't be together again. She must get away. She must!

'I'll find some way of getting out of here,' she told him defiantly. 'Some way out of that contract. This is the twentieth century. There's no way you can hold me prisoner indefinitely.'

'No?' The amusement, the arrogant self-confidence in his voice made her uneasy. 'I wasn't going to tell you this. It could have been against my own interests, but not now, I think. The only way you could be released from that contract is if you were to become pregnant. Obviously a stuntwoman in that condition would be very little use.'

She stared at him. Oh, the irony of it.

'On the other hand . . .' His eyes roved over her in a considering way that brought an involuntary, convulsive flutter to her stomach muscles. 'Pregnancy could keep you here just as effectively. Either way I win. Wouldn't you agree?' Then, before she could answer, 'I'd like a son.'

'That's something you'll have to . . . to apply to Marcha for.' She nearly choked on the words. If he had been deliberately seeking for some way in which to hurt her he couldn't have succeeded better. If he only knew it, she would like nothing better than to give him the son he wanted. It might bind him to her and it would mean as much to her in other ways, but it just wasn't possible.

'Marcha?' Unaware of her mounting distress, he was smiling broadly. 'Marcha is a career woman. She wouldn't dream of risking her future ... or her figure.'

'Not even for the chance of marrying you?' she couldn't help asking and felt the immediate rejection in him.

'I've no intention of marrying Marcha,' he said coldly.

'Or anyone else?' she returned shrewdly, and felt a chill within herself as he dipped his dark head in agreement.

'But Gina ...' he began, holding out his hand to her.

'No!' She didn't let him finish. Dared not. Every nerve in her body was still highly sensitised. Now that she had known intimacy with him, she knew that if he attempted a repetition of his lovemaking she would succumb just as easily. 'You've said enough, Tod. I get the picture, quite clearly ... and I want you to know this. I despise you. Oh yes ...' as he seemed about to protest, 'I despise you ... But I despise myself just as much. When my marriage broke up, I swore I'd never risk getting involved with another man, that I'd never marry again. So in a way I can understand how you felt about Maria. Marriage is an entanglement, it's an inextricable relationship painful to get out of, to forget. Just for a while there, you made me forget my resolution and I'm bitterly ashamed of myself. Sex without love, without commitment, is just lust and we've just been guilty of one of the deadliest sins.'

'Gina, wait a moment. I ...'

'No!' she said again. She backed towards the door. 'You may think you've got the upper hand. But I'll break that contract somehow. I won't stay here, give you a chance to catch me off guard again ...'

'And if you become pregnant?' His words were cut off as she began to laugh, wildly, hysterically.

'Even *you* aren't man enough for that!' she cried, despair in her voice.

'Why! You little...'

'Oh, don't worry! Much as I'd like to dent your intolerable ego, I don't stoop to insults of that kind. What you don't realise ... what I've never told anyone else ...' she was sobbing jerkily now, 'is that I can't get pregnant ... not by you ... or any other man. I'm barren. Do you hear me, barren. I'm no use to anyone ... not even to myself ... and certainly no use to you! Look elsewhere for your son ...'

With these words she fled and, such was the shock she'd dealt him, his reactions were delayed long enough for her to reach her own room, to lock its door against intrusion.

CHAPTER NINE

AFTER not expecting to sleep at all, Gina overslept. Groggily, she supported herself on one elbow in order to look at the bedside clock she'd forgotten to set, wondering what *had* finally woken her.

The sound of voices raised in altercation drifted up from the courtyard below. Wide awake now, for surely one of those voices didn't belong here, she ran to the window, threw it open and leant out. A curious little tableau was being enacted.

Tod's car stood, doors still wide open. In his wheelchair, beside the car, sat Rusty, Tod's hand on his shoulder as, together, they faced Marcha's spitting venom.

'So this is what it's all about. This crippled brat! A fine pack of lies I dare say he's told you ... he and Gina between them.'

'Don't you dare say anything against Gina, you bitch!' Rusty began, but Tod silenced him.

'No, Rusty! She's not worth your breath. Gina,' he continued harshly, not shouting, but overriding Marcha's frustrated mewls of rage, 'Gina has more decency and loyalty in her little finger than you possess in your whole body. She hasn't a malicious bone in her. What I've learnt about you, Marcha, has been from other sources, merely confirmed by Rusty here. I wondered how anyone could be so callous as to subject a boy of Rusty's age to such a dangerous risk and, in spite of what you told me, I couldn't reconcile that kind of behaviour with what I've learnt of Gina's character.'

'It was at Rusty's own insistence.' Marcha managed to insert the excuse.

'Maybe! But as his next-of-kin you had the power to veto it. Gina begged that it shouldn't be allowed, but you welcomed the risk, didn't you?' His tone became contemptuous. 'As far as you were concerned it was one well worth taking, and not just for the sake of your programme ratings. Only it didn't quite come off, did it?'

'I don't know what you mean.' Marcha was trembling visibly now, not with rage, but with what seemed to the watching Gina to be an ague of fear.

'Piecing together what Rusty's told me, plus information from your late father's solicitor ... that your father left everything to your stepbrother ... it seems to me Rusty's death would have been very convenient for you. No wonder you couldn't wait to get away from the scene of the accident. Even you, my dear Marcha, weren't hard boiled enough to witness the outcome of your "calculated" risk. I wonder what it felt like, for those few hours until they told you Rusty would live, to feel like a murderess?'

'This is all rubbish, guesswork,' Marcha cried shrilly. 'How could I know there would be such a dreadful accident? You can't prove a thing like that.'

'No,' Tod agreed, 'you couldn't know, but you could hope ... And no, I haven't any proof, luckily for you. But I'm certain enough in my own mind. Get out of my house, Marcha! You've got an hour.'

'I've also got a contract,' she cried triumphantly. 'I still have two more films to do. I could sue you.'

'Go ahead! It would be worth the money to be rid of you. But I don't think you'll succeed. In fact I don't think you'll even try, just in case I let a few rumours leak out.'

Breathlessly, Gina waited for her cousin's reaction. Would it be one of further defiance? But it seemed the older girl realised she had lost. Yet she retained sufficient of her normal hauteur to enquire,

'I presume I'm allowed to use the telephone to make my arrangements?'

'Obviously you'll need to call a taxi,' Tod said, 'since I've no intention of chauffeuring you anywhere.'

Gina felt like cheering as Marcha turned away and flounced out of sight, back into the house, but her main concern now was with showering, getting dressed and going downstairs to see Rusty. It was obvious what he was doing here. Tod had brought the boy to confront his stepsister, so Marcha could be in no doubt that Tod possessed all the facts he claimed. But how long had Tod known that Rusty was Marcha's stepbrother?

En route to search for her young cousin, Gina heard Marcha using the library telephone.

'OK.' Her voice sounded angry, sulky. 'So the moment's finally come. Yes, today! I've only got an hour.' Obviously she was making use of her access to the telephone to call friends, as well as the necessary taxi. It seemed she had been expecting her cards sooner or later, and yet, only a few weeks ago, Marcha had seemed so positive she would be marrying Tod. At any rate it had seemed certain that she would retain her position as '*maîtresse en titre*'.

'Hallo, Rusty darling!' She had tracked them down to the breakfast room, where morning coffee was being served. There was a host of other people milling about, for which Gina was relieved. There would be no opportunity for Tod to approach her, to give the conversation a personal turn; and, by the time the last of the film crew had filtered away, she would have done likewise, for she had made her plans, knew how she was going to escape.

'Gina! Gosh, am I glad to see you. I've got so much to tell you, you wouldn't believe.' The words fairly cascaded out of the excited boy and Gina tried to look suitably surprised as he related the conversation, most of which she'd already overheard. 'And Tod says I'm to *live* here . . . actually live *here*, as if it was my real home, and only go to the hospital for my treatment. He's a great guy, Gina!' Rusty gazed with admiring eyes at Tod as he stood talking to one of his crew.

As if she didn't know that, Gina thought miserably. In her eyes he was damned near perfect, except for one thing, his reluctance to marry again. Yet, in fairness, she couldn't blame him for an aversion she'd once held herself.

'He's been to visit me almost every day since that first time. We've been making all kinds of plans, you can't imagine. And he says you'll be staying here, too, Gina. Is that right?'

'No,' she said curtly, then, at the boy's surprised look, softened her tone, 'I'm afraid that's impossible. You know how busy I am . . . and the flat's my home.'

Rusty's freckled face was downcast, but not for long.

'Oh, well,' he said cheerfully, 'I guess he must have got it wrong. But I dare say you'll still come and visit me?'

'Oh . . . I . . .' But before she could think of a suitably non-committal reply which would satisfy the boy, there was a general interruption.

Sally rushed into the room, face and figure both expressive of agitation.

'Oh, Mr Fallon! Thank goodness I've found you all together. Now you'll all be able to look for her.'

'Look for whom?' Tod asked sharply. 'You don't mean . . .'

'Yes! Melanie! I can't find her anywhere.'

'When did you last see her?'

'About half an hour ago. We discovered her kitten was missing. She was so upset. I . . . I told her to stay in her room while I looked for him. But this is such a big house and he's such a tiny thing. I didn't realise I'd been gone so long and . . . and when I got back to the nursery, Melanie wasn't there.'

'Did it never occur to you that she's probably hunting for the damned thing herself? I *knew* the dratted animal would cause trouble of some sort.' An indignant Gina received the full force of his irritated scowl. 'We'll soon find her, Sally. Don't worry. Some of us will search the house and others the garden.'

This was her chance, Gina thought. Every inclination told her she, too, ought to join in the search for Melanie but, as Tod had said, it shouldn't prove a long one and for once she was going to put herself first.

'I'll try the garden,' she murmured and, in the general hubbub of noise and movement, she slipped out of the house.

Moving slowly at first, pretending to look about her, she finally reached the trees, then began to run, only emerging from cover when she reached the edge of the airstrip. Sliding back the door, she entered the hangar. Would the Cessna have enough fuel for her to reach a suitable place to land, far enough from Tod's clutches? She scrambled into the cockpit, flicked switches and anxiously inspected dials. She drew a breath of relief. The tanks were full.

Just to think, flying had once been a source of terror to her and now it was to prove a means of salvation. She taxied out on to the runway and was soon airborne. She had no idea where she was headed. Her main preoccupation had been to take off before Tod got wind of her plan and prevented it.

Her flight path took her over the house and the main gate and she was just heaving a wistful little sigh of nostalgia, when something strange arrested her attention. The large iron gates which, when shut, completed the circuitry of electronic warning devices, were standing open, unattended.

Forgetting her former urgency, Gina circled. Her curiosity was rewarded as two figures emerged from the gatehouse, a woman and a child ... Marcha and Melanie!

Gina's first thought was that Marcha had magnanimously postponed her departure, put aside her own feelings to help search for the missing child. But this conjecture didn't stand up to inspection. Marcha didn't like children; she wasn't the sort to forgive and forget a slight, much less a direct attack upon herself and the discovery of her past action. And Tod had made it pretty clear what he thought of her perfidy towards Rusty. No, Marcha might be said to have a score to settle.

She'd had nearly an hour in which to carry out her revenge and fate seemed to have played into her hands with the missing kitten. Or ... Gina didn't believe in coincidence ... had Marcha contrived that disappearance?

Living and working here, the older girl would obviously know about the gatehouse control system. She would know, as Gina did, that Andy and Greg were bound to join in searching house and immediate grounds. Nothing easier than for her to reach the control point unobserved. But how had she persuaded Melanie to accompany her, when their dislike was mutual? Of course! Simple! She had only to pretend she'd seen the kitten wandering down the drive!

But, puzzled Gina as she circled again, how did Marcha intend to proceed from here? It would be pointless to just walk out. Once the break in security was discovered, it would be no time at all before Marcha was overtaken, particularly as she would be hampered by the slower speed of the child. The taxi! Marcha's telephone call!

Marcha was standing by the gates, obviously waiting, one hand restraining Melanie, who appeared to be struggling. Then two things happened simultaneously. A large limousine raced up the road, halting in the gateway long enough to bundle woman and child into the interior. Then it proceeded *onwards, into the grounds of Mallions*! That was no taxi!

The second occurrence gave Gina the clue to this apparently strange proceeding. To her right, and slightly above her, appeared a helicopter. There was every indication that it was descending towards the airstrip, from which she herself had taken off only minutes before.

Gina's swift thought processes had made her the successful businesswoman she was. Within an instant of recognising the intruder's intentions, surmising that this was another attempt by the Mantalinis, aided and abetted by Marcha, she was heading the Cessna back towards base, faster than the helicopter could travel.

The black limousine had reached the airstrip and was stationary, its occupants waiting for the helicopter to land. No use Gina setting down. She hardly imagined herself to be a match for the men in it. It was as the helicopter neared the ground that she realised what she must do. She must stop anyone leaving the car, she must undertake the most dangerous stunt of her career to date, low-level flying. But she didn't think twice about it.

Down she plummeted, then she began to fly backwards and forwards over the car, dipping first one wing then another, keeping between car and helicopter. She wasn't unduly surprised to hear the crack of bullets, to learn that the would-be kidnappers were armed. A bullet hit and ricocheted off the bodywork of the Cessna and she was thankful it hadn't struck the cockpit window. After several runs, she was beginning to wonder how much longer she could continue before a bullet found its target . . . her.

But help was at hand. Two or three cars were now streaming towards the airstrip: Tod's and those she recognised as belonging to Greg and Andy. The breach in their defences had been discovered. She made one more overhead pass and then, the pilot obviously opting for discretion rather than valour, the helicopter took off. Without its support, the occupants of the car seemed to decide it was futile to continue and, as Gina circled again, gaining height, she was relieved to see Marcha and Melanie pushed from the car, which then took off at great speed.

Greg and Andy drove in pursuit, but Tod was out of his car, running to where his daughter was just scrambling up from the grass. Gina waited only long enough to see that the child was safe, then she turned the aircraft away, not seeing Tod's frantic signals, flying blind for a moment or two as tears stung her eyes, tears at the memory of Tod with Melanie in his arms. Did he even realise who had played such a large part in his daughter's rescue? Did he care?

'Well Miss ... Mrs? ... Ah, Miss Darcy, I don't know if this is good news or bad.'

Gina sat on the edge of her seat, hands tightly clasped. Her throat worked convulsively as she awaited the verdict.

'It's quite conclusive. You are pregnant! Oh dear! Oh dear, dear!' The doctor's homely features contorted into lines of distress as Gina burst into tears. She rounded her desk, proffering a box of tissues, a glass of water, kindly platitudes.

'H-how is it possible?' Gina gulped after a while, after she had told the other woman of her utter delight, that her tears were those of happiness. 'Th-they told me I'd never get pregnant again, never.'

Doctors had been wrong before, this sympathetic one told her. Sometimes things changed, righted themselves. There were so many imponderables in the human physiology. 'But I don't think we need trouble ourselves with all that, do you? The next obvious step is to provide for your welfare and the baby's. Is yours a professional name, my dear? Are you married?'

'No, I'm not married and the father isn't going to know anything about it. This baby is going to be mine . . . just mine.'

If Tod ever found out, he would surely claim it, particularly if it turned out to be a boy.

It was just six weeks since Gina had flown away from Mallions and had been fortunate enough to secure permission to land on another private strip. She'd been uncertain at first whether it was safe to return to her flat, or whether she should move out, covering her tracks. But with Tod's resources it was unlikely she could evade him forever, so she might as well save herself the trouble. In the event, he had made no attempt to contact her and gradually she relaxed. He wasn't going to follow up his seduction of her. She ought to feel relief, and in one sense she did, but it was mingled with pique that his attraction towards her should have been so transitory, his pursuit of her so easily abandoned. But worse than the pique was the ache in her heart, in her body. How long did it take for such pains to ease?

Two weeks ago, certain symptoms which, taken in conjunction with other facts, had added up to a suspicion, an unlikely circumstance, which at first she had discarded as being totally impossible. But the signs had persisted and she had decided to consult a gynaecologist.

She hadn't worked since she'd returned to London. There had been no point in contacting TLM Enterprises, since Tod held sway there. But now, though she was by no means impoverished, she knew she must think of her baby's future. The GD Agency was still running profitably and, rather than just sit back and receive the proceeds, Gina decided she would return there, take up the reins once more herself. With a brief break for her child to be born, she would be fully occupied, with no time to brood about Tod Fallon, to wonder whom he had found to fill Marcha's place, the place he had invited her, Gina, to take.

'Hallo? Gina Darcy speaking!'

She had heard the telephone's insistent ring as she'd stepped out of the lift and inserted her key in the front door of the flat.

'Oh, Miss Darcy, thank goodness!' It was her secretary. 'Just after you left the office, we had a client call in. He said he had a most urgent request to make and he insisted he would only speak to you.'

Gina sighed wearily. It had been a long day and she was tired and hungry. She seemed to have less stamina these days.

'Did you get his number? I'll ring him.'

There was a slight hesitation at the other end, as if the girl expected a reprimand for what she was about to say.

'He ... he wouldn't give me a telephone number. He said he wanted to speak to you, face to face.'

'You didn't give him my address?' Gina snapped out the question. Her staff had strict instructions, but this girl was new.

'He ... he said he knew where you lived, that he'd call round. I said I'd telephone you, warn you to expect him, but he said I wasn't to. He ... he was quite fierce. I was worried. Miss Darcy, do you want me to call the police? ... Miss Darcy? ... *Miss Darcy*?'

'Yes? Oh, sorry! No, Babs, I don't think that will be necessary. But you did right to warn me. Thanks.'

What had begun as an irritating interruption to her free time had, while the secretary spoke, assumed a more menacing aspect. It was Tod. It had to be. Only he and Jimmy Riley knew her home address and Jimmy wasn't aware that she was back in London.

Thanks to her secretary she had a few precious moments in which to decide her course of action. She could pretend to be out or she could make it an actuality: leave her flat and spend the evening elsewhere. But why should she run away, be driven out of her own home? And any evasive action she took would only give her a temporary reprieve.

Tod, as she had cause to remember, could be very persistent. Better to get the encounter over, make it quite clear that she never wanted to see him again. It wasn't true of course. Underlying her determination to outface him was a nagging curiosity to know the purpose of his visit and, even stronger, an insidious longing to see him.

The doorbell rang and her heart skipped a beat. He was here and she hadn't even had time to do anything about her appearance. She was still wearing the smart, but rather severe grey dress she affected for office work. Her make-up was probably non-existent and her hair! She groaned. She had meant to wash it tonight.

What did any of that matter? she asked herself sternly, as she went to answer the bell's now more insistent summons. But she couldn't resist a swift assessment of herself in the hall's full length mirror. Anxiously, she ran her hands over her hips, the slight curve of her belly. She didn't think her condition showed yet.

The ringing had ceased and now her caller was raining blows on the front door.

'Gina! Open up! I know you're in there, damn you!'

She flung the door open, surprising him with his fists still raised.

'For heaven's sake. Do you want all the neighbours to hear?'

'In this place?' he scoffed, inserting himself into the hallway so adroitly she couldn't have prevented him from doing so even if that had been her intention. 'I bet it's so well soundproofed you could commit murder without being overheard.'

She turned around, leaving him to shut the door, and preceded him into the living area. It was taking every ounce of her determination to appear cool and poised when, inwardly, she was a mass of nervous speculation. She seated herself on a chair so that, if he wanted to sit down, he would be forced to place himself some distance from her. The only trouble was he showed no inclination to settle anywhere, roaming to and fro restlessly.

Gina was determined she wouldn't be the first to open the subject of his visit. She sat quietly, hands folded, eyes steady, giving a deceptive impression of cold disinterest.

Hell's bells! Tod thought, shooting a glance at her from beneath lowering brows. Why did she have to make it so difficult for him to begin? Why didn't she say something, ask why he was here, even get mad at him, so that he had an excuse to take hold of her, an action which had obsessed him mentally and physically for some considerable time? She was even lovelier than he remembered. Despite her obvious end-of-day fatigue, there was some indefinable luminous quality about her, an added serenity which he longed to disturb.

'Aren't you going to ask me why I'm here?' He shot the question at her suddenly, abruptly, when the silence had become too strained to endure.

'No, since I've no doubt you'll enlighten me eventually.' Her tone was maddeningly remote and Tod took a grip of himself. He must match her coolness. With this intention, he threw himself down in the sunken lounging area and looked up at her, his view a distorted one, beginning with her primly folded legs, long and shapely in sheer nylon. He swallowed, averted his eyes.

'I want to thank you for what you did, for your part in rescuing Melanie.'

'A letter would have done,' she told him quietly.

Confound it. He couldn't sit down here, at a disadvantage. He got up and came to stand over her.

'A letter would *not* have done! You took a considerable risk, flying so low. The least I could do was to thank you personally.'

'It took you long enough,' she observed, with no apparent signs of rancour. Didn't she mind that he hadn't come to her sooner? If she didn't then his cause was lost before he'd begun. Well, he wasn't going to grovel. He'd come the first moment he'd been able to.

'The men who tried to kidnap Melanie were apprehended. There were proceedings taken against them . . . and Marcha. Then I flew out to Italy, to see my father-in-law.'

He had Gina's interest now, at least. She was leaning slightly forward in her chair, even though she didn't speak.

'Mantalini was behind the attempt. Marcha *did* spend that holiday of hers in Italy . . . at La Spezia. Debbie and Steph were right; they did see her there.'

'But why?' Gina could keep silent no longer. 'Why should Marcha co-operate with him? How could she plot against you when she expected to marry you? It must have been planned before . . . before . . .'

'Before you came to Mallions and ousted her in my affections? Yes.'

'Then . . .'

'Marcha didn't intend her part in the kidnap to be known. That was part of her bargain with Mantalini. She didn't like children, didn't want to be bothered with mine. For some reason she believed she'd succeeded where others had failed, that she'd get me to marry her. With Melanie safely out of the way, she wouldn't have had to share my attention.'

'She admitted all that?'

'Not at first, no. Not until after I'd seen the Mantalini boys, heard their version. The sons weren't involved. They'd lost interest in their father's vendetta, so he'd relied on Marcha being on the inside ... and some hired bully boys.'

'How did he know about Marcha, contact her?'

'She knew about him, sought him out. She knew about his earlier attempts. Mantalini promised her money, too ... a great deal of it.'

'A circus performer with money?'

'Not only a performer ... a circus owner. He owned several. I say owned, because Mantalini is dead. Apparently when he heard about the failure of his latest coup, he flew into a rage which brought on a heart attack.'

'Good riddance!' Gina said feelingly and, at Tod's look of amazement, 'I can't feel sorry for him, or for Marcha. They've both caused too much trouble, too much heartache to people I ...'

'Yes?' Tod said tensely as she broke off, her face flushing. Then, as she continued to stare up at him speechlessly, 'I suppose you weren't, by any chance, going to say "to people you love".'

She must brazen it out. There was a piece of sophistry she could employ.

'I adore Rusty, you know that ... and I became very fond of Melanie,' she added primly. Somehow she managed to look away from those penetrating dark eyes.

'Is that all?' His voice was harsh.

'What else should there be?' A nice, understated little note of surprise, she congratulated herself.

'Where do I come into all this?' he demanded and her stomach seemed to achieve several rapid backflips. Automatically, she rested her hand upon it, thinking of the growing life within, found Tod watching the gesture and as hastily withdrew it.

'I'm sorry, of course, that you had all that worry. But it's over now, isn't it?'

'Not by a long way!' He ground the words out savagely and bent forward leaning over her, his hands grasping her shoulders. 'I've had some worry in my life ... but nothing worries me so damned much as you do.'

She refused to look at him, felt she couldn't speak. But that insidious trembling had begun to agitate her body and he must be aware of it. She must say something, if only to divert his attention, to give herself breathing space.

'What I can't understand,' she said, amazed at the controlled note of her own voice, as if she were merely discussing some academic problem, 'is why you wanted me as Marcha's stand-in, when she was so against it.'

The diversion worked, temporarily. His grasp relaxed a little.

'Whatever her opinion,' he said simply, 'she needed you. There was no one else who resembled her so closely to be found at such short notice, and there was no way I could get her to perform her own stunts. When she realised I didn't intend to back down, she added to what she'd already told me of your background a very elaborate tissue of lies and insinuations, so that I'd be very disinclined to believe anything you might have let slip about *her*. If it hadn't been for young Rusty ... I'm glad I decided to visit him again.'

'Why did you?'

'For his own sake, initially ... I liked the lad, admired his guts ... and to find out more about you. In so doing, I uncovered Marcha's lies, her true nature. And now, Gina, let's stop shilly-shallying. When are you

coming back to Mallions ... to Rusty ... to *me*?' The
blunt, uncompromising question took her by surprise.

'Never! There's no reason why I should. I completed
my part of your film and I told you I wouldn't work for
you again, even if you did try to sue me for breach of
contract.'

'Gina! Being a businesswoman seems to be bad for
you. Will you please stop looking at everything in terms
of pounds and pence? I don't care a damn if you never
appear in another film, and one thing's certain, there'll
be no more stunting for you.'

'Why?' she asked suspiciously, disregarding the first
part of his sentence. Had he any idea? No, he couldn't
have.

'Because I've watched one woman I love kill herself. I
don't intend to let that happen again.'

It was not stubbornness, nor was it pique that kept
her silent now. He had, effectively, taken away her
breath.

'Did you hear what I said?' he demanded, giving her
a little shake.

'I heard!' she managed to say.

'Well?'

'Well what? Do you expect me to fall at your feet in
gratitude? I've told you, on several occasions, I don't
like your ideas about love. OK. So you're rid of
Marcha ... well rid. You must know plenty of other
women who are panting to take her place. But I'm not
one of them.'

'Is it this damned stupid idea you have that you're
first and foremost a career woman? Because, if so, I'll
tell you now, I won't interfere with that. You can keep
your agency, be financially independent if you like. You
can act ... you can do anything you damned well
please, just so long as you come back to me.'

He was making it very difficult for her. He was
offering her everything she had ever wanted, except for

one thing. He wanted her on his terms, without commitment, without marriage. She was glad he didn't know about the baby. He might have felt compelled to offer marriage then, just to gain control of his future son or daughter. But she wouldn't have wanted those sort of terms either.

'Gina!' His voice grated huskily in his throat. 'Come back. I want you with me. I need you.' He pulled her up out of the chair, so that they stood breast to breast, thigh to thigh. 'I'll *make* you come back,' he told her savagely. 'I'll make you want me again. If I have to I'll even resort to Mantalini's tricks, I'll abduct you. If I once get you back to Mallions, you'll never escape me again. I'll keep you where you belong, in my bed, until you give in.' He scooped her up, ignoring her protesting cries, but instead of heading for the door, as she had feared, he carried her in the direction of her bedroom.

As he dumped her on the bed he looked around him.

'Very pretty! But it's a woman's idea of what a bedroom should be. It's obvious no man has ever been in here. Well I can think of a far better setting in which to make love to you, but for now, this will do!'

It was of no avail to struggle, to protest. She couldn't overcome his determination that way. She'd failed before. She had to use a surer deterrent, one which would appeal to his reason.

'OK,' she said wearily. 'I know in this kind of situation I lose out. I know you can make me want you . . . you've proved that often enough. But however many times you do that, you'll always end up the loser, because however much I might enjoy your lovemaking, however much I might crave for it, you'll never get me back to Mallions willingly.' She flung out her arms dramatically. 'Well . . . go on then . . . get on with it . . . and then go.'

'Damn you, Gina!' He sat down on the edge of the

bed. 'You certainly know how to turn a man off. For God's sake, I don't want to take you against your will. I want your co-operation, not . . . not a sacrificial victim. Just tell me what you've got against me, why you can't love me as well as want me? Is it my past, the women since . . . since Maria? I can tell you, they didn't mean a damned thing. They were just to . . . to save me from going out of my mind.'

'And that's all I'd be.' She sat up. 'Don't you see, Tod? I don't want that casual kind of relationship. I don't want to be something you just use when your body is in need. My ideal is to be a companion to a man, friend as well as lover, to have shared interests, respect . . .'

'Hold on! Hold on!' There was a queer kind of urgency in his voice. 'What you're trying to tell me is that *you* want marriage?'

'Yes. And since you don't . . .'

'Shut up! What the hell do you think I've been trying to say all this time . . . the last time we made love? I told you then that I loved you. I think I must have been in love with you for a long time, only I'd forgotten what the sensation felt like.'

'You said,' Gina told him disbelievingly, accusingly, 'that you'd no intention of marrying . . . Marcha or anyone else.'

'That's true, but you didn't let me finish. I meant anyone else but you. But you got hysterical. You let me see just why you had this block against men, because you could never get pregnant. Gina, I know I told you I wanted a son, but it doesn't matter. It's not important, not as important as having you. I've got one child. We'll share her. I'll . . . I'll adopt Rusty. I'd thought of it anyway. Gina, please say you'll marry me. Put me out of this torture I've been going through for the last few weeks, not able to come to you, wondering if you were all right. I didn't even know for a while whether you'd landed that blasted plane safely, if I'd ever see you again. And now I'm here, now I've found you, I'm no better off. It ... it's like beating my head against a brick wall.'

'Tod!' She'd said his name twice already, trying to stem the flow of his words. Now, finally, 'Shut up!' Surprised into silence, he did. 'Shut up, Tod, and let me get a word in. If you hadn't gone raving on, you could have had at least five minutes less uncertainty. I haven't got a block against men, certainly not against one particular man ... you. I love you, Tod, and if you'd said "marry me" as soon as you walked through that front door, instead of ... well ... Anyway, I'd have said "yes" right away.'

He swallowed.

'You would?' Then, with more certainty, 'You would, Gina?'

'It was all I wanted to hear, idiot!' she told him affectionately.

'I *am* an idiot, aren't I?' he admitted. 'But it never occurred to me that your response to me was anything other than a physical one.'

'It seems to me,' she said softly, 'that there's only one way I can prove it to you.' She held out her arms and he came down into them willingly. Her mouth sought his, warmly, eagerly. 'I love you, Tod Fallon. I loved you long before I even *liked* you.'

He could not doubt her sincerity as he felt the shudders that began to run through her, as she sought to pull him closer. Exultantly he gathered her up, demonstrating the full force of his arousal as they kissed until both were breathless.

Without relinquishing her mouth, he began to undo the buttons of the severe grey dress, dispensed with her bra, his fingers caressing with tactile intimacy.

'Gina?' It was a question that needed no enlargement.

'Yes!' she whispered. 'Oh, yes, Tod. Oh Tod, I *ache* so. Please ... please ...'

Gently he removed her clothes, swiftly discarded his own, lowered his weight upon her once more.

'I never intended to fall in love again,' he said ruefully between kisses, 'but I think I knew right from the first that I was lost, only I wouldn't admit it to myself. I thought it was just physical ... for both of us. But I know now this *is* love. Gina, please tell me you believe me.'

'I believe you,' she told him.

Then he made love to her, a desperate, starved, devouring love, their gasps turning to groans of delight at the pleasures that racked their bodies, pleasure neither had thought to know again ... together. Then he entered her warmth, raised her, possessed her, his movements increasing their rapidity as she urged herself against him, ending in a shuddering, convulsive climax that transcended even their first coming together, since now they both knew the ecstasy was born, not only of wanting, but of love.

They lay still for a while, glorying in the continuing contact.

'Happy?' Tod asked after a while.

'Completely. You're my whole life, from this moment on.'

He laughed softly, a gentle, contented sound, but it held disbelief.

'Knowing you, I'll have to move over to leave room for that career of yours.'

'Maybe! But not for a while. I think my time will be pretty full, between you ... and your son.'

'My son?' He raised himself to look at her. 'Gina, if you only knew how I wish ... A child of our love. But you told me it was impossible.'

'I know. I thought it was. But it seems it isn't. Oh, Tod ...' Her eyelids fluttered down shyly. 'I'm ... I'm six weeks pregnant.'

An urgent hand grasped her chin.

'Is this true?' he rasped. 'Why didn't you tell me before? God, if I've harmed you . . .'

'Harmed me?' Her green eyes were brilliant with happy tears. 'Tod, your love can only do me good, better than any medication. In fact . . .' Her mouth curved into a wicked little smile as her hands issued an unmistakable invitation.

'Witch! Temptress!' he gasped. 'Oh, Gina, my love. You can't want it any more than I do. But are you sure?'

'Quite sure,' she said serenely.

He was gentle this time, reverent almost, but nonetheless satisfying to her senses, to his own.

'You were misnamed,' he whispered, as once more they lay in peaceful aftermath. 'Not fantasy, but fantastic . . . *my* Fantastic Woman!'

New This spring

Harlequin Category Romance Specials!

New Mix

4 Regencies—for more wit, tradition, etiquette . . . and romance

2 Gothics—for more suspense, drama, adventure . . . and romance

Regencies

A Hint of Scandal by Alberta Sinclair
She was forced to accept his offer of marriage, but could she live with her decision?

The Primrose Path by Jean Reece
She was determined to ruin his reputation and came close to destroying her own!

Dame Fortune's Fancy by Phyllis Taylor Pianka
She knew her dream of love could not survive the barrier of his family tradition....

The Winter Picnic by Dixie McKeone
All the signs indicated they were a mismatched couple, yet she could not ignore her heart's request....

Gothics

Mirage on the Amazon by Mary Kistler
Her sense of foreboding did not prepare her for what lay in waiting at journey's end....

Island of Mystery by Margaret M. Scariano
It was the perfect summer job, or so she thought—until it became a nightmare of danger and intrigue.

Don't miss any of them!

BPA-CAT87-1

Take
4 novels
and a
surprise gift
FREE

ATTRACTIVE, SPACE SAVING BOOK RACK

Display your most prized novels on this handsome and sturdy book rack. The hand-rubbed walnut finish will blend into your library decor with quiet elegance, providing a practical organizer for your favorite hard-or soft-covered books.

Only $9.95

Approximately 16" x 8" when assembled

Assembles in seconds!

To order, rush your name, address and zip code, along with a check or money order for $10.70* ($9.95 plus 75¢ postage and handling) payable to *Harlequin Reader Service*:

Harlequin Reader Service
Book Rack Offer
901 Fuhrmann Blvd.
P.O. Box 1325
Buffalo, NY 14269-1325

Offer not available in Canada.

BKR-1R

*New York residents add appropriate sales tax.

What the press says about Harlequin romance fiction...

"When it comes to romantic novels...
Harlequin is the indisputable king."
— *New York Times*

"...always with an upbeat, happy ending."
— *San Francisco Chronicle*

"Women have come to trust these
stories about contemporary people,
set in exciting foreign places."
— *Best Sellers*, New York

"The most popular reading matter of
American women today."
— *Detroit News*

"...a work of art."
— *Globe & Mail*, Toronto

Harlequin Presents

Coming Next Month

975 DARK ENCHANTMENT Helen Bianchin
A young Australian's feelings for the man she's to marry veer crazily
between attraction and resentment. The match would cement a
financial empire. Love—for him anyway—seems entirely incidental.

976 A WILLING SURRENDER Robyn Donald
It's love versus family loyalty for an au-pair girl who falls in love with the
man who broke up her brother's marriage. Her head urges caution. But
her heart cries out "Surrender."

977 AN IDEAL MATCH Sandra Field
They might be the perfect match—a music teacher who can't have
children and a widowed professor with three of his own. The attraction is
there. So why does he warn her not to fall in love with him?

978 DESIRE FOR REVENGE Penny Jordan
Love at first sight…. It all seems possible when a London editor comes
face-to-face with a sapphire-eyed stranger at a masquerade ball. But
fantasy collides with reality when she returns to the real world….

979 A LONG WAY FROM HEAVEN Susanne McCarthy
A hotel owner in the Grenadines is left in financial arrears when her
husband dies. Her only way out is marriage to a man she once loved—a
man whose pride wanted her, not his heart!

980 BEYOND RANSOM Sophie Weston
An agronomist in South America is kidnapped by revolutionaries and
forced to pose as the leader's woman for her own safety. But she feels
decidedly unsafe when she no longer has to *pretend* to love him.

981 PASSION'S DAUGHTER Sara Wood
It's one thing for a Gypsy girl to love the lord of the manor, quite another
to think their marrying would bring happiness—no matter what he says
in the heat of the moment.

982 FANCY FREE Karen van der Zee
An adventure tour company owner thinks she has it all until she falls for
a dynamic but conservative man. He wants a wife and children, but
seems willing to settle for a long-distance affair in the meantime.

Available in May wherever paperback books are sold, or through
Harlequin Reader Service:

In the U.S.
901 Fuhrmann Blvd.
P.O. Box 1397
Buffalo, N.Y. 14240-1397

In Canada
P.O. Box 603
Fort Erie, Ontario
L2A 5X3